INDEX OF
MARRIAGE LICENSES,
PRINCE GEORGE'S COUNTY, MARYLAND
1777-1886

By
HELEN W. BROWN

CLEARFIELD COMPANY

March 1996
$22.50

First Printing
College Park, Maryland, 1971

Reprinted
Genealogical Publishing Co., Inc.
Baltimore, 1973

Reprinted for
Clearfield Company, Inc. by
Genealogical Publishing Co., Inc.
Baltimore, Maryland
1995

Library of Congress Catalogue Card Number 73-012384
International Standard Book Number 0-8063-0579-7

FOREWORD

Index *of* *Marriage* *Licenses*, *Prince* *George's* *County*, *Maryland*, *1777-1886* provides the genealogical researcher with a convenient list of over 13,000 male and female names, which are recorded in five hand-written books at the Hall of Records, Annapolis, Maryland. Anyone wishing a copy of the original entry should give the name and date of license which he finds in this index, and send $1 with his request to the Hall of Records.

History and Description

At the February 1777 session of the Maryland General Assembly "An Act concerning marriages" was passed. Among the outlined specifications it states that "no person is to marry without a license." And that "thirty shillings of current money shall be paid." In one of the articles it further states that "returns shall be made by the clerk annually in November and sent to the Treasurer of his Shore." At that time the clerk was to pay the treasurer "25 shillings current money for each License by him granted, retaining five shillings on each License for his Trouble." The first marriage license recorded in Prince George's County after this law became effective was issued May 31, 1777 to James Nevitt and Ruth Conn.

The first three license books are approximately 7 by 9 inches and are nicely bound in red. They consist of pages, now laminated, from various types of notebooks written in numerous styles of hand-writing, some of which are barely legible. I believe the names have been copied from other accounts, sometimes more than once. Since names were spelled the way the name sounded to the writer, the researcher should imagine variant spellings of a name if he doesn't immediately find the name he is looking for in this index.

1. The first book covering May 31, 1777 to October 30, 1797 and May 2, 1818 to October 5, 1826 is titled on the first page;

Marriage Records
John Read Magruder, Clerk
Prince George's County Court, commencing
20th May Anno 1777.

The records beginning May 2, 1818 are not as neatly inscribed as those kept by Mr. Magruder and the name of the clerk is not given. Several pages have been crossed out and recopied in book #3.

2. The second red book contains two notebooks, the first being licenses granted by Benjamin Beall from May 4, 1798 to September 28, 1803. The second notebook (slightly larger in size with no clerk's name given) covers licenses granted May 16, 1804 to April 22, 1818.

3. The third red book covers the period from January 7, 1797 to April 16, 1817. After the first 73 pages were written, evidently a new clerk was appointed, for the book was reversed and pages 1 through 188 cover licenses issued from November 7, 1826 to November 26, 1880. On page 185 is the following personal account of

A. Beall in a/c with B. Beall
Loaned you in Court to pay deposit of   262.
Loaned you for mother   40.
Paid N. Beall for Jn? S. Belt   4.50
1828 Ditto you balance on Jn? Wards license   6.00
Oct. 30 Ditto you by Jn? S. Belt retail license 12.00
Ditto by Ordinary License   18.00
1829 Ditto by Ditto Ordinary License   15.00
Feb'y Ditto by Ditto   "   "   5.00
Ditto for (?)   3.00
Ditto paid for proper Stage fare   .50

The remaining books are larger in size than those described above, the fourth being 14-1/4 by 17-1/4 inches. It is a leather-bound, canvas covered ledger. The fifth book is 8-3/4 by 14 inches.

4. The fourth book of licenses from 1865 to 1867 has columns for age, color, condition (meaning widower, single or widow), occupation,

and residence of the persons. One clerk wrote "healthy" in the condition column. This recording of extra information concerning the licenses, helpful to the researcher, was unfortunately kept for two years only.

The fifth book for <u>December 11, 1879 to June 23, 1886</u>, gives the names of the ministers performing the marriages. In the following index I have indicated these ministers' names with parentheses.

It is possible, due to various circumstances, that people were married in Prince George's County without recorded licenses during the period covered by these records. Therefore, one should consult existing church registers of this period before giving up a search. However, I believe the names indexed here will be useful to many persons, and the hours which I have spent on this project will prove worthwhile for them.

Helen W. Brown

4704 Fordham Road,
College Park, Maryland, 20740

ABAGILL, Sarah R. & William A. Dicus 11-4-1841
ABBIGILL, Thomas & Sarah Hughes 2-4-1788
ABIGAIL, James R. & Mary C. Tucker (Hatterway) 10-16-1873
  Richard & Ellen Riddle 2-4-1818
ABIGILL, James & Catherine V. Beall 3-10-1863
  Wm. B. & Caroline E. Sansbury 12-24-1878 (Mercer)
ABRAHAM, Mary & Henry Williams 4-7-1879
ABRAMS, Emory & Rachel Johnson (Price) 6-16-1874
  George Washington & Harriet Ann Johnson col., both reside in
  Ann Arundel County 12-23-1881
  James & Maria Smith 11-28-1883
ACTON, Eleanor & Robert Clements 2-15-1832
  Emanuel Frances of Charles County & Charlotte P. Gibbons of P. G.
  County, by Rev. Josiah Perrie 11-24-1880
  F. B. & Mrs. Mary Nothy (Kershaw) 1-11-1870
  Hepsey & William Coates 12-31-1817
ADAMS, Amny & Zachariah Canter 12-12-1797
  Ann & Joseph Peake 1-26-1818
  Ann & George T. Underwood 1-18-1870
  Arsidius James & Sohpia Locker (Welsh) 9-4-1874
  Charles & Georgianna Hall (Father Cotton) 6-29-1885
  Charles H. & Laura Selby (Gordon) 12-23-1876
  Charles Henry & Maria Smallwood (Gordon) 3-27-1869
  Charles Henry & Frances Brooks (Rev. Mr. Wilson) 12-27-1879
  Eleanor & Robert Davis 5-28-1806
  Elizabeth & Isaac Grimes 3-23-1799
  Elizabeth & George Naylor 1-23-1802
  Elizabeth & John Worrell 12-16-1833
  Elizabeth & William Griffin (Langford) 5-15-1869
  Eliz.th A. & Hepburn S. Berry 11-5-1825
  Emma A. & Daniel E. Webster (Fowler) 6-3-1869
  George & Mary Wright 1-21-1783
  Harriet & John Henry Kittle col. Rev. Dr. Gordon 12-24-1881
  Ignatius & Ariana Scott 1-16-1811
  Ignatius & Sarah Ann Sansbury 1-22-1816
  Ignatius D. & Mary Beall 2-6-1844
  Ignatius D. & Sarah L. Jones 4-24-1851
  J. S. & Jane A. Magruder (Begue) 1-3-1871
  Jenny D. & John S. Davis 3-18-1825
  John & Ann Thompson 2-1-1803
  John Q. & Rachel Kittle (Gordon) 12-28-1878
  Joseph & Ann Nevitt 11-5-1791
  Josephus & Eliz.a Watson 10-24-1777
  Judy & John Barten 6-1-1792
  Leticia & James S. Howell 12-12-1832
  Leuisa & Thomas Barton Smith 1-16-1788
  Lewis B. & Martha A. E. Naylor 12-15-1846
  Littleton T. & Mary Ann Estep 12-13-1827
  Littleton T. & Elizabeth J. Weems 9-3-1834
  Lewis B. & Mary C. Naylor 2-16-1866 Age 41 of Baltimore, Md.
  widower-labourer, m. at Thomas Naylor's, Prince George's County
  Luke & Susanna Thorn 6-2-1781
  Marg. Ann & Edward Butler 10-28-1870
  Maria & Nathan Dunlop Hall 6-18-1806
  Mary & Perry Boen 1-20-1814

ADAMS, Mildred D. & John E. Ware (Smith) 4-8-1868
  Robert & Sarah Ann Brown col.^{d} (Call) 4-20-1867
  Rose & William Chambers Rev. Mr. Brooks 3-14-1885
  Samuel T. & Sarah A. Beavin 12-27-1836
  Sarah & James Webster 3-3-1819
  Sarah Ann & Richard Sansbury 2-6-1823
  Sarah Ann & George H. Martin (Kershaw) 6-4-1867
  Susannah & John Perrie 1-1-1801
  Susannah & Thomas Perrie 12-8-1807
  Thomas & Sarah Estep 3-30-1814
  Thomas & Ambler Glascow (Rev. N. C. Brown) 9-18-1883
  Thomas W. & Martha M. Shaff (Linthicum) 12-28-1870
  Vendalia & William Waters (Watson) 2-6-1872
  William & Rebeccah Howard 7-12-1796
  Wm. F. & Emily Caroline Berry 9-1-1828
ADDETON, Richard & Elizabeth Clarke 4-25-1787
ADDISON, Aaron & Margaret Williams col. 6-25-1865
  Anthony & Rebeccah Murdock 6-26-1794
  Edmund & Eliza D. Bowie 10-7-1828
  Eleanor & Garland Callis 12-22-1779
  Eleanor & John Tolson 12-18-1806
  Emily & Henry Johnson (Kershaw) col.^{d} 6-11-1869
  Emily & Henry Sprigg (O'Dwyer) 5-22-1875
  Frank Girault & Ellen Bowie (Rev. Stanley) 10-11-1884
  Frederick & Mary C. Sprigg (Carroll) 9-21-1878
  Hannibal & Christiana Calvert 5-2-1874
  Harriet & Dr. John H. Bayne 12-15-1841
  Henry & Eliz. Clagett 2-22-1794
  James & Charity Key (Pindell) 2-10-1870
  James L. & Bettie Tolson 12-3-1860
  John & Mary C. Jones col.^{d} 8-2-1871
  Mary & Samuel Ridout 12-21-1790
  Mary B. & William Tyler 7-18-1809
  Rebecca & Thomas H. Hanson 3-21-1778
  Roderick & Elisabeth Contee col.^{d} (Gordon) 8-1-1868
  The Rev. Walter D. & Rebecca Mackall 2-2-1814
ADKINS, Thomas & Lucy Berry 3-11-1780
AILSEA, Eliz.^{a} & William Proctor 1-11-1868
AIST, Adam G. & Catherine A. Clark 2-2-1853
  Annie C. & M. J. Kaldenback Jr. (Seat) 3-19-1877
  Fannie & J. Edward Pyles 2-12-1882 (Rev. Mr. Townshend)
  Katie & J. Edward Pyles 9-9-1884
AITCHESON, Diana (age 17) & Benj. P. McKnew 11-30-1865
ALBY, Ann & Thomas Higdon 6-10-1797
ALBEY, William & Keziah Riston 1-21-1778
  Aminta & Elisha Risson 1-11-1779
ALBRITTAIN, Catherine E. & Jas. T. Padgett (Rev. M. M. Lewin) 1-3-1884
ALDER, Caroline & William Atchison 9-30-1815
  Elizabeth & Robert Fry 12-13-1792
  George & Lucy Ann Wynn 10-31-1778
  James & R ebecca Atchison 1-6-1790
  James & Eleanor Tippett 3-24-1815
  James H. & Penelope Latimer 11-23-1827
  Joanna & Philip Ryon 3-23-1778
  Susanna M. & Green S. Atcherson 3-15-1831

ALDRIDGE, Ann & Benjamin Hall 2-19-1838
   Caroline & John Wineberger 10-31-1836
   Christiana & William Trunnell 12-19-1832
   Eleanor & Richard Belt 12-5-1803
ALEXANDER, Eliz.ª & Electius Thompson 8-14-1780
   Green & Mary Ann DeVaughn (Porter) 2-22-1866
   James T. & Mary E. Plummer (Rev. Mr. Brooks) 5-9-1885
   Rachel & William Hayes 9-5-1795
   Sarah & John Matthews (Watts) 12-29-1874
   Thomas S. & Priscilla Ghiselin 11-30-1830
ALLEN, Amanda M. & Henry Fry 12-27-1865
   Ann & Haswell Magruder 4-18-1802
   Ann Amelia & John D. Moore 11-27-1838
   Benjamin W. & Sarah Smith Hilleary 12-2-1817
   Charles & Matilda Lindsay 11-25-1806
   Charles & Susannah Thomas 2-9-1822
   Dennis & Mary Dorsey col.ᵈ (Wheeler) 8-5-1871
   Edmund T. & Margaret Thompson (Kershaw) 12-25-1866 aged 23 of
   Prince Georges's County, - farmer
   Eliza Jane Olivia & R. T. Lusby 9-7-1863
   Elizabeth & William Arnold 7-30-1786
   Elizabeth A. & George P. Walker 8-1-1833
   George & Sarah Lowe 1-5-1782
   George & Maria Henson (Townshend) 1-3-1874
   Henson & Margaret Ennis(MacDonald) 8-23-1872
   James & Susan Ann Smith 12-28-1840
   John A. & Jane Sophia Bigges 1-3-1860
   Joseph & Sarah Ball 3-19-1851
   Julia A. & Alpheus C. Hoopes 2-8-1866 Age 32, resident of P. G. Co.-
   seamstress
   Kitty Jane & John Francis Dent 12-10-1870
   Levi & Louisa Matilda Allen (Begue) 4-18-1870
   Mar. Vincentia & John E. Biggs 1-23-1860
   Mary & Marsham Moore 12-7-1842
   Mary Elizabeth & George M. Moore (Martin) 5-15-1869
   Mary F. & James G. Grimes (Berry) 11-10-1868
   Mary L. & Jerre Herbert (Green) 5-8-1876
   Reasen & Charity Young 12-25-1818
   Robert & Mary Henson (Dwyer) 9-6-1873
   Sarah E. & Jno. F. Dannerson 8-29-1862
   Sarah Louisa Josephine & William Marden King (West) 4-30-1875
   Susan & John Chase 3-21-1873
   Susannah & Dennis Sweeny 12-12-1807
   Thomas & Jemima Piles 10-11-1786
   Tobias & Matilda Jones (Beque) 2-1-1866
   Walter & Sarah Ann Piles 2-13-1830
   William T. & George A. Sweeney (Kershaw) 11-21-1867
ALLENS, Susan & Thomas Boteler col. 8-3-1871
ALLIEN, Sarah & James G. Wood 12-4-1798
ALLEY, Levi & Rachel Hopkins 12-30-1807
   Walter & Elizabeth Smith 2-26-1783
ALLINGHAM, Stephen & Jemima Richards 3-30-1781
ALLISON, Daniel F. & Mary P. Cadle 5-21-1839
   Mary & George T. Edelen 1-13-1847
ALNUTT, James & Juliet Jackson 11-12-1811

ALNUTT, Zachariah & Elizabeth Osborn 11-26-1805
ALRIGHT, Richard & Susan Hayden 1-29-1822
ALVEY, Eliza & Horatio Newman 1-13-1813
  Eliz.thAnn & John Cross 3-3-1851
  Jno. W. & Marrion E. Lowe 11-19-1849
ALVY, Elizabeth & Samuel W. Ball (Rev. LaRoche) 9-11-1882
  John & Rebecca Suit 2-11-1824
  Mary E. E. & Wm. A. Walker 12-21-1848
AMAN, Emma A. & Samuel T. Weaver 7-17-1883
AMBLER, Elizabeth & Thomas Pearce 1-21-1783
  Mary & Richard Lee 11-9-1779
AMBLIN, Josephuas & Elizabeth Pearce 10-16-1787
AMERICA, Annie & Rueben Clark colored 5-5-1866 Age 20 of Ann Arundel
  County- servant
AMMON, Ronne Barbara (widow) & Henry Knock 5-7-1866
ANDERSON, Absalom & Ann Burrell 6-6-1794
  Amelia & Mordecai S. Finny 12-29-1845
  Ann & George B. Scagges 5-15-1834
  Ann M. & Christopher C. Stone 3-20-1850
  Asa & Elizabeth Wells 1-3-1822
  Asa & Eliza Williams 2-3-1829
  Benjamin & Beno Davis 2-12-1800
  Benjamin F. & Elizabeth H. Carrick (Stanley) 5-23-1876
  Celey & Edmund Faryey col. 6-11-1867
  Comfort & John Sam. Peters 2-27-1779
  Edward C. & Catherine Downs 11-10-1853
  Eliza Jane & Henry Soper 3-29-1848
  Elizabeth & Henry P. Armstrong (Cross) 1-15-1879
  Elizabeth U. & Wm. Thomas 7-11-1842
  Ellen & John R. Brooks (Rev. Mr. Walker) 12-27-1882
  Francis & Eliz.^a Duvall 1-3-1818
  George & Barbara Sutherland 4-18-1788
  George & Laura Lee (Stanley) 10-25-1870
  Doct. George W. & Carrie Morsell 10- 1-1855
  Georgeanna & William F. Gray 9-25-1876
  Henry & Elizabeth Lindsey 12-22-1815
  Hezekiah & Elizabeth Cooke 12-22-1819
  James G. & Mary Johnson 12-28-1877
  Jane & John B. Edelen 10-15-1834
  Jesse & Mary Riley 7-19-1800
  Jocephas & Mary H. Chaney 9-20-1873
  John & Alice Duvall 1-30-1811
  John & Matilda Walker 12-14-1824
  John Varnall & Mary Hurley 10-21-1807
  Katie & David Butler (Rev. Mr. Brooks) 2-9-1886
  Lydia & John Stewart 12-18-1822
  Lydia A. & Zadock Duvall 12-22-1835
  Margaret Emma & Louis C. Gray 12-2-1885
  Maria W. & Fielder C. Duvall (Rev. H. Stanley) 4-12-1883
  Mary & Jacob Riddle 2-1-1819
  Mary A. & Nicholas Shaw 9-4-1856
  Mary Jane of Lauranceville, N. J. aged 28 years & James Watts, age 31
  years, born in England 2-16-1881, Rev. James Lasey, Bladensburgh
  N. D. & Carrie V. Shipps 7-13-1864
  Rachael & Francis L. Newman 12-20-1848
  Rebecca & Tongue - (Rev. Mr. Howard) 6-16-1886

ANDERSON, Rezin & Ann Stevenss 2-19-1803
Richard T. & Jane Brown (Harper) 2-7-1870
Richard W. of Ann Arundel County & Edith Tayman of P.G. Co. 3-28-1881
Samuel & Martha Taylor 2-19-1787
Samuel B. & Elizabeth Hall 12-10-1833
Samuel E. & Maria A. Williams 6-10-1846
Sarah & Jacob Riddle 2-26-1819
Sarah Ann & Wm. Jesse Suit 11-25-1844
Dr. Thomas & Eleanor Lowndes 11-29-1841
Tobias & Mary Ann Riddle 1-5-1842
William C. & Mabel Waters 10-7-1835
William E. & Sarah A. Mitchell (Chesley) 4-10-1869
William F. & Lucy Brashears 12-14-1842
Wm. F. & Martha Ann Lanham 7-2-1844
ANDERWIG, Lancelot & Sarah Turner 12-19-1797
ARELL, Christiana & James Rector Magruder Lowe 1-11-1803
ARMEGER, Ann & Zadock Brashears 3-23-1819
ARMIGER, Benjamin F. & Elizabeth C. Tippett (Perry) 12-10-1877
Elizabeth & Elisha Howes 2-18-1834
John & Tessha Gardiner 1-27-1829
John & Ann Dove 9-21-1831
John W. & Virginia Wayson 10-20-1879
Mary J. & Benjamin Craig 12-28-1846
Rachel & Thomas Greenwell 2-5-1823
Sarah E. & James F. Greenwell 12-24-1856
Thomas A. & Georgianna Duckett (Trapnell) 4-15-1872
ARMISTED, Mary & Landon Carter 1-1-1800
ARMSTRONG, Henry P. & Elizabeth Anderson (Cross) 1-15-1879
Wm. & Emma Griffith 10-6-1879
ARNELL, Louise & Samuel Generals col? (Chesley) 9-17-1869
ARNOLD, Barbara & Benjamin Harvey 12-9-1823
Christopher & Verlinder Glasgow 11-23-1801
EDward & Margaret Wells 5-25-1854
John & Nancy Davis 12-16-1817
Joseph & Mary Elizabeth Belt 10-22-1853
Jo. N. & Mary E. King 4-11-1844
Lucy & Thomas Standage 9-13-1817
Mary E. & Hebrew T. Fletcher (Rev. Mr. Walker) 4-4-1883
Richard & Susannah Talbert 10-16-1800
Rosella & James Harris 12-4-1838
Samuel & Mary Sheriff 11-9-1826
William & Elizabeth Allen 7-30-1786
William & Sarah Ridgeway 2-28-1842
William & Mary Ridgeway 5-29-1858
ARTHUR, Maggie & J. T. W. Ourand 8-6-1857
ARVIN, Elisha & Henrietta Courts 10-29-1808
Margaret & Ignatius Windsor 12-23-1809
Ruth & Charles Courts 1-16-1808
ASH, Charles & Mary C. Wilson (Dr. Lowrey) 10-25-1869
Sarah Ann & Leonard Maddox (Marbury) 10-28-1871
ASHCOM, George & Eleanor Eversfield 11-20-1815
ASKEY, Mary & Nathan Wells 1-14-1785
Priscilla & Gideon Hinton 12-24-1798
ATCHERSON, Celia & Nicholas Blandford 12-21-1822
George F. & Jennie Neal (Harper) 12-21-1870

ATCHERSON, George G. & Barbara P. Taylor 7-14-1834
  Green S. & Susanna M. Alder 3-15-1831
  Ignatius W. & Sarah Caroline Atcherson 12-10-1833
  Mildred & Thomas Jenkins 11-10-1787
  S. E & Daniel C. Johnson 12-4-1837
  Sarah Caroline & Ignatius W. Atcherson 12-10-1833
ATCHESON, Chloe & Caleb Vernem (Vernon?) 11-30-1790
ATCHINSON, James & Ann Davis 2-8-1783
ATCHISON, see Etchison
  George H. & Hellen Ball 9-11-1849
  John E. & Eda Vermillion 12-11-1811
  Sarah A. & Michael J. Slayman 2-6-1865
  Rebecca & James Alder 1-6-1790
  Susanna & Robert H. Procter 1-25-1859
  William & Caroline Alder 9-30-1815
ATKERSON, James W. & Mary Hoye 1-12-1847
ATHEY, Elizabeth & George Dement Robey 12-16-1791
  Hezekiah & Rebeccah Tilley 12-10-1799
  Hezekiah & Barbara Coe 2-19-1806
  Presley N. & Mary E. Massey 6-6-1843
  Mary E. & John Higdon 11-20-1841
  Rhodie & James Thompson 11-25-1788
  Zephaniah & Lucy Duckett 11-11-1790
ATLEE, John Yorke & Ann Jennette Klock (Rev. Wm. Brayshaw) 10-3-1883
ATTCHISON, Henry & Susannah Hilton 2-17-1800
ATWELL, Benjamin & Sarah Ann Dodson 11-25-1837
  James & Elizabeth Owens 9-16-1799
AUGUR, Andrew J. & Laura Middleton 11-21-1878
AUSTIN, Andrew & Sarah Swaine 8-23-1832
  Eleanor & Baston Naylor 11-6-1778
  Elizabeth & Benjamin Robinson 2-7-1793
  Samuel & Anne Davis 1-18-1793
  Sarah & Jacob Wheeler 2-10-1786
  Thomas A. & Matilda J. Whitney 6-6-1811
  William & Ann Steel 1-23-1801
AVANS, Sarah & John Barnes 2-19-1785
AWL, Martha & James Daugherty 6-9-1795
AYERS, Francis & Catharine Ann Johnson 2-22-1881
AYRES, Robert & Ann Hardy 9-10-1784
AYTON, Richard & Ann Berry 12-18-1817

BACON, Benjamin & Elizabeth Downer 12-23-1797
BADDY, Charity & John Larkins (Watkins) 12-19-1878
  Clarissa & Gusty Brooks (Watkins) 12-19-1878
BADEN, Alexander & Mary Steel 6-3-1797
  Alexander & Sarah Gibbons 3-31-1804
  Amanda M. & Robert Henry Robinson (Marbury) 7-24-1872
  Aquila & Elizabeth Barnes 11-25-1818
  Aquila & Mary Eleanor Glascow 1-15-1833
  Benj. J. &Mary Ann Webster 2-6-1844
  Catherine E. & George D. Grimes 2-24-1864
  Clement & Eleanor Waring 8-30-1821
  Elizabeth & John Marlow 10-29-1791
  Elizabeth & Henry Emberson 12-31-1800

BADEN, Elizabeth & Colmore Augustus Swaine 12-2-1826
  Elizabeth & William Carr 3-19-1834
  Eliza S. & Zadock Robinson 1-18-1840
  Eliz.th T. & Dennis M. Williams 7-8-1836
  George A. & Martha Naylor 3-30-1832
  George W. & Rosa A. Garner (Lenaghan) 12-29-1873
  Ida & John A. Goldsmith (Rev. Perrie) 1-26-1880
  James & Susannah Gibbons 12-4-1799
  James & Ruth Davis 2-5-1811
  Jeremiah T. & Susanna J. Baden 7-5-1849
  John & Milley Robinson 4-17-1802
  John & Eleanor A. G. Townshend 1-21-1857
  John Jr. & Elizabeth Naylor 3-24-1814
  John Thomas & Margaret Baden 12-7-1813
  Joseph N. & Sarah S. Hawkins 11-28-1826
  Jn.° & Willimina M. Maulden 1-12-1782
  Lottie & Guy Carlton (Williams) 4-23-1878
  Margaret & John Thomas Baden 12-7-1813
  Margaret E. & James S. Morsell Jr. 4-30-1839
  Martha & Samuel Mitchell 1-1-1816
  Martha & Joshua Naylor 12-2-1799
  Martha & John Cooksey 11-18-1856
  Mary E. & William N. Burch 2-13-1846
  Rebecca & John L. Townshend 5-15-1838
  Rebeccah & Richard Noble 9-26-1796
  Robert & Elizabeth Gover 5-12-1796
  Robert Jur. & Frances Gover 11-10-1779
  Robert E. & Bessie Thomas (Leneghan) 1-18-1873
  Robert W. G. & Margaret C. Earley 1-2-1838
  Sarah & Thomas Cater 8-31-1791
  Sarah Gover & Josias Gibbons 10-18-1819
  Sarah M. & William M. Baden (Rev. Mr. Dame) 12-15-1885
  Susanna Eliz.th & James Harrison 10-7-1823
  Susanna J. & Jeremiah T. Baden 7-5-1849
  Susannah & Zacheus Davis 12-29-1804
  Thomas & Sarah Dorsett 2-6-1797
  Thomas of Benj.ⁿ & Martha Griffen 6-7-1811
  William M. & Sarah M. Baden (Rev. Mr. Dame) 12-15-1885
BAILEY, George & Maria Wrigman 3-1-1843
BAINE, Quintin & Mary Brewer 9-13-1792
BAKER, Chloe Lee & Overton Carr 4-21-1807
  Mary E. & John F. Tucker (Robey) 12-20-1870
  Mary E. & Edward M. Ulle (Rev. E.Robey) 10-1-1883
  Philip Thomas & Maria A. Bayly 12-19-1799
  Samuel H. & Elizabeth Paca 6-30-1797
  Thomas & Catharine Dyer 8-28-1811
  William & Susannah Greenfield 5-1-1789
BALDWIN, Amelia & Stephen Bright 9-21-1796
  Ann & Thomas Joshua Clark 9-3-1807
  Ann & Nathan Cooke 12-21-1814
  Catherine & Robt Simmons 5-9-1781
  Dorcas & Stephen Osbourn 2-3-1829
  Edmund & R achael Godman 12-8-1835
  Elie & Mary Eleanor Harvey 1-3-1826
  Elie S. & Mary Suit 2-19-1834

BALDWIN, Elizabeth & John Higgins 3-31-1814
  Elizabeth E. & John T. Ranten 12-28-1838
  George H. & Annie M. Blaine (Rev. Mr. Brashaw) 7-31-1882
  Jason & Elizabeth E. Mullikin 6-4-1833
  Kitty & Francis Smith (Father Maher) 5-27-1869
  Lillie E. & Joseph Walter (Rev. Mr. Brayshaw) 6-8-1886
  Margaret A. B. & Owen Norfolk 5-17-1847
  Martha S. & Richard H. Kendrick 5-14-1834
  Mary & William Tucker 1-15-1803
  Mary E. & Robert Taylor 7-23-1846
  Nancy & Theodore Ryon 2-4-1823
  Roena & Samuel Godman 12-18-1820
  Rhody & Benjamin Carrick 1-26-1815
  Sophia & Samuel Clarke 11-21-1809
  Susanna & Wm. B. Brooks 7-1-1851
  Susannah & Samuel Riddell 12-2-1791
  Thomas & Christian Webster 7-23-1790
  William & Elizabeth Sheriff 12-7-1799
  William & Sarah Savington 11-9-1811
  William & Mary Ann Brady 1-21-1853
  Wm. O. & Jane E. T. Smith 3-21-1848
  Zach^{a} & Marg^{t} Beckett 2-21-1783
  Zach^{a} & Flavilla Chaney 5-18-1839
  Zacharia & Mary Ann Meeke 4-1-1822
  Zachariah W. & Jemiah Fairall 4-14-1827
BALL, Ann Busey & Richard Bryan 1-27-1786
  Bennett & Ann Morriss 1-6-1789
  Dionysius & Priscilla Jane Fowler (Kershaw) 1-23-1868
  Druscilla & Moses Jones 11-30-1790
  Elizabeth & William Ridgway 12-29-1812
  Elizabeth & George R. Posey 7-17-1852
  Elizabeth E. & John W. Richardson (Gwynn) 10-7-1879
  Hellen & George H. Atchison 9-11-1849
  Henry & Eleanor Swann 5-21-1831
  Isaac & Mary Leach 4-20-1799
  Isaac & Eliza Jane Walker 12-5-1865
  John & Ann Fowler 4-4-1795
  John & Sarah Ann Maddox 2-4-1802
  John & Sarah Brashears 1-23-1812
  John & Elizabeth Mayhew 1-9-1822
  Louisa & Francis E. Moore (Porter) 1-2-1866 age 18
  Lucissi Ellen & William Oliver (Kershaw) 6-10-1873
  Mary & Grafton Beall (Williams) 2-19-1873
  Mary E. & Joseph Craig 1-5-1870
  Mary F. & Luther E. Watson 8-19-1881
  Mary Jane & John R. Fowler (Chesley) 3-7-1870
  Meeky & Henry Brian 1-20-1802
  R^{d} D. & Mary E. Thorn 12-19-1864
  Robert T. & Emma J. Piles (Kirby) 12-10-1872
  Samuel W. & Elizabeth Alvy (Rev. La Roche) 9-11-1882
  Sarah & Joseph Allen 3-19-1851
  Susan & John Fisal (West) 12-13-1875
  Thomas & Eleanor Beane 6-15-1799
  Thomas & Maria Swain 1-20-1842
  Thos of Thos & Rachael Ann Tubman 10-28-1854

BALL, Thomas A. T. & Rosana Lusby 9-30-1852
  Thomas E. & Mary Jane Tubman 3-9-1857
  Thomas E. & Eliza A. Gibbons (Marbury) 1-7-1870
  Thomas H. & Susannah R. Perrie 8-9-1841
  Thomas Henry & Mary C. Rawlings 9-12-1853
  Walter & Esther Walker (Griffin) 10-9-1876
  Wm. H. & Mary Jones 5-31-1862
BALLETT, John & Joanna Gloyd 11-29-1782
BANKS, Henry & Rachel Ford (Evans) 9-9-1871
  Lettie & Philip Plater col^d (Fowler) 6-2-1869
BARBER, Luke Philip & Jane Bruce Yates 2-20-1803
BARBOUR, Daniel & Sarah Herbert (Green) 11-6-1876
  John S. & Susan S. Daingerfield (Marbury) 10-16-1865
BARCLAY, Th: J. & Elizabeth D. Jackson 1-9-1855
  William & Mary Evans 12-17-1794
BARKER, Daniel of Wash^n City & Mary E. Holland 8-28-1868
  Joseph A. & Emma Sansbury (Linthicum) 11-16-1870
  Joseph P. & Mary Elizabeth Connick 4-30-1849
  Wm. R. & Charity Ann Gil 12-30-1828
BARNARD, Edward F. & Rachel B. Conway 11-9-1847
  John J. & Kate H. Keech 11-7-1863
BARNE, Oliver & Sarah Wilson 2-8-1785
BARNES, Basil & Mary Lanham 1-22-1791
  Benedict & Sally Lanham 3-7-1801
  Daniel & Ann Wilson 2-21-1783
  Eleanor & David Knowles 1-18-1805
  Elizabeth & Aquila Baden 11-25-1818
  Emma & John Henson 10-9-1879
  George A. & Susan C. Phillips 1-8-1821
  George A. & Lucy Ann D. Beck 5-25-1828
  Henry & Ann Lanham 2-3-1790
  John & Sarah Avans 2-19-1785
  Martha C. & Horatio Beall 1-2-1843
  Mary & John Lindsay 7-31-1818
  Mary A. & Ja^s C. Wilson 2-1-1782
  Millicent & Hezekiah Berry 12-19-1797
  Ruth A. & William Clem Tuck 8-14-1861
  Tracy & Edward Magruder 2-15-1813
BARNEY, George & Rebecca C. Beall 5-8-1825
  Harriet Ann & Henry Parran (Rev. Mr. Aquilla) 12-26-1881
  Rachel Ann & William Griffin (Rev. Mr. Aquilla) 12-26-1881
BARNS, Alexander & Harriet Diggs (Gordon) 11-2-1867
BARRETT, Ann & William Mulliken 3-25-1780
  Elizabeth & John H. Dowell 8-9-1864
  James D. & Lucy Beall 2-2-1818
  John & Mary Price 12-11-1781
  Jonathan & Margaret Gilpin 3-20-1779
  Richard & Lucy Brown 12-18-1784
  Sarah & Charles M. Spicknall 10-14-1811
  Sarrah & Isaac Loveless 1-7-1791
BARRETTE, Lucinda & John Tolson 2-12-1839
BARRICK, Jane & Andrew Herbert both col^d 4-28-1865
BARRON, Daniel & Mary Ann Yost 12-6-1839
  Elizabeth & William Yost (Evans) 9-13-1877
  Emma & Thomas Clarke Duvall 12-14-1809

BARRON, Harriot & Horatio Beall 1-3-1803
  Maria & Henry L. Carlton 2-22-1831
  Martha & John Tilley 12-9-1808
  Ninian B. & Adelia W. Scott 4-14-1829
  Oliver & Elizabeth Beall 5-28-1800
  Rebecca & Benjamin Burch 9-6-1784
  Ruth & William B. Gailor 11-11-1822
  Samuel & Rebecca J. Davis 3-13-1821
  Zachariah & Ann Mulliken 12-14-1809
BARROT, Isaac & Barbara Tilley 11-29-1809
BARROTT, Ann & Richard Campbell 4-29-1812
  Jamima & Philip Suit 10-14-1815
  John & Catharine Newman 1-8-1799
  Nancy Ann & Colmore Thompson 1-11-1808
  Richard & Sarah Smallwood 10-14-1812
  Sarah & Thomas Webster 2-11-1805
BARRS, Mary Ellen & Robert Fry 2-18-1862
BARRY, Fannie & James F. S. Bryan 12-1-1865
  William & Mary Ann Smith 6-19-1778
  William W. & Henrietta Underwood (Toles) 2-9-1872
BARSE, George P, & Georgianna Vermillion (Kershaw) 9-6-1877
BARTEN, John & Judy Adams 6-1-1792
BARTLETT, Edward & Rebecca Parker (Butler) 12-24-1878
BARTLEY, George & Mary Cross 1-26-1798
  Peter Q. & Sabina Emerson 11-20-1830
  Sarah & Thomas Cross 11-1-1798
BARTLY, Elizabeth & Zadock Riston 1-7-1786
BARTON, George & Eliza Ann Rhodgers 7-8-1834
  James Hanson & Eliza Ann Elizabeth Johnson (McDonald) 1-7-1870
  Jane & Dennis Fletcher (Wheeler) 6-3-1871
  Pinkney & Fanny Matthews (Jackson) 12-1-1879
  Richard & Anne Chitham col^d (Stanley) 8-22-1868
  Richard & Sarah Johnson 2-27-1875
BASFORD, Alverdus H. & Sarah Ann Neghen 5-14-1839
  Elizabeth & Abraham Jones 2-12-1820
  George W. & Alice Mullikin (Kershaw) 1-6-1869
  John & Mary Duvall 6-11-1808
  Susan & Richard Sheckells 1-8-1840
  Thomas & Mary Freeman 12-27-1831
BASSFORD, Benjn J. & Susan Cordelia Tydings 1-16-1877
  Chrissy & Thomas Ferrell 12-4-1794
  Ezekiel & Dinah Chaney 6-16-1815
  Henry & Catharine Mullikin 2-21-1839
  Jacob & Permella Woodward 12-14-1814
  John & Sarah Isaac 6-2-1826
  Julia A. & John Thos Hardesty 1-6-1848
  Thomas & Casandra Waters 4-2-1784
BATCHELLER, Elizabeth & J. B. Beasley (Martin) 8-16-1870
BATSON, Basil & Rachel Ann Docket col^d (Langford) 1-22-1870
  Elizabeth & David Peck 9-17-1810
  Leana & George Buchanan 12-27-1823
  Nancy & Robert Jackson (O'Dwyer) 10-6-1871
  Rachel Ann & Nathaniel Scott (Carroll) 12-27-1877
  Renia & William E. Dent 1-9-1873
BATT, Dorcas & William Turner 2-21-1784

BATT, Elizabeth & Thomas Quinn 5-26-1792
BATTY, Angeline & Henry Sevoy col. (Watkins) 11-28-1878
  John & Mary Batty 8-10-1872
  Julia A. & John Mills col? (Watkins) 11-28-1878
  Mary & Charles Duckett col? 10-16-1869
  Mary & John Batty 8-10-1872
BATZEL, Rebecca & Ignatius Hutchins 12-20-1844
BAUSE, George & Ann Sparrow 9-24-1796
BAVIN, Rachel Ann & Henry Burroughs 5-5-1841
BAYLY, Maria A. & Philip Thomas Baker 12-19-1799
BAYNE, Amelia & Daniel Hurley 12-21-1784
  Clara & Woodbury Wheeler (Martin) 10-26-1869
  Daniel & Ann Pope 2-4-1795
  Eleanor H. & Hanson G. Catlett 11-7-1832
  Elizabeth & Lancelot Crow 11-26-1794
  Elizabeth Ann & John S. Marlowe 12-1-1819
  George & Ann Jones 4-20-1779
  Grace B. & Robert W. Hunter Jr. 6-28-1852
  Hector & Elizabeth Palmer 2-23-1802
  Dr. John H. & Harriet Addison 12-15-1841
  John H. & Amelia L. Moore (Kershaw) 3-24-1868
  John H. & Ellen R. Darcey 2-28-1881
  Josephine E. & Benjamin F. Marbury 6-2-1856
  Martha & Henry Howsley 4-14-1783
  Martha E. & Alfred Tolson 2-11-1834
  Mary & Thomas Noland 6-13-1796
  Milly & Josias Talburt 6-11-1796
  Prescilla & John Masters 6-3-1778
  Rector & Susanna Jones 12-25-1805
  Robert E. & Ellen G. Wright (Smith) 9-6-1867
  Sarah & George D. Moore 12-16-1795
  Sarah A. & Charles Harbin 1-12-1870
  Wm. B. & Mary E. Hunter 6-1-1844
  William Jr. & Nannie Halley (J. O. Dorsey) 6-19-1877
BAYNES, Chloe & Thomas Fenley 1-29-1791
  John & Catharine Beall 11-2-1784
  Mary Fell & Philip Stuart 12-15-1792
BEACH, William & Mary Medley 5-9-1797
BEALE, Elizabeth & John Wells 1-18-1824
BEALL, Alethea & Jesse Dorsey 1-7-1797
  Alethea & Jacob Riddle 6-11-1836
  Alethea Elizabeth & Archibald Vanhorn 7-26-1797
  Alice Virginia & John W. Wood (Miller) 5-19-1877
  Allison F. & Elizabeth E. Coe 12-15-1806
  Alpheus & Jane Walker 12-10-1841
  Amelia H. & Leonard H. Chew 10-29-1835
  Andrew & Mary Beall 11-9-1782
  Andrew & Mary Ann Ridgely 12-7-1832
  Ann & Thomas Wilson 9-7-1783
  Ann E. & John S. Higdon 12-12-1806
  Ann Rebecca & Septimus J. Cook 12-22-1829
  Ann Rebecca & Philip F. Nally 9-3-1863
  Aquilla & Sophia Duvall 12-21-1798
  Azel & Martha Soper 4-13-1801
  Azel & Lucy E. Smith 6-17-1833

BEALL, Basil & Eleanor Jane Harvey 9-7-1853
Benjamin H. & Mary A. Jones (Rev. Mr. Butler) 2-20-1882
Buchanan & Helen M. Hill (Kershaw) 9-27-1875
Carrie W. & John B. Clark 10-8-1879
Catharine & John Baynes 11-2-1784
Catherine & William Beanes 12-20-1788
Catherine & Chas. Edward Hamilton (Young) 10-12-1867
Catherine R. E. & Rich. Hopkins 12-20-1849
Catherine V. & James Abigill 3-10-1863
Charles & Mary E. Young 2-5-1862
Charles & Hellen Carrick (Scott) 5-14-1875
Charles & Graceanna Smith (DeWolf) 2-9-1880
Charlotte Ann & George W. Brady 3-5-1863
Christopher & Ann Brooke 1-11-1780
David F. & Elizabeth McDaniel 1-28-1800
Dionysius & Charity Ann Harvey (Kershaw) 6-16-1868
E. Thomas & Mary J. Mayhew (Cotton) 4-15-1872
Eleanor & Robert Macgill 4-28-1789
Eleanor W. & Richard I. Morsell 4-29-1816
Elema & Maria Jones 1-16-1822
Elizabeth & Peter Brown 5-11-1781
Elizabeth & Zadock Duvall 4-1-1791
Elizabeth & James Craufurd 6-11-1799
Elizabeth & Oliver Barron 5-28-1800
Elizabeth & George Beall 9-13-1800
Elizabeth & James Shaw 6-24-1805
Elizabeth & Jesse Soper 1-20-1813
Elizabeth & Edward Penn 6-2-1820
Elizabeth & Joseph Wright 5-2-1831
Elizabeth & Rezin Shaw 12-21-1842
Eliz.th E. & Loveless Henson 11-26-1850
Elizabeth F. & Dennis F. Brown (Kershaw) 1-25-1868
Ellen Genever & Joseph Jackson Suit (Rev. Mr. Cooke) 1-14-1885
Emily Jane & Basil Brown 12-24-1839
Estelle M. & Wallace L. Martin 12-31-1875
George & Elizabeth Beall 9-13-1800
George & Rebecca Godman 3-23-1805
George & Dorcus Hellen 12-24-1807
George & Pamelia Hayes 10-20-1813
George & Eliza Bowie 9-2-1817
George & Charity Ann Quander (Dwyer) 10-1-1873
George of Ninian & Deborah L. Jones 9-28-1830
Geo. D. & Martha Kidwell 4-4-1850
George W. & Mary Ann Sophia Beall 11-3-1862
George W. & Mary Lavinia Scott (Cotton) 9-20-1873
George W. & Rebecca F. Hall (McDonald) 1-24-1877
George W. & Jennie Moore (Rev. Mr. Butler) 2-4-1880
George Washington & Martha Beall 12-11-1846
Grafton & Mary Ball (Williams) 2-19-1873
Harriot & John Iglehart 2-11-1807
Henrietta & John Ray 12-8-1804
Henrietta E. & John F. Chasley 5-13-1846
Horatio & Harriot Barron 1-3-1803
Horatio & Martha C. Barnes 1-2-1843
James & Ann Mitchell 5-9-1787

BEALL, James & Caroline Carrick 1-15-1834
  James Francis & Susan Contee (Lankford) 12-30-1870
  James W. & Frances L. Nally (McDonald) 5-27-1872
  Jennie E. of Beltsville & Rev. George V. Leech of Harrisburg, Va.
    2-23-1861
  John & Elizabeth G. Perrie 12-18-1826
  John & Ruth Ellen Beall 9-23-1835
  John & Mary S. Walker 1-19-1838
  John & Ruth Ann Beall 1-3-1840
  John D. & Ruth Barrow Onion 1-5-1842
  John F. & Margaret B. Hanson 4-4-1787
  John H. & Sarah Gantt 4-7-1808
  John H. & Ann P. Clarke 12-27-1817
  John H. & Amelia Jenkins 1-11-1836
  John H. & Margaret E. Vermillon 1-5-1859
  Jonathan & Elizabeth Williams 5-6-1794
  Joseph Lemuel & Henrietta Kidwell (Chesley) 3-9-1869
  Joshua & Elizabeth Waring 2-3-1787
  Joshua & Priscilla Ann Fowler 11-6-1854
  Joshua F. & Hetty A. Small (Rev. Mr. Hyland) 11-1-1881
  Josias Augustus & Elizth Mary Beanes Clagett 12-2-1825
  Josias Fendall & Ann Middleton Marlowe 1-18-1804
  Lethea & Samuel B. White 2-21-1781
  Levin & Henrietta Magruder 1-6-1802
  Levinia & Joshua Shipley 12-4-1878
  Lewis C. & Jennie C. Martin 12-30-1874
  Lucy & James Selby 2-16-1808
  Lucy & Francis Edelen 1-19-1814
  Lucy & James D. Barrett 2-2-1818
  Lucy Virginia & John William Bowling colored (Rev. Perry) 5-11-1880
  Margaret Rosine & William E. Phillips (Stanley) 1-29-1874
  Marian L. & John D. Stone 6-7-1855
  Martha & Thomas Harvey 1-20-1841
  Martha & George Washington Beall 12-11-1846
  Martha A. & Benjamin Mullikin (Gordon) 11-18-1872
  Martha Ellen H. & Richard B. Beans 1-30-1844
  Mary & Andrew Beall 11-9-1782
  Mary & John Duvall 3-29-1793
  Mary & Hiram Belt 10-6-1796
  Mary & Trueman Lanham 10-18-1825
  Mary & Ignatius D. Adams 2-6-1844
  Mary & Louis R. Wood 10-2-1876 (Major)
  Mary Ann & Otho Beall 5-16-1850
  Mary Ann & Basil B. Brown 12-14-1858
  Mary Ann Sophia & George W. Bean 11-3-1862
  Mary B. & Thomas B. Dashiell 11-1-1816
  Mary B. & N. C. Harbry (Rev. Mr. Butler) 12-27-1884
  Mary E. & Albert Brooke 8-30-1873
  Menassah & Mary Price 1-25-1819
  Nancy & Sandford Renn 4-2-1805
  Nancy & William W. Berry 3-2-1807
  Ninian & Angeline Beckett 12-28-1844
  Otho & Mary Ann Beall 5-16-1850
  Otho Berry & Mary Brashears 1-16-1813
  Pierce & Caroline Simpson (Rev. Wm. C. Butler) 10-8-1885
  Priscilla & John Crow 10-25-1780

BEALL, Priscilla B. & James Somervell Jr.   12-15-1846
R. W. & Tabitha A. Taylor (Kershaw) 9-2-1867
Rachel G. & Rich. Harvey 7-16-1845
Rachael Teresa Virginia & Richard Henry Willet 10-9-1860
Rebecca & James F. Millar 7-28-1832
Rebecca C. & George Barney 5-8-1825
Rebeccah & Tobias Belt 1-31-1798
Rezin & Catherine Harris 1-6-1868
Richard & Rebecca Harvey 12-18-1850
Richard Jun. & Cassandra Hilleary 12-16-1794
Richard Henderson & Martha Ann Beanes 2-6-1839
Robert B. & Elizabeth E. Berry 1-5-1791
Rosa & Richard Loveless (Billup) 6-2-1873
Rosa & Wm. J. Bowie 10-17-1876
Ruth & Samuel N. Smallwood 2-28-1801
Ruth & Basil Brown 8-5-1803
Ruth Adelle & Jno. Grafton Hall 2-2-1878
Ruth Ann & John Beall 1-3-1840
Ruth Ellen & John Beall 9-23-1835
Sallie J. & J. Henry Swope 1-29-1864
Saml & Sofa Beall col? (Stanley) 6-5-1867
Samuel & Maggie Brooks (Rev. Henry) 10-14-1884
Sarah & Humphrey Williams 1-21-1794
Sarah & Samuel Hanson 6-9-1795
Sarah & Elisha Harrison 3-25-1796
Sarah & Nathaniel Pope 1-12-1802
Sarah M. Beall & Joshua B. Disney 4-19-1877
Sarah Rebecca & Henry Warring Grimes 7-4-1863
Shadrach & Jane R. Howell 2-6-1841
Sofa & Saml Beall col? (Stanley) 6-5-1867
Sophia & William Smith 2-11-1809
Sophiah & George Page 8-26-1813
Sprigg O. & Sarah A. Sansbury (Rev. Mr. Brayshaw) 1-26-1881
Susanna & Ninian Willett 11-5-1827
Sylvester & Louisa Murray col. (Langford) 6-12-1869
Tabitha & William Lanham 11-21-1820
Taris & John Duker Brashears 11-5-1788
Terrence & Alexander Mockbee 12-24-1810
Theodore & Catharine Jones 8-13-1860
Thomas & Catherine Brown 1-13-1779
Thomas & Jane Magruder 12-28-1839
Thomas & Mary Ann Onions 12-2-1845
Thomas & Sarah King (Kershaw) 12-14-1872
Thomas W. & Margaret J. Wilson 1-9-1818
Upton & Louisa Ogle 10-9-1837
Walter Brooke & Jane Waring 5-1-1794
Walter Trueman Greenfield & Amelia Beall Van Horn 6-2-1818
Washington J. & Mary A. Magruder 7-8-1840
William & Mary Ellen Shaw 12-19-1846
William D. & Sarah A. Brooke 8-30-1786
William O. & Matilda Cox (Rev. Mr. Hyland) 1-10-1883
William Thomas & Mary Ann Beans 12-9-1841
William Thomas & Elizabeth H. Hardey (Gordon) 12-7-1871
William Thos. & Minnie E. Duckett (Rev. Dr. Spangler) 3-12-1884
Zachariah B. & Mary R. Hatton 10-26-1846

BEALL, Zephaniah & Virlinda Fergusson 1-5-1783
BEALLE, Martha S. & D. W. Townshend (Dorcey) 1-19-1875
BEAN, Benj? & Rebecca Evans 12-8-1779
  Benjamin & Artermecia Soper 11-16-1840
  Catharine Emma & John T. Brown (Chesley) 12-21-1868
  Edward & Ann E. McKee 4-13-1827
  Emily & Benjamin Stockett 11-20-1855
  James E. & Mary C. Brady (Butler) 12-18-1878
  Jane & William Harvey 10-15-1817
  Mary & Charles Clarkson 11-6-1802
  Mary Ann & John Clarke 2-28-1871
  Susan & William Simmes col? (Chesley) 10-21-1865
  Thomas & Ann Demar 10-13-1837
  Thomas & Annie L. Harvey (Rev. Mr. Hamilton) 12-14-1875
  Trueman & Elizabeth Ida Brady 12-20-1876
  William O. & Eliza E. Moore (Williams) 4-11-1871
  Wm. & Sarah E. Greenfield 5-8-1825
BEANE, Easther & Thomas Pennefield 7-20-1790
  Ebbsworth & Mary McDaniel 12-12-1798
  Eleanor & Thomas Ball 6-15-1799
  Elizabeth & Philip Lewin Webster 5-20-1793
  George & Maranda Prather 5-13-1820
  John & Rebecca Brightwell 3-10-1784
  Millicent & James A. Magruder 6-10-1794
  Rebecca & Thomas Lucker 2-7-1785
  Rhoda & Richard Peirce 2-8-1819
  Thomas & Sarah Brown 1-13-1794
BEANES, Catharine & John H. Clagett 1-15-1838
  Colmore & Millicent Tyler 4-10-1778
  Eleanor & James Milliken 3-30-1781
  Henrietta & Robert Bradley Tyler 12-1-1779
  John H. & Henrietta Dyar 12-23-1785
  John H. & Harriott Clagett 5-20-1795
  John H. & Catharine Edelen 1-29-1817
  Martha Ann & Richard Henderson Beall 2-6-1839
  Mary & Jeremiah Cooke 12-14-1785
  Mary B. & Baruch Duckett 1-11-1783
  Polly Bowie & Thomas Magruder 11-21-1803
  Rebecca & William Mattingley 2-7-1838
  William & Catherine Beall 12-20-1788
  William & Catharine Fairall 10-25-1818
  William Bradley & Eleanor Brown 4-20-1809
BEANS, Catherine & Levi Young 6-20-1850
  Elzear & Eliza Dent 4-6-1869
  Joseph & Maria Brown col? (Young) 7-22-1865
  Mary Ann & William Thomas Beall 12-9-1841
  Richard B. & Martha Ellen H. Beall 1-30-1844
BEARD, Anthony & Sarah Mockbee 11-14-1801
  Charles & Margaret Ketling 7-19-1852
  Mary Ann & Dennis Magruder 11-21-1820
  Thomas & Caroline Finley 2-7-1837
  William C. & Matilda H. Johns 8-7-1821
BEASLEY, Elizabeth Alice & John Hunter (Martin) 5-22-1867
  J. B. & Elizabeth Batcheller (Martin) 8-16-1870
  Joseph & Hattie M. Boswell (Rev. Father Clarke) 11-17-1884

BEASLEY, Virginia & George Compton (Kershaw) 10-21-1872
BEASON, Jane & William Sasscer 5-3-1779
BEATHY, Mary Jane & Levi Smith (Gordon) 2-14-1876
BEATTER, Richard T. & Mary L. Coats 10-12-1877
BEATTEY, Sallie & John Peacock (Rev. Mr. Gordon) 3-3-1881
BEAVEN - see also Beavin, Beavins, Bevan, Bevin
  Benjamin & Elizabeth Cooksey 2-18-1814
  Charles & Sarah Sasscer 1-13-1778
  Eliz.ᵃ & William Sasscer 12-5-1781
  Elizabeth & George Wright 1-13-1814
  Henrietta & William Cooke 8-28-1777
  Henry & Mary Cooksey 3-28-1815
  Juliet & Benjamin Watson 2-3-1819
  Martha & Benjamin Naylor 12-23-1793
  William & Ann Ellixen 2-2-1787
BEAVIN, Ann & Henry Trueman 4-3-1790   BEAVIN, John & Virlinda
  Ann & Charles L. Boteler 1-12-1813   Gibbons 12-6-1796
  Catharine & Samuel Cooksey 12-23-1813   BEAVIN, Mary & James
  Charles & Amy Sasscer 12-13-1791   Watson 12-25-1799
  Charles & Catharine Long 3-28-1793
  Elizabeth E. & William Strickland 6-20-1814
  James & Susan Watson 12-22-1837
  Sarah A. & Samuel T. Adams 12-27-1836
  William N. & Martha E. Grimes 9-23-1850
BEAVINS, John & Ellen Ellis 3-5-1835
BECK, Arabella & Dr. Grafton Hanson 10-21-1818
  Elizabeth & Middleton Belt 3-16-1832
  James & Ann Duckett 6-10-1806
  James H. & Louisa V. Higgins 5-14-1855
  John & Sarah Hamilton 11-18-1778
  Lemuel G. & Susan Ann Hall 12-10-1822
  Lucy Ann D. & George A. Barnes 5-25-1828
  Mary & Henry Jones 11-24-1834
  Rezin & Elizabeth Ann Walker 11-11-1822
  Ruth & William Williams 12-11-1792
  Samuel D. & Martha Webb 8-19-1793
  Sarah & John Turner 2-5-1799
  Sarah & James Pumphrey 9-15-1821
BECKET, Mary & Jeremiah Wells 12-20-1819
BECKETT, Ann & William Thomas 9-27-1830
  Angeline & Ninian Beall 12-28-1844
  Benj. & Sarah Ann Duvall 12-10-1836
  Benjⁿ H. & Ann R. Duvall 11-30-1852
  Caroline & Richard G. Cross 9-29-1837
  Easter & Henry Clarke 12-20-1777
  Eleanor & John Clubb 4-5-1817
  Elizabeth & William Wallace 3-30-1831
  Emma & Richard Hawkins 12-18-1878
  Humphrey & Mary Shreeves 2-22-1786
  Humphrey & Geneva A. Lanham (Hadaway) 9-17-1873
  John & Mary Walker 9-29-1778
  John & Barbara Wood 5-1-1804
  John & Elizabeth Dixon (both free colored) 4-25-1855
  Josephine & Charles Chase 7-22-1876
  Lucy & Amon Duvall 3-31-1817

BECKETT, Margaret R. & Charles Clarke 11-12-1861
  Marg. & Zach. Baldwin 2-21-1783
  Martha & Jesse Duvall 2-23-1829
  Matilda & Henry Smith 12-8-1874
  Sarah & William Newcome 12-19-1780
  Sarah Ann & Rich. G. Cross 7-12-1843
  Sarah E. & Basil C. Talbert 7-11-1849
  Susan & John White 12-23-1822
  Ursula M. & Benjamin Hopkins 12-23-1826
  Walter & Deborah Lowe 4-21-1813
  William & Rosener S. Duvall 11-29-1821
BECKWITH, Rezin & Mary Hopkins 3-31-1798
  Wm. & Priscilla Jenkins 9-23-1778
BEDDER, Caroline & Miley Butler (Cotton) 3-25-1875
  Elizabeth & Thomas Hooper 8-18-1784
  Jonathan & Martha Hooper 5-25-1778
  Nancy Ann & John Henry Jones (Lanahan) 8-13-1866
  Thomas & Sarah Sullavan 1-8-1785
BEDDO, Ann & Hezekiah Taylor 6-15-1806
  Richard & Mary Riggins 1-29-1816
BEDDOE, Allen & Catherine Rawlings 6-27-1787
BEDDOW, Lenny & John Pool 1-7-1804
  Milley & William Hooper 12-19-1805
BEDLE, Annie & Daniel Frisby col. (Fr. Young) 10-26-1867
BEERS, Isaac & Milly Webster 12-21-1818
BELL, Alice & William Norton (Dwyer) 2-16-1870
  Frank & Alice Levinia Deuvan (Billop) 9-9-1875
  Margery & William W. Berry 6-29-1802
  Sallie & Wilson Plater (Smith) 6-10-1867
  Saul & Lethe Fleet (Rev. Mr. Walker) 11-3-1883
  William & Isabel Lansdale (Maher) 10-23-1869
BELT, Ann C. & John H. Hardesty 6-10-1837
  B. Lee & Amelia Mary Bowie (Rev. Dr. Stanley) 2-2-1882
  Benjamin & Ann Wilson 1-25-1820
  Benj. W. & Elton Smith Drane 9-4-1817
  Charles & Annie Porter col. (O'Dwyer) 6-10-1873
  Dreyden G. & Rob't B. Tyler 3-17-1783
  Edward W. & Eleanor Douglas Hardesty 1-16-1860
  Eleanor Ann & William Hawkins (McDonald) 6-1-1870
  Eleanor Lansdale & Benjamin Lee 12-14-1824
  Elizabeth & John Magill 11-13-1786
  Elizabeth Bowie & Samuel Lane Smith 11-26-1799
  Ella (age 28) & Thomas Berry 11-3-1866
  Esther & Alexander Soper 11-9-1796
  Hiram & Mary Beall 10-6-1796
  Humphrey Sen. & Elizabeth Vincent 3-3-1804
  Humphrey Jun. & Elizabeth Tyler 2-4-1792
  Isabel & Alexander Henson (Walker) 2-28-1877
  Isabella & Samuel Scissell 2-21-1806
  James & Elizabeth Lansdale 12-2-1794
  James Jun. & Mary Gordon McGill 12-14-1813
  Jas. B. & Rebecca Lane 1-18-1842
  Jeremiah Jun. & Priscilla Gantt 3-4-1778
  John S. & Ann C. Courts 12-13-1831
  Joseph & Rachel Brashears 1-12-1791

BELT, Joseph Sprigg & Sarah Burgess 4-28-1790
  Lucy & Thomas Watkins 12-6-1779
  Margaret & Thomas Bowie 1-23-1794
  Margery & Beale Duvall 4-28-1800
  Mary & William John Jackson 4-29-1788
  Mary & William Clarke 2-12-1828
  Mary E. & Trueman D. Cross 3-30-1859
  Mary Elizabeth & Joseph Arnold 10-22-1853
  Mary S. & Caleb C. Magruder 5-28-1833
  Middleton & Elizabeth Beck 3-16-1832
  Osborn Jun? & Sarah Turner 2-10-1807
  Pamelia & Zadock C. Chesley 9-27-1838
  Philip T. & Eveline E. Duvall 2-7-1835
  Pinkney & Eleanora Clifton (Hooman) 6-5-1878
  Rachel & John Wilks Pratt 2-12-1803
  Rachell & Elisha Duvall 6-17-1785
  Richard & Eleanor Aldridge 12-5-1803
  Rufus & Mollie S. Ryland 11-10-1866   Age 24 - lawyer, married at
    rector's house - J. Earnest, minister
  Samuel T. & Autridge Isaac 2-20-1832
  Sarah & Benjamin Elliott 6-30-1813
  Sarah V. & William O. Harvey 9-27-1853
  Stephen & Rebecca Hilleary 1-18-1786
  Stephen & Celestia Gwynn 11-17-1846
  Susan T. & William Talbert 1-15-1828
  Thomas & Sarah Hodges 7-25-1787
  Tobias & Rebeccah Beall 1-31-1798
  Trueman & Eliz?th Ann Ross 4-9-1828
  Violetta Lansdale & Marsham Waring 12-11-1824
  Wm. J. & Ellen N. Bowie 1-14-1823
  William S. & Elenora B. Lee 11-18-1851
BENCE, Oliver & Arra Jane Williams col? (Thompson) 10-16-1867
BENHAM, Calhoun & Betty D. Marbury 4-27-1855
BENJAMIN, J. E. & Florence Smith (William) 3-2-1878
  Lizzie & Samuel W. Simms (Rev. Mr. Van Arsdale) 1-18-1882
BENNETT, Mary & John Rhodes 1-30-1782
  Mary & John Ridgway 11-27-1811
BENSON, Anne Caroline & John Tho? Padgett 3-3-1851
  Basil & Milly Sibley 2-19-1850
  C. M. R. & John F. Sweeney 3-28-1864
  Cephas M. & Harriet T. Wall 10-5-1828
  Cephas Renaldo & Mary Harvey 1-26-1829
  Cephas R. & Maria V. Dye 4-24-1855
  Cepheas W. & Amelia Harvey 12-24-1806
  Eliza & Jn? Harrison 10-23-1848
  Elizabeth E. & Jacob Feagahine 11-21-1864
  James & Martha Brookes (Young) 8-30-1866
  Lucinda & John W. Scott 6-4-1836
  Maria Frances & Basil McKnew 11-21-1864
  Mary Ann & Wm. H. Stinchecum Age 22 - weaver 6-21-1866
  Sarah & Zach? Danielson 12-29-1777
  Thomas & Margaret Tate 2-11-1790
BENTENING, Benj? Smith & Susanna Willett 5-15-1783
BENTON, Nathaniel & Mahala Wills 6-8-1811
BERCKLEY, Henry & Frances Nicholdson 11-22-1788

BERRY, Albert B. & Jane W. Budd 1-4-1858
Ann & Mareen D. Walker 1-15-1787
Ann & Samuel Berry 1-30-1810
Ann & Richard Ayton 12-18-1817
Ann & Robert Marshall 2-25-1820
Ann E. & John Mayo 10-20-1818
Anne Maria & Clement B. Hill 11-22-1830
Annie M. & Benjamin J. Berry 12-24-1883
Ariana & John Osborn Jun. 1-2-1809
Augustus F. & Henrietta L. Davis 12-26-1849
Barbara A. & Robert C. Brooke 12-13-1832
Benjamin & Margaret Duvall 12-12-1833
Dr. Benjamin & Fanny A. Jhons 2-17-1857
Benjamin J. & Annie M. Berry 12-24-1883
Benjamin Sen. & Barbara Lane 12-19-1815
Benjamin of Wm. & Elizabeth C. Sasser 10-23-1818
Brook M. & Emma Magruder 1-25-1816
Deborah & Thomas Ramsey Hodges 12-30-1797
Dorinda E. & Thomas Sasser 12-21-1818
Eleanor & George Naylor 6-2-1785
Eleanor & Benjamin Berry Jefferies 10-18-1791
Elisha & Deborah Summers 7-28-1818
Eliza & Zachariah Walker 12-11-1817
Eliza & Henry McGregor 3-6-1829
Elizabeth & Gabriel Swain 1-3-1798
Elizabeth & Thomas E. Berry 12-12-1838
Elizabeth E. & Robert B. Beall 1-5-1791
Elizabeth Jane & John E. Turton 3-21-1860
Eliz.th H. & John Wolfe 1-25-1829
Ellen A. & Charles S. Worthington (Rev. Wm. Brayshaw) 9-30-1884
Emily & Richard L. Thompson 12-11-1826
Emily Caroline & Wm. F. Adams 9-1-1828
Dr. Geo. W. Berry & Miss Mary H. Dorsett 6-1-1864
Georgie W. & Charles S. Early (Maher) 2-21-1870
Harriet & John Eversfield 4-12-1814
Harriet & Jeremiah Douglass (Gordon) 2-10-1876
Hepburn S. & Eliz.th A. Adams 11-5-1825
Hezekiah & Millicent Barnes 12-19-1797
Isabella F. & Sebastian Sasscer (McDonald) 2-24-1873
James & Ella H. Huntt (Rev. Mr. LaRoche) 5-5-1884
Jane E. & Stephen B. Ward 4-9-1834
Jarret H. & Margaret E. Maddox 1-31-1826
Jesse T. & Mary Thomas 10-27-1868
John & Sarah Jackson 1-1-1812
John & Kitty Pinkney (Gordon) 12-12-1874
John & Charlotte Ann Spencer (Mr. Walker) 4-21-1883
John T. & Ann Sophia Smith 1-25-1827
John T. & Mary Jeffries 2-10-1836
John T. & Louisa Talbert 1-16-1840
Laura L. & William M. Stewart 8-18-1865 Age 30 of P. G. County
Lucy & Thomas Adkins 3-11-1780
Lucy C. & Fendall Marbury Jr. (Rev. Dr. Lewin) 9-10-1883
M. E. & J. M. Meginnis 5-28-1836
Margaret & Thomas Waring 3-21-1795
Maria & Dr. John Vare 11-4-1858

BERRY, Martha & William O Neel 12-7-1814
  Martha J. & Thomas G. Turton 7-20-1853
  Mary & Robert Gordon Wall 2-7-1801
  Mary & Richard Wells Brashears 2-9-1804
  Mary Ann E. & Robert W. Brooke 11-1-1839
  Mary M. & Joseph R. Cassin 1-31-1861
  Matilda & Richard Young 10-24-1815
  Melvina H. & Allen P. Bowie 12-27-1831
  Nicholas & Elianor Eversfield 6-16-1784
  Priscilla & James Goddard 12-30-1815
  Rebecca & John Hodges of Thomas 1-12-1799
  Roger Bernard & Mary Elizabeth Thomas (Lewin) 10-27-1879
  Rosanna & John Hollyday (Langford) 5-15-1869
  Samuel & Ann Berry 1-30-1810
  Sam⁝ H. & Ann R. Mundell 12-22-1846
  Samuel T. & Susan Ann Middleton 12-29-1840
  Sarah A. & Theophilus M. Brooke 6-21-1858
  Sarah C. & Fendall Marbury (Chesley) 4-7-1869
  Susan Ann & Samuel Patterson colored (Lawson) 11-11-1880
  Susanna C. & John H. Cox (Charles County) 12-13-1862
  Thomas & Elizabeth Tolson 12-7-1810
  Thomas & Mary Williams 6-5-1815
  Thomas & Ella Belt (Kershaw) 11-3-1866   Age 32, planter, married at
    Trinity Prot. Ep. Church by Henry J. Kershaw
  Thomas E. & Elizabeth Berry 12-12-1838
  Th⁝ O. & Nannie C. Budd 6-1-1864
  Washington & Eliza T. Williams 6-17-1822
  William & Martha Watts 4-7-1792
  William & Henrietta Guy 10-6-1815
  William & Mary Osbourn 2-7-1826
  William & Kate C. Billop (Billopp) 10-13-1874
  William E. & Elizabeth Harwood 3-23-1799
  William J. & Sarah Eliza Clagett 5-18-1835
  William J. F. & Eliza N. Perrie (Perry) 12-22-1831
  William P. & Caroline P. Plater (Rev. Mr. Gordon) 10-24-1882
  William W. & Margery Bell 6-29-1802
  William W. & Nancy Beall 3-2-1807
  Zachariah Jr. & Priscilla M. Gantt 5-13-1820
BESLEY, Oliver G. & Mary Jane Ives 12-2-1864
BETTS, Joanna & Joseph T. Hopkins 10-18-1875
  Marshall & Harriet A. Carr 9-5-1844
BEVAN, Albert H. & Mary J. Hopkins (Cotton) 1-31-1873
BEVIN, Elizabeth & Nathan Magruder 8-12-1790
BEVINS, Mary Ridout & William Cooke Ogle 12-15-1834
BEYER, Victor & Lucy Duvall 1-10-1827
BIAS, Frank & Mary Wallace (Rev. Mr. Howard) 5-19-1884
  John & Susan Starks 9-9-1874
  John Henry & Georgianna Powell (Rev. Mr. Howard) 5-7-1885
  Victoria & John Powell (Rev. Joshua Barnes) 2-22-1883
BICK, Mathias & Frances Krehh 2-10-1857
BIER, George H. & Mary R. Carter (Chesley) 12-6-1867
BIEYS, James P. of A. A. County & Lilly D. Hodges (Rev. Richard Brown
  4-15-1881
BIGGANAN, Jane & Alexander Smith 2-10-1835

BIGGES, Anna Maria & Josias Kidwell 10-26-1859
Jane Sophia & John A. Allen 1-3-1860
BIGGS, John & Susanna King 12-11-1779
John E. & Mar[t] Vincentia Allen 1-23-1860
Priscilla & Henry Bottler 2-9-1789
BIGNALL, John & Jane Gates 11-14-1818
John & Catherine Weeder 8-21-1786
BILLINGS, Daniel & Jane Thompson 9-26-1791
BILLOPP, Charles F. & Mary B. Brooke (Billopp) 11-2-1874
Ellen & George W. Brooke (Billop) 4-10-1875
Kate C. & William Berry (Billopp) 10-13-1874
BING, Ann & Thomas May 4-1-1816
BINGHAM, Annie & William Watson (Langford) 10-9-1869
BINNEX, Benjamin Franklin & Emma Jane Kagle (Rev. Mr. Dr. Laney) 10-18-1880
BIRCH, Eva A. & John S. Killman (Cross) 1-7-1878
Julia & Rufus E. Rawlings (Mr. Chesley) 7-1-1884
Margaret & Richard Trueman Skinner (Sliner) 1-6-1873
BIRD, Benjamin & Mary Mills 2-9-1801
Benjamin L. & Emily Duvall 11-7-1837
Benjamin L. Jr. & Nannie O. Hodges (Hodges) 6-8-1868
Jacob W. & Ellen Hodges (Rev. Wm. C. Butler) 6-5-1886
John & Elizabeth Swain 9-5-1788
Joshua & Sarah Upton 2-10-1806
Thomas & Jemima Wheeler 12-14-1780
BIRKMAN, Sophia & William E. Mangun (Gordon) 8-8-1872
BISCOE, Ann A. & Richard H. Williams 7-26-1830
Ann Fitzhugh & Charles Steuart 11-1-1814
Eliz[a] & Edward H. Calvert 2-29-1796
George W. & Hannah Sophia Oden 9-28-1812
John R. & Elizabeth Gourly 5-27-1858
Maria A. & Frisby F. Chew of Zazoo, Missi. 2-28-1837
Mary Bond & George Wilson 3-3-1802
BISHOP, Florence V. & Louis Brown col[d] (Rev. Butler) 1-26-1881
Rosa A. & Wilbur A. Dodge 4-27-1886
BLACKBURN, Barbara & Levin Greer 11-18-1815
John & Elizabeth Magruder 2-4-1787
Lena W. & Rich[d] A. Perrie 7-5-1816
BLACKFORD, Wm. F. of Washington County & Emma M. Grove of Washington County (Williams) 4-6-1878
BLACKISTONE, Harriet & Benjamin James (C arroll) 6-29-1877
Letty & Sandy Smith (Maher) 1-8-1870
BLACKLOCK, Leathy Ann & Walter Gassaway 12-19-1846
Nicholas & Elizabeth Cawood 11-24-1786
Thomas & Sarah Sansbury 1-30-1783
Thomas & Ann Wynn 11-22-1783
BLACKSTON, Susannah (Maher) & Louis Carroll 11-1-1870
BLACKWELL, Clarissa & Warner Terry 2-27-1869
BLAINE, Annie M. & George H. Baldwin (Rev. Mr. Brashaw) 7-31-1882
BLAIR, Sarah & Francis West (Towles) 5-19-1873
BLAKE, Clarissa & James Douglass (Watkins) 2-4-1878
John H of Calvert County & Flavilla Marriott 5-22-1862
Lizzie & Benjamin Burroughs 5-19-1885
BLANDFORD, Ann L. & Wm. H. Lindsay 2-15-1858
Elizabeth & Thomas Lewis 6-17-1815

BLANDFORD, Elizabeth & Horatio Dyer 1-12-1839
  George W. & Laura V. Bowen 2-28-1859
  Nicholas & Celia Atcherson 12-21-1822
  Rebecca & Charles H. Driver (Rev. T. H. Brooks) 4-7-1884
  Sarah Ann & Henry B. Darnall 6-19-1838
  Stanislaus & Mary S. Lackland 11-18-1832
  Thomas S. & Catherine C. Spalding 8-3-1857
  Thomas Sprigg & Sarah E. Hill (Father Call) 10-30-1865
  Henrietta & Henry Miles 6-9-1783
  Rebecca & William White 10-11-1783
BLANFORD, Susan & Francis Hamilton 1-27-1785
BOARMAN, Alfred & Amanda Deakins 6-16-1858
  Carroline M. & John B. Edelin 7-29-1819
  George & Lucy Dyer 2-7-1812
  Jannette R. & Solomon G. Chaney 2-8-1849
  Joseph & Mary Ann Edelen 1-9-1801
  Juliann & Michael Mudd 4-19-1819
  Mary M. & Horatio Dyer 1-28-1825
  Ralph & Teressa Ann Hill 12-12-1801
  Rebecca & George Edelen 12-31-1790
  Thomas C. & Jannette R. Manning 12-12-1847
BOCOCK, C. Anna & James S. Jones (Ritter) 6-17-1876
  Eugenie E. & William F. Palmer (Fowler) 2-3-1870
  John H. & Sarah E. Clements 12-26-1859
BOEN, Perry & Mary Adams 1-20-1814
BOHEN, Charles C. of Montgomery County & Annie R. Hodges of Prince
  George's County (Rev. Dr. Lewin) 12-12-1879
BOHLEBER, Louisa F. & L. O. Wissman Age 22 - widow lic. 9-20-1866
  m. 9-25-1866
BOLDING, George & Mittie Briscoe (Waters) 1-13-1870
  Laura & Walter Harris 9-18-1878
  Moses T. & Sarah Ann Prouts (Stanley) 7-3-1872
BONAFIN, Sarah & Adam Havener 12-12-1792
BOND, Edward & Sarah Glascow (Marbury) 12-27-1866
  Edward & Ann Maddox (Wells) 2-9-1877
  Frederick & Sarah Hawkins (Gordon) 12-6-1871
  Matilda & David Koones 5-22-1810
BONEFANT, Keziah & Wm. Townshend 10-12-1795
BONES, Mary & Moses Wood (Rev. Mr. Walker) 5-19-1883
BONIFANT, Elizabeth & Joshua Davis 12-24-1793
  Mary & Thomas Gray 6-2-1781
BONNAFILL, Ann & Basil Riston 12-4-1787
BOOCOCK, Elizabeth M. & George W. Spencer 12-19-1842
BOONE, Alectius & Anna Statia Martin 11-8-1806
  Ann & John Gray 2-9-1802
  Ann Hedwick & Thomas Clagett Scott 12-8-1806
  Caroline & Robert Hardesty 12-23-1854
  Eleanor & James Spalding 12-16-1797
  Electius & Mary Smith 1-8-1779
  Elizabeth Ann & James Conner 7-18-1825
  Francis & Henrietta Neale 8-13-1795
  Georgianna & William H. Okey (O'Dwyer) 4-17-1875
  Ignatius & Martha Boone 4-21-1790
  Ignatius & Eleanor Sansbury 1-14-1796
  John & Ann Hardey 1-12-1782

BOONE, Joseph & Priscilla Boone 1-3-1795
  Laura A. & George S. Jarboe 10-29-1885
  Margaret & Benedict Jameson 3-12-1796
  Marion & Wm. N. Burgess 8-12-1857
  Martha & Ignatius Boone 4-21-1790
  Nace & Susan Williams col? (Maher) 7-12-1869
  Oswald & Ann Jenkins 4-14-1800
  Priscilla & Joseph Boone 1-3-1795
  Rozella Ann & William H. Gwynn 1-25-1825
  Stanislaus & Eleanor Gardner 1-2-1796
  Susannah & Samuel Mitchell 1-2-1794
  Sylvester & Elizabeth Mudd 11-11-1827
  Terrisa & Oswald Jamison 1-8-1805
  Walter & Mildred Edelen 10-9-1783
BOOSE, Elizabeth & Leonard Storm 4-20-1813
  Matilda & Simon Brown (Hooman) 5-10-1879
BOOTH, George & Martha Hoye 10-14-1805
  Harriet Ann & Benjamin Lawson 1-19-1856
  Mary Catherine & Henry Thomas Butler 1-19-1878
BOOTHE, Alfred & Sophia Smith (Fowler) 1-13-1870
  Charles & Georgianna Hawkins 4-13-1869
  George A. & Rose Ann Hawkins 1-17-1866
  Hanna & Richard West (McDonald) 9-4-1869
  Matilda & Lloyd Johnson col? (Smith) 8-9-1867
  Wm. H. & Jenny Henson 12-6-1875
BOOTHES, Isabella of Ann Arundel County & Washington Tyler of same
    county (Rev. Daniel Aquilla) 6-22-1881   colored
BOOZE, Henrietta & James Newman 12-12-1818
  Rosa Ann & James H. Moore (Rev. Mr. Williams) 9-25-1884
BOREN, Wm. H. & Harriet A. E. Williamson 2-22-1864
BORSELL, Elia & William H. Cook 2-6-1839
BOSLEY, Rebecca M. & Oden B. Carrick 3-5-1881
BOSTON, Ella & Francis Rozier (Carroll) 4-20-1878
  Sarah & Michael Garner 12-19-1798
  Sarah & Robert Dulaney 2-19-1803
  Viana & John Hickman 11-3-1798
BOSWELL, Alberta & Charles Harris (Rev. Mr. Shoaff) 12-22-1880
  Caroline & Thomas P. H. Cawood 10-17-1821
  Clement & Eleanor Collard 5-18-1796
  Debby S. & Quincy H. Boswell (Rev. Mr. Peters) 2-25-1884
  Eleanor & Daniel E. Havener 1-28-1826
  Eliz.th & John Hall 9-22-1830
  Elizabeth E. & Cornlius Morley 3-28-1873
  Emma M. & Julius Vermillion 5-19-1880
  George & Susannah Spalding 6-21-1811
  George & Catharine Spalding 1-2-1817
  Harrison E. & John Thomelson (Leneghan) 7-27-1869
  Hattie M. & Joseph Beasley (Rev. Father Clarke) 11-17-1884
  Hendley & Henrietta Johnson 12-15-1792
  Henry & Eleaner Pickrell 1-30-1811
  Henry & Matilda Wells 3-31-1834
  Henry C. & Eliz.h H. Wade 11-21-1826
  James H. & Deborah S. Jones 5-29-1858
  James H. & Mary Hall 8-25-1875
  Jane M. & Mordecai F. Smith 2-8-1810

BOSWELL, John Giles Lilburn & Mary M. Marlow 2-10-1826
  John T. & Mary Lambert 12-16-1831
  John T. & Eliz.th A. Taylor 11-6-1838
  Joseph & Martha A. Thomas 12-18-1862
  Joseph T. & Ann Underwood 1-7-1876
  Josephine & George W. Smith (Smith) 1-8-1868
  Leon^{d} H. & Elizth Garner 1-29-1849
  M. Matilda & Cornelius Morgan 3-28-1864
  Maly Celestia & John Fielder Grimes (Lanham) 12-8-1873
  Maria & Joseph L. Dunlop 8-13-1822
  Martha Ann & Peter G. Burch 7-17-1861
  Mary & George W. Taylor 2-9-1881
  Mary Priscilla & Robert Windsor (Rev. Josiah Perry) 3-29-1880
  Mordecai L. & Julia Watson (White) (Rev. Cross) 12-22-1879
  Mordecai Taylor & Mary Kidwell (Smith) 5-28-1872
  Peter & Ann Findley 5-4-1783
  Quincy H. & Debby S. Boswell (Rev. Mr. Peters) 2-25-1884
  Sarah A. M. & John L. Lederer 1-29-1858
  Trueman E. & Ann Venable 12-16-1833
  Washington G. & Tilly Curten 2-8-1817
  Wm. & Elizabeth F. Monroe 11-8-1851
  Wm. Henry & Mary A. Milburn 11-2-1864
BOTELER, Ann & Thomas Smith Cox 2-2-1785
  Ann & John Taylor 1-25-1832
  Caroline & Levin W. Skelly 12-20-1823
  Catherine & Philip Selby 8-24-1778
  Charles & Sarah Robinson 1-22-1785
  Charles & Sarah Jones 2-21-1806
  Charles & Harriott Brashears 1-25-1799
  Charles L. & Ann Beavin 1-12-1813
  Edward & Elizabeth Saunders 1-31-1781
  Edward J. & Elizabeth E. Deason 7-13-1842
  Edward L. & Eliz.th Ann Davis 4-1-1830
  Eliza Ann & Edward J. K. Scott 2-25-1840
  Eliza S. & Thomas Hodgkin 10-10-1836
  Elizabeth & James Price 1-28-1779
  Elizabeth J. & George B. Scaggs 10-25-1837
  Emily & Randall Moore (Smith) 12-20-1867
  Henderson S. & Susannah G. Hawkins 11-7-1799
  Henry & Rachel Boteler (Evans) 1-20-1872
  Jane A. & Chapman Savoy (Lanahan) 12-30-1867
  Joseph & Sarah Reynolds 12-22-1783
  Julia Ann & William Hurley 12-30-1850
  Levi & Mary Ann Willcoxen 11-25-1820
  Lucinda & Jno. H. Dodson 12-24-1836
  Margaret & Leonard John Brooke 10-29-1793
  Mary & James Naylor 12-31-1800
  Mary Ann & Joseph Estep 8-25-1787
  Mary Ellen & William Holly 1-17-1853
  Milly & Alexander Lovejoy 9-6-1794
  Rachel & Henry Boteler (Evans) 1-20-1872
  Reazin & Jane Poston 10-7-1807
  Rezin & Jane Campbell 4-20-1803
  Rezin Harry & Elizabeth Eleanor Windsor 12-2-1844
  Sarah & Nace Brookes (Hicks) 8-3-1866

BOTELER, Theophilius A. & Margaret Waddell 5-8-1860
    Thomas & Ann Clarke 5-24-1784
    Thomas & Susan Allens col? 8-3-1871
    William & Elizabeth Osbourn 2-5-1816
    William & Priscilla Crandel 9-29-1853
    William N. & Susan Warner 12-16-1841
BOTTLER, Henry & Priscilla Biggs 2-9-1789
BOUNDS, Sally Ann & Selby B. Scaggs 6-17-1850
BOURNE, John & Elizabeth S. Hodgkin 6-3-1862
    Maria E. & William E. Duvall (Gordon) 4-12-1869
    Mary E. & Alexander B. Hodgkin 10-26-1861
BOUSE, John M. & Eliza E. Talbott (Kershaw) 9-2-1874
BOWEN, George Y. & Mary Ann Robertson 2-4-1826
    John & Alice Seitz 12-21-1878
    Kate M. & John P. Driscoe (Perry) 11-22-1879
    Laura V. & George W. Blanford 2-28-1859
BOWIE, Alice & T. Owen W. Roberts 11-8-1876 (St anley)
    Alice R. & Francis Tolson 11-30-1857
    Allen P. & Melvina H. Berry 12-27-1831
    Amelia Mary & B. Lee Belt 2-2-1882 (Rev. Dr. Stanley)
    Ann & John Smith Brooke 10-31-1780
    Ann & Philemon Lloyd Chew 10-27-1790
    Benjn H. C. & H. Clotilda Hilleary (McDonald) 11-23-1871
    Camilla & John Somervell 11-29-1825
    Caroline L. & Osborn Sprigg 12-22-1840
    Catherine & Daniel Clarke 6-4-1833
    Catherine Waring & Thomas Jefferson Clagett 12-31-1881 (Rev. Dr. Gordon)
    Charles & Eliza L. Coombes 5-15-1828
    Cora & Edmund Clare Fitzhugh (Washington Territory) 5-15-1861
    Crista S. & Colin Mackenrie 11-28-1853
    Edith P. & Joseph K. Roberts Jr. (age 21) 6-6-1866 (Kershaw)
    Eliza. & George Beall 9-2-1817
    Eliza Coombs & Edgar Patterson McCeney (Billup) 11-17-1873
    Eliza D. & Edmund Addison 10-7-1828
    Elizabeth & Thomas Brooke 3-21-1803
    Elizabeth Ann & Edmund Cooledge 11-14-1832
    Elizabeth Margaret & John Waring Jr. 12-30-1800
    Elizabeth Susanna & Joseph Howard 3-31-1809
    Ellen & Frank Girault Addison (Rev. Stanley) 10-11-1884
    Ellen N. & Wm. J. Belt 1-14-1823
    Emily C. & Richard A. C. Magruder 10-25-1824
    Fielder & Barbara Susannah Parker Lane 12-16-1811
    Fielder & Rebecca Mackall 3-10-1835
    Francis & Alice Dodson (Carroll) 9-19-1876
    Francis M. & Sarah M. Courts 10-17-1833
    Francis M. & Ida M. Hill (Hooman) 1-14-1879
    James E. & Frances Whitemore 12-21-1860
    John & A. M. L. Gantt 10-21-1833
    John Burgess & Catharine Hall 10-15-1803
    John F. & Susanna A. Hawkins 4-23-1784
    Juliet & Charles Edward Hanson (Rev. Mr. Lawson) 6-6-1881
    Juliet M. & James B. Brookes 10-17-1812
    Kate & Wesley Hanson 3-29-1869 (McDonald)
    Lizzie & Harry Brooks (Rev. Mr. Brooks) 1-12-1886
    Margaret & Isaac Duckett 1-24-1792

BOWIE, Marg<u>t</u> Eliz<u>a</u> & Roderick M. McGregor 10-12-1866 (Rev. H. J. Kershaw)
   Age 22 married 10-16-1866
Margaret H. & William W. Hemsley 8-23-1869 (Stanley)
Margaret S. & Benj<u>n</u> Brookes Jun<u>r</u> 12-24-1785
Maria L. & James Owens Junior (Stanley) 8-9-1867
Martha M. & Benton Tolson 12-15-1860
Mary & Thomas Franklin (Stanley) 10-17-1870
Mary & John T. Wall (Lewin) 11-17-1880
Mary Ann & William D. Clagett 2-4-1828
Mrs. Mary Jane & Samuel N. Smith (Mark) 3-29-1866
   m. 4-1-1866 age 28 res. S. N. Smith, Presbyter E. Church
Mary M. & Turner Wootton 3-27-1794
Mary M. & Reverdy Johnson Esq. 11-15-1819
Mary M. & Samuel C. Moran 10-8-1833
Mary M. & Thomas Clagett Jr. (Kershaw) 10-26-1869
Mary Margaret & Grafton Tyler Jr. 1-8-1836
Michael & Jane Jefferson 11-6-1851
Mollie & James Campbell col<u>d</u> (Fowler) 3-22-1871
Oden & Alice Carter 12-3-1851
Priscilla & Richard L. Ogle 12-16-1846
Rachel & Louis Gott (Rev. Mr. Barnes) 12-27-1883
Richard W. & Margrt Somervill 5-20-1836
Richard W. W. & Elizabeth L. Waring 7-23-1852
Robert & Margaret French 2-21-1826
Robert & Eleanor B. Magruder 12-9-1850
Robert of Walter & Julia V. Waring (Marbury) 5-17-1872
Robert W. & Catharine Lansdale 3-28-1818
Simeon F. & Mary E. Burgess (Lenahan) 3-25-1867
Thomas & Margaret Belt 1-23-1794
Thomas Contee & Mary Mackall Wootton 2-7-1801
Thomas F. & Catherine H. Waring 11-18-1830
Thomas F. Jr. & Elizabeth M. Worthington 12-15-1856
Thomas T. S. & Agnes W. McGregor (Kershaw) 12-2-1868
W. Worthington & Ellen V. Clagett (Rev. Dr. Lewin) 9-23-1885
Walter & Amelia Margaret Weems 11-24-1812   BOWIE, Walter W. W.
William & Kitty Duckett 12-13-1802   & Adeline Snowden
William B. & Ann A Clarke 7-15-1837   9-1-1836
William D. & Eliza M. Oden 2-8-1825
William D. & Mary Oden 1-3-1854
Wm. J. & Rosa Beall 10-17-1876
William M. & Martha Magruder 10-30-1809
William M. & Mary Trueman Hilleary 11-29-1814
Wm. S. & Eliz<u>a</u> Sprigg 12-18-1781
BOWLDING, Jane & James H. Calvert 11-15-1875 (Major)
BOWLING, Alcysius B. & Ann Maria Summers 2-12-1838
Basil & Mary Hardey 12-31-1799
Bradley & Eliza Murray (Gordon) 10-15-1875
E. R. & T. Baker Dyer 10-29-1867
Elizabeth C. & Charles S. Contee 6-1-1860
Emily M. & Thomas McWilliams 4-28-1858
Fanny & George Forbes Jr. 11-25-1872 (Dwyer)
Helen & G. Douglass Mercer 11-10-1874
Henry & Margaret Morton 12-23-1859
John & Christiana Jemima Plummer (Edelen) 12-15-1868
John D. & Eliz.<u>th</u> Gill 4-9-1832

BOWLING, John William & Lucy Virginia Beall colored (Revd. Mr. Perry) 5-11-1880
Laura E. & Henry Chapman (Pinkney) 1-28-1874
Levinah & Charles Nevitt 1-18-1780
Margaret & Clarence Hall 2-19-1884
Mattie C. & Henry W. Clagett 11-18-1863
Sarah & Jacob Clements 1-5-1810
Thomas & Ann Nevill 8-4-1783
BOWSER, Louisa & John Crawford (Fr. Cotton) 5-17-1872
BOWZER, James & Martha Brown (Father Cotting) 4-7-1885
BOYCE, Marion & Hilleary Matthews 1-17-1868 (Smith)
BOYD, Abraham & Elizabeth Igleheart 1-23-1800
Andrew & Cecelia Jackson 7-23-1870 (Fr. McDonald)
Archibald & Ann Scott 11-9-1777
Benjamin & Lettecia Pinkney 2-27-1872 (Fowler)
Dennis & Elizabeth M. Lansdale 11-4-1809
Eleanor & Cephas Shekells 9-27-1796
Eleanor G. & Nicholas L. Queen 1-1-1801
James & Martha Dorsett cold. 1-11-1867 (Lenahan)
James H. & Susanna A. Hodrick 12-9-1843
Joseph & Elizabeth Tait 1-14-1800
Joseph & Sarah Duvall 8-15-1814
Matilda & Richard Chany 2-9-1825
Rebecca & Richard Taylor 1-14-1801
Richard D. & Matilda Duvall 4-18-1814
Thomas Junr & Mary Magruder 10-13-1788
William & Jemima Igleheart 12-29-1802
BRACE, William Henry & Fennie Hedge cold. 8-8-1868
BRADDY, John & Mary Gross 9-2-1882
BRADFORD, Eleanor & Isaac Walker 7-27-1790
BRADLE, Mary Isabella & John F. Curtain 12-13-1866 (Marbury)
Thomas & Martha Jane Curtain 12-13-1866 (Marbury)
BRADLEY, Catharine & Abraham Williams 12-13-1794
Susanna & Daniel Jones 11-16-1779
Wesley P. & Sarah M. Hill 2-25-1862
BRADY, Elizabeth Ida & Trueman Bean 12-20-1876
Frances Rebecca & James Wesley Fowler 12-31-1873 (Gordon)
George & Amelia Jones 7-24-1845
George D. & Sarah Ann Phellps 4-22-1851
George W. & Charlotte Ann Beall 3-5-1863
James & Margaret Ford 5-19-1870 (Stanley)
James H. & Sarah Priscilla Taylor 3-11-1868
James Owen & Jane Walter Fuller 12-31-1850
John & Caroline Phelps 1-25-1848
John A. & R. E. Henry 11-20-1884 (Rev. Mr. Stanley)
John W. & Sarah E. J. Morris 12-26-1882 (Rev. Wm. C. Butler)
Joseph H. & Mary A. Brady 12-17-1878 (Hooman)
Mary & John Wm. Egling 10-9-1884 (Rev. Mr. Brashaw)
Mary A. & Joseph H. Brady 12-17-1878 (Hooman)
Mary Ann & William Baldwin 1-21-1853
Mary C. & James E. Bean 12-18-1878 (Butler)
Mary Jane & Jno. W. Selby 12-20-1848
Richard L. & Ellen Frances Hayes 4-15-1868 (Chesly)
Stephen & Sarah Jane Buckler 2-5-1874 (Townshend)
Zachariah & Margaret Farr 1-3-1853

BRANDT, Gerard W. & Anne T. Dixon (MacDonnell) 1-31-1870
BRANDTT, Richard & Lucy Ann Mitchell 12-15-1792
BRANHAM, Mary & Richard White 11-14-1798
BRANT, Jemima & Samuel Hepburn 7-7-1871 (Stanley)
  Margaret & Richard Tarman 2-12-1795
BRASHEARS, Angelina & Joshua Currico 12-16-1842
  Benedict & Sarah Godman 1-25-1810
  Caroline A. & J. L. Thomas 2-6-1872 (Mr. Gordon)
  Cassia & Charles Duvall 3-27-1778
  Columbus & Susan M. Fletcher 6-4-1874
  Dorca G. & Thomas Harvey 1-29-1851
  Eleanor & William Laten 1-20-1802
  Eliz? & Basil Ridgway 1-18-1779
  Elizabeth & Moses Orme 2-27-1795
  Elizabeth & Theodore Sansbury 10-8-1803
  Elizabeth Ann & John Lloyd Sweeny 3-29-1848
  Frances E. & John H. Martin 7-4-1870 (Kershaw)
  George & Mary Crompton 2-10-1802
  Green & Mary Hyatt 8-20-1806
  Harriet & Charles Boteler 1-25-1799
  Henrietta & Elisha Hoskinson 7-21-1777
  Henry & Aggy Ferguson 4-7-1792
  James L. & Sarah E. Cator 1-4-1848
  Jemima & William Wells of George 10-2-1816
  Jeremiah & Margaret Soper 4-30-1803
  John & Mary Sheriff 1-8-1805
  John Duker & Taris Beall 11-5-1788
  John P. & Ann Pumphry 12-9-1778
  Jonathan & Mary Brown 6-12-1781
  Joseph & Mary Cross 12-10-1780
  Lucy & Joseph Cross 5-20-1783
  Lucy & William F. Anderson 12-14-1842
  Margaret & Fielding Cross 12-12-1794
  Martha & James Hodhe 1-22-1790
  Martha & Trueman Duvall 11-19-1801
  Mary & Levin Wilcoxon 2-11-1780
  Mary & Plummer Latten 1-25-1798
  Mary & Nathan Thomas 1-17-1799
  Mary & Thomas Latton 2-12-1806
  Mary & Otho Berry Beall 1-16-1813
  Mary E. & Wm. R. Mitchell (Robey) 1-3-1867
  Nathaniel & Mary Page 2-17-1792
  Osburn & Martha Oden 6-1-1785
  ..burn & Elanor Procter 2-14-1795
  Otho & Nancy L. Cator 10-20-1853
  Otho R. & Dorinda V. Mangun 3-20-1848
  Rachel & Joseph Belt 1-12-1791
  Rebeccah & Walter Ray 12-31-1791
  Richard G. & Dorens S. Turner 2-21-1835
  Richard Wells & Mary Berry 2-9-1804
  Ruth & Frederick Miles 2-11-1784
  Sarah & John Ball 1-23-1812
  Wilkinson & Hannah Brown 2-4-1788
  Wilkinson & Angeline Hoye 12-17-1834
  Wilkinson & Jane N. Clarke 5-25-1853

29

BRASHEARS, Zachariah & Ann Cutchly 1-22-1785
  Zadock & Elizabeth Drane 2-9-1790
  Zadock & Ann Armeger 3-23-1819
BRAWNER, Jas. & Matilda A. Parker 10-30-1825
  Josephine & Jno. Wm. Thomas colᵈ 2-27-1871 (Linthicum)
  Pembroke A. & Matilda Semms 10-13-1857
BRAY, George W. & Ann Eliza Townshend 6-6-1842
BRENT, Ann & Edward Roberts 12-29-1797
  Francis Neale & Mary Jane Anna Magill 11-17-1858
  George T. & Barbara E. Taylor 2-6-1883 (Rev. Father Cunnane)
  George Taney & Laura Eugenia French 1-16-1866
    Age 25 - farmer (P. B. Lenaghan, Catholic Priest)
  Moses & Julia Hamilton 12-22-1865 (Beque)
  Virlinda & Fielder Watson 2-28-1817
  Wm. Henry & Matilda A. Galloway colᵈ 12-16-1865
BRENTT, Mary & Robert Sewell 2-16-1789
BREWER, Mary & Quintin Baine 9-13-1792
  Wilson & Lizzie Chase 12-13-1867 (Beque)
  Wilson & Rose Ross 1-5-1884 (Rev. Wm. C. Butler)
BRIAN, see Brien, Bryan
  Henry & Meeky Ball 1-20-1802
  Rachel & Joseph Wheat 12-12-1791
  William & Sarah Padgett 1-13-1787
BRICE, Anna & Stephen W. Butler 2-2-1870 (McDonald)
  Anthony & Harriet Ann Robinson 9-9-1876 (Green)
  Charles & Letty Carter 1-3-1871 (Gordon)
  Edward W. & Christianna Hall 9-6-1877 (Carroll)
  Lemuel & Louisa Hager 10- 4 -1879
  Mary Jane & Patrick Scott colᵈ 10-12-1868 (Langford)
  Richard & Hannah Isaac 11-22-1781
  William & Jane Courts 2-28-1848
BRIDGET, Eleanor & James Fergusson 5-22-1807
BRIEN, M.A. & James G. Pumphrey 2-18-1841
BRIGHT, Stephen & Amelia Baldwin 9-21-1796
BRIGHTWELL, Allen & Jane Pearce 3-13-1802
  Ann & Thomas Ratcliff 1-9-1805
  Benjamin T. & Hetta Ann Edelen 2-17-1842
  Catherine & John Wood 4-23-1825
  Elizabeth Juliet & John Ellis 2-7-1814
  Emma & John William Winsor 10-26-1876 (Gordon)
  Hetta Ann & Henry Mangun 2-7-1851
  John & Henrietta King 2-9-1803
  John & Letitia Mahew 1-25-1804
  John Lawson & Sophinia Brightwell 2-15-1802
  Levin Broten & Sarah Lamar 1-3-1820
  Martha & William Pickeren 9-17-1806
  Mary & James Thompson 4-2-1803
  Rebecca & John Beanes 3-10-1784
  Richard & Mary Purce 5-3-1785
  Richard L. & Fanoni Thomas 12-26-1794
  Sophinia & John Lawson Brightwell 2-15-1802
  Susanna & Charles Smith 8-4-1866 (Hoover)
  Thomas G. & Willy Stamp 1-5-1821
BRINTALL, Francis & Catherine Jane Shipley 8-15-1867
BRISCOE, Annie & Benjamin Hall 12-25-1876

BRISCOE, Aquilla & Jane Robinson 4-4-1795
  Bettie A. & George E. Orme 3-5-1869 (Lanahan)
  Edmund &.Caroline Sophia Marshall 12-2-1844
  John F. & Jane Gray 10-19-1876
  John P. & Kate M. Bowen (Perry) 11-22-1879
  John P. & Susie Flutcher 12-24-1873 (Dwyer)
  Margaret A. & James W. Johnson 12-29-1879 (Rev. Mr. Wilson)
  Mittie & George Bolding 1-13-1870 (Waters)
  Thomas & Catharine Dockett 10-24-1879 (Wills)
  William & Annie Holland 7-31-1878 (Hooman)
  William & Ellen Pinkney col? 12-9-1880 (Rev. Mr. Lawson)
BROGDEN, Henry H. & Annett Carter 11-16-1880
  Priscilla & Thomas J. Wilson 3-3-1852
BROMLEY, William & Sarah Sansbury 1-29-1794
BROOK, see Brooke, Brookes, Brooks
  Julia & Robert Douglas 5-19-1868 (Langford)
BROOKE, Albert & Mary E. Beall 8-30-1873
  Ann & Christopher Beall 1-11-1780
  Ann & Joseph Wheeler 4-23-1785
  Augustus D. & Margaret A. S. French 5-25-1853
  Barbara & John Eversfield 6-2-1778
  Catharine & Isaac Lansdale 3-27-1792
  Clement & Ann Eleanor Whitaker 4-2-1801
  Edmund Jr. & Ellen M. Young 2-1-1817
  Eleanor Ann & Francis Ridgeway 1-6-1868 (Fr. Call)
  Felley (Felleci) & George W. Dunlop 5-27-1831
  George W. & Ellen Billopp 4-10-1875 (Billopp)
  George W. & Annie L. Butler 11-22-1881 (Rev. W. C. Butler)
  Harriet & Clarence Hawkins 4-9-1873
  Harriot & Luke Howard 8-21-1824
  Henry & Hariot S. Brown 1-13-1798
  Henry & Eleanor Waring 10-8-1798
  Henry & Eliza J. Worthington 5-28-1834
  Hetta & Henry Hill Jun? 4-23-1781
  Ida Julia & William W. Waring 6-8-1871 (McDonald)
  Isaac & Sarah Anne Magruder 10-20-1780
  James & Mary Ann Hill 10-24-1814
  John B. & Araminta Carroll 9-18-1821
  John Smith & Ann Bowie 10-31-1780
  Leonard John & Margaret Boteler 10-29-1793
  Lethe Ann & James M. Edelen 10-4-1872 (Dwyer)
  Mariah A. & Wm. Kelly 11-30-1820
  Mary & Joseph Manning 11-5-1857
  Mary B. & Charles F. Billopp 11-2-1874 (Billopp)
  Mary M. & Robert Ellis 4-5-1824
  Nancey & Benjamin Randell 11-25-1867 (Fr. Young)
  Richard & Elizabeth Otway 6-5-1800
  Robert C. & Barbara A. Berry 12-13-1832
  Robert W. & Mary Ann E. Berry 11-1-1839
  Samuel & Laura C. Hill 11-4-1858
  Sarah A. & William D. Beall 8-30-1786
  T. Blake & Florence Contee 11-20-1863
  Theophilus M. & Sarah A. Berry 6-21-1858
  Thomas & Elizabeth Bowie 3-21-1803
  Thomas F. & Ann Duckett 6-20-1791

31

BROOKE, Washington & Margaret Harvey 2-15-1819
BROOKES, Alice & Isaac Woodard 1-13-1870 (Lankford)
  Benjamin & Sarah Johnson 11-7-1782
  Benjʔ Junr & Margaret S. Bowie 12-24-1785
  Benjamin & Elizabeth Halkerstone 2-18-1799
  Bettie & Brooke Mackall 2-29-1884 (Rev. C. W. Walker)
  Charity & Charles Jackson (Wills) 11-15-1879
  Frances & George Reeder colᵈ 12-21-1869 (Marbury)
  James & Rosetta Gray 12-26-1865
  James B. & Juliet M. Bowie 10-17-1812
  John & Eleanor H. Waring 12-21-1841
  John Smith & Eleanor Harwood 6-3-1786
  Louisa & Richard B. B. Chew 11-23-1853
  Martha & James Benson 8-30-1866 (Young)
  Martha & Peter Reeder 5-15-1877 (Perry)
  Nace & Sarah Boteler 8-3-1866 (Hicks)
  Thomas R. & Susan R. Waters 12-7-1844
BROOKS, Addie C. & Whittingham Bryan 11-25-1878 (Williams)
  Anne B. & George M. Henault 8-20-1874 (Pickney)
  Annie & John R. Hawkins 12-9-1884 (Rev. John R. Henry)
  Bettie & Lemuel Lyons colᵈ 6-25-1870 (Evans)
  Bettie & Amos Butler colᵈ 12-14-1880 (Rev. Mr. Watkins)
  Chas. & Sallie Green 11-29-1884 (Rev. Mr. Brooks)
  Cornelia & John Maddox 4-11-1874 (Tennent)
  Edward P. & Eva Lizzie Whetters 10-10-1877
  Fr ances & Charles Henry Adams 12-27-1879 (Rev. Mr. Wilson)
  George & Susan Johnson 5-19-1847
  Gusty & Clarissa Baddy 12-19-1878 (Watkins)
  Harry & Lizzie Bowie 1-12-1886 (Rev. Mr. Brooks)
  Henry & Harriet Eliza Gray both colᵈ 4-27-1865
  Jeremiah & Mary Butler 12-17-1872 (Marbury)
  John R. & Ellen Anderson 12-27-1882 (Rev. Mr. Walker)
  Leander & Ann Maria Bukney colᵈ 4-4-1882 (Rev. Mr. Gordon)
  Maggie & Samuel Bealle 10-14-1884 (Rev. Henry)
  Martha & Robert Fleet 12-20-1884 (Rev. Mr. Brooks)
  Mary & John Thomas Contee 12-26-1876 (Carroll)
  Mary J. & Elkanah N. Waters 11-3-1876 (Williams)
  Pinkney & Laura Swain 4-14-1879 (Gordon)
  Saulsbury & Mary West 4-3-1885 (Father Cotton)
  Teresa & George W. Butler 1-6-1849
  William & Lizzie Carter 9-14-1878 (Lenaghan)
  Wm. B. & Susanna Baldwin 7-1-1851
  Wm. P. & Mary S. McCormick (Rev. Mr. Brayshaw) 10-22-1880
BROOM, Samuel & Harriet Taylor 1-9-1883 (Rev. Henry Waters)
BROOMFIELD, Nathan & Elizabeth A. Oneale 1-15-1840
BROWN, Adam C. & Susan Tucker 2-17-1834
  Agnes & John Brown 1-31-1879 (Hooman)
  Agnes C. & H. M. Ryon 5-3-1886
  Alice & Albert Shorter 12-14-1872 (Ankward)
  Alice M. & Noah Frye 4-29-1885 (Rev. Cooke)
  Allen & Adeline Galloway 5-9-1868
  Almira & Samuel G. Mulloy 10-26-1875
  Alsa & James M. Suit 3-11-1867
  Andrew & Margaret Crawford 3-14-1797
  Andrew & Ann Jarman 4-11-1812

BROWN, Andrew & Mary B. Sansbury 7-13-1876 (Kershaw)
  Ann & Samuel Hutchinson 6-3-1786
  Anna & Aquilla Webb 11-27-1802
  Antony & Annie White 5-30-1872 (McDonald)
  Basil & Ruth Beall 8-5-1803
  Basil & Charity Ann Moore 5-14-1833
  Basil & Emily Jane Beall 12-24-1839
  Basil B. & Mary Ann Beall 12-14-1858
  Basil T. & Miss Julia Lynch 12-9-1862
  Brittania A. & Alfred R. Forman 9-22-1859
  Carrie R. & Samuel R. Young 11-18-1862
  Catharine & John Hawkins 2-14-1876 (Wiget)
  Catherine & Thomas Beall 1-13-1779
  Catherine & Richard Ryon 12-19-1825
  Catherine & William Turner 1-22-1873 (McDonald)
  Charles & Mary Simmons 8-8-1879 (Crowley)
  Charles C. & Mary A. Isaacs 7-15-1867 (Stanley)
  Charles H. C. & Henrietta Green 10-9-1884
  Charles W. H. & Louisa Queen colored 11-19-1880 (DeWolfe)
  Charlotte & Robert Marshall 2-25-1839
  Clement & Camilla Jackson col'd 8-5-1869 (Maher)
  David & Eliza Gibson 11-30-1824
  Dennis & Elizabeth Talbert 1-10-1827
  Dennis F. & Elizabeth F. Beall 1-25-1868 (Kershaw)
  Dinah & Laurence Wood col'd 1-18-1866 (Call)
  Dollie & Frederick A. Tschiffely Jr. 2-15-1873 (Ernest)
  Edward & Catherine Speake 3-8-1780
  Eleanor & William Bradley Beanes 4-20-1809
  Eliza & James Howell 7-30-1834
  Eliza Jane & Theodore Owens col'd 12-17-1880
  Elizabeth & John Hooper 7-7-1788
  Elizabeth & Richard King 2-11-1795
  Elizabeth & Thomas Ryon 12-7-1832
  Elizabeth & Samuel Smith 11-24-1865
  Elizabeth & Mitchell Liberty 9-11-1871 (Wheeler)
  Elizabeth & Jacob Denney 10-10-1876
  Elizabeth & William Butler 2-11-1886 (Rev. Father Cotton)
  Eliz.th & Samuel Townshend 2-8-1831
  Ellen & Mack Johnson 12-7-1869 (Maher)
  Emily & Andrew Smith 4-29-1867
  Fanny & Thomas Jackson 8-17-1866 (Call)
  Francis & Lucy Gates 7-13-1802
  George & Ann McDowell 5-27-1799
  George & Cornelia Jane Tucker 8-13-1866 (Griffith) Married at
    Mr. Tucker's, Sam'l H. Griffith, minister E. Church. Age 23-farmer
  Geo. T. & Juliana Hardey 8-11-1825
  Gustavus R. & Mary C. Hatton 8-21-1816
  Hannah & Wilkinson Brashears 2-4-1788
  Hariot S. & Henry Brooke 1-13-1798
  Harriet E. & William T. Prince 7-12-1853
  Harriet Georgianna & James R. Lawson 11-26-1861
  Henrietta & Jesse Fowler 2-20-1802
  Henry & Jane Wood col'd 2-6-1868 (Chesley)
  Henry & Alice Mitchell 11-4-1871 (McDonald)
  Henry & Mary West 2-14-1874

BROWN, Henry & Lizzie Chitham 5-15-1876
  Henry & Julianna Dorsey cold 4-8-1882
  Henry W. & Sophia Knox 8-11-1881
  Hepzebah & John Griffen 5-30-1807
  Isaac & Bettie Carroll 6-8-1871 (McGuire)
  Isaac G. & Mary Mangun 3-28-1818
  James F. & Lillie M. Naylor 4-26-1851
  Jane & Richard T. Anderson 2-7-1870 (Harper)
  Jane & Frederick McClane 2-5-1873
  Jennett & Charles John Carroll 5-26-1795
  Jennie A. & George W. Gray 6-6-1883 (Rev. Mr. Walker)
  Jerry & Margaret Robinson 2-11-1870 (Wheeler)
  John & Sarah Ann Rhodes 11-25-1835
  John & Agnes Brown 1-31-1879 (Hooman)
  John & Emily Carroll 12-30-1885 (Rev. Enoch Peters)
  John Arthur & Mary Jane Jackson 2-15-1871 (Father McDonald)
  John D. & Casino Sears 8-1-1876 (Kershaw)
  John Henry & Lucy Ann Brown col. 4-27-1867 (Fr. Call)
  John Preston & Maggie Plummer colored 12-17-1879 (Rev. Henry Plummer)
  John R. & Mary Minker 8-26-1880
  John T. & Catharine Emma Bean 12-21-1868 (Chesley)
  John W. & Sarah Miller 5-11-1829
  Joseph & Sophia Rideout 4-22-1871 (Wheeler)
  Joseph & Emma Ida Webster 8-15-1882 (Rev. Mr. W. K. Boyle)
  Joseph Henry & Clora Ann Crack - both colored people 4-15-1865
  Julia & John Vinson cold 12-21-1869 (Maher)
  Letitia & John Wheeler 12-11-1792
  Lizzie & Thomas Young cold 8-21-1869 (Maher)
  Lloyd & Drusilla Elliott 11-30-1841
  Lloyd & Henrietta West cold 10-21-1865 (Father Call)
  Lloyd & Harriet Owens 1-6-1877 (Walker)
  Louis & Florence V. Bishop col. 1-26-1881 (Rev. Mr. Butler)
  Louisa & Isaac Fletcher cold 9-16-1869 (Maher)
  Lucy & Richard Barrett 12-18-1784
  Lucy & Robert Digges 12-22-1866 (Kershaw)
  Lucy Ann & John Henry Brown 4-27-1867 (Fr. Call) cold
  Margaret & David Larkins col. 12-24-1881 (Rev. Mr. Butler)
  Margery B. & John Urnshaw 1-23-1843
  Maria & Joseph Beans cold 7-22-1865 (Young)
  Martha & James Bowzer 4-7-1885 (Father Cotting)
  Martha Ann & Llewellen Lodge 5-21-1832
  Mary & John White 12-20-1780
  Mary & Jonathan Brashears 6-12-1781
  Mary & Abraham Fowler 2-2-1801
  Mary & Julius Jones cold 6-15-1870 (Maher)
  Mary & James Madison Carrick 2-11-1873 (Stanley)
  Mary & Paul Heightman 9-3-1875 (Green)
  Mary A. & Charles J. Watson 3-15-1865
  Miss Mary E. & James W. Clubb 6-1-1864
  Mary E. & Edward Hollins 12-20-1877 (Homan)
  Mary Elizabeth & James Henry Wright 5-23-1874 (Maybury)
  Mary Ellen & James Hagan 5-21-1866 (Fr. Call)
  Mary Ellen & Thomas Brown 1-11-1868 (Call)
  Matilda & John Calvery cold persons 6-6-1865
  Milley & David Chase 7-5-1872

BROWN, Milly & Joseph Riley 7-23-1794
　Nancy & George Washington Whitaker 6-16-1801
　Nancy & George Washington Talbott 2-26-1814
　Nicholas & Mary Frisby 4-20-1872 (McDonald)
　Osborn & Rachel Ann Brown 11-16-1870 (Maher)
　Patrick & Maria Wills 1-9-1875 (Lenaghan)
　Peleg & Emily Wallingsford 8-3-1836
　Peoly & Rebecca D. Magruder 1-12-1822
　Peter & Elizabeth Beall 5-11-1781
　Pinkney & Ariana Stewart 1-28-1870 (Langford)
　Pinkney & Christiana Naylor 5-10-1876 (Carroll)
　Pinkney & Elizabeth Henson col? 10-10-1881 (Rev. Mr. Wilson)
　Priscilla & John Hunt 1-10-1789
　Priscilla E. & James E. Woodall 6-28-1854
　Rachel Ann & Osborn Brown 11-16-1870 (Maher)
　Rebecca & Henry Jackson col? 12-7-1878 (Wheeler)
　Rebecca & William Henry Stewart 1-31-1880 (Rev. M. Quiller)
　Richard F. & Judith M. Gravath 4-11-1866 (Chesly) m. at Ormes by
　Jno. W. Chesley, clergyman Pr. E. Ch. Age 26, widower, carpenter
　Robert & Elizabeth Webster 10-31-1808
　Robert & Agnes Edelen 10-27-1876 (Green)
　Sally & William Powell 2-13-1830
　Samuel & Amelia Daton col? 9-8-1866 (Fr. Call)
　Samuel & Louisa Digges 2-8-1868 (Fr. Call)
　Samuel & Mary Digges 11-12-1873 (Dwyer)
　Sarah & William Manley 1-7-1789
　Sarah & Thomas Beane 1-13-1794
　Sarah & Ebbin Parmer 4-4-1801
　Sarah & John Donald 11-2-1877 (Perry)
　Sarah Ann & Jeffry Suit 11-9-1831
　Sarah Ann & Robert Adams col? 4-20-1867 (Call)
　Sarah E. & John T. Sansbury 5-16-1853
　Sarah Jane & James Porter 12-26-1868 (Begue)
　Simon & Matilda Boose 5-10-1879 (Hooman)
　Susan & Warren (?) Waugh 1-7-1845
　Susan & George Waters 10-5-1872
　Thomas & Mary Lowe 11-9-1778 　　BROWN, Thomas &
　Thomas & Mary Ann Taylor 6-4-1802 　　Sarah Taylor 6-29-1777
　Thomas & Elizabeth Summers 8-3-1854
　Thomas & Ellen S. Shields col? 8-7-1865 Age 30yrs 8 mo. Ditcher
　　Adam R. Dolly, minister
　Thomas & Mary Ellen Brown (Call) 1-11-1868
　Thomas & Isabella Parker 2-19-1870 (Maher)
　Tillie & Philip Watkins 11-18-1884 (Rev. Mr. Howard)
　Walter & Ruth Sheriff 12-21-1799
　Walter F. & Josephine Smith 8-5-1851
　Wesley & Hester Harrison 8-27-1875
　William & Eliza Degors 2-12-1835
　William & Anna Gant col? 9-22-1866 (Fr. Call)
　William & Cornelia Wilson (Wells) 1-1-1875
　William Francis & Martha A. Forrest 10-27-1876 (Gordon)
　William H. & Alice V. Henson 2-11-1886 (Rev. Father Cunane)
　William W. & Adelaide Robey 4-5-1851
　Zachariah & Jane Ricketts 4-4-1787
BROWNE, Elbertene Elizabeth & Septimas J. Cook 3-7-1848

BROWNING, Edward & Aurelia Clarke 10-16-1837
  George & Nuly Mangum 3-16-1885
BRUCE, Albert & Susan Quander col? 12-8-1869 (Maher)
  Alice & W. Benjamin Dockett 2-15-1872 (Gordon)
  Ann E. & Thomas S. Wright 3-26-1851
  Charles & Lucy Dunlop 6-20-1831
  Elizabeth & William H. Lyles 1-22-1830
  Rebecca & William Johnson col? 6-10-1867 (Fr. Call)
  Richard & Mary M. Ross 10-9-1883 (Walker)
  Upton & Sarah M. Clagett 11-5-1800
  Upton & Charity Tolson col? 9-28-1867 (Gordon)
BRUNT, Thomas & Verlinda Smith 8-2-1796
BRYAN, Ann & Thomas Jenkins 9-4-1832
  Edward H. & Mary E. Lanham 11-18-1833
  Eleanor & Osborn Bryan 12-6-1815
  Eleanor Ann & Walter Parker Griffin 9-27-1853
  Eliz? & Thomas Church 12-6-1777
  Elizabeth & Henry Mahew 7-10-1800
  Eliz.th A. & Charles F. Dement 11-17-1843
  Erasmus & Martha A. Hunt 6-11-1855
  James & Mary Johnson 7-21-1866 (Fr. Call)
  James Henry & Elizabeth Hawkins 10-20-1875 (Green)
  James F. S. & Fannie Barry 12-1-1865 married by P. B. Lenaghan,
    Catholic Priest. No age given, Planter
  John & Elizabeth Lawson 11-19-1802
  Joseph S. & Maggie Dodson 3-19-1886
  Kitty & Edward Harrison 4-15-1876 (Maddox)
  Lewis & Marg.t Church 1-16-1779
  Margaret & William W. Manning 6-30-1800
  Mary Ann & James Jones 2-15-1826
  Osborn & Eleanor Bryan 12-6-1815
  Rebecca A. M. & Edward S. Plummer 10-7-1856
  Richard & Ann Busey Ball 1-27-1786
  Richard & Mary Steel 9-29-1796
  Richard & Catherine M. Maddox 4-1-1844
  Rinaldo & Estelle V. Hall 2-29-1884 (Father Cunnane)
  Sally & George Jones 1-18-1824
  Sarah Ann & Paul Talbutt 3-4-1791
  Sarah Ann & Benjamin Fowler 1-26-1835
  Thomas & Mary Dixon 4-24-1805
  Thomas & Sarah Webb 12-15-1807
  Whittingham & Addie C. Brooks 11-25-1878 (Williams)
  William & Susannah Selby 11-11-1802
  William & Sarah Lanham 6-24-1809
  William & Susanna P. Lanham 2-28-1827
  William of Tho.s & Filla Thorn 4-1-1839
  William Tho.s & Lucy Smith 3-23-1778
BRYANT, Jan & William Steuard 6-6-1783
  Rev? Joseph G. & Elizabeth Medley col? 5-15-1882 (Rev. Chesley)
  Mary & John Davis 8-20-1779
  Rev.d William & Emma Herbert 11-10-1837
BUCEY, Ann & Samuel Smith 1-4-1845
BUCHAN, Margaret & Kidd Morsell 3-29-1803
BUCHANAN, Elizabeth & David C. Stewart 8-11-1803
  George & Leana Batson 12-27-1823

BUCHANAN, Mary & Robert Pottinger 2-15-1785
  Sophia & Richard Jacob Duckett 3-30-1795
  Susannah & Thomas Johnston 5-26-1807
BUCKINGHAM, Nancy & Dennis Curting 2-13-1797
BUCKLAND, William & Ann Lynn 11-24-1795
BUCKLER, Sarah Jane & Stephen Brady 2-5-1874 (Townshend)
BUDD, Jane W. & Albert B. Berry 1-4-1858
  Martha W. & Major Harry Cook Cushing 6-6-1868
  Nannie C. & Th$ O. Berry 6-1-1864
BUKNEY, Ann Maria & Leander Brooks col$ 4-4-1882 (Rev. Mr. Gordon)
BUNNELL, Catharine E. & Joseph S. Ward 2-20-1882 (Rev. Dr. Lewin)
  George H. & Christie Pumphrey 1-12-1870 (Kershaw)
  George H. & Louisa Cowle Pumphrey 1-25-1877 (McNeer)
  Reubin W. & Mary J. Mullikin 4-25-1840
BURCH, Ann & Samuel Godfrey 7-3-1798
  Ann N. & Nathaniel Hatton 2-15-1816
  Benjamin & Mary Townsend 2-22-1784
  Benjamin & Rebecca Barron 9-6-1784
  Benjamin & Jennett Harvey 7-1-1803
  Benjamin & Christiana Spalding 1-2-1809
  Cassandra & Patrick Kinen 1-1-1808
  Catharine & Smith Martin 4-1-1822
  Edward & Ann Spinks 10-15-1779
  Elizabeth & Lewin Talbott 11-17-1794
  Elizabeth T. & William L. Weems 8-1-1814
  Francis & Penelope Vermilion 1-24-1783
  Jane & And^W Hamilton 4-17-1783
  Jane & James Naylor 7-11-1826
  John & Martha Thompson col$ 10-10-1868 (Fr. Lenaghan)
  Jonathan H. & Margaret Newton 6-11-1810
  Joseph Newton & Sarah Calvert 10-10-1812
  Joseph N. Jr. & Susanna Townshend 6-7-1837
  Lizzie M. & John H. Thomas 11-21-1867 (Leneghan)
  Margaret A. & John R. Richardson 5-30-1879 (Perrie)
  Marg^t & Thos Humphries 11-22-1781
  Mary & Benjamin Sheckles 2-6-1819
  Peter G. & Martha Ann Boswell 7-17-1861
  Samuel & Susannah Wilson 12-22-1809
  Susan R. & John F. Latimer 1-4-1825
  Thomas & Susanna Talburt 7-26-1780
  Thomas & Lenny Harvey 9-5-1794
  William N. & Sarah R. Townshend 1-14-1834
  William N. & Susan L. Talbert 6-21-1842
  William N. & L. E. M. Parker 12-21-1839
  William N. & Mary E. Baden 2-13-1846
BURGEE, Thomas & Sarah Chaney 12-13-1804
BURGEN, Francis & Sophia Kerby 12-18-1871 (Stanley)
BURGESS, Ann & William Sansbury 9-8-1803
  Annie & George Thompson 4-1-1872 (Skinner)
  Annie E. & Henry C. Davis 1-6-1885 (Father Clarke)
  Charles & Sarah Sansbury 2-4-1807
  Charles & Ellen Stewart col$ 9-8-1866 (Rev. Father Young)
  Edward Cornburns & Mary Margaret Norfolk 7-4-1885
  Eleanor A. & John H. Selby 1-12-1856
  Elisabeth & Edward Clifton 1-9-1870 (Gordon)

BURGESS, Elisha & Mary Harvey 1-29-1820
  Enoch & Mary Pinkney 2-8-1868 (Fr. Call)
  Grace & Dennis F. Ryon 3-21-1867 (Griffith)
  Henderson & Terisa Dunlop 3-9-1830
  James & Emily White 2-2-1853
  James W. & Elizabeth Gates 12-18-1858
  James William & Mary Emily Thompson 1-2-1832
  Jas. W. & Mary A. Thompson 2-27-1845
  John H. & Ann Nothey 2-13-1854
  John M. & Eleanor Magruder 10-18-1779
  John M. & Eliz^a Cooledge 2-26-1794
  Joseph & Sarah Gray 12-31-1779
  Keziah & Henry Walker 12-8-1780
  Mary & Christopher C. Moore 2-5-1870 (Chesley)
  Mary Ana & Barney Clarke 12-24-1870 (McDonald)
  Mary C. & Benjamin Sprigg 12-26-1804
  Mary E. & Simeon F. Bowie 3-25-1867 (Lenahan)
  Mary Eleanor & James White 12-29-1856
  Mary J. & James W. Tucker (Butler) 3-10-1879
  Massey & James Steward 12-30-1790
  Matilda & William J. Millard 6-7-1862
  Mildred & Allen White 7-9-1785
  Rachel & Richard Thompson 10-20-1779
  Richard & Sarah Walker 1-12-1802
  Robert & Susanna Gates 2-7-1874
  Robert & Mary Alice Gates 11-29-1876 (Green)
  Sarah & Joseph Sprigg Belt 4-28-1790
  Susan N. & Eli Randall 12-27-1883 (Rev. Jas. Chaney)
  Wm. N. & Marion Boone 8-12-1857
BURK, Thomas & Hessey Courts 12-19-1828
BURKE, Sarah Jane & William James Smith 2-7-1854
  Teresa & David Pratt col^d 12-24-1852
BURKETT, Ann & Francis Means 9-25-1779
BURLEY, Joseph & Lizzie Eastern 12-27-1883 (Rev. Mr. Barnes)
  Philip & Laura Magruder 6-7-1884
BURLS, Louis & Dolly Sewall 12-13-1877 (Homan)
BURLY, Thomas & Francis Mitchell 10-14-1885 (Rev. M. Howard)
BURNELL, Ann H. & John T. Rantin 12-24-1836
  James & Eliza E. A. W. Ward 6-14-1839
BURNES, Elizabeth & Josiah Wilson 4-1-1789
  Margaret & John Lane 2-21-1781
BURNILL, John & Louisa Gutterice 9-8-1810
BURNS, Benjamin & Margaret Gibson 3-8-1833
  Lavinia M. & Daniel Connick 10-15-1849
  Walton & Charlotte Dare col^d 6-22-1869 (Thomas)
BURRAUGHS, Benjamin & Lizzie Blake 5-19-1885
BURRELL, Allen & Susannah Wood 3-18-1789
  Ann & Absalom Anderson 6-6-1794
  Mary & James Wells 2-6-1795
  Sarah & John Denoon 1-17-1798
BURROUGHS, C. Ella & Charles N. Simms 6-22-1880 (Rev. Mr. Gordon)
  Frederick & Mary Jackson col^d 4-18-1870 (Lenaghan)
  George & Rebeccah Wailes 7-6-1792
  Henry & Rachel Ann Bavin 5-5-1841
  James & Mary Hawkins 6-22-1875 (Scott)

38

BURROUGHS, Ruth E. & Jno. H. Yost 2-13-1864
BURY, William & Mary Cole 12-18-1797
BUSEY, Ann & Benjamin Walker 6-13-1798
  Eleanor & Thomas Littleford 2-12-1797
  Elizabeth & Zach⁑ Howse 11-3-1779
  James & Sarah Ann Gibbons 12-28-1805
  Mary & Caleb Vermillion 12-20-1794
  Samuel & Sarah Roberts 7-13-1777
BUSH, Martha N. & James R. Lawson 12-27-1855
  William & Martha Rebecca Lawson 9-25-1824
BUSHELL, Ruth Rosana & William W. Danenhower Jr. 12-30-1873 (Williams)
BUTLER, Alfred & Emily Sweeting 11-10-1879
  Amos & Bettie Brooks col⁹ 12-14-1880 (Rev. Mr. Watkins)
  Andrew & Emily Imes 7-14-1877 (Wheeler)
  Ann & William Garner 12-30-1799
  Annie & John W. Ford 8-29-1879
  Annie L. & George W. Brooke 11-22-1881 (Rev. W. C. Butler)
  Caroline & Robert Waters 11-30-1868 (Lenaghan)
  Cecelia E. & John H. Jackson 12-29-1865 Age 17, black
  Cecie & Marcellus Newman 10-3-1874 (Welsh)
  Charles & Emma Cecelia Suit 11-14-1881 (Father De Wolf)
  Charles Henry & Chloe Watson 1-11-1868 (Greenleaf)
  Charles L. & Margaret A. Garner 12-3-1877 (Perry)
  Chloe A. E. & Patrick C. Scott col⁹ 2-10-1881 (Rev. Mr. Lawson)
  David & Katie Anderson 2-9-1886 (Rev. Mr. Brooks)
  Edward & Marg⁺ Ann Adams 10-28-1870 (Evans)
  Edward & Gracie Chesley 5-1-1875 (Matthews)
  Edward H. & Georgia Crandell 12-4-1872 (Mercer)
  Eliza & Ignatius Langster 2-10-1872 (O'Dwyer)
  Eliza & Lucian Green 12-26-1885 (Rev. Mr. Brookes)
  Elizabeth & Henry Jones 1-3-1820
  Elizabeth & Albert H. Scott 12-28-1835
  Eliz^th & Lawson Hurley 10-30-1848
  Elsie & John R. Johnson 8-27-1885 (Rev. Mr. Wills)
  Francis Llewellyn & Caroline Healley 12-13-1869 (Lenghan)
  Gabriel & Sarah Catherine Suit 5-4-1880 (Father Cotten)
  George & Catherine Douglass 12-7-1883 (Rev. N. C. Brown)
  George Henry & Lizzie Butler 5-1-1876 (Homan)
  George W. & Teresa Brooks 1-6-1849
  Gusty & Rachel Hagan 9-27-1873 (Fowler)
  Harriet & John Crawford 2-26-1877
  Harriet Virginia & Henry Proctor 2-9-1875 (Welch)
  Henry & Mary Butler 6-18-1855
  Henny & Edward Skinner 1-6-1873 (Walker)
  Henry & Martha Ennis 10-13-1875 (Peter)
  Henry Thomas & Phillippena Newman 1-12-1852
  Henry Thomas & Mary Catherine Booth 1-19-1878
  Henson & Ann Mathes 11-15-1884 (Rev. Mr. Towles)
  Hettie Louisa & George Allen Simpson 12-26-1868 (Langford)
  Israel & Laura Harvey 2-28-1880 (Aquilla)
  James & Priscilla Wenn 2-22-1867 (Hicks)
  James & Susannah Harrison col⁹ 6-27-1868 (Fr. Lilly)
  James & Jane Richardson 4-19-1871 (McDonald)
  James Robert & Mary Margaret Estep 3-29-1845
  Josias & Mary Savoy col⁹ 10-7-1856

BUTLER, Lizzie & George Henry Butler 5-1-1876 (Homan)
   Lucretia & Robert Jackson 5-29-1873 (Dent)
   Mary & Henry Butler 6-18-1855
   Mary & Andrew Crawford col? 1-29-1870 (Langford)
   Mary & Jeremiah Brooks 12-17-1872 (Marbury)
   Mary Ann & Daniel Gibbons 1-16-1830
   Mary Caroline & Owen Starting of A. A. County 11-8-1880
     (Rev. Father D. Woolf)
   Miley & Caroline Bedder 3-25-1875 (Cotton)
   Nancy & George Jackson 10-1-1884 (Rev. C. O. Cook)
   Noble & Matilda Holly col? 7-26-1852
   Richard & Margaret Jane Franklin 1-20-1886 (Rev. Mr. Howard)
   Richard Francis & Annie Hamilton 1-1-1876
   Rinaldo & Emily Mitchell 12-30-1885 (Rev. Frank Wills)
   Sarah & Hopewell Ford 12-30-1880 col?
   Stephen W. & Anna Brice 2-2-1870 (McDonald)
   Thomas H. & Sarah A. Wignall 12-24-1881 (Rev. Mr. Hyland)
   William & Elizabeth Brown 2-11-1886 (Rev. Father Cotton)
   William Albert & Elizabeth Ann Procter 1-9-1875 (O'Dwyer)
   William T. & Jennie Starlings 1-22-1868 (Chesley)
BUTT, Eleanor & Samuel Philips 1-12-1790
BUTTELER & Jemima Davis 12-15-1785
BUTTERWORTH, Wm. & Eliz? Darbyshire 1-31-1779
BUTTON, John S. & Mary F. Lambert 3-12-1873 (Kershaw)
BYER, Victor & Sarah Duvall 4-24-1819

CADDINGTON, Walter L. & Catherine F. Ridgdway 9-20-1876 (Dorsey)
CADLE, Caroline Elizabeth & Jesse Obleton Phelps lic. 1-22-1866
    m. 1-26-1866 (Father Lanahan)
   Delilah & James Murray 1-2-1839
   Elizabeth & Thomas Grimes 12-16-1833
   James G. & Charlotte L. Lewis 11-11-1839
   James R. & Anna E. King 5-28-1875 (Welch)
   Jno. W. & Alice Piles 1-2-1877 (McNeer)
   Mary P. & Daniel F. Allison 5-21-1839
   Richard R. & Jane C. Lewis 11-25-1833
CAGE, Elizabeth & Robert Paddy 1-15-1817
   Elizabeth A. & Theodore W. Watson 6-25-1879 (Perry)
   Jane & George T. Wood 12-26-1814
   Leonard P. & Sarah Ann Davis 12-2-1852
   Martha A. & James A. Murray 5-21-1876 (Tennant)
   Mary & William Mayhew 4-7-1794
   Mary Susanna & Benjamin Lawson 12-26-1828
   Peter B. & Mary Parker 1-20-1783
   Rosa B. & J. Hedges Sparklin 3-22-1880 (Cross)
   Sarah F. & Henry J. Hawkins 6-9-1876
   Susannah & Benjamin Watson 2-6-1809
   Thomas S. & Susanah Lawson 1-21-1817
   Verlinda P. & John Paddy 1-26-1813
   William & Mary Mahew 12-18-1777
   William & Sarah Ellen Campbell 1-14-1851
   William Wilson & Verlinda Mahew 12-22-1807
CAHALEY, Thomas & Mary Sansbury 12-3-1807
CAHALL, Margaret & William Tyler 8-2-1824

CAHALL, Thomas & Elizabeth Russell 5-21-1822
CAHOE, Elizabeth S. & Wm. W. Richardson 1-18-1851
  Mary & Thomas Harrison 4-15-1805
CAIN, Michael & Elizabeth Craver 1-27-1800
CALDWELL, Anna M. & Sam! Hamilton 10-25-1847
  Harriet E. & Robert Wright 10-11-1830
CALIS, Marrion & Virginia Thomas 1-9-1843
CALLAHAN, Catharine & Philip O'Mara 9-8-1798
  Eleanor & John Newton 5-27-1781
  Rosamond & Zach? Prather 3-2-1778
CALLAHANE, John & Susanna Sherwood 2-21-1778
CALLELY, Andrew & Catharine MacColgin 3-9-1801
CALLICOE, Joseph & Amelia Demar 12-5-1781
  Sally & Clement Craycroft 10-14-1818
CALLIS, Garland & Eleanor Addison 12-22-1779
  Henry Addison & Chloe Ann Tolson 2-20-1810
  Henry A. & Eleanor H. Hanson 8-28-1832
CALVERT, Ann & Ignatius Lovelis 12-23-1799
  Annie & Sandy Forrest 1-11-1883 (Rev. Mr. Walker)
  Attaway & George Grandon Mead 8-16-1873
  Bettie S. & Daniel Parke Peter 7-19-1870 (Kershaw)
  Caroline Maria & Thos W. Morris 5-18-1823
  Cecelia & John Worthington Dulaney 2-19=1873 (McGuire)
  Christiana & Hannibal Addison 5-2-1874
  Edward H. & Eliz? Biscoe 2-29-1796
  Ela S. & Duncan G. Campbell 8-29-1861
  Eliza & Peter Greenleaf 1C-28-1874 (O'Dwyer)
  Elizabeth & Charles Steuart 6-14-1780
  Elizabeth Jane & Erasmus Gantt 12-26-1865 (Kershaw) Age 18, dark
    housemaid
  Fielder & Lucy Wells 11-16-1876 (Gordon)
  James H. & Jane Bowlding 11-15-1875 (Major)
  Joseph & Garthey Ann De Neil 3-17-1877 (Carroll)
  Julia & Richard H. Stuart 5-6-1833
  Julia & Dennis Green 10-22-1870 (Wheeler)
  Richard & Susan Clarke 2-2-1877 (Carroll)
  Sarah & John Cord 4-24-1804
  Sarah & Joseph Newton Burch 10-10-1812
  Sarah Stuart & Christian Matthew Hines 9-9-1871
  Washington Custis & Sophia Oden Mullikin 6-17-1851
  William T. & Sarah Hall 7-26-1875
CALVERY, John & Matilda Brown col? persons 6-6-1865
CAMMELL, Mary Elizabeth & James V. Logan 1-21-1866 Age 43 of Howard Co.
CAMPBELL, Ann & Alexander McKay 12-16-1778
  Arthur & Ann Lovejoy 12-29-1788
  Cecelia & George Humphries 9-22-1868
  Duncan G. & Ela S. Calvert 8-29-1861
  Ellen & Charles Parker 7-13-1876 (Major)
  George & Jane Coats 8-20-1869 (Stanley)
  George Washington & Harriet Stoddert 7-17-1812
  James & Mollie Bowie col? 3-22-1871 (Fowler)
  Jane & Rezin Boteler 4-20-1803
  Richard & Ann Barrott 4-29-1812
  Sarah & Josias Lovejoy 2-19-1789
  Sarah Ellen & William Cage 1-14-1851

CANTER, John & Mary Ann Richardson 12-29-1840
  John Samuel & Joanna Curtain 6-18-1884
  John W. & Ann S. Smith 7-6-1878 (Perry)
  Julia Ann & Wm. Henry Phillips Kidwell 5-17-1871 (Lenaghan)
  Priscilla & Samuel Walker 5-5-1814
  Zachariah & Amny Adams 12-12-1797
CAPRON, Horace & Louisa Snowden 6-5-1834
CARLIN, Katie & Edward T. Young 2-4-1884 (Rev. Mr. LaRoche)
CARLTON, Alice E. & William M. Clark 9-23-1869 (Harper)
  Clara D. & Robert S. Fountain 1-13-1879 (Harper)
  Guy & Lottie Baden 4-23-1878 (Williams)
  Henry L. & Maria Barron 2-22-1831
CAROLL, John T. & Eleanor Littleford 3-17-1846
CARR, Dabney & Elizabeth Carr 6-28-1802
  Eleanor B. & Samuel Carr 4-28-1795
  Elizabeth & Dabney Carr 6-28-1802
  Elizabeth & Charles Erekrison 12-16-1841
  Harriet A. & Marshall Betts 9-5-1844
  John & Rachell Purnell 2-8-1779
  Linny & John Chaney 2-13-1840
  Mary Ann & Zachariah Mangun 11-17-1847
  Overton & Chloe Lee Baker 4-21-1807
  Rachel & James Errickson 4-8-1846
  Rachael Ann & Thomas Stallings 12-23-1833
  Rich.ᵈ & Eliza J. Mangun 11-8-1848
  Samuel & Eleanor B. Carr 4-28-1795
  William & Elizabeth Baden 3-19-1834
CARRICK, Adaline & Dennis Jackson col.ᵈ 12-21-1869 (Leneghan)
  Adiline & Richard W. Crook 12-29-1858
  Alberta M. & Thomas A. King 2-15-1856
  Amos & Susanna Ryon 3-29-1853
  Ann & John Warfield 12-19-1784
  Benjamin & Rhody Baldwin 1-26-1815
  Mrs. Carlene N. & William H. Slack 11-25-1869 (Dr. Hancock)
  Caroline & James Beall 1-15-1834
  Caroline & John H. Loveless 6-20-1855
  Darcus & Joshua Thomas Clarke 2-13-1833
  Dorcas & Valentine Keiser 8-31-1867
  Elizabeth & John Gallyham 11-27-1841
  Elizabeth H. & Benjamin F. Anderson 5-23-1876 (Stanley)
  Franklin F. & Amy Ann Frances Hood 9-15-1876 (Major)
  Hellen & Charles Beall 5-14-1875 (Scott)
  Henry & Eleanor Ryon 12-24-1832
  Henry & Elizabeth E. Edelen 10-1-1862
  Isaac & Maranda Duvall 1-23-1833
  James Madison & Mary Brown 2-11-1873 (Stanley)
  John R. of R.ᵈ & Lavinia A. Gray 6-1-1869 (Kershaw)
  Joseph M. & Margaret Ann Young 11-10-1856
  Julian & Elmira Pinkney col.ᵈ 12-16-1868
  Mareen & Mary Duvall 2-23-1791
  Mareen & Margaret Webb 1-17-1795
  Margaret Eliza & Richard Hardey 2-6-1860
  Mary & Wm. Downes 6-2-1827
  Mary E. & Thomas Houston 2-9-1861
  Mira M. Rebecca Jane & Jas. H. Curtain 5-10-1864

CARRICK, Nettie & Jefferson Hawkins 12-29-1874 (Scott)
  Oden B. & Rebecca M. Mosley 3-5-1881
  Richard & Sarah Duvall 1-13-1836
  Sarah & Thomas Carroll 3-8-1788
  Sarah & Richard Hardey 2-3-1838
  Sarah Ann & William A. Lusby 1-30-1856
  William & Eliz^{a} Shreeves 2-13-1795
  William & Mary Powers 1-8-1844
  William Henry H. & Rosa M. Loveless 3-1-1860
  Zachariah & Eliza Jane Wedding 2-2-1859
CARRICO, Ann & William Cage Rawlings 2-17-1807
  Elizabeth & Thomas C. Davis 12-28-1816
  Jno. H. & Mary Jane Knott 2-20-1865
  Martha & Elijah Ellis 7-27-1809
CARROLL, Alexander C. & Julia Pinkney 11-19-1882 (Mr. Walker)
  Alice & Dominic Carroll 7-1-1873 (Dwyer)
  Ambrose & Ann R. Pinkney col^{d} 8-17-1883 (Rev. Mr. Mills)
  Araminta & John B. Brooke 9-18-1821
  Benjamin & Sarah Jane Crawford col^{d} 8-1-1871
  Bettie & Isaac Brown 6-8-1871 (McGuire)
  Bradley & Harriet Mackall 9-12-1871 (Evans)
  Catharine A. & John M. Martin 1-24-1846
  Charles John & Jennett Brown 5-26-1795
  Dominic & Alice Carroll 7-1-1873 (Dwyer)
  Emily & John Brown 12-30-1885 (Rev. Enoch Peters)
  Emma & John Addison Johnson 7-24-1874 (Gordon)
  George W. & Hester S. Padgett 1-14-1885
  Henry & Kitty Hawkins 6-12-1869 (Maher)
  Ignatius & Jane Lynch 12-15-1800
  James & Susannah Galwith 4-6-1792
  James H. & Priscilla Ann Littleford 12-21-1852
  Jane Ann & Wm. H. Martin 2-18-1851
  John & Mary Duvall 11-8-1800
  John Edward & Mary Ella Underwood 5-8-1882 (Rev. Father Clarke)
  Louis & Susannah Blackston 11-1-1870 (Maher)
  Mary & Patrick Sim 7-11-1777
  Mary & Ignatius Fenwick 6-10-1780
  Mary & Richard Hall 12-29-1846
  Mary J. & James E. Underwood 2-15-1873 (Leneghan)
  Michael B. & Jane M. Worthington 10-9-1822
  Naomi & Christopher Cooper 9-30-1871 (Wheeler)
  Patrick & Mima Hayes 12-31-1794
  Rachael & Henry Hardesty 10-20-1846
  Robert & Charity Travers 10-2-1869 (Langford)
  Robert & Lavinia Carter 3-3-1877 (Carroll)
  Selesta & Oliver Hawkins col^{d} 5-11-1869 (Langford)
  Sophy & Thomas Hatton 12-2-1875
  Thomas & Sarah Carrick 3-8-1788
  Thomas & Susannah Cheney 11-14-1804
  William Thomas & Sally Sprigg 10-7-1828
CARSON, Elizabeth & James Johnson 9-12-1800
CARTER, Alice & Oden Bowie 12-3-1851
  Ann E. & James R. Davis 1-30-1845
  Annett & Henry H. Brogden 11-16-1880
  Elijah & Ann Ford colored 5-21-1866 (Rev. Mr. Gordon)
    Age 36, fisherman, m. parsonage St. Thomas Parish

CARTER, Elizabeth & George Kilton 9-23-1796
 Elizabeth Van Suverugh & Tilghman Scott 2-28-1822
 Ella & Samuel K. George Jr. 6-11-1863
 George & Ruth Gibbons 4-19-1815
 George & Amanda Chatton 9-6-1872 (Marbury)
 Grace & Andrew Hillman 1-13-1866 (Call)
 Henry H. & Mary M. Gunton 10-9-1873 (Stanley)
 Jesse & Christiana Moore 4-2-1804
 Landon & Mary Armisted 1-1-1800
 Lavinia & Robert Carroll 3-3-1877 (Carroll)
 Letty & Charles Brice 1-3-1871 (Gordon)
 Lizzie & William Brooks 9-14-1878 (Lenaghan)
 Louisa & Robert Digges col? 10-21-1865 (Father Call)
 Mary R. & George H. Bier 12-6-1867 (Chesley)
 Richard F. & Catharine Kidwell 2-17-1814
 Rosalie E. & Francis M. Hall 5-29-1851
 Rozena & John Tippett 9-1-1834
CARTWRIGHT, Jonathan & Rachel Scott 5-9-1843
CASE, Susan & James Williams 12-28-1840
CASEY, John & Philorlea Edgeworth 8-12-1778
CASHELL, Richard H. & Margaret O. Havenner 4-7-1865
CASSELL, John & Sarah Ann Simpson 12-8-1801
 Mary & Isaac Swain 12-21-1787
CASSIN, Joseph R. & Mary M. Berry 1-31-1861
CASTEEL, Edmond & Mary Hardey 4-4-1801
 Amine & Basil Ridgeway 12-18-1798
CASTLE, Mary Estella & Benjamin Franklin Shaffer 5-30-1885
 Philip P. & Emily Jane Curley 8-22-1883
CATENDON, Charles H. & S. M. Cox 1-9-1877
CATER, Absalom & Ann Hutchinson 1-7-1807
 Benjamin & Mary Clubb 2-16-1801
 Elizabeth & Thomas Swan 2-11-1793
 Elizabeth & John Ritchie 1-8-1816
 George & Mary Moore 12-23-1815
 John & Mary Tarman 1-23-1805
 Mary & Nathaniel Weeden 12-16-1794
 Sarah & Thomas Thompson 2-7-1785
 Thomas & Sarah Baden 8-31-1791
 Thomas & Mary Winkler 1-9-1821
 Thomas & Caroline Locker 1-3-1825
 William & Elizabeth Clubb 2-1-1792
CATLETT, Hanson G. & Eleanor H. Bayne 11-7-1832
CATON, Sarah Ann & Alexander Hutcherson 4-21-1840
 William & Susan Hamnan 9-29-1832
CATOR, Elizabeth & Thomas O. White 8-4-1857
 George & Priscilla E. Wilson 12-28-1830
 Mary & Joseph Parker 11-13-1862
 Mary & Thomas M. Taylor 2-12-1874 (Gordon)
 Mary Emily & John Prather 6-2-1856
 Nancy L. & Otho Brashears 10-20-1853
 Sarah E. & James L. Brashears 1-4-1848
 William A. & Mary F. Sheckolls 12-28-1858
CATTERTON, Benjamin F. & Carrie E. Dalrymple 1-13-1886 (Rev. Elridge)
 Eliza R. & Samuel E. Tippett 1-15-1873 (Townshend)
CATTINGTON, James & Jane Greer 12-19-1805

CATTNAN, Lucretia & Samuel Knighten 1-8-1823
CAVE, Elizabeth & Henry Lee 12-15-1781
  Mary & Thomas Caleb 12-29-1784
  Sarah & Leonard Eddis 8-21-1780
  Sary & John Adam Rallings 4-10-1787
  Thomas & Elizabeth Peirce 11-18-1786
CAWOOD, Ann Rebecca & Joseph M. Kendrick 9-6-1869 (Fowler)
  Benjamin & Martha Sheid 5-8-1798
  Catherine E. & Thomas S. Marlow 1-20-1844
  Elizabeth & Nicholas Blacklock 11-24-1786
  James E. & Annie Josephine Horton 11-27-1866 (Smith)
  Mary & Samuel Lindsay 7-8-1807
  Sarah Eleanor A. L. & John Lindsay 10-11-1815
  Stephen & Elizabeth Ann Fendall 6-13-1792
  Thomas P. H. & Caroline Boswell 10-17-1821
CAYWOOD, Eleanor & Washington Wright 8-31-1842
CECIL, see also Ceicel, Cessell, Cicel, Cissell
  Elizabeth & James Sibley Jr. 4-6-1814
  Julius D. & Sarah J. Stewart 12-30-1882 (Rev. Mr. Gordon)
  Virlinder & James Wales 11-5-1817
CEICEL, Susannah & Clement Wilson 9-5-1778
CESSELL, William & Margery Cole 12-2-1793
CHAMBERS, Martha & Charles H. Johnson 8-21-1861
  William & Rose Adams 3-14-1885 (Rev. Mr. Brooks)
  Wm. & Alice Ward 10-5-1870 (Gordon)
CHANEY, Abraham & Dianna Woodfield 9-22-1797
  Allen W. & Anna E. Vermillion 12-9-1872 (Mercer)
  Amos & Rachel Mitchell 3-12-1807
  Beckie & Thomas Simpson 12-24-1867 (Stanley)
  Dinah & Ezekiel Bassford 6-16-1815
  Eliza Ann & John Henry Turner 9-7-1853
  Elizabeth F. & James F. Purdy 12-4-1876 (Stanley)
  Emma & Wm. Wesley King 1-5-1876 (McNear)
  Flavilla & Zach? Baldwin 5-18-1839
  George Wesley & Edith Deall 4-21-1881 (Rev. Mr. Butler)
  Jesse & Martha Ann Clarke 12-22-1835
  John & Linny Carr 2-13-1840
  Mareen & Mary V. Stone 2-2-1875 (Mercer)
  Mary Ann & Charles Shaw 12-18-1850
  Mary Ellen & James Phelps 12-17-1862
  Mary H. & Jocephas Anderson 9-20-1873
  Pamelia & John Leach 5-16-1807
  Rebecca & John Shepherd 2-27-1797
  Samuel & Medora Whittington 3-24-1880 (Chaney)
  Sarah & Thomas Burgee 12-13-1804
  Solomon G. & Jannette R. Boarman 2-8-1849
  Solomon G. & Caroline Heflebower 11-21-1860
  Somerville & Caroline Loveless 9-2-1862
  Susie A. & Eugene H. Shags 1-23-1882 (Rev. Mr. Stanley)
  Theodore & Othella Jones 9-22-1874 (Mercer)
CHANY, Richard & Matilda Boyd 2-9-1825
CHAPIN, Harman & Cath? V. Dement 5-30-1849
CHAPLIN, Isaac & Julia Latimer 8-18-1834
CHAPMAN, Charity & Henry Gross 9-14-1871 (Evans)
  Charlotte & Isaac Hawkins 9-14-1871 (Evans)

CHAPMAN, Eleanor & James Glasgow 2-19-1868
  Eliza & Edward Jackson 1-13-1872 (Dwyer)
  Henry & Laura E. Bowling 1-28-1874 (Pinkney)
  Jennie & Calvert Contee 5-24-1873 (Townshend)
CHASE, Charles & Josephine Beckett 7-22-1876
  David & Milley Brown 7-5-1872
  Flora Belle & James L. Schaaff 6-16-1885
  John & Susan Allen 3-21-1873
  Lizzie & Wilson Brewer 12-13-1867 (Beque)
  Mary A. & Samuel Hawkins col? 12-1-1865
  Thomas & Charlotte Galloway 12-27-1866 (Greenleaf)
  William & Catharine West 9-14-1868 (Fr. Lilly)
CHATHAM, Ann & Joseph Parsons 7-22-1798
CHATTON, Amanda & George Carter 9-6-1872 (Marbury)
CHENEY, Ann & John Shekells 8-14-1799
  Ann & Osborn Conoway 11-25-1812
  Deborah & Joseph Russell 5-16-1797
  Eleanor & William Wells 3-30-1793
  Henrietta & John Hardesty 7-23-1788
  John & Elizabeth Ferrell 12-12-1780
  Rebecca & William Watson 12-19-1793
  Susannah & Thomas Carroll 11-14-1804
CHESELDINE, Mary L. & James E. Thompson 12-21-1883
  Philip Thomas & Mary Elizabeth Estella Oxley 8-10-1885 (Highland)
CHESLEY, Daniel S. & Mary C. Scott 10-3-1867 (Kershaw)
  Gracie & Edward Butler 5-1-1875 (Matthews)
  Jennie P. & James G. Wildman 3-4-1871 (Fowler)
  John F. & Henrietta E. Beall 5-13-1846
  John F. & Annie R. Tolley 10-29-1861
  Mary Ellen & Constant Craig 10-17-1878 (Watkins)
  Mary Margaret & William Hanson Thomas 4-1-1881
  Thomas O. & Ann Sophia Piles 12-21-1871 (Kershaw)
  Zadock C. & Mary Clagett 8-31-1831
  Zadock C. & Pamelia Belt 9-27-1838
CHESTER, Maria & Frederick Lyles 4-20-1866 (Fr. Call)
CHEW, Amelia & William Hanson 2-28-1877 (Snowden)
  Ann & Levi Perry 2-20-1797
  Anne & Archibald Shorter 10-26-1867 (Fa. Bayne)
  Bettie Ann & John Sparrow 2-10-1849
  Frisby F. of Zazoo, Mississippi & Maria A. Biscoe 2-28-1837
  Henry M. & Sarah P. Layman 4-9-1828
  Katie & James H. Gilligan 9-9-1878 (Robey)
  Leonard H. & Amelia H. Beall 10-29-1835
  Margaret S. B. & William H. Tuck 6-22-1843
  Mary & Upton S. Key 2-13-1844
  Michael & Ellen Proctor 10-26-1868 (Lilly)
  Philemon Lloyd & Ann Bowie 10-27-1790
  Richard B. B. & Louisa Brookes 11-23-1853
  Walter & Martha J. Cobb 7-8-1833
  William Bowie & Harriet Eversfield 10-7-1828
CHILDER,Mary E. & Alexander P. 4-26-1845
CHILDS, Cephas & Martha Elson 4-4-1801
  Joseph & Eleanor Soper 6-20-1793
  Samuel & Elizabeth Ann Lamar 5-4-1824
  William & Mary Willett 12-13-1781

CHISLEY, Philip & Juliet Edelen 12-24-1866 (Marbury)
CHITHAM, Anne & Richard Barton col? 8-22-1868 (Stanley)
  Lizzie & Henry Brown 5-15-1876
CHITTAM, Charlie & Sarah Jackson (Cotton) 5-11-1875
CHRISTIAN, William & Elizabeth M. Marbury 9-23-1858
CHRISTMAN, Horace & Sarah Matilda Magruder 10-4-1876 (Williams)
CHURCH, Elizabeth & Richard Smith 1-12-1785
  Joseph & Ann Fossett 12-23-1800
  Marg^t & Lewis Bryan 1-16-1779
  Rebecca & James Godfrey Jones 1-10-1823
  Susanna & Jonathan Mobley 2-5-1793
  Thomas & Eliz? Bryan 12-6-1777
CICEL, Rachel J. & James D. Cobb 4-10-1817
  Sam? & Mary Summers 1-8-1828
CISSELL, Ann C. & John S. King 6-11-1859
  Mary S. & William Tracy 9-18-1777
  Samuel & Rebecca V. Williams 5-9-1817
  Sarah & Richard Jones 12-13-1808
CLAGETT, Adeline & Henry J. Kershaw 12-16-1874 (Pinkney)
  Allison & Maria Hawkins 9-8-1876 (Gray)
  Ann H. P. & Richard T. Hall 6-28-1827
  Caroline M. & William Lyles 1-4-1831
  Charles & Mary Mulliken 11-12-1846
  Charles Wyckliffe & Mary H. Sasscer 11-21-1866 (Lenahan)
  Edw? Luther & Susan A. Hall 11-2-1867 (Dr. Marbury)
  Eleanor & Benj? Hall Clarke 10-2-1809
  Eliz^a & Henry Addison 2-22-1794
  Elizabeth L. & Josias Young 1-22-1833 (written above Mary W. Clagett)
  Eliz^th Mary Beanes & Josias Augustus Beall 12-2-1825
  Ellen V. & W. Worthington Bowie 9-23-1885 (Rev. Dr. Lewin)
  George T. & Sarah Ann Hall 9-22-1827
  Harriet E. & John Henry Hardesty 11-29-1833
  Harriott & John H. Beanes 5-20-1795
  Henrietta Maria & Richard Hall 6-20-1810
  Henry W. & Mattie C. Bowling 11-18-1863
  John H. & Catharine Beanes 1-15-1838
  Lethea Ann & Basil Huntt 10-21-1871
  Lucy & Frederick Sasscer Jr. 6-10-1884 (Rev. Dr. Lewin)
  Lucy Ann & Polydore E. Scott 2-11-1840
  Margaret & Thomas D. Marlow 3-10-1787
  Mary & Edward Scott 2-9-1790
  Mary & Patrick McElderry 6-5-1789
  Mary & Thomas Duckett 1-5-1796
  Mary & Zadock C. Chesley 8-31-1831
  Mary Ann & John Eversfield 2-22-1800
  Polly Bond & George Tyler 4-11-1803
  Priscilla & Thomas Wood 3-10-1787
  Rachel & Thomas White 12-26-1811
  Rachel & Charles James Kinsolving 7-11-1870 (Kinsolving)
  Rebecca & Philip R. Edelen 12-25-1848
  Richard H. & Grace H. C. Waring 11-15-1837
  Sarah Ann & John Duvall 7-9-1831
  Sarah Eliza & William J. Berry 5-18-1835
  Sarah Ellen & Joseph Howard 10-19-1841
  Sarah H. & Dr. Edgar W. Wood 1-17-1870 (Kershaw)

CLAGETT, Sarah M. & Upton Bruce 11-5-1800
  Sarah Magruder & Thomas Ramsey Hodges Jr. 3-14-1805
  Saulsbury & Pliney Green (Ankward) 12-24-1872
  Susanna & Charles Hill 6-29-1818
  Thomas & Eliza Courts 8-31-1824
  Thomas & Adeline Mandell 11-13-1838
  Thomas Jr. & Mary M. Bowie 10-26-1869 (Kershaw)
  Thomas H. & Christianna H. Oden 11-8-1831
  Thomas Henry & Henrietta Beanes Marbury 11-16-1804
  Thomas Jefferson & Catherine Waring Bowie 12-13-1881 (Rev^{d} Dr.Gordon)
  Thomas Magruder & Martha Scott 3-12-1805
  Thomas W. & Susan G. Harry 12-24-1833
  William B. & Kate Croswell Duckett 12-3-1883 (Rev. Dr. Lewin)
  William D. & Mary Ann Bowie 2-4-1828
  Wm. H. & Elizth H. Hardesty 12-1-1828
  Wiseman & Priscilla Lyles 1-16-1779
CLARK, Catherine A. & Adam G. Aist 2-2-1853
  Daniel & Mary Ann Duvall 1-11-1825
  David & Eleanor Hall 3-25-1788
  Eliza Ann & Andrew Crawford 6-20-1874 (Maybury)
  Elizabeth & Philip Hopkins 1-9-1830
  Fannie & John C. Jones 5-31-1869 (Chesley)
  George W. & Eveline McCarling 11-26-1848
  Henry & Cornelia Sprigg 9-9-1874 (Wiget)
  John B. & Carrie W. Beall 10-8-1879
  Joseph T. & Elizabeth A. Selby 4-6-1857
  Joshua G. & Rachel Celestia Pumphrey 2-2-1856
  Juliet A. & Dennis W. Ferrall 5-18-1841
  Lemuel & Catherine Hyatt Middleton 5-17-1866 (Dr. McCabe)
    Age 28 of Baltimore City, merchant, m. Hyattsville, Presby. minister
  Martha & Alexis Wood 1-30-1817
  Moses & Zilphy Gray col^{d} 11-24-1866 (Fa. Young) Age 25, laborer
    m. home Mrs. Eliza Grahams, Md. by N. D. Young, Catholic Priest
  Rueben age 23, colored, laborer of Ann Arundel County, married by
    Jas. Alex Young at Laurel, Presbyterian P. E. Church to
    Annie America age 20, colored of Ann Arundel County, servant
    5-5-1866
  Samuel & Mary Elizabeth Wood 4-24-1848
  Thomas & Ann Hall 12-21-1781
  Thomas & Ann Wailes 10-29-1791
  Thomas & Eleanor Mitchell 12-9-1797
  Thomas & Elizabeth Jones 9-20-1799
  Thomas Joshua & Ann Baldwin 9-3-1807
  William & Susan West col^{d} 10-12-1867 (Fr. Call)
  William & Rachel Franklin col^{d} 9-3-1881 (Rev. Daniel Aquilla)
  William M. & Alice E. Carlton 9-23-1869 (Harper)
CLARKE, Abraham & Priscilla Willett 12-14-1786
  Abraham & Maria Clarke 10-12-1818
  Airy & Horace Jones 12-18-1869 (Mahr)
  Alben & Sarah Mudd 8-13-1812
  Ann & Wm. Mockbee 2-29-1780
  Ann & Thomas Boteler 5-24-1784
  Ann & James H. Denson 5-21-1830
  Ann A. & William B. Bowie 7-15-1837
  Ann N. & Jeddidiah Gittings 11-22-1843

CLARKE, Ann P. & John H. Beall   12-27-1817
  Anne & Richard King   11-5-1839
  Ann Sophia & Dennis Wells   1-31-1833
  Aurelia & Edward Browning   10-16-1837
  Baley L. & Marseleen Duvall   5-1-1827
  Barney & Mary Ana Burgess   12-24-1870   (McDonald)
  Benjᵃ Hall & Eleanor Clagett   10-2-1809
  Bessie J. & F. L. Wellford   1-8-1885   (Father Cotton)
  Bettie & Joseph B. Sipe   4-29-1882   (Rev. Dr. Stanley)
  Catharine & Thomas Duckett   11-12-1840
  Charles & Margaret R. Beckett   11-12-1861
  Christopher C. & Catherine E. Pumphrey   6-15-1857
  Clara E. & John C. Sheriff   11-25-1882   (Rev. Mr. Chew)
  Daniel & Margaret Duckett   1-13-1812
  Daniel & Catherine Bowie   6-4-1833
  Eleanor & Lewis Hopper   2-7-1804
  Eleanor & Thomas Sandford   12-23-1816
  Eleanor & Leonard Kidwell   12-15-1826
  Elizabeth & Richard Addeton   4-25-1787
  Elizabeth & John Wood   12-31-1850
  Ellen & Richard H. Duvall   9-18-1838
  Ellen Ann & Nicholas L. Darnall   9-30-1834
  Frances colᵈ & James Jackson   4-19-1867
  George & Matilda Duvall   2-27-1850
  Miss Georgia & G. M. Serpell   9-13-1869   (Ross)
  Hannah & Robert Hawkins   10-9-1869   (Mahr)
  Harriet Ann & James Roberts   2-23-1867   (Young)
  Henry & Easter Beckett   12-20-1777
  James & Rachel Hagan   2-9-1781
  James & Ellen Wells   4-18-1837
  James & Sarah Elizabeth Mitchell   12-3-1855
  James & Phillis Wood colᵈ   9-1-1870   (McDonald)
  Jane N. & Wilkinson Brashears   5-25-1853
  John & Cathᵉ Lowe   10-20-1843
  John & Mary Ann Bean   2-28-1871
  John L. & Eleanora Williams   5-9-1832
  Joshua T. & Margaret A. Hardey   1-17-1874   (Wigget)
  Joshua Thomas & Darcus Carrick   2-13-1833
  Levin & Elizabeth Gibbons   12-13-1796
  Louisa & John Jackson   3-13-1877   (Carroll)
  Margaret & Colmore Duvall   1-3-1789
  Margaret & John Mockbee   12-26-1833
  Maria & Abraham Clarke   10-12-1818
  Martha & Chrisᵗ Parrott   1-20-1781
  Martha Ann & Jesse Chaney   12-22-1835
  Mary & Elisha Green   3-1-1783
  Mary & Thomas Magruder   1-4-1800
  Mary & Richard Higgins   12-17-1806
  Mary & Burnett Meaguyn   6-11-1827
  Mary Ann & George Cole   8-7-1816
  Mary Ann & Walter Ryon   12-22-1830
  Mary Anna C. & Addison Murdock   4-13-1805
  Matthias & Mary H. Mackabee   2-17-1879   (Major)
  Milley & Caleb Taylor   9-17-1803
  Robert & Ruth Beall Walker   8-21-1810
  Samuel & Sophia Baldwin   11-21-1809

CLARKE, Sarah & Christopher Hyatt 9-3-1793
  Sarah E. & Wiley Smith 5-19-1868 (Kershaw)
  Sarah Elizabeth & William Albert Turner 12-24-1881 (Fr. Cotton)
  Stephen & Mary M. Jones 3-6-1878 (Hooman)
  Susan & Richard Calvert 2-2-1877 (Carroll)
  Susana & Edward Perry 7-12-1777
  Susanna & William Pickins 6-17-1777
  Thomas & Jane D. Wall 12-21-1810
  Walter Smith & Sarah Perkins 12-23-1808
  William & Mary Belt 2-12-1828
  William D. & M. M. Forbes 6-9-1859
  William H. & Joanna Wells 2-11-1863
  Willicy & John Riley 8-2-1790
  Willy Ann & William Lanham 4-4-1814
CLARKSEN, Elizabeth & Ignatius Spink 12-16-1794
CLARKSON, Charles & Mary Bean 11-6-1802
  Joseph & Jane Eaglin 4-11-1788
  Sarah & George Dyer 5-27-1784
  Sarah & Leonard Jenkins 2-12-1814
  Thomas & Tracey Edelen 11-18-1797
CLARVOE, Mary Ann & John R. Dyer 8-17-1812
CLASON, Elizabeth & Mordecai Ridgeway 4-17-1832
CLASTON, Findel & Elizabeth Soper 3-31-1821
CLAUD, Ephana & John Grant 10-21-1777
CLAYTON, George & Lucy Williams 12-30-1870 (Stanley)
  John & Elizabeth Hodges 4-2-1814
CLEMENTS, Anne Augustus & William M. Fowler 12-10-1872 (McDonald)
  E. Anna & Henry A. C. Wheatley 4-1-1861
  Edward & Mary Jenkins 10-14-1806
  Edward H. & Minty Sansbury 1-15-1796
  Francis H. & Henrietta E. Gardiner 9-2-1843
  Francis H. & Margaret Clements 10-16-1848
  George H. & Mary E. Dixon 11-21-1857
  Jacob & Sarah Bowling 1-5-1810
  Judson S. & Catherine A. F. Martin 2-17-1873 (Toules)
  Margaret & Francis H. Clements 10-16-1848
  Martha & John Grimes 1-11-1785
  Martha & Joshua Osborn 10-21-1814
  Mary Ann & Perry Dowden 11-9-1835
  Mary Anna & Robert Edelen 11-10-1855
  Mary C. & J. B. Osbourn 2-10-1870 (Myer)
  Robert & Eleanor Acton 2-15-1832
  Sarah E. & John H. Bocock 12-26-1859
  Virginia & Dr. Joseph A. Mudd 2-11-1867 (Lenahan)
CLEMMENS, Catherine & Samuel Wright 1-9-1786
CLERK, John & Amela Willett 12-18-1788
CLIFFORD, Miledor & Charles McEver 10-17-1778
CLIFT, Henry D. & Martha A. R. Tate 7-28-1842
CLIFTON, Edward & Elisabeth Burgess 1-9-1870 (Gordon)
  Eleanora & Pinkney Belt 6-5-1878 (Hooman)
  Peggy & Charles Smith col^{d} 12-24-1868 (Stanley)
CLOUD, Joseph & Eliz.th Hughes 11-7-1826
CLUB, Harriet & Dennis Herbert 2-6-1823
  Horatio & Mary Nothie 12-11-1810
  Horatio & Elizabeth Smallwood 10-19-1821

CLUB, James & Eliza Smith 8-16-1842
  John & Sarah Taylor 12-23-1799
  Levin & Rhoda Short 8-25-1786
  Martha A. & Wm. Domine Nothey 12-24-1861
CLUBB, Ann & William Tucker 6-26-1824
  Ann Maria & Charles H. Tayler 1-9-1837
  Elizabeth & William Cater 2-1-1792
  Elizabeth Jane & William M. Gallyhan 12-18-1860
  Emily & William Clubb 4-4-1826
  Henrietta & Benoni Sansbury 7-7-1873 (Coe)
  James W. & Miss Mary E. Brown 6-1-1864
  John & Eleanor Beckett 4-5-1817
  John & Susan Jane Simpson 9-13-1836
  Kissey & Harrison Grimes 3-10-1831
  Mary & Benjamin Cater 2-16-1801
  Mary & Darius Gray 1-23-1819
  Mary & Charles Crook 9-21-1837
  Rebecca E. & Uriah Goldsmith 11-12-1859
  Rebeccah & John Mitchell 1-29-1791
  Sarah & Nathan Wells 11-2-1815
  Sarah & Cornelius Langly 12-23-1818
  Sarah & George N. Walls 1-16-1824
  Sarah Ann & John Thomas 1-12-1839
  William & Ann Nothey 1-2-1797
  William & Emily Clubb 4-4-1826
CLUM, Robert A. & Irene M. Shiby 2-17-1881 (Rev. Chester of W. D.C.)
COALE, Alfred & Sarah Ann Hopkins 2-2-1831
  Comfort & William L. Duvall 9-27-1831
  Ellen Rebecca & Archibald Roberts 5-19-1870
  James & Martha Forbes 6-4-1875
  Joseph H. & M. Virginia Wilson 7-24-1877 (Kershaw)
  Joseph H. & Lucy F. Ennis 6-18-1884 (Rev. Father Cunanne)
  Wm. A. & Alice J. Lowe 2-4-1867 (Kershaw)
COATES, Ann Matilda & Thomas Griffin 7-24-1874
  Felix & Anne Lancaster col⁴ 4-22-1868 (Lenaghan)
  Lucretia & Charles Hayes 11-20-1845
  William & Hepsey Acton 12-31-1817
  William & Fannie Agnes Gross colored 12-7-1880 (Rev. Mr. Watkins)
COATS, Ann Rebecca & Henry Henson 11-12-1868 (Langford)
  Annie & William Tyler 2-28-1880 (Aquilla)
  Charles D. & Josephine Galloway 10-17-1868 (Price)
  Jane & George Campbell 8-20-1869 (Stanley)
  Mary L. & Richard T. Beatter 10-12-1877
  Mollie & Thomas Sellman 12-26-1878 (Wheeler)
COBB, Elkanah & Martha Jones 9-8-1813
  James D. & Rachel J. Cicel 4-10-1817
  John S. & Ann Elizabeth Pierce 2-1-1870 (Harper)
  Martha J. & Walter Chew 7-8-1833
COBERTH, Priscilla & William Howard 6-12-1821
COCKLER, John & Ann Shoemaker 5-13-1799
COE, Ann Elizabeth & William N. Thomas 2-1-1851
  Barbara & Hezekiah Athey 2-19-1806
  Eleanor & Jno. S. Davis 10-17-1818
  Elijah & Ann Smallwood 10-23-1779
  Elizabeth E. & Allison F. Beall 12-15-1806

COE, James D. & Mary Tippett 11-12-1827
  John A. & Susan E. McPherson 10-20-1843
  John A. & Ann Dorman 11-18-1856
  Marsilva & Bayne Smallwood 12-19-1780
  Milburn & Mary Tongue 1-8-1783
  Richard & Margaret Wood 5-8-1784
  Samuel & Ellen Hardy 12-20-1879
COFFIN, Susan & Daniel Fowler 8-4-1840
COFFREN, George F. & Mary Jane Mills 11-24-1869 (Linthicum)
  Jeremiah & Rebecca Dove 9-8-1866 (Gordon) Age 23, Married Lodge,
    P. G. Co. Md. - Samuel R. Gordon, Presby. minister
  John W. & Susan H. Parsons 5-30-1849
  Julius E. & Martha A. E. Littleford 12-26-1878 (Lewin)
  Marg: Ellen & James T. Selby 1-23-1872 (Gordon)
  Mary Elizabeth & Edward Wallace Sweeny 2-7-1876
  Thomas & Elizabeth Ann Monk 5-25-1854
COFFRIN, Sarah A. & J. Kelley Mangum 1-29-1880 (Rev. Dr. Lavin)
COGHLAN, Dennis & Rebecca Smith 7-18-1777
COLDENSTROTH, Maggie C. & Henry C. Knock 3-29-1880
COLE, Elizabeth & Manoah Scott 2-9-1803
  Eveline & Williams Hopkins 1-20-1836
  George & Priscilla Hooker 5-6-1778
  George & Mary Ann Clarke 8-7-1816
  Margery & William Cessell 12-2-1793
  Mary & Mordecai Jacobs 6-6-1789
  Mary & William Bury 12-18-1797
  Priscilla & William Sansbury 3-29-1811
COLEMAN, Ellen & Frank Jackson col? 12-22-1880
COLLARD, Eleanor & Clement Boswell 5-18-1796
  Elizabeth & Francis Kirby 1-11-1783
COLLEA, William & Ann Trass 11-7-1786
COLLIER, Theresa J. & Charles W. Hawke 6-16-1873 (McKenney)
COLLINGS, Elizabeth & Samuel Silk 7-26-1779
  Sarah & Cephas Hoye 12-27-1784
COLLINS, Elizabeth & James Right 7-27-1796
  Horatio B. & Ellen Suit 2-2-1825
  Mary & James Hardey 2-10-1827
  Sarah & Thomas Davis 3-8-1791
COLMAN, Sarah & Daniel Stevenson 10-2-1875 (Green)
COLTON, Walter & Mary E. Stone 1-17-1873 (Marbury)
COMPTON, George & Virginia Beasley 10-21-1872 (Kershaw)
  Henry T. & Ann Swann 11-17-1797
  John T. D. & Mary S. Key 10-10-1850
  Margaret & William A. King 11-19-1883 (Rev. LaRoche)
  Mary & John Higgins 5-16-1853
  William H. & Sarah W. Scott 10-24-1855
CONAWAY, Addison & Eleanor Hyatt 1-4-1804
  Wesley & Rachael Duvall 4-8-1833
CONLEY, Adera & William Newhouse 1-10-1786
  Ann & Brian Mahew 6-19-1779
CONN, Ruth & James Nevitt 5-31-1777
CONNELL, John & Sarah White 12-7-1801
CONNER, James & Elizabeth Ann Boone 7-18-1825
  John & Eleanor W. Tracy 12-1-1778
  Martha E. & Andrew Haislip 11-17-1845

CONNER, Rifa Ann & George Walker 5-17-1807
Thomas & Elizabeth Hutchinson 2-13-1781
Thomas & Susannah Jones 3-31-1804
Violetta & Joshua Piles 10-24-1827
CONNICK, Anna Sophia & Alfred Benjamin Mudd 2-10-1855
Columbus F. & Rebecca M. Scott 12-14-1859
Daniel & Lavinia M. Burns 10-15-1849
Edward B. F. & Sarah A. Cook 1-6-1858
Elijah & Darkey Gibbons 11-20-1827
Elizabeth S. & James Naylor of Wm. 6-12-1886 (Rev. Wm. C. Ross)
Emma V. & James E. Keys 1-2-1884 (Rev. Mr. LaRoche)
James W. & Nancy Caroline Stewart 10-23-1847
Margaret J. & John M. Jameson 7-21-1863
Maria L. & Joseph W. Kerby 5-24-1849
Mary Ann & Daniel E. Havener 5-19-1830
Mary Elizabeth & Joseph P. Barker 4-30-1849
Robert & Marion R. Naylor 5-11-1867 (Brown)
CONNIE, Clement R. & Sophia A. Stallings 1-12-1825
CONNOCK, William & Elizabeth Ryon 1-31-1798
CONNOR, Violetta Ann & Addison Hardesty 4-19-1847
CONNOWAY, John & Rachel Ann Sharps 12-27-1878
CONOWAY, Osborn & Ann Cheney 11-25-1812
CONSTABLE, John & Ann Fuller 12-4-1780
CONSTANCE, Alice & Charles C. Goddard 11-21-1883 (Rev. LaRoche)
CONTEE, Ann & Dennis Magruder 9-23-1779
Arianna & James B. Ford col[d] 12-13-1879 (Rev. Dr. Lewin)
Calvert & Jennie Chapman 5-24-1873 (Townshend)
Caroline & James Spriggs 12-10-1884
Charles S. & Elizabeth C. Bowling 6-1-1860
Eleanor & Michael Wallace 8-18-1780
Elisabeth & Roderick Addison col[d] 8-1-1868 (Gordon)
Eliza & Fred. Jackson 5-3-1879 (Hooman)
Elizabeth G. & Dennis Magruder 5-29-1805
Eloise & Richard Wootton 3-23-1874 (Billup)
Florence & T. Blake Brooke 11-20-1863
George & Margaret Mackall 10-17-1885 (Rev. Brooks)
Henrietta & John Smallwood 12-3-1869
Jane & Hanson Penn 4-29-1824
Jennie & George Douglass 6-15-1886 (Rev. Mr. Price)
John & Eliza Duckett 12-28-1813
John & Ann Louisa Snowden 2-16-1824
John Thomas & Mary Brooks 12-26-1876 (Carroll)
Lucy & Moses Hathman col[d] 7-17-1880 (Fr. Voltz)
Margaret & Nicholas H. Shipley 2-19-1844
Mary L. & William W. Plummer 8-31-1865 (Stanley)
Nancy & Thomas Fowler col[d] 11-2-1881 (Rev. J. C. Bryan)
P. A. L. & Sarah F. Kent 3-28-1837
Rich[d] A. & Mary Crauford 6-16-1785
Sarah & David Slater 5-29-1790
Sophia & Thomas Henry Ford 12-28-1876 (Carroll)
Susan & James Francis Beall 12-30-1870 (Lankford)
CONWAY, Mamie & George W. Fowler 8-18-1884
Rachel B. & Edward F. Barnard 11-9-1847
COOK, Celia & Francis Rawlings 12-27-1871 (Gordon)
Elizabeth & John Henry Sprigg 6-10-1867 (Kershaw)

COOK, Jacob & Jane Jones 11-25-1806
  James & Ruth Deakins 1-11-1820
  Joseph & Rachel Tucker 11-29-1866 Age 20 - farmer, married at
    St. Barnabas Ch. Prot. Ep. - John W. Chesley, Minister
  Louis & Lizzie Wilson 4-8-1871 (Gordon)
  Martha & Charles C. Ridgeway 6-22-1852
  Mary Ann & Robert Hardisty 1-23-1821
  Mary Catherine & Frederick Pinkney 8-13-1875
  Richard & Margaret Ann Montgomery 9-18-1821
  Rosa N. & Joseph M. Garner 6-11-1862
  Sarah A. & Edward B. F. Connick 1-6-1858
  Septimus J. & Ann Rebecca Beall 12-22-1829
  Septimus & Barsina Duvall 1-21-1834
  Septimas J. & Julia A. Magill 4-23-1845
  Septimas J. & Elbertene Elizabeth Browne 3-7-1848
  Theodore & Eleanor Mulliken 7-22-1819
  Walter R. & Hannah M. Gibson 12-2-1885 (Rev. Mr. Butler)
  William Francis & Sarah A. R. Davis 3-25-1853
  William H. & Eliza Borsell 2-6-1839
  Wm. & Sarah Fry 9-4-1848
COOKE, Ann & Ralph Sherlock 2-13-1805
  Delila & Zachariah Gentle 12-22-1802
  Eliza & John Grimes 1-26-1808
  Elizabeth & Joseph Hinton 12-22-1796
  Elizabeth & Hezekiah Anderson 12-22-1819
  Ellen R. & Jn⁰ Tucker 3-18-1844
  Jeremiah & Mary Beanes 12-14-1785
  John & Elizabeth Hinton 6-25-1801
  John & Deborah Hopper 12-22-1802
  Joseph Junr & Elizabeth Russell 12-11-1792
  Nathan & Ann Baldwin 12-21-1814
  Rebecca & Michael Deakins 10-7-1779
  Robert & Henrietta Hogan 7-27-1790
  Ruth & James Deakins 2-8-1812
  Samuel & Rebecca A. Wilkins 11-11-1839
  Sarah A.E.M. & Austin Montgomery 11-25-1839
  William & Henrietta Beaven 8-28-1777
  William & Elizabeth Mudd 5-28-1796
  William Henry & Anne R. Forbes 11-13-1885 (Rev. Mr. Chesley)
  Wm. L. & Elizabeth Matilda Davis 11-12-1849
  Zadokiah & Hetty King 12-26-1794
COOKSEY, Andrew & Sarah Perrie 2-18-1800
  Ann & Elijah Ellis 7-9-1802
  Benjamin & Sarah Watson 2-23-1827
  Elizabeth & John Ellis 12-7-1808
  Elizabeth & Benjᵃ Beaven 2-18-1814
  Elizabeth A. & W. W Ives 4-23-1862
  George R. & Catherine R. Martin 11-24-1852
  John & Martha Baden 11-18-1856
  John & Mary A. Ryon 6-12-1871
  Jonathan & Susannah Robinson 12-27-1816
  Joshua J. & Mary Jane Watson 4-15-1859
  Julia Ann & George H. Waters 9-13-1831
  Margaret Perrie & Philip Cooksey Watson 12-12-1817
  Mary & Henry Beaven 3-28-1815

COOKSEY, Mary M. & Wm. H. White 1-9-1867 (Smith)
  Nathaniel T. & Martha Kidwell 12-10-1821
  Samuel & Catharine Beavin 12-23-1813
  Sarah & Leonard Watson 1-7-1792
  Sarah & Hugh Perrie 7-12-1817
  Sarah & William Smith 9-23-1817
  Sarah D. & John W. Eastwood 2-13-1813
  Susan & Benjamin Garner 1-29-1853
  William & Eleanor Waring 1-10-1826
  William H. & Mary Jane Paine 8-19-1858
COOLEDGE, Edmund & Elizabeth Ann Bowie 11-14-1832
  Eliz^a & John M. Burgess 2-26-1794
COOLEY, Ann Maria & Edward Cooley 2-18-1834
  Benjamin & Mary Hows 12-17-1816
  Edward & Ann Maria Cooley 2-18-1834
  Jane & Benjamin Earley 1-27-1789
COOLIDGE, Samuel Judson & Mary Hepburn 2-20-1798
COOMBES, Eliza L. & Charles Bowie 5-15-1828
  Joseph & Dorothy Sherkliff 5-4-1783
  Joseph & Mary Lyles 10-23-1797
  Terissa & Nathan Hardey 5-16-1783
COOMBS, Henry L. & Louisa D. Seaton 8-15-1822 lic. 8-2-1822
COOPER, Christopher & Naomi Carroll 9-30-1871 (Wheeler)
  Elizth & Richd E. Cropley 5-28-1838
  James & Matilda Padgett 6-3-1820
  John & Rebecca Ferrall 11-14-1845
CORD, John & Sarah Calvert 4-24-1804
CORFRIES, Francis & Henrietta Greer 10-14-1821
CORRICK, Alice & John M. Roberts 2-8-1868 (Marbury)
COUGHLAND, Richd Johnson & Eliz^b Mitchell 2-28-1785
COURTS, Ann C. & John S. Belt 12-13-1831
  Charles & Ruth Arvin 1-16-1808
  Charles C. & Sidney Hawkins 1-27-1838
  Elijah & Lettie Tolson 12-23-1867 (Gordon)
  Eliza & Thomas Clagett 8-31-1824
  Henrietta & Elisha Arvin 10-29-1808
  Hessey & Thomas Burk 12-19-1828
  Jane & William Brice 2-28-1848
  Sarah M. & Francis M. Bowie 10-17-1833
  William & Eliza Lyles 5-17-1808
  William & Eliza Mitchell 1-19-1822
COUSEY, George W. & Mary A. Sexton 10-30-1869 (Mahr)
COVINGTON, Alexander & Harriot Magruder 12-16-1797
  Levin & Rebecca Mackall 3-25-1796
  Priscilla & Charles Stewart 10-10-1877
COWAN, James Seymore & Ellen Clay Wright 6-20-1867 (McCabe)
COWLES, William & Ann Earlie 7-29-1777
COX, Ann R. & Richard L. Goddard 1-3-1866 (Martin)
  Charlotte & Daniel W. Pumphrey 1-16-1878
  Chloe Ann & Alfred Thomas Sheriff 12-28-1840
  John & Annie Vermillion 9-23-1869 (Kershaw)
  John H. (Charles County) & Susanna C. Berry 12-13-1862
  Mackall S. & Susannah Sasser 12-6-1808
  Matilda & William O. Beall 1-10-1883 (Rev. Mr. Hyland)
  S. M. & Charles H. Catendon 1-9-1877

COX, Sarah & Henry N. Tall 1-5-1824
  Sarah & Charles Rob. Grimes 12-24-1842
  Sarah Ann & Richard Harwood 10-28-1799
  Thomas J. & Josephine Duckett 6-15-1870 (Harper)
  Thomas Smith & Ann Boteler 2-2-1785
  Walter B. & Ann Hollyday 11-19-1778
  William & Charlotte Taylor 5-25-1796
COXE, Elizabeth & John Palmer 4-30-1844
COXEN, Georgianna & James H. Jones 11-21-1866 Age 18 (white) (Kershaw)
  James Henry & Mary Catharine Ryon 3-25-1862
COYLE, Francis & Matilda Spalding 5-15-1813
CRABB, Charles & Susannah Smith 2-13-1792
  Priscilla & Stephen Drane 12-24-1793
CRACK, Clora Ann & Henry Joseph Brown 4-15-1865 both colored people
  John William & Eliza Jane Savoy 3-4-1868 (Gordon)
CRACKLIN, Nancy & Samuel Crooke 1-1-1806
  Susan Rebecca & John T. Osbourn 4-28-1856
  Susannah & Walter Crooke 1-26-1811
CRACROFT, John & Ann Watson 1-11-1808
CRAEGG, Ann & James P, White 1-26-1857
CRAIG, Benjamin & Mary J. Armiger 12-28-1846
  Constant & Mary Ellen Chesley 10-17-1878 (Watkins)
  George W. & Mary Hodges 2-21-1860
  Joseph & Mary E. Ball 1-5-1870
  Julia & Geo.Wm. Mills 4-23-1879
  Margery & Luke Galloway 4-19-1873
  Mary & James Henry Garner 1-13-1876 (Tennant)
  Robert & Mary Fowler 2-12-1869 (Langford)
CRAIN, Sarah & Hezekiah Schrucner 7-21-1874 (Price)
CRAINE, Robert Alex. & Elizabeth Wood 2-4-1814
CRAMPKIN, Alice & John Francis 11-5-1781
CRANDALL, Elizabeth & Edward Mitchell 1-19-1814
  Sarah & Thomas M. Dorsett 9-3-1799
  Thomas & Hessey Smith 1-23-1804
CRANDEL, Priscilla & William Boteler 9-29-1853
CRANDELL, Elizabe th & Thomas Fry 6-29-1795
  F. Dysen & Annie V. Ryon 10-8-1881
  George Emory & Rebecca King 11-18-1873 (Dwyer)
  Georgia & Edward H. Butler 12-4-1872 (Mercer)
  Henry S. & Elizabeth A. Kidwell 12-11-1855
  Susan E. & James N. Wells 9-30-1867
  Susie R. & William H. Suit 11-15-1877 (Miller)
  Thomas & Annie E. Gibson 7-5-1881 of Ann Arundel County
CRANDLE, James H. & Elizabeth E. Rantin 1-9-1845
CRANFORD, see also Crauford, Crawford, Crawfurd
  Benjamin & Mary Hook 11-1-1871 (Skinner)
  George T. & Josephine Suit 10-31-1855
  Mary Ann & Octavius Young 2-20-1854
  Richard & Maggie De Vaughn 9-14-1874 (Kershaw)
  Rosa & Robert Tayman 12-28-1885 (Rev. Mr. Chesley)
  Samuel B. & Elizabeth Ryon 11-13-1861
CRAUFORD, Anna V. & William L. Wall 2-13-1857
  Barbara Jane & Loyd Sweeney 2-17-1862
  Elizabeth & James Kerr 6-4-1870 (Harper)
  Georgie L. & Samuel O. Tayman 12-30-1879 (Fr. De Wolf)

CRAUFORD, Mary & Richd A. Contee 6-16-1785
  Sarah J. & Daniel R. Wall 12-1-1855
  Thomas & Miss Alice Sweeney 4-27-1880 (Rev. Mr. Boteler)
CRAUFURD, Emily & Tyler Wilson 1-28-1828
  Harrison & Ann Maria Nalley 8-8-1867 (Fa. Call)
  James & Elizabeth Beall 6-11-1799
  Martha & George Walker 12-16-1794
CRAVER, Elizabeth & Michael Cain 1-27-1800
  Jacob & Ann Evans 4-13-1800
CRAWFORD, Andrew & Mary Butler col^d 1-29-1870 (Langford)
  Andrew & Eliza Ann Clark 6-20-1874 (Maybury)
  Basil B. & Airey Beall Cross 2-24-1813
  Cator & Elizabeth Anne Crawford 3-5-1877 (Carroll)
  Elizabeth Anne & Cator Crawford 3-5-1877 "
  Hugh & Mary Jeans 11-28-1780
  James & Priscilla Taylor 11-9-1801
  James Lemuel & Nancy Smothers 2-26-1870 (Maher)
  John & Louisa Bowser 5-17-1872 (Fr. Cotton)
  John & Harriet Butler 2-26-1877
  Lucy & Henry Tyler 2-9-1870 (Begue)
  Margaret & Andrew Brown 3-14-1797
  Mary Ann & James Reynolds 12-9-1834
  Mary E. & Jno. H. Sansbury 5-1-1850
  Rachel & Theodore Jones 1-25-1821
  Robert & Mary Weems 2-22-1872 (Gordon)
  Sarah A. & Esmond J. Soper 11-23-1883 (Dr. Harvey Stanley)
  Sarah Jane & Benjamin Carroll col^d 8-1-1871
  Thomas & Cecelia Harrison col^d 12-20-1870 (Begue)
  Tilghman & Martha Ann Isaacs 4-1-1822
  Tilghman & Mary E. Isaacs 4-14-1857
  W. B. & Mary Ferrall 8-31-1845
CRAWFURD, Mary & Thomas Suit 11-13-1826
  Priscilla & Daniel Lee 5-21-1829
CRAYCROFT, Ann & Theodore Demar 10-10-1815
  Annie E. & James E. Thompson 1-25-1868 (Marbury)
  Clement & Elizabeth Lamar 3-7-1812
  Clement & Sally Callicoe 10-14-1818
  Columbus P. & Emma S. Tucker 1-22-1876 (Tennent)
  George & Eliza Taylor 7-24-1820
  Mary & Elijah Ellis 12-20-1814
  Mary E. & Benj. N. Robinson 2-2-1864
  Mary S. & Richard M. Scott 6-25-1863
  Perry & Mary E. Oliver 6-20-1840
  Susan & Benjamin Robertson 12-22-1827
CREATON, John & Massey Ann Lanham 2-21-1783
CREEK, Margaret & Thomas Gray 4-5-1801
  William H. & Christianna Sims 9-16-1878
CRIMPTON, Thomas & Margery Waring 1-28-1779
CRIST, Robert C. & Mary J. C. Hood 9-15-1876 (Major)
CROCKETT, John & Susan Wheatley 6-6-1848
CROMPTON, Mary & George Brashears 2-10-1802
CRONER, Margaret G. & Edward Edmonston 6-27-1800
CROOK, Alice C. & Jeremiah Duckett Jr. 8-19-1879 (Townshend)
  Cassandra & Somervell Nicholson 1-29-1850
  Celistia Ann & Charles A. Duvall 10-18-1853

CROOK, Charles & Mary Clubb 9-21-1837
  Eleanor & Noah Wheat 9-24-1804
  John J. & Jane Loveless 12-22-1858 CROOK, Mary Ann &
  Mary & John Taylor 2-16-1798   William Wakeham 11-24-1843
  Richard W. & Adiline Carrick 12-29-1858
  Susannah & Thomas Goldsmith 1-31-1828
CROOKE, Amelia & William Diggins 8-15-1840
  Ann Maria & MacCeeny Howes 11-13-1854
  Eleanor & Trueman Robey 11-25-1805 (Robey)
  John & Cassandra Gray 12-23-1797
  John & Eleanor Hopkins 1-13-1810
  Samuel & Nancy Cracklin 1-1-1806
  Susannah & Henley Curting 2-23-1811
  Walter & Susannah Cracklin 1-26-1811
CROPLEY, Richd E. & Elizth Cooper 5-28-1838
CROSBY, Alice & Ashby C. Owens 1-19-1886
  Harriet & William Stallings 2-3-1838
  John & Margaret Jones 2-22-1881
  Walter & Ann Ryon 11-16-1799
  Walter & Sarah Ann Dove 3-21-1831
CROSS, Airey Beall & Basil B. Crawford 2-24-1813
  Cecelia & Fielder Cross 1-13-1838
  Dennis B. & Camilla Duvall 2-21-1827
  Edward & Elizabeth Scott 6-19-1780
  Eleanor & Jacob Simmons 4-19-1780
  Elizabeth & Robert H. Stewart 4-5-1820
  Elizabeth & Anthony C. Page 1-13-1838
  Elizabeth & Nathan Watson 4-6-1844
  Elizabeth Ann & William Theodore Watson 11-10-1862
  Fielder & Cecelia Cross 1-13-1838
  Fielder Jr. & Harriet T. Wall 1-30-1856
  Fielding & Margaret Brashears 12-12-1794
  George & Martha Trueman 6-5-1879 (Quinn)
  Howerton & Susan Willett 2-21-1831
  Isabella & Frank Slingluff 7-13-1880 (Rev. Mr. Butler)
  John & Mary Lamar 4-26-1813
  John & Deleley Kidwill 12-24-1836
  John & Elizth Ann Alvey 3-3-1851
  John L. & Maggie J. Fowler 12-22-1873 (Gordon)
  John L. & Ella V. Fowler 5-16-1876 (Kershaw)
  Joseph & Lucy Brashears 5-20-1783
  Joseph & Cecelia Duvall 2-15-1817
  Joseph & Sophia Duckett 12-8-1823
  Joseph & Mary Ann Watson 12-23-1834
  Joseph & Amelia Kitwell 6-15-1867 (Smith)
  Maria Louisa & Strong J. Thomson 12-22-1846
  Mary & Joseph Brashears 12-10-1780
  Mary & George Bartley 1-26-1798
  Mary & William Cross 5-16-1808
  Mary & John F. Watson 4-8-1834
  Mary & N. C. Darnall 9-23-1876 (Williams)
  Mary Ann & Benjamin N. Duckett 10-18-1824
  Osbourne & Louisa Duvall 12-15-1832
  Richard G. & Cornelia Duvall 5-11-1830
  Richard G. & Caroline Beckett 9-29-1837

CROSS, Richd G. & Sarah Ann Beckett 7-12-1843
  Richard Henry & Mary Emma Fowler 5-3-1877 (Kershaw)
  Sarah A. & John H. Williams 1-6-1873 (Marbury)
  Thomas & Eliz? Vermilion 10-14-1780
  Thomas & Sarah Bartley 11-1-1798
  Trueman D. & Mary E. Belt 3-30-1859
  William & Mary Cross 5-16-1808
  William & Arabella Gibbons 8-15-1845
CROUSE, Hugh V. & Jenevive Ridgely 2-27-1878 (Hooman)
CROW, John & Priscilla Beall 10-25-1780
  Lancelot & Elizabeth Bayne 11-26-1794
  Margaret & Garston Powell 10-10-1811
CROWLEY, Rosanna D. & Oliver B. Magruder 11-22-1842
CROWN, Charles & Annie Owens 12-31-1880 cold (Rev. Mr. Butler)
  Elizabeth & Edward Deale 3-2-1878 (Gray)
  Joseph & Anne Guy 5-12-1795
  William & Jenet Ferguson 10-9-1799
CRUTCHLY, Delia & Samuel Popham 12-25-1783
CULLEY, Burdy & Cora Harris 4-6-1877
CULVER, Catherine & Christopher C. Hyatt 2-25-1824
  Henry & Permelia Jones 1-25-1827
  Samuel & Margaret Ann Thompson 10-30-1822
CUNNINGHAM, John & Margaret Simms 8-4-1792
  John & Eleanor Tippett 8-28-1811
CURCAURD, Mary J. & Theodore Hodgkin 4-9-1787
CURLEY, Emily Jane & Philip P. Castle 8-22-1883
CURRICO, Joshua & Angelina Brashears 12-16-1842
CURTAIN, Albert & Susannah Taylor 2-18-1878 (Kershaw)
  Elizabeth & Michael Lovejoy 2-10-1808
  Elizabeth & John T. Simpson 1-9-1839
  George W. & Joanna R. Smith 8-13-1884 (Rev. Mr. Chesley)
  Hezekiah & Martina Langley 12-22-1817
  James & Elizabeth Kidwell 4-16-1863
  Jas. H. & Mira M. Rebecca Jane Carrick 5-10-1864
  Joanna & John Samuel Canter 6-18-1884
  John F. & Mary Isabella Bradle 12-13-1866 (Marbury)
  Martha Jane & Thompson Bradle 12-13-1866 (Marbury)
  Richard H. & Catherine R. Selby 3-15-1866 Age 23, farmer, married by
    A. J. Porter, minister
  Rosanna & Richard Winsor 8-25-1863
  Susanna & James R. Seabourne 1-3-1870 (Gordon)
  William & Elizabeth Lamar 2-6-1813
CURTEN, Celesta Ann & John J. Winsor 2-21-1846
  Tilly & Washington G. Boswell 2-8-1817
  William & Elizabeth Kidwell 4-14-1873
CURTIN, Dennis & Teresa Moreland 8-25-1813
  Eliza E. & Leonard D. Wilson 12-24-1839
  Harriet & William H. Hall 12-14-1853
  Mary & David Jones 3-26-1806
  Richard & Harriett Loveless 12-21-1839
  Wᵐ & Pamelia Cutts 12-9-1817
CURTING, Dennis & Nancy Buckingham 2-13-1797
  Henley & Susannah Crooke 2-23-1811
CURTIS, Charles & Mary Jane Gardiner 6-28-1856
  William T. & Jane W. Hoker 12-27-1884

CUSHING, Major Harry Cook & Martha W. Budd 6-6-1868
CUSTIS, William H. & Eliza B. Wheeler 4-27-1829
CUTCHES, Margaret & William Dulany 12-17-1819
CUTCHLY, Ann & Zachariah Brashears 1-22-1785
CUTTS, Pamelia & Wm. Curtin 12-9-1817

DABNEY, Mary & Charles Young Jr. 8-17-1796
DAILEY, Moses & Ann Wiley 10-7-1797
DALE, John R. & Rebecca L. Orme 10-31-1849
DALRYMPLE, Carrie E. & Benjamin F. Catterton 1-13-1886 (Rev. Elridge)
DAINGERFIELD, Maly C. & Rice W. Hooe 8-2-1873
  Susan S. & John S. Barbour 10-16-1865 (Marbury)
  William Allen & Maria H. H. Rozer 12-12-1807
DANENHOWER, Charles & Mary Elizabeth Jones 10-30-1872
  William W. Jr. & Ruth Rosana Bushell 12-30-1873 (Williams)
DANFORTH, Mrs. Nancy & John M. White 10-30-1797
DANGERFIELD, Henry & Harriot Rozer 5-19-1810
DANIELSON, Benjⱱ & Drusilla Pearce 10-26-1779
  Zach. & Sarah Benson 12-29-1777
DANISON, John F. & Martha Anne Phelps 9-8-1857
DANNERSON, Jno. F. & Sarah E. Allen 8-29-1862
DANNISON, Rhody & Walter Fearall 12-2-1801
DARBY, Ann F. & Nathan Masters 10-26-1885 (Rev. Mr. Hyland)
DARBYSHIRE, Elizᵃ & Wm. Butterworth 1-31-1779
DARCEY, Ann & Nathan Soper 11-21-1791   See also Dorsey
  Ellen R. & John H. Bayne 2-28-1881
  Elizabeth & William Young 12-20-1826
  John & Rebecca Hardey 11-21-1786
  John & Lucy Vermillion 12-3-1825
  Lucy & Ignatius Lott Hardey 7-1-1803
  Margueretta Eugenia & Wm. E. R. Suit 2-23-1881 (Rev. Brayshaw)
  Mary & Colemore Fry 2-12-1821
  Nathan & Mary Young 9-26-1828
  Rebecca & Joseph Osborn 1-18-1803
DARCY, Edward L. & Mary A. Fergusson 4-3-1850
  Francis & Rebecca Darnall 6-21-1817
  Ida M. & Frank Gordon 6-17-1878 (Dorsey)
  Mary & William Wellen 1-30-1793
DARE, Charlotte & Walton Burns colᵈ 6-22-1869 (Thomas)
  John & Mary McPherson 11-5-1834
  Dr. John & Maria Berry 11-4-1858
DARNALL, Charles J. & Ann Rebecca Davis 2-15-1825
  Elizabeth & Philip C. Watson 1-3-1820
  Francis & Mary Hill 4-9-1818
  Gerrard & Sarah Hurley 1-31-1781
  Henry & Ann Maria Gross 12-29-1873 (Pinkney)
  Henry B. & Sarah Ann Blandford 6-19-1838
  John & Barsheba Hurley 12-11-1782
  John S. & Elizabeth Darsey 11-21-1809
  Mary & Robert Wigfield 6-29-1805
  Mary & James Davis 5-14-1812
  N. C. & Mary Cross 9-23-1876 (Williams)
  Nicholas L. & Ellen Ann Clarke 9-30-1834
  Rachel & John Dodson Jr. 9-10-1803

DARNALL, Rebecca & Francis Darcy 6-21-1817
  Sarah & Edward Jones 1-21-1804
  Susan J. & M. L. Wilson 4-26-1847
  Susanna & George Owen 1-25-1783
  Susannah & Philip Mockbee 12-24-1808
  William & Elizabeth Soper 2-20-1819
DARSEY, Elizabeth & John S. Darnall 11-21-1809
  George & Milly Scarce 12-27-1798
DASHIELL, Thomas B. & Mary B. Beall 11-1-1816
DATON, Amelia & Samuel Brown col^d 9-8-1866
DAUGHERTY, James & Martha Owl 6-9-1795
DAVIDSON, Henry & Annastacy Reynolds 12-30-1795
  Henry & Jemima Hatton 10-18-1825
  Plinny & Mary Henry Harrison 8-31-1793
DAVIS, Alfred & Mary Clare Young 12-23-1875
  Ann & John Talbott 10-1-1777
  Ann & James Atchinson 2-8-1783
  Ann & Thomas Leitch 1-8-1806
  Ann Rebecca & Charles J. Darnall 2-15-1825
  Anne & Samuel Austin 1-18-1793
  Beno & Benjamin Anderson 2-12-1800
  Caroline A. & William A. Quynn 2-18-1835
  Catharine & John King 9-23-1847
  Eleanor & Zach^g Thompson 12-9-1783
  Eleanor & Levin Wailes 10-28-1796
  Elizabeth & George Holdsworth Gantt 7-5-1806
  Elizabeth & Cornelius Watson 3-19-1807
  Elizabeth & John A. Dixon 1-6-1855
  Elizabeth Matilda & Wm. L. Cooke 11-12-1849
  Elizth Ann & Edward L. Boteler 4-1-1830
  Ellen S. & Joseph R. Waters 2-13-1870 (Leneghan)
  George & Lizzie Locker 4-11-1873 (Dwyer)
  George T. & Henrietta Garner 4-7-1846
  George Washington & M. Jones 2-22-1886 (Rev. Mr. Brooks)
  Henrietta L. & Augustus F. Berry 12-26-1849
  Henry & Mary Norman Morris 10-23-1790
  Henry C. & Annie E. Burgess 1-6-1885 (Father Clarke)
  James & Mary Darnall 5-14-1812
  James Fred^k & Mary Elizabeth Gray 3-20-1884 (Rev. Mr. Wills)
  James R. & Ann E. Carter 1-30-1845
  Jane & James Gross 9-10-1869 (Lenaghan)
  Jemima & Walter Butteler 12-15-1785
  John & Mary Bryant 8-20-1779
  John F. & Margaret W. Williams 2-3-1882 (Rev. Mr. La Roche)
  John Henry & Maria Jackson col^d 1-29-1870 (Begue)
  John R. & Rebecca Lucas 9-26-1881
  John S. & Jenny D. Adams 3-18-1825
  John Wesley & Eleanora Hawkins 10-22-1873 (Townshend)
  Jno. & Sarah A. Hyde 11-1-1841
  Jno. F. & Mary Ann Digges 4-13-1864
  Jno. S. & Eleanor Coe 10-17-1818
  Jno. W. A. & Pricey A. Young 12-28-1885 (Rev. Geo. W. Dame)
  Jonathan & Sarah Watson 12-26-1787
  Jos. & Annie White 3-18-1875
  Joshua & Elizabeth Bonifant 12-24-1793

DAVIS, Josiah & Mary M. Greer 2-14-1817
  Leonard & Polly Mitchell 12-26-1812
  Lethe & Jonathan Hardey 4-19-1837
  Marcus Lafayette & Annie Ruth Goodrick 7-16-1883 (Rev. Mr. Fowler)
  Martha Ann & Levin Sasser 7-23-1834
  Mary & William Cage Rawlings 7-25-1809
  Mary T. & Edward Wyvill 11-26-1832
  Minty & Henry Swann 1-8-1789
  Nancy & John Arnold 12-16-1817
  Polly & John Proctor 9-18-1815
  Rebecca & Marlowe Wynn 2-12-1811
  Rebecca J. & Samuel Barron 3-13-1821
  Robert & Eleanor Adams 5-28-1806
  Ruth & James Baden 2-5-1811
  Sarah & Walter White 1-14-1789
  Sarah A. R. & William Francis Cook 3-25-1853
  Sarah Ann & Leonard P. Cage 12-2-1852
  Sophia & William Green 2-26-1778
  Sophy R. & Lemuel H. Henry 1-12-1861
  Susannah & Perry Stallings 1-29-1816
  Thomas & Sarah Collins 3-8-1791
  Thomas A. & Rebecca P. Gibbons 11-25-1856
  Thomas C. & Elizabeth Carrico 12-28-1816
  William T. & M. R Fuller 12-2-1869 (Kershaw)
  Wm. & Sarah Osborn 8-5-1816
  Zacheus & Susannah Baden 12-29-1804
DAVY, Leonard & Artridge Phipps 1-30-1867
DAY, Amey & Leonard Fry 12-8-1803
  Eleanor & Robert Simmons 12-6-1805
  Eliz? Ana & Noah Lusby 12-3-1868 (Berry)
  Frank & Lizzie Smithson 1-22-1876 (McNeer)
  Harriet R. & John Shaw 6-22-1876
  John & Ann Winkler 11-29-1831
  Margaret & Samuel Dunning 11-26-1803
  Margaret R. & Nicholas C. Stephen 6-10-1849
  Martha & Francis Jenkins 10-28-1780
  Martha & Levi Sheakells 2-3-1833
  Richard H. & Elizabeth Millar 11-7-1832
  William & Harriet R. Duvall 1-2-1867 Age 25, farmer – married at
    Davidsonville, A. A. County by C. R. Nelson, minister P. E. Church
DAYLEY, Thomas & Bini Jones 8-23-1793
DEACON, John & Elizabeth E. DeVaughn 1-23-1865
DEAKINS, Amanda & Alfred Boarman 6-16-1858
  Caroline A. R. & George McLeod 5-7-1835
  Elizabeth D. & John Heath 3-20-1819
  Ellen F. & Henry T. Trueman 8-19-1878 (Perry)
  Emily & Theodore Wilburn 11-19-1832
  Emily R. & James M. Wood 2-14-1855
  James & Ruth Cooke 2-8-1812
  Mrs. Mary & John L. Thompson 3-2-1874
  Michael & Rebecca Cooke 10-7-1779
  Rebecca & Bennett Lowe 12-7-1819
  Ruth & James Cook 1-11-1820
  Walter & Rebecca Upton 2-7-1821
DEAL, Catherine & Oden Williams 12-13-1875

DEAL, Edward & Kitty Simms 5-15-1874 (O'Dwyer)
  Richard Franklin & Ella Rebecca Hardy 12-27-1875 (McNeer)
  Sylvester & Kate Gummer 5-31-1873
  Thomas H. & Susan Tydings 1-7-1852
DEALE, Edith & George Wesley Chaney 4-21-1881 (Rev. Mr. Butler)
  Edward & Elizabeth Crown 3-2-1878 (Gray)
  Ella & John H. Tidings 4-19-1875 (Kershaw)
  Henry & Ally Proctor 12-20-1802
  Phoebe & Richard Wells 4-19-1830
DEAN, Charles H. & Lizzie Straining 10-18-1879
  Robert & Barbara Moore 3-30-1861
DEANER, Michael & Elizth Powers 8-4-1818
DEASON, Elizabeth E. & Edward J. Boteler 7-13-1842
DeBUTTS, Mary Ann & John P. Dulaney 5-18-1812
DEGORS, Eliza & William Brown 2-12-1835
DEGRAFF, Margaret & Edward McCubbin 8-16-1826
DEJEAN, Peter & Henrietta McPherson 5-11-1816
DELANEY, Johanna & Patrick Quick Jr. 1-9-1874 (Cotton)
DELEHAYE, Joseph & Mary Mills 6-22-1788
DELLAPLANE, George W. & Margaret Willett 12-28-1831
DELMEGE, Patrick A. & Elizabeth Piles 8-8-1868
DEMAR, Amelia & Joseph Callicoe 12-5-1781
  Ana Price & William L. Gibbons 1-17-1882 (Rev. Mr. LaRoche)
  Ann & Thomas Bean 10-13-1837
  Charles & Sarah H. Hunter 7-11-1828
  Elizabeth & James Watson 9-15-1815
  Georgianna & James E. Joy 12-11-1883 (Rev. Mr. Sutherland)
  I. V. & Ida Demar 5-8-1883
  J. V. & Sarah A. Richards 1-4-1865
  John & Martha Demar 1-25-1847
  John Thomas & Marg^{t} Elizabeth Richardson 2-3-1877
  Martha & John Demar 1-25-1847
  Martha E. & Benj. F. Richardson 1-8-1862
  Mary & Samuel Selby 1-25-1832
  Mary Ann & Thomas Demar 8-1-1838
  Mary E. & J. A. Selby 2-16-1862
  Nannie & John W. Lamar 8-25-1883
  Sarah & James Richardson 1-22-1817
  Sarah P. & Robt. Mathaney 12-9-1851
  Theodore & Ann Craycroft 10-10-1815
  Thomas & Mary Ann Demar 8-1-1838
  Thomas & Elizabeth Oliver 12-30-1847
DEMCEY, John & Margaret Frowmay 11-7-1784
DEMENT, Benj. Franklin & Mary Martha Starbuck 11-19-1866 (Rev. Lanahan)
  Cath^{a} V. & Harman Chapin 5-30-1849
  Charles F. & Elizth A. Bryan 11-17-1843
  Jane E. & William Tolson 9-28-1835
  Julia A. & Joseph Smoot 4-5-1841
  Richard & Catharine McDaniel 3-1-1811
DEMPSEY, George R. & Hattie A. Harman 4-7-1877
DeNEIL, Caroline & Alfred Woodward 2-8-1877 (Carroll)
  Garthey Ann & Joseph Calvert 3-17-1877 (Carroll)
DENNISON, John F. & Sarah Francis Fowler 8-20-1866 Age 30, widower,
    Gardner, m. near Forestville, Henry J. Kershaw, minister, P. E. Church
    Upper Marlboro

DENNEY, Jacob & Elizabeth Brown 10-10-1876
DENOON, John & Sarah Burrell 1-17-1798
DENSON, James H. & Ann Clarke 5-21-1830
DENT, Cloe Hanson & Thomas James Stoddert Jr. 9-21-1790
  Eleanor & George Hatton 6-27-1786
  Eliza & Elzear Beans 4-6-1869
  Frank & Emily Hodge 5-18-1872 (Trapwell)
  Grace Ann & Henson Young 12-26-1867 (Greenleaf)
  Henson & Rose Scott 5-14-1884
  Hezekiah & Georgina Hodges 5-25-1869 (Father Maher)
  John A. & Margaret Goldsmith 12-18-1874 (Scott)
  John Francis & Kitty Jane Allen 12-10-1870 (Gordon)
  Laura & David Miles 5-20-1873 (O'Dwyer)
  Lelie C. & Francis O. St. Clair of Wash. D. C. 10-24-1866 Age 25
  Louisa & James Hawkins 6-22-1875
  Margaret & Ruffian Holmes 9-21-1866
  Mary Priscilla & James Alfred Hawkins 12-17-1879 (Rev. Samuel Gordon)
  Patrick & Susannah G. Wood 7-22-1809
  Sandy & Josephine Jackson 5-25-1867 (Fr. Call)
  William E. & Renia Batson 1-9-1873
De POINCY, Jane Mary Sebastian Zephirine Javain & John Constantine
  Marsollan Generis 6-2-1804
DEUVAN, Alice Levinia & Frank Bell 9-9-1875 (Billop)
DEVAN, Elennora West & Richard Henry Tayman 12-18-1883 (Rev. LaRoche)
  George Washington Holliday & Marianna Hyde 12-31-1862
  James T. & S. J. Robey 6-4-1884 (Rev. Mr. Chesley)
  Michael & Barbara Richards 12-29-1812
DEVAUGHN, Benjn T. P. & Delilah A. Rowell 2-17-1844
  Elizabeth E. & John Deacon 1-23-1865 Age 21
  Ella A. & B. F. Rawlings 4-25-1871
  James R. & Elizth N. Ratcliff 9-3-1830
  Maggie & Richard Cranford 9-14-1874 (Kershaw)
  Mary & George Garner 1-2-1868
  Mary C. & Peter Wood Richards 1-6-1879
  Susannah & John Johnson 2-2-1788
  Walter Josephus & Mary Tayman 6-13-1877 (Gordon)
DEVEAL, John & Mary Ellen Thomas 2-8-1883 (Rev. Mr. Walker)
DeVEIL, Isaac & Rachel Tolson 10-23-1875 (Mayberry)
  Matthew & Sophia Nichols 7-22-1871 (Evans)
DEVILLE, Caroline & Dorothy Stewart 1-28-1870 (Langford)
DEVON, John Thomas & Rebecca Hyde 3-17-1857
  Mary Susannah & Elijah Thomas Garner 12-28-1859
  Michael & Eleanor Estep 2-23-1824
DICK, Mary & John Laird 1-28-1797
DICKERSON, Catherine V. & Douglass Freeland 12-24-1884 (Rev. LaRoche)
DICKEY, P. S. & Maria H. DuVal 8-30-1879 (Stanley)
DICUS, William A. & Sarah R. Abagill 11-4-1841
DIE, John & Maria Warner 11-22-1842
DIGGES, Ann & John Plummer 11-28-1780
  Ann Maria & Robert LeRoy Livingston 6-29-1811
  Baley & Elizabeth Lawson 3-1-1821
  Daniel C. & Juleima Forrest 11-22-1842
  Daniel C. & Elizabeth C. Glass 11-27-1856
  Elias & Elizabeth Richardson 1-27-1870 (Marr)
  Elizabeth & Emanuel Wood col^d 1-6-1881 (Rev. Mr. Lawson)

DIGGES, George & Charlotte Simmins 11-18-1874 (O'Dwyer)
  Harriet & Stephen Williams 11-22-1867 (Fr. Call)
  Henry & Matilda Jackson 9-12-1867 (Chesly)
  Jane & John Fitzgerald 1-2-1779
  John & Maria King 3-27-1875 (Maguire)
  John H. & Rachel Ann Hall col^d 12-31-1859
  Lizzie & David Moore 6-5-1870 (Mahr)
  Louisa & Samuel Brown 2-8-1868 (Fr. Call)
  Louisa & John Owens 12-20-1869 (Mahr)
  Louisa & Jeremiah Hunt 6-30-1871 (McDonald)
  Lucy & John Green 10-30-1873 (Snowden)
  Mary & Samuel Brown 11-12-1873 (Dwyer)
  Mary Ann & Jno. F. Davis 4-13-1864
  Norah T. & James E. Morgan 6-10-1854
  Robert & Louisa Carter col^d 10-21-1865 (Father Call)
  Robert & Lucy Brown 12-22-1866 (Kershaw)
  Sarah & John Jones col^d 7-31-1868 (Father Begue)
  Sarah & John Dockett 2-14-1872
  Terissa & Ralph Forster 5-27-1783
  William & Matilda Mahoney 2-19-1876 (Green)
  William T. & Margaret C. Webster 6-16-1858
DIGGINS, William & Amelia Crooke 8-15-1840
DIGGS, Harriet & Alexander Barns 11-2-1867 (Gordon)
  Joana & John Dodson 2-7-1822
  Lucy & Frank Harrum 6-16-1886 (Father Cunnane)
  Nace & Cecelia Matilda Robinson 3-30-1874
  Nancy & Louis Albert Hill 2-6-1885
  Susan & Alfred Nebbit 7-29-1875
DIJEAN, Peter & Letitia Dent Stoddert 1-18-1785
DISNEY, Joshua B. & Sarah M. Beall 4-19-1877
  Maggie A. & Frank B. Luers 2-13-1884
  Nicholas M. & Rachal L. Disney 4-19-1877
  Rachel L. & Nicholas M. Disney 4-19-1877
DIXON, Amelia & Zachariah Webster 1-5-1832
  Annie T. & Gerard W. Brandt 1-31-1870 (MacDonnell)
  Barbara & George Lanham 1-27-1818
  Catherine & Joseph L. Murphy 4-11-1859
  Edward & Elizabeth Lanham 1-27-1818
  Edward E. & Ann Louisa Mudd 1-4-1827
  Elizabeth & Samuel Jones 8-30-1815
  Elizabeth & John Beckett both free col^d 4-25-1855
  George & Ally Munroe 8-25-1824
  John A. & Elizabeth Davis 1-6-1855
  John A. & Celestia M. Spencer 11-25-1872 (O'Dwyer)
  Jno H. & Henrietta Thompson 9-25-1848
  Mary & Thomas Bryan 4-24-1805
  Mary E. & George H. Clements 11-21-1857
  Rachel E. & William H. Roland 3-5-1845
  William & Martha Ann Wall 12-24-1811
DOCK, David & Anna Hill 3-22-1877
DOCKET, Rachel Ann & Basil Batson col^d 1-22-1870 (Lankford)
DOCKETT, Catharine & Thomas Briscoe 10-24-1879 (Wills)
  Frederick & Martha Weems col^d 5-11-1869 (Langford)
  John & Sarah Digges 2-14-1872 (Evans)
  John H. & Mary M. Henderson 12-9-1878 (Hooman)

DOCKETT, Mary Jane & Robert Smith 2-6-1872 (Evans)
  W. Benjamin & Alice Bruce 2-15-1872 (Gordon)
DODGE, Wilbur A. & Rosa A. Bishop 4-27-1886
DODSON, Alice & Francis Bowie 9-19-1876 (Carroll)
  Ann & Henry Fulks 10-24-1822
  Charles & Laura Gross 6-25-1886 (Rev. Father Cunnane)
  Elizabeth & Samuel Dodson 7-2-1803
  Geo. & Jane Gray 6-3-1876
  John & Joana Diggs 2-7-1822
  John Jr. & Rachel Darnall 9-10-1803
  Jno. H. & Lucinda Boteler 12-24-1836
  Maggie & Joseph S. Bryan 3-19-1886
  Pearce & Annie Jennifer 12-24-1875 (Tennant)
  Robert & Rebecca Duvall 3-9-1803
  Samuel & Elizabeth Dodson 7-2-1803
  Sarah & James Draine 12-20-1826
  Sarah Ann & Benjamin Atwell 11-25-1837
DOING, Scott B. & Addie Kelley 4-2-1883 (Rev. E. Robey)
DONALD, John & Sarah Brown 11-2-1877 (Perry)
DONALDSON, Thomas G. & Laura V. Swann 1-19-1876 (West)
DONALLY, Dr. William & Lizzie Schaaff 10-26-1875 (Sweet)
DONLEVY, Charles & Eleanor Newton 8-12-1799
DOOLEY, Ann E. & Samuel P. Hook 12-8-1880
  Sarah J. & George W. Rawlings 11-17-1880 (Rev. Solomon German,
    Brandywine P. G. County)
DOOLING, Martin & Ann Sarah Jenkins 12-16-1822
DORMAN, Ann & John A. Coe 11-18-1856
DORNEY, Maria & Benjamin T. Watson 9-24-1832
DORSETT, Amelia Jane & John W. Lyons 10-15-1857
  Fielder & Jane Joan G. Young 4-19-1794
  Lamuel & Mary Skinner 1-4-1794
  Martha & James Boyd col? 1-11-1867 (Lenahan)
  Miss Mary H. & Dr. Geo. W. Berry 6-1-1864
  Samuel & Priscilla Fowler 4-4-1818
  Sarah & Thomas Baden 2-6-1797
  T. Somerville & Isabella McGregor 12-2-1868 (Kershaw)
  Thomas & Ann Selby 12-16-1784
  Thomas M. & Sarah Crandall 9-3-1799
  Wm. N. & Amelia H. Somervell 12-18-1827
DORSEY, Ann Elizabeth & Philip Soper 12-27-1842
  Clem & Bettie Owings col? 8-28-1880 (Rev. Mr. Wheeler)
  Edward & Hannah Peacock 12-28-1799
  Eliza & Charles Toye 9-13-1872
  Eliza Jane & John Sewall 5-6-1876 (Carroll)
  Henrietta Dorsey & Thomas Nevett 1-3-1798
  James E. & Savannah Herterly 4-15-1884 (Rev. Mr. Brashaw)
  James W. & Emily Harris col?, both of Ann Arundel County, married
    9-11-1880 by Rev. Mr. Quiller
  Jesse & Alethea Beall 1-7-1797
  Jno. Henry & Anna Forrest 12-23-1865 (Fa. Call)
  Joshua & Martha Hall 12-17-1798
  Juliana & Henry Brown col? 4-8-1882
  Lucy & Charles A. Jones 12-20-1865 (Marbury) Age 16, black, housekeeper
  Mary & Dennis Allen col? 8-5-1871 (Wheeler)
  Rezin & Celie Jones 9-18-1876 (Gordon)

DORSEY, Sallie & Francis Hawkins 10-9-1884
  William & Ann Hardy 1-7-1804
DOUGHLAS, Richard & Ellen Hawkins 12-23-1868 (Martin)
DOUGLAS, Joseph R. & Violetta S. A. Smallwood 12-4-1859
  Lemuel & Elizabeth Parks 1-12-1878 (Weems)
  Robert & Julia Brock 5-19-1868 (Langford)
  Sullivan & Mary Larkins 5-19-1868 (Langford)
DOUGLASS, Catherine & George Butler 12-7-1883 (Rev. N. C. Brown)
  Elizabeth & Gavin Hamilton 7-26-1800
  George & Sarah Williams 8-15-1871 (McDonald)
  George & Lucy Glascow 12-26-1882 (Mr. Brown)
  George & Jennie Contee 6-15-1886 (Rev. Mr. Price)
  Hennie & Francis Tolson 11-18-1871
  Hennie & David Glascow 7-18-1881 (Rev. Mr. Brown)
  James & Clarissa Blake 2-4-1878 (Watkins)
  Jeremiah & Harriet Berry 2-10-1876 (Gordon)
  Joanna & Edward B. Gray col⁴ 11-23-1867 (Blankford)
  Mary E. & R. Magruder 12-27-1884 (Rev. W. Williams)
  Robert & Lucy Savoy 12-23-1867 (Lankford)
  Webster & Margaret Smothers 11-6-1878
DOVE, Amy E. & Wm. J. Sunderland 1-11-1856
  Ann & John Arminger 9-21-1831
  B. Frank & Alice Humphreys 12-28-1874 (Chaney)
  Deborah & Joshua Pearce 4-16-1785
  Eliz⁴ & Philip Russell 2-17-1781
  Elizabeth & John Hooper 6-6-1779
  Elizabeth & Charles Fendley 12-5-1797
  George S. & Alice C. Sansbury 2-28-1878 (Miller)
  Isaac & Darkey Hardey 12-20-1802
  Isaac & Elizabeth Fairall 1-18-1806
  James H. & Maria A. Moulden 1-14-1853
  James W. & Mary Ann Littleford 4-6-1864
  Mary & John Stewart 2-3-1790
  Mary Ann & John Hooper 2-20-1784
  Maxcy & Michael Dugans 5-5-1835
  Rebecca & Jeremiah Coffren 9-8-1866 Age 30 (Gordon)
  Samuel B. & Martha A. Phipps 1-5-1867 (Geo. Hildt)
  Sarah & Noble Lindsay 1-18-1813
  Sarah Ann & Walter Crosby 3-21-1831
  Sarah J. & Joshua Humphries 2-17-1873
  Thomas & Elizabeth Hopkins 12-18-1797
  William & Ellen Lambert 3-2-1835
  William & Mary Mangun 2-18-1839
DOWDEN, Perry & Mary Ann Clements 11-9-1835
DOWEL, Laura Jane & Alfred Kidwell 1-1-1847
DOWELL, Francis S. & Eliz⁴ Naylor 12-15-1826
  John H. & Elizabeth Barrett 8-9-1864
  Richard & Margaret Journey 4-4-1795
  William & Fanny Stallings 2-19-1822
DOWNER, Elizabeth & Benjamin Bacon 12-23-1797
DOWNES, Amey & Thomas Holley 1-29-1800
  Daniel & Eleanor Taffe 12-30-1802
  Lucy & John Halsal 2-15-1779
  Wm. & Mary Carrick 6-2-1827
DOWNING, Ann M. & Thomas Tomlinson 7-2-1834

DOWNING, Elizabeth A. & Richard A. Hyde 7-2-1834
  Esther & John Garner 7-16-1839
  John Z. & Elizabeth Richardson 1-24-1867 (Marbury)
  Joseph & Elizabeth Webster 12-26-1815
  Mary W. & Henry Greer 2-10-1816
  Robert & Georgeanna Markwood 9-24-1850
  Sarah & William Grahame 12-30-1807
  William & Catherine Webster 1-12-1847
DOWNS, Alpheus & Mary A. Murray 12-13-1882 (Rev. Mr. Towles)
  Catherine & Edward C. Anderson 11-10-1853
  Catherine & Edward C. Anderson 11-17-1853
DOXY, Susannah & Lewis W. Plum 11-2-1799
DRAGE, Maria & Humphrey Keadle 12-1-1828
DRAINE, James & Sarah Dodson 12-20-1826
DRANE, Ann & Richard Lamar 11-9-1790
  Anthony & Ann Smith 12-23-1778
  Anthony & Catharine Scott 3-29-1792
  Eleanor & George Moore 11-19-1792
  Eliz^a Piles & John Woodward 11-9-1796
  Elizabeth & Zadock Brashears 2-9-1790
  Elton Smith & Benj^a W. Belt 9-4-1817
  James & Priscilla Lamar 2-18-1789
  Stephen & Priscilla Crabb 12-24-1793
  Thomas & Martha Wells 2-4-1786
DRIVER, Charles H. & Rebecca Blandford 4-7-1884 (Rev. T. H. Brooks)
  George & Virginia West 10-30-1872 (Gordon)
DRUMMOND, Elizabeth & Josiah Prather 10-6-1803
  Hugh & Rebecca Prather 5-16-1803
  Hugh W. & Matilda Walker 1-1-1824
DRURY, Charles & Mary Hardesty 1-21-1815
  Helen & Henry O'Neale 9-5-1850
DUCKETT, Adeline & Francis Mullikin 8-20-1856
  Ann & Thomas F. Brooke 6-20-1791
  Ann & James Beck 6-10-1806
  Ann Eliza & John Kingsbury 11-10-1856
  Annie C. & Edward Minor 11-23-1885 (Rev. Mr. Smith)
  Baruch & Mary B. Beanes 1-11-1783
  Basil T. & Sophia E. Hill col^d 1-25-1853
  Benjamin L. & Rebecca Kingsbury 1-26-1857
  Benjamin N. & Mary Ann Cross 10-18-1824
  Catharine & Thomas Queen col^d 12-24-1859
  Catherine & Nicholas Greenleaf colored persons 11-16-1861
  Catharine & Henry Robinson 2-15-1868 (Kershaw)
  Charity & Josiah Moore 4-21-1778
  Charles & Mary Batty col^d 10-16-1869 (Langford)
  Cornelius & Eliza Sprigg col^d 11-23-1867 (Blankford)
  Daniel & Chloe Ann Tolson 2-22-1877
  Eleanor & Thomas Lyles 4-10-1779
  Eliza & John Contee 12-28-1813
  Elizabeth & Thomas Soper 1-5-1802
  Elizabeth & Fielder Smith Ryon 1-12-1818
  Elizabeth & Erasmus Mullikin 12-11-1854
  Emily & Anthony Plummer 5-15-1872
  Emma & William E. Earnshaw 4-20-1880 (Rev. Mr. Thomas)
  Francis & Martha Harvey 1-28-1850

DUCKETT, Francis Jr. & Fannie Smith col? 3-13-1882
  Georgianna & Thomas A. Armiger 4-15-1872 (Trapnell)
  Harriet & Richard H. Dyson 12-8-1881 (Rev. F. Wills)
  Isaac & Margaret Bowie 1-24-1792
  Jacob & Mary McElderry 5-4-1799
  James & Susannah Ryon 12-29-1815
  James & Catherine Onion 1-18-1844
  James & Mary Ellen Nally 5-21-1863
  James M. & Elizabeth E. Grimes 2-6-1877 (McNeer)
  Jane & Stephen Waters 3-25-1794
  Jeremiah & Louisa Harvey 12-13-1842
  Jeremiah Jr. & Alice C. Crook 8-19-1879 (Townshend)
  Johanna & William Smith 12-17-1869 (Pindell)
  John & Sarah Willett 4-18-1816
  John & Mary Magruder 1-10-1868
  John H. & Eliza McGregor col? 1-17-1852
  John H. F. & Letitia Greenleaf col? 9-22-1869 (Langford)
  Josephine & Thomas J. Cox 6-15-1870 (Harper)
  Kate Croswell & William B. Clagett 12-3-1883 (Rev. Dr. Lewin)
  Kitty & William Bowie 12-13-1802
  Lucy & Zephaniah Athey 11-11-1790
  Margaret & Daniel Clarke 1-13-1812
  Margaret E. & William T. Duvall 2-11-1856
  Marion & Gabriella Augusta DuVal 8-6-1879 (Stanley)
  Mrs. Mary & William Wickham 6-15-1870 (Cotton)
  Mary Ann & Israel M. Jackson 11-28-1817
  Mary Frances & Osceola Piles 1-3-1859
  Matty & Levi Ridgeway 12-22-1801
  Minnie E. & William Thos. Beall 3-22-1884 (Rev. Dr. Spangler)
  Nettie & J. E. Stamp 2-11-1885
  Richard & Elizabeth M. Waring 6-2-1856
  Richard Jacob & Sophia Buchanan 3-30-1795
  Robert V. & Alice J. King 8-10-1876 (McNeer)
  Samuel & Elenor Wellins 2-18-1820
  Sophia & Joseph Cross 12-8-1823
  Sophronia & Edward S. Walker 5-15-1877 (McNeer)
  Stephen W. & Rose E. Soper 2-15-1879
  Susannah & Daniel Rawlings 3-27-1806
  Thomas & Mary Clagett 1-5-1796
  Thomas & Catharine Clarke 11-12-1840
  Thomas & Jennie Frye 3-22-1884 (Rev. Mr. Brashaw)
  Walter & Susie Ritchie 1-23-1882
DUGANS, Michael & Maxcy Dove 5-5-1835
DUGIND, Robert & E. Newman 10-7-1856
DUHAYS, William & Sarah Moore 12-24-1803
DUKE, Mary & William More 3-6-1780
DULANEY, Benjamin Tasker & Eliza Rozer 2-13-1796
  Henry & Lucinda King 12-24-1877 (Weems)
  John Worthington & Cecelia Calvert 2-19-1873 (McGuire)
DULANY, Eleanor & John Rusten 10-29-1802
  John P. & Mary Ann DeButts 5-18-1812
  Mary & Henry W. Rogers 6-23-1813
  Mary A. & John McNemus 11-12-1867 (Burry)
  Robert & Sarah Boston 2-19-1803
  William & Margaret Cutches 12-17-1819

DULEY, John & Mary Wilson 6-14-1800   DULEY, Norval Edwin & 5-24-1875
  Sophia & Nathan Wells 11-12-1798   Mary Ann Taylor
DULY, Enoch George & Margaret Ann Sansbury 4-5-1853
DUNKIN, Grace & William Shaw 12-13-1797
DUNLOP, George & Catharine Oden 6-27-1818
  George W. & Felley (Felleci) Brooke 5-27-1831
  Joseph L. & Maria Boswell 8-13-1822
  Lucy & Charles Bruce 6-20-1831
  P. Carter & Mary A. Magruder 8-14-1830
  Terisa & Henderson Burgess 3-9-1830
DUNN, Elizabeth & Joseph Moore 7-11-1798
DUNNING, Samuel & Margaret Day 11-26-1803
  Zachariah & Jane Nothey 12-28-1816
DUNNINGTON, John Enoch & Catharine Elizabeth Piles 1-25-1860
DURITY, Sarah & Joseph Joy 7-4-1795
  William & Mary Hurdle 1-13-1798
DUSIEF, Wm. & Cath. A. Talbert 11-2-1847
DUTTON, Dora R. & Ferdinand Neitzey 3-24-1880
DUVALL, Airy & Richard Duvall 1-31-1803
  Alice & John Anderson 1-30-1811
  Altzena & Thornton Hall 8-9-1842
  Amanda S. & John E. Wilson 10-19-1848
  Amelia & William Hall Wilson 7-6-1802
  Amon & Mary Fairall 1-30-1811
  Amon & Lucy Beckett 3-31-1817
  Ann & Frederick Jones 12-5-1809
  Ann R. & Benj. H. Beckett 11-30-1852
  Barsina & Septimus Cook 1-21-1834
  Barten & Marg. Duvall 10-30-1830
  Barton & Hannah Isaac 11-26-1811
  Barton & Miranda Isaac 12-23-1822
  Beale & Margary Belt 4-28-1800
  Beale & Elizabeth Williams 4-11-1806
  Benjamin & Eleanor Higgins 7-4-1787
  Benjamin Jr. & Rebecca Soper 5-16-1821
  Benjamin F. & Susan J. Sasscer 11-22-1854
  Camilla & Dennis B. Cross 2-21-1827
  Cecelia & Joseph Cross 2-15-1817
  Charles & Cassia Brashears 3-27-1778
  Charles & Jemima Ann Duvall 4-3-1804
  Charles & Flavilla Waters 12-20-1808
  Charles A. & Celistia Ann Crook 10-18-1853
  Colmore & Margaret Clarke 1-3-1789
  Cornelia & Richard G. Cross 5-11-1830
  Cornelius & Eleanor Ann Duvall 2-23-1802
  Edward W. & Mary Miller 7-11-1837
  Eleanor of Samuel & John W. Williams 2-15-1802
  Eleanor Ann & Cornelius Duvall 2-23-1802
  Elisha & Rachell Belt 6-17-1785
  Elisha & Mary E. Fitzgerald 12-22-1832
  Eliza & Francis Anderson 1-3-1818
  Elizabeth & Samuel H. Hamilton 5-7-1833
  Emily & Benjamin L. Bird 11-7-1837
  Eveline E. & Philip T. Belt 2-7-1835
  Fielder C. & Maria W. Anderson 4-12-1883 (Rev. H. Stanley)
  Gabriel & Henrietta W. Moran 11-6-1833

DuVAL, Gabriella Augusta & Marion Duckett 8-6-1879
DUVALL, George Washington & Elizabeth Hill Soper 1-15-1820
  George W. of D. & Mary M. Lanham 6-28-1872 (Williams)
  Harriet R. & William Day Age 20 1-2-1867 (Dr. Nelson)
  Henry & Elizabeth Godman 1-17-1803
  Henry & Emily Mitchell 1-27-1885 (Father Cotton)
  James & Elizabeth Hall 1-31-1884 (Rev. Mr. Butler)
  James E. & Mary C. Loveless 1-14-1867 (Begue)
  Jemima Ann & Charles Duvall 4-3-1804
  Jesse & Martha Beckett 2-23-1829
  John & Mary Beall 3-29-1793
  John & Priscilla Bowie Eversfield 2-20-1805
  John & Sarah Ann Clagett 7-9-1831
  John M. & Sarah Ann Sandford 5-27-1837
  Joseph Jr. & Mary Redden 8-26-1800
  Joseph J. & Mary A. Mitchell 5-12-1851
DuVAL, Kate M. & Daniel M. Kent 9-21-1872 (Stanley)
DUVALL, Laura & Emanuel Eckenrode 12-23-1870 (McDonald)
  Laura V. & William H. Griffith 11-19-1856
  Lavinia & Henry Mitchell 11-22-1830
  Lewis of Thomas & Mary Perkins 12-20-1802
  Louisa & Osbourne Cross 12-15-1832
  Lucy & Victor Beyer 1-10-1827
  Macksey & William B. Ranken 9-15-1806
  Mahala & Judson W. McNew 12-20-1824
  Maranda & Isaac Carrick 1-23-1833
  Mareen & Mary Duvall 10-26-1780
  Marg & John Sweeney 10-4-1819
  Margaret & Benjamin Berry 12-12-1833
  Marg.t & Barten Duvall 10-30-1830
DuVAL, Maria H. & P. S. Dickey 8-30-1879 (Stanley)
DUVALL, Maria L. & John N. Walker 10-5-1874 (Stanley)
  Mark & Mary Miller 1-11-1825
  Mark Brown & Sarah Duvall 1-14-1793
  Marseleen & Baley L. Clarke 5-1-1827
  Marsh M. & Susanna Jeams 6-4-1785
  Marsham & Mary Hyatt 8-5-1801
  Martha & Fielder Cross 12-22-1817
  Mary & Mareen Duvall 10-26-1780
  Mary & Mareen Carrick 2-23-1791
  Mary & John Carroll 11-8-1800
  Mary & John Basford 6-11-1808
  Mary & Richard B. Walker 10-28-1823
  Mary & Alfred Scaggs 3-18-1826
  Mary & Geo. A. Mitchell 5-2-1848
  Mary Ann & Daniel Clark 1-11-1825
  Mary E. & Robert B. Seabourn 1-4-1882 (Rev. Dr. Gordon)
  Mary H. & John B. Lucas 11-22-1836
  Mary Jane & George Leonard Thompson 1-8-1859
  Mary M. & Benj. G. W. Phelps 10-27-1864
  Mary Susannah & George W. Smith 8-13-1859
  Massum & Rebecca Walker 1-27-1809
  Matilda & Richard D. Boyd 4-18-1814
  Matilda & George Clarke 2-27-1850
  Philip B. & Mary Ann Hopkins 2-26-1838

DUVALL, Rachel & John Lucas 9-12-1787
  Rachael & Thomas W. Fitzgerald 4-20-1832
  Rachael & Wesley Conaway 4-8-1833
  Rachel & Lloyd Logan 1-30-1802
  Rebecca & Robert Dodson 3-9-1803
  Richard & Airy Duvall 1-31-1803
  Richard H. & Ellen Clarke 9-18-1838
  Richard J. & Sarah A. Duvall 9-28-1833
  Rosener S. & William Beckett 11-29-1821
  Ruth & William Marica 10-29-1778
  Samuel & Eliza Hall 11-29-1826
  Samuel B. & Elizabeth Moran 12-15-1831
  Sarah & Mark Brown Duvall 1-14-1793
  Sarah & Joseph Boyd 8-15-1814
  Sarah & Victor Byer 4-24-1819
  Sarah & Richard Carrick 1-13-1836
  Sarah A. & Richard J. Duvall 9-28-1833
  Sarah Ann & Benj. Beckett 12-10-1836
  Sarah Ann & Ignatius Rawlings 1-5-1846
  Sarah E. & F. W. Whittelsey 9-25-1862
  Sarah E. Peach & Benjamin Fairall Jr. 12-16-1812
  Sarah J. & Middleton F. Mitchell 12-9-1867 (Beque)
  Sophia & Aquilla Beall 12-21-1798
  Sophia & Charles Perrie 10-20-1830
  Susan Bowie & John A. Langston 8-14-1826
  Tabitha & Mortimer H. Mullikin 11-7-1831
  Thomas Clarke & Emma Barron 12-14-1809
  Tobias & Sarah Willett 2-5-1795
  Tobias & Rebecca Onions 3-5-1831
  Trueman & Martha Brashears 11-19-1801
  Violetta & Tobias Tyler 2-3-1816
  William E. & Maria E. Bourne 4-12-1869 (Gordon)
  William L. & Comfort Coale 9-27-1831
  William N. & Lucy Smith 2-15-1814
  William T. & Margaret E. Duckett 2-11-1856
  Willy & Edward Hall 2-18-1814
  Wm. E. & Ann S. Mitchell 7-24-1830
  Zadock & Elizabeth Beall 4-1-1791
  Zadock & Lydia A. Anderson 12-22-1835
DYAR, George R. & Elizabeth Underwood 2-8-1862
  Henrietta & John H. Beanes 12-23-1785
DYE, Martha V. & Cephas R. Benson 4-24-1855
DYER, Aaron Jr. & Sarah Thompson 6-22-1821
  Ann Eliza & John Guyn 2-8-1820
  Annie & George Marshall col^{d}. 12-22-1869 (Langford)
  Catharine & Thomas Baker 8-28-1811
  Daniel R. & Mary C. French 5-14-1861
  Dorsey & Jane Sedricks 12-7-1871 (Wheeler)
  George & Sarah Clarkson 5-27-1784
  George & Sally Edelen 2-6-1802
  George & Eleanor Lindsay 4-20-1815
  Henny & James Fenley 2-7-1800
  Horatio & Mary M. Boarman 1-28-1825
  Horatio & Elizabeth Blandford 1-12-1839
  John R. & Mary Ann Clarvoe 8-17-1812

DYER, Julia Ann & John Rowland 4-9-1819
Lucy & George Boarman 2-7-1812
Maria & Leonard Shertliffe 1-30-1833
Martha Ann & Nicholas Smith 10-23-1790
Mary Henrietta & Jno. H. Gibbs 7-20-1778
Milley & Alexander Johnson 12-24-1798
Robert & Lucy Speake 1-21-1800
Sarah Ann & John G. Summers 2-8-1820
Susan & Henry Gates 5-6-1814
Susanna H. & John S. Edelen 3-22-1830
T. Baker & E. R. Bowling 10-29-1867
Wm. Henry & Mary Washington 7-3-1866 (Hicks)
DYSON, Elizabeth & Patrick A. Murphy 1-9-1847
George H. of St. Mary's County & Mary E. Freeland of Calvert County 4-24-1865
Henderson & Ann Shanan 5-30-1868 (Langford)
Richard H. & Harriet Duckett 12-8-1881 (Rev. F. Wills)
William & Mary J. Mackell 9-16-1876 (Green)

EAGLEN, Thomas & Sarah Hinton 7-25-1795
Jane & Joseph Clarkson 4-11-1788
EALES, Susannah & Thomas Henry Stallons 12-21-1798
EARLE, John & Barbara Hodgkins 6-9-1798
EARLEY, Ann & Theophilus Turton 12-24-1803
Benjamin & Jane Cooley 1-27-1789
Benoni & Martha Marlow 2-22-1816
Catherine Jane & Thomas Shearlock 11-11-1823
Dorinda E. & Joseph G. Hatton 6-22-1841
Margaret C. & Robert W. G. Baden 1-2-1838
Thos. & Willemina Slye 1-1-1784
Willicia & John Harvey 12-13-1814
EARLIE, Ann & Williams Cowles 7-29-1777
EARLY, Charles S. & Georgie W. Berry 2-21-1870 (Maher)
Cornelia A. E. & O. C. Harris 5-23-1850
Leonard H. & Margaret Waters 8-7-1816
Malvina & Thomas J. Turner 12-11-1850
Martha & Francis Piles 4-6-1795
Thomas & Mary Stephens 2-8-1810
EARNSHAW, B. Benjamin & Catharine O. Edelen 9-24-1870
William E. & Emma Duckett 4-20-1880 (Rev. Mr. Thomas)
EARP, Mary Ann & Joseph N. Vermillion 6-5-1873
EASTERN, Lizzie & Joseph Burley 12-27-1883 (Rev. Mr. Barnes)
EASTON, Eliza. & Allen Preston 4-5-1779
EASTWOOD, Ann & Hugh Perrie 1-24-1806
Eliza. & Alexander Watson 1-9-1796
John W. & Sarah D. Cooksey 2-13-1813
Sarah & William Rawlings 10-9-1799
EATON, Alfred A. & Martha Eleanor Hill 12-31-1844
Ann & Roderick McGregor 12-20-1831
ECKENRODE, Emanuel & Laura Duvall 12-23-1870 (McDonald)
EDDIS, Leonard & Sarah Cave 8-21-1780
EDELEN, A. W. & Georgianna Young 2-27-1867 (Marbury)
Agnes & Robert Brown 10-27-1876 (Green)
Aloysius & Eleanor Kirby 7-14-1831

EDELEN, Ann Sophia & John W. F. Hatton 12-13-1881 (Fr. Clark)
Benedict & Johanna Posey 11-21-1854
Caroline & Wm. Mason 6-30-1817
Caroline R. A. & George W. Thompson 9-1-1869 (Kershaw)
Catharine & John H. Beanes 1-29-1817
Catharine A. & George H. Hunter 9-18-1843
Catharine O. & B. Benjamin Earnshaw 9-24-1870
Catherine & Joseph Edelen 2-26-1788
Celestia & Samuel C. McPherson 7-15-1828
Clara E. & Joseph B. Edelen 1-7-1850
Clary & Jesse Edelen 2-7-1800
Clement & Ann Simpson 11-6-1780
Edmonia & John B. Semmes 1-27-1860
Edward C. & Sarah Moore 12-8-1801
Edward H. & Sydney Weightman 7-11-1829
Eleanor & Thomas Mitchell 11-9-1778
Eliza & Thomas H. Edelen 1-11-1831
Elizabeth & Ignatius Hagan 1-28-1792
Elizabeth & Dennis Osborn 9-9-1801
Elizabeth & George H. Hunter 7-18-1857
Elizabeth E. & Henry Carrick 10-1-1862
Elizabeth Emily & Benedict J. Semmes 11-11-1823
Ellen V. & Bennett F. Gwynn 1-31-1843
Francis & Lucy Beall 1-19-1814
Francis & Christianna Kirby 12-9-1834
Francis S. & Elizabeth Robinson 3-25-1837
George & Rebecca Boarman 12-31-1790
George T. & Mary Allison 1-13-1847
Harriet Ophelia & Dr. Edgar D. Hurtt 1-24-1874 (Welsh)
Henrietta & Charles C. Osbourn 1-29-1817
Henry D. & Judith T. B. Robinson 1-16-1832
Hetta Ann & Benjamin T. Brightwell 2-17-1842
Horatio & Eleanor C. Tolson 2-13-1827
Jacob & Mary Osborn 12-23-1806
James & Margaret Tolson 12-28-1829
James M. & Lethe Ann Brooke 10-4-1872 (Dwyer)
James R. & Eveline Hunter 10-4-1872 (Dwyer)
James R. & Mary E. L. Richards 4-28-1879 (Gordon)
James Richard & Mary Josephine Robey 1-12-1882 (Rev. Mr. Hyland)
Jeremiah & Sally Jenkins 2-11-1792
Jesse & Clary Edelen 2-7-1800
Jesse of Thomas & Mary Hatton 2-7-1800
Jesse R. & Mary R. Hunter 9-9-1871 (McDonald)
John B. & Mary Anne J. Latimer 1-1-1831
John B. & Jane Anderson 10-15-1834
John S. & Susanna H. Dyer 3-22-1830
Joseph & Catherine Wathen 4-4-1786
Joseph & Catherine Edelen 2-26-1788
Joseph B. & Clara E. Edelen 1-7-1850
Joshua James & Sarah Ann Lynch 2-13-1836
Juliet & Philip Chisley 12-24-1866 (Marbury)
Margaret & John A. Hamilton 11-8-1867 (Fr. Lanahan)
Margaret Matilda & Theodore Wm Maurice 7-16-1819
Martha & Leonard Jenkins 2-10-1798
Mary & Jackin Jenkins 2-18-1784

74

EDELEN, Mary & Joseph Hunter 1-13-1844
  Mary A. R. & Walter A. Edelen 5-20-1833
  Mary Ann & Joseph Boarman 1-9-1801
  Mary Catharine & Henry G. Murray 2-22-1838
  Mary Helen & Edward W. Young 6-24-1871 (O'Dwyer)
  Mary Olivia & Thomas F. Semmes 6-1-1835
  Mary P. & John J. R. Steed 5-14-1861
  Mildred & Walter Boone 10-9-1783
  Olivia A. & Joseph M. Parker 4-15-1844
  Paulina E. & Francis M. Finotti 11-4-1879 (Father Edelen)
  Philip R. & Sarah M. Hill 5-30-1845
  Philip R. & Rebecca Clagett 12-25-1848
  Rebecca & Bennett Gwinn 8-29-1807
  Richard A. & Mary O. Swann 12-17-1850
  Robert & Mary Catharine Hardy 1-2-1816
  Robert & Mary Anna Clements 11-10-1855
  Sally & George Dyer 2-6-1802
  Samuel & Mary Smith 12-14-1787
  Sarah & Henry Rozer Jun.ʳ 9-13-1779
  Sarah & James Webster 11-19-1821
  Sarah Ann R. & James N. Watson 8-1-1860
  Thomas H. & Eliza Edelen 1-11-1831
  Tracey & Thomas Clarkson 11-18-1797
  Walter A. & Mary A. R. Edelen 5-20-1833
  Walter A. & Emily Gwynn 10-15-1849
  William & Catherine Wilson 2-2-1843
  William J. & Harriet A. Lewis 11-26-1843
EDELIN, John B. & Carroline M. Boarman 7-29-1819
  Laura R. & Richard S. Jenkins 1-3-1840
EDELON, Elizabeth & Hezekiah Mudd 5-12-1779
EDEN, Wm. P. & Emma Lowe 8-28-1862
EDGEWORTH, Philorlea & John Casey 8-12-1778
EDMOND, Charlotte & Joseph Galloway 3-14-1877 (Carroll)
EDMONDS, William & Rebecca A. Waring 12-28-1832
EDMONSTON, Edward & Margaret G. Croner 6-27-1800
  Horatio L. & Elizᵗʰ Ann Lowndes 11-5-1828
  Nathan & Deborah Welsh 12-19-1788
EDWARDS, Charles W. & Eliza Walker 5-1-1878 (Cotton)
  James H. & Sallie M. Hogue 8-15-1882 (Rev. Wm. L. Hyland)
EGLING, David & Barbara Ann Smith col.ᵈ 4-20-1867 (Greenleaf)
  John Wm. & Mary Brady 10-9-1884 (Rev. Mr. Brashaw)
EIGLEHEART, Martha & Benjamin Farall 2-16-1787
EKTON, John & Sarah Lanham 4-12-1816
ELDER, Ruth Hawkins & William Haye 1-6-1798
ELERY, Charity & David Trigg 1-11-1796
ELLEN, Anne & Edward Magruder 10-23-1800
ELLEXON, Hannah & Benjamin Swain 2-1-1794
ELLIOTT, Alfred & Mary Lanham 2-7-1873 (Evans)
  Benjamin & Sarah Belt 6-30-1813
  Drusilla & Lloyd Brown 11-30-1841
  Thomas & Sarah Wells 1-28-1812
  Thomas & Lidia Ann House 2-4-1851
  William T. & Elizabeth Mayhew 3-1-1859
ELLIS, Ann & Owen Ellis 6-9-1813
  Elijah & Susanna Watson 12-27-1779

ELLIS, Elijah & Ann Cooksey 7-9-1802
  Elijah & Martha Carrico 7-27-1809
  Elijah & Mary Craycroft 12-20-1814
  Ellen & John Beavin 3-5-1835
  John & Ann Leatch 12-22-1806
  John & Elizabeth Cooksey 12-7-1808
  John & Elizabeth Juliet Brightwell 2-7-1814
  Leonard & Jane Peirce 11-15-1780
  Owen & Ann Ellis 6-9-1813
  Robert & Mary M. Brooke 4-5-1824
  Sarah & Jack Smith 4-17-1867
ELLIXEN, Ann & William Beaven 2-2-1787
  Mary & Samuel Thomas 4-18-1797
ELLOTT, Anne & John Smith 2-11-1796
ELSNER, Edward & Catherine Heult 2-24-1855
ELSON, Arch? & Hannah Roberts 11-2-1782
  Joseph P. & Caroline M. Isaac 1-30-1795
  Martha & Cephas Childs 4-4-1801
  Rachel & Zadock Moore 11-22-1782
  Sarah & John Baptist Kirby 9-23-1779
EMBERSON, Henry & Elizabeth Baden 12-31-1800
  John & Rebecca Simpson 10-25-1790
EMERSON, Sabina & Peter Q. Bartley 11-20-1830
EMMERSON, Aquila & Susannah Simpson 11-13-1792
ENGLISH, Zeph. & Julia A. Tolson 12-17-1859
ENNIS, James Rob? & Dorcas Thomas 2-10-1876 (McNeer)
  Lucy F. & Joseph H. Coale 6-18-1884 (Rev. Father Cunanne)
  Margaret & Henson Allen 8-23-1872 (MacDonald)
  Martha & Henry Butler 10-13-1875 (Peter)
  Peter & Maria Twine 7-26-1871 (McDonald)
  Rachel & Sandy Sprigg col? 7-27-1867 (Call)
  Rebecca of Ann Arundel County & Henry Hayman colored
    12-13-1880 (Rev. Dr. Gordon)
  Susan & John Hardesty 12-26-1828
  William & Henrietta Lee 4-26-1872 (McDonald)
EREKRISON, Charles & Elizabeth Carr 12-16-1841
ERRICKSON, Elizabeth & William N. Smith 10-14-1815
  James & Rachel Carr 4-8-1846
ESCOTT, Amy & J. William Wallis 11-15-1870
ESSEX, Francis & Deborah Shekell 8-21-1792
ESTEP, Ann Maria & Leonard C. Oliver 12-5-1853
  Benjamin & Sarah Tayler 9-27-1793
  Benjamin & Jane Wood 1-22-1827
  Catharine & John B. Trueman 2-8-1819
  Catharine & John T. Wall 5-19-1823
  Eleanor & Michael Devon 2-23-1824
  Elizabeth Ann & John L. Pierce 1-15-1822
  Henry & Sarah Garner 12-4-1798
  Jane & John Tarvin 1-8-1834
  John & Kitty B. Wailes 5-30-1795
  John L. & Mary Ann Selby 12-8-1821
  John L. & Mary Jane Naylor 4-26-1856
  Joseph & Mary Ann Boteler 8-25-1787
  Mary Ann & Littleton T. Adams 12-13-1827
  Mary Margaret & James Robert Butler 3-29-1845

ESTEP, Priscilla & Wm. Richardson 10-20-1821
  Sarah & Michael Oden 3-12-1796
  Sarah & Thomas Adams 3-30-1814
  Susan & Johnson Moran 2-25-1824 also listed 3-4-1824
  Susanna & Richard A. Peirce 1-24-1787
  Thomas & Mary Letchwalt 3-4-1797
  Vilinder & Charles Taylor 11-22-1819
EASTUP, Thomas & Paycy Rawlings 12-12-1804
ETCHISON, Ignatius & Susanna Permillion 11-19-1808
EVANS, Alexander & Marg⁺ Mullikin 2-19-1812
  Alice Ann & Thomas Weaver 12-24-1870 (Gordon)
  Ann & Jacob Craver 4-13-1800
  Casandra & John T. Fraser 8-30-1777
  Catherine & Samuel Philips 6-4-1839
  Charles & Catherine Hall 8-22-1882 (Rev. Mr. Butler)
  Cornelius & Mary Thomas 1-16-1869 (Langford)
  Elizabeth A. & Zadock W. McNew 10-12-1830
  Guy & Christian Swain 9-16-1779
  James & Jennie Tucker 9-17-1878 (Butler)
  Jesse & Cassandra Soper 1-13-1816
  John & Norlinda Wilcoxon 12-19-1786
  John & Elizabeth Wright 8-25-1798
  John & Catharine Wallace col⁵ 6-30-1866
  Mary & William Hurley 8-12-1778
  Mary & William Barclay 12-17-1794
  Philip & Mary Hurley 1-9-1786
  Rebecca & Benj⁻ Bean 12-8-1779
  Ruth & Thomas Smith 8-18-1777
  Sarah & John Hurley 12-19-1787
  William B. & Mary Frances Pumphrey 8-2-1853
EVENS, Thomas & Mary Virginia Gray 6-5-1876 (Price)
EVERETT, Thornley J. & Eliza Lyles 9-17-1851
EVERHEART, Casper & Mary Keadle 12-11-1792
EVERSFIELD, Bowie & Elizabeth Bowie Lane 12-13-1804
  Charles & Elizabeth Gantt 2-13-1786 .
  Charles E. & Annie M. Suter 8-17-1852
  Eleanor & George Ashcom 11-20-1815
  Elianor & Nicholas Berry 6-16-1784
  Elizabeth Gantt & Charles Smith Perrie 1-18-1808
  Harriet & William Bowie Chew 10-7-1828
  John & Barbara Brooke 6-2-1778
  John & Mary Ann Clagett 2-22-1800
  John & Harriet Berry 4-12-1814
  Priscilla Bowie & John Duvall 2-20-1805
  Sarah & Richard Roberts 5-3-1847
  Thomas & Mary Ann Hodges 2-11-1822
  Virlinda & Thomas Mundell 2-28-1794

FAIR, Ann & Hezekiah Gray 1-2-1782
FAIRALL, see also Farall, Fearall, Farrall
  Benjamin Jr. & Sarah E. Peach Duvall 12-16-1812
  Catharine & William Beanes 10-25-1818
  Elizabeth & Isaac Dove 1-18-1806
  Elizabeth & Joshua Gates 2-20-1821
  Elizth & John F. Jacobs 12-26-1825
  Elizth A. & George W. Mullikin 1-13-1846
  Jemiah & Zachariah W. Baldwin 4-14-1827
  John & Elizabeth Hopkins 12-13-1822
  Martha & Henry Wilson 12-5-1820
  Mary & Amon Duvall 1-30-1811
  Mary Ann & Charles Lynch 5-28-1833
  Priscilla & John Turton 12-6-1809
  Stephen & Drusella Johnson 9-12-1806
FAIRFAX, Albert & Caroline Eliza Snowden 4-7-1828
  Archibald B. & Sarah C. Herbert 11-10-1832
  Donald MacNeill & Virginia Cary Rayland 6-5-1854
  Henry & Ann Caroline Herbert 10-8-1827
FAIRO, Cincinatis & Ann Elizabeth Tracey 11-5-1828
FAR, Mary & Elias Gray 4-11-1785
FARALL, Benjamin & Martha Eigleheart 2-16-1787
FARR, Bennett & Elizabeth Hall 11-28-1795
  Bushrod W. & Ann Elizabeth Hays 1-11-1858
  Elizabeth & Henry Warner 12-29-1794
  George & Frances Maddox 2-12-1798
  George D. & Anna T. Phillips 10-23-1865 (Stanley)
  James E. & Alice E. Stone 1-18-1876
  John Baptist & Mary Vermilion 11-23-1780
  Joshua & Margaret Hull 11-8-1800
  Joshua W. & Emma Moore 6-14-1866 Age 30, cabinet maker, married
    Upper Marlboro, H. J. Kershaw minister Pr. Ep. Church
  Margaret & Zachariah Brady 1-3-1853
  Nicholas & Tabitha White 2-13-1805
  Nicholas & Elizabeth McDaniel 2-20-1816
  Priscilla & Benjamin Vermillion 1-8-1787
  Samuel & Rachel Isaac 10-17-1795
FARRALL, John & Susannah Wheeler 1-13-1786
  William & Elizabeth Hyatt 2-26-1783
FARVEY, Edmund & Celey Anderson col^d 6-11-1867
FAZIER, Emeline & Thomas White 3-30-1853
FEAGAHINE, Jacob & Elizabeth E. Benson 11-21-1864
FEARALL, Jason & Mary Ann Johnson 2-4-1800
  Walter & Rhody Dannison 12-2-1801
FELTER, Margaret & William Wood 12-22-1818
FENDALL, Elizabeth Ann & Stephen Cawood 6-13-1792
FENDLEY, Charles & Elizabeth Dove 12-5-1797
FENLEY, James & Henny Dyer 2-7-1800
  Mary & Joseph Gill 12-16-1794
  Thomas & Chloe Baynes 1-29-1791
  Walter& Susanna Lindsey 1-31-1821
FENLY, Elizabeth & John Sutton 12-21-1797
FENTON, Sarah & Andrew Norris 10-16-1800
FENWICK, Ignatius & Mary Carroll 6-10-1780
FERGERSON, Clay & Anna Shandle 4-26-1882 (Rev. M. Bryan)

FERGURSON, Sarah & Dominick Habiner 11-13-1790
FERGUSON, Aggy & Henry Brashears 4-7-1792
  Jenet & William Crown 10-9-1799
  Jennett & Henry Wirt 1-15-1795
  Ruth & Joseph Wilson 10-5-1793
  Ruth & Samuel Young 12-8-1798
FERGUSSON, Ann S. & Joseph Wilson 8-29-1777
  Elisha B. & Amelia Hays 10-28-1858
  James & Ruth Halsall 8-23-1780
  James & Eleanor Bridget 5-22-1807
  John & Sarah Fergusson 2-4-1808
  Mary A. & Edward L. Darcy 4-3-1850
  Rebecca & William Wilson 10-1-1777
  Sarah & John Fergusson 2-4-1808
  Susanna & Farquire McCray 4-21-1781
  Thomas S. & Elizabeth Shearlock 12-22-1856
  Virlinda & Zepheniah Beall 1-5-1783
FERRAL, Fielder Hawkins & Ann Lan Ham 3-5-1819
FERRALL, Dennis W. & Juliet A. Clark 5-18-1841
  Jennie A. & C. L. Lieberman 10-17-1867
  John A. & Sarah M. Young 2-7-1872 (Marbury)
  Mary & W. B. Crawford 8-13-1845
  Rebecca & John Cooper 11-14-1845
  Thomas S. & Margaret E. Higgins 6-16-1841
FERRELL, Ann & George Killrigle 11-24-1810
  Elizabeth & John Cheney 12-12-1780
  Rebeccah & Archibald Upton 12-30-1795
  Thomas & Chrissy Bassford 12-4-1794
FIELDS, Elisha & Margaret Naylor 2-12-1780
  Letta & Benjamin Tarman 3-7-1791
  Margaret & John Wills 12-24-1788
FILLIUS, Augustus & Elizabeth Ann Ricketts 3-6-1857
FINCH, George F. & Ruth Janes 3-7-1879 (Gordon)
FINDLEY, Ann & Peter Boswell 5-4-1783
FINDLY, James & Letty Young 12-8-1801
FINLEY, Caroline & Thomas Beard 2-7-1837
FINNOTTI, Gustavia M. & Emily R. Hill 6-16-1851
FINNY, Mordecai S. & Amelia Anderson 12-29-1845
FINOTTI, Francis M. & Paulina E. Edelen 11-4-1879 (Father Edelen)
FISAL, John & Susan Ball 12-13-1875 (West)
FISHER, Alfred & Alice Owens of Anne Arundel Co. 5-21-1877 (Wheeler)
  Daniel & Elizabeth Millar 9-15-1835
FITZGERALD, Elizabeth & Francis Lightfoot Lee 4-7-1807
  Elizabeth & Jesse Moran 11-24-1817
  Frances & Dennis Magruder 10-4-1817
  James & Elizabeth Suit 2-3-1812
  Jane & Francis Lightfoot Lee 2-2-1810
  John & Jane Digges 1-2-1779
  Mary & John Keeffe 7-10-1864
  Mary E. & Elisha Duvall 12-22-1832
  Rachel & William Russell 1-6-1795
  Thomas W. & Rachael Duvall 4-20-1832
FITZHUGH, Edmund Clare (Washington Territory) & Cora Bowie 5-15-1861
  Johnson & Lily Keech 7-13-1869
FLANDERS, Mattie A. & Samuel Gray 12-22-1884

FLEET, Charles & Jane Hodge 12-27-1881 (Rev. Mr. Wilson)
 James W. & Margaret A. Hamilton 12-29-1879 (Rev^d Dr. Gordon)
 John S. & Maria E. Scott 11-21-1871 (Gordon)
 Lethe & Saul Bell 11-3-1883 (Rev. Mr. Walker)
 Mary Emma & John R. Hawkins 1-29-1884 (Rev. Mr. Walker)
 Robert & Martha Brooks 12-20-1884 (Rev. Mr. Brooks)
 Thomas & Ida Forbes col^d 9-16-1881 (Rev. Dr. Gordon)
FLEMMIN, Frederick & Anne Hogan 12-18-1798
FLETCHER, Benj. & Sarah Johnson 11-12-1880 (Rev. Mr. Lawson)
 Benjamin Jr. & Maria Hamilton 5-18-1871 (Stanley)
 Caroline & Stephen Perry (Crowley) 9-19-1879
 Dennis & Jane Barton 6-3-1871 (Wheeler)
 Gabriel H. & Virginia Randall 2-2-1886
 Hebrew T. & Mary E. Arnold 4-4-1883 (Rev. Mr. Walker)
 Isaac & Louisa Brown col^d 9-16-1869 (Maher)
 James & Nellie Powers 12-21-1870 (Begue)
 Jane & Peter Marshall 11-2-1870 (Maher)
 John & Maria Wood 1-4-1873 (Cotton)
 John & Maria Smith 10-14-1875 (Green)
 John Fielder & Margaret Ann Watson col^d 9-20-1869 (Langford)
 Margaret & John Thomas E. Jackson 9-25-1868 (Begue)
 Mary & James Howard col^d 1-20-1866
 Mary Jane & Isaac Henry 5-29-1868 (Begue)
 Mary V. & James James 12-24-1872 (Evans)
 Michael D. & Jane Hawkins 12-27-1872 (Fr. Cotton)
 Robert & Martha Ann Mitchell col^d 8-9-1867 (Begue)
 Sophy & Benedict Lansdale 12-24-1870 (Wheeler)
 Susan & Thomas Sheppard 5-26-1876
 Susan M. & Columbus Brashears 5-4-1874
 William & Elizabeth Mudd 1-8-1808
FLING, James & Rebecca Frazer 4-20-1783
FLORENCE, Joseph & Saully Jones 6-6-1806
FLUTCHER, Susie & John P. Briscoe 12-24-1873 (Dwyer)
FOARD, Charlotte & Buttler Marlow 12-21-1782
 Mary & Benjamin Ward 7-17-1784
FOLLER, James & Elisse Gray 12-30-1868
FOOTE, William Hayward & Cecilia Rozer 1-8-1801
FORBES, Anne R. & William Henry Cooke 11-13-1885
 Eliza & Horatio C. McElderry 10-29-1816
 George Jr. & Fanny Bowling 11-25-1872 (Dwyer)
 Henrietta & John Sims 5-11-1875 (O'Dwyer)
 Ida & Thomas Fleet col^d 9-16-1881 (Rev. Dr. Gordon)
 Isaiah & Mary E. Jones 8-10-1884 (Rev. P. H. Green)
 James & Eleanor Lane 3-16-1805
 Jane & Daniel of St. Thomas Jenifer 7-5-1810
 John & Emily Hinson 4-11-1874
 M. M. & William D. Clarke 6-9-1859
 Martha & James Coale 6-4-1875
FORBS, Serena & Chas. Henry Harper colored persons 6-3-1865
FORD, Adeline & John Thomas Smith 4-3-1874 (Gordon)
 Ann & Elijah Carter colored Age 30, widow, cook 5-21-1866 (Gordon)
 Caroline Age 25, mulatto, laborer & Emanuel Hawkins, black
  9-5-1866 (Rev. Fr. Young)
 Chloe Ann & Porter Wills 10-3-1885 (Rev. Mr. Wills)
 Edward & Action Howard 6-17-1856

FORD, Eleanor & James Padgett 11-22-1817
  Gassaway & Mary Harrison (colored persons) 4-15-1865
  Hopewell & Sarah Butler col? 12-30-1880
  James & Mary Knighton 12-11-1804
  James B. & Arianna Contee col? 12-13-1879 (Rev. Dr. Lewin)
  John W. & Annie Butler 8-29-1879
  Joseph Francis & Ann R. Greenleaf 12-27-1882 (Rev. Mr. LaRoche)
  Julia & Jeremiah Holland 12-24-1875 (Tennent)
  Lizzie & Lewis Heet 4-3-1869 (Gordon)
  Lucinda & Elias Gardiner col? 10-4-1866 (Stanley)
  Margaret & James Brady 5-19-1870 (Stanley)
  Nat. & Helen Purvy 11-21-1868 (Kershaw)
  Nathanial & Rebecca Savoy 11-20-1882 (Mr. Walker)
  Priscilla & Robert Patterson 2-25-1873
  Rachel & Henry Banks 9-9-1871 (Evans)
  Rachel & John Tolson 8-15-1879 (Gordon)
  Richard & Mary Smothers 6-6-1882
  Thomas Henry & Sophia Contee 12-28-1876 (Carroll)
FOREACOIS, John Thomas & Mary Jennette Harvey 9-27-1881 (Rev. Mr. Thomas)
FORMAN, Alfred R. & Brittania A. Brown 9-22-1859
FORREST, Anna & Jno. Henry Dorsey 12-23-1865 (Father Call)
  Anna Maria S. & Charles G. Wilcox 10-4-1843
  Julius & Sophia Ogle 11-23-1824
  Martha A. & William Francis Brown 10-27-1876 (Gordon)
  Mary M. & John A. Kearney 12-5-1835
  Mary M. & Charles W. Gordon 10-14-1879 (Crowley)
  Sandy & Annie Calvert 1-11-1883 (Rev. Mr. Walker)
  Zuleima & Daniel C. Digges 11-22-1842
FORRESTER, Plummer & Mary J. Randall 12-10-1884
FORSTER, Ralph & Terissa Digges 5-27-1783
  John & Linny Smith 2-11-1792
  Richard & Priscilla Tyler 4-5-1784
  Thomas & Mary Magruder 6-2-1794
FOSSETT, Ann & Joseph Church 12-23-1800
FOSTER, Mary & Leonard Kidwell 8-1-1798
FOUNTAIN, John H. & Mary Savoy 8-29-1878 (Carroll)
  Robert S. & Clara D. Carlton 1-13-1879 (Harper)
FOWLER, Abraham & Willey Stamp 12-23-1790
  Abraham & Hester Mills 11-28-1794
  Abraham & Mary Brown 2-2-1801
  Ann & John Ball 4-4-1795
  Benjamin & Sarah Ann Bryan 1-26-1835
  Benjamin & Jane Swaine 12-10-1839
  Daniel & Susan Coffin 8-4-1840
  Elizabeth & Frederick Price 10-27-1798
  Elizabeth & Lloyd Simpson 7-18-1819
  Elizabeth & John H. Selby 5-23-1833
  Eliz.th Ann & Wm. S. Ryon 10-16-1827
  Elizabeth Ann & William A. Jarboe 2-23-1841
  Ella V. & John L. Cross 5-16-1876 (Kershaw)
  George W. & Mamie Conway 8-18-1884
  James & Henrietta Norton 1-1-1852
  James Wesley & Frances Rebecca Brady 12-31-1873 (Gordon)
  Janet & James H. Ritchie 11-4-1870 (Williams)
  Jemima & Jno. Sappington 1-29-1781

FOWLER, Jeremiah & Elizabeth Scott 7-16-1879 (Perry)
Jesse & Henrietta Brown 2-20-1802
John & Lucy Moore 12-30-1802
John & Rachel Isaac 12-16-1813
John & Margaret Sweeny 1-3-1840
John & Harriet Mangler 7-16-1842
John & Elizabeth Sweeney 1-2-1844
John R. & Mary Jane Ball 3-7-1870 (Chesley)
John W. & Sophia M. Gray 12-18-1878 (Perry)
Joseph & Elizabeth Minis 1-15-1810
Joseph & Lucinia Ann Lewis 4-8-1820
Joseph & Milison Louisa Robey 6-2-1828
Joseph & Zulemma Swaine 10-25-1832
Joseph of Wm. & Elizabeth Pumphrey 1-16-1824
Joseph H. & Deborah A. V. Griffen 3-12-1833
Josephine M. & Josiah B. B. Wilson 11-11-1878 (Quinn)
Letitia & John R. Smallwood 12-27-1832
Lucy V. & Noah Fry 7-23-1862
Maggie J. & John L. Cross 12-22-1873 (Gordon)
Margaret & Philip Hopkins 6-6-1794
Margaret & Benjn Swann 5-3-1847
Mary & Martin Wells 1-5-1799
Mary & John Walker 2-24-1830
Mary & Robert Craig 2-12-1869 (Langford)
Mary E. & George W. Swann 8-2-1854
Mary E. & Samuel O. Wells 11-9-1878
Mary Emma & Richard Henry Cross 5-3-1877 (Kershaw)
Mary F. & George Fraas 2-22-1867
Matilda & Paul Talbert 3-10-1823
Priscilla & Samuel Dorsett 4-4-1818
Priscilla Ann & Joshua Beall 11-6-1854
Priscilla Jane & Dionysius Ball 1-23-1868 (Kershaw)
Rich^{d} & Ann Summers 1-16-1779
Samuel & Margaret Selby 2-2-1798
Samuel & Elizth Ann Perrie 8-4-1825
Samuel & Margaret A. Talbert 11-26-1833
Saml B. & Virginia Rawlings 6-5-1850
Samuel H. & Elizth Jane Hardey 1-12-1832
Sarah Francis & John F. Dennison 8-20-1866 (Kershaw)
Susannah & James Ireland 12-22-1806
Thomas & Draden Leatch 4-14-1804
Thomas & Elizabeth Murphy 10-21-1812
Thomas & Nancy Contee col^{d} 11-2-1881 (Rev. J. C. Bryan)
Walter & Fanny Glascow 12-22-1876
William & Eleanor Lovejoy 2-24-1786
William & Lydia Sanders 11-25-1788
William & Priscilla Simpson 1-29-1799
William M. & Anne Augusta Clements 12-10-1872 (McDonald)
FOX, Amos & Lucy Hardey 5-12-1809
William & Letty Wade 11-18-1794
FRAAS, George & Mary F. Fowler 2-22-1867
FRANCIS, Alex^{r} & Millicent Ann Loveless 12-22-1783
John & Alice Crampkin 11-5-1781
John H. & Mary Hamilton 11-12-1870 (Fr. Maher)
Peter & Matilda Suit 2-22-1850

FRANK, Catharine & James Green 11-9-1796
FRANKLIN, Augustus & Chloe Mackall 7-21-1855
  Revd Benjⁿ & Emma Winsor 4-12-1847
  Cassie & Richard Waters 4-15-1876 (Chaney)
  Elizabeth & John Moss 11-30-1866 (Young)
  Esther & William Waters col^d both of A. A. Co. 1-31-1881 (Chaney)
  Fanny & Daniel Pshawder 1-12-1874
  Joseph & Susan Hanson 12-20-1879 (Rev. E. Peters)
  Joseph C. & Sophia Tayman 1-31-1883
  Margaret Jane & Richard Butler 1-20-1886 (Rev. Mr. Howard)
  Mary & Felix Giles 12-26-1884 (Rev. Mr. Hendricks)
  Nancy & Thomas J. Franklin 7-7-1853
  Rachael & Franklin Waters 4-30-1833
  Rachel & William Clark col^d (Rev. Daniel Aquilla) 9-3-1881
  Samuel & Mary Waters 1-17-1807
  Sarah Ellen & James Green 12-22-1874 (Oberly)
  Thomas & Mary Bowie 10-17-1870 (Stanley)
  Thomas J. & Nancy Franklin 7-7-1853
  William & Mary Murray 4-7-1877
FRASER, Andrew & Catharine Lanham 12-31-1791
  Archibald & Sarah Tucker 5-20-1833
  John A. & Georgianna Pumphrey 1-4-1870 (Harper)
  John T. & Casandra Evans 8-30-1777
  Mary E. & Henry F. Thorn 12-3-1833
  Nelly & John Southerland 12-20-1777
  Simon & Mary Pumphrey 1-10-1825
FRAZER, Elizabeth & Henry Frazer 2-19-1805
  Henry & Elizabeth Frazer 2-19-1805
  Rebecca & James Fling 4-20-1783
FRAZIER, Annie & John W. Tyler 1-9-1877 (Walker)
  Archibald & Sarah Taylor 4-15-1800
  Elizabeth & George Harbin 1-4-1821
  Emeline & John H. Osbourn 10-13-1840
  John L. & Elizabeth Sarah Lovelace 5-21-1821
  Mary & James F. Robinson 9-28-1825
  Mary & Fendall Sansbury 2-10-1845
  Sarah & George Lindsay 12-6-1798
FREE, Elizabeth & Samuel Scott 4-19-1796
  John & Sarah Wallace 1-25-1796
FREELAND, Douglass & Catherine V. Dickerson 12-24-1884 (Rev. La Roche)
  George & Hannah Ann Tolson 11-30-1885 (Rev. Mr. Brooks)
  Isabel & Charles Perry 12-26-1874
  Jennie & Thomas Williams 12-27-1884 (Rev. Mr. Brooke)
  Mary E. of Calvert County & George H. Dyson of St. Mary's County
    4-24-1865
  Sml. H. & Mary C. Rawlings 6-23-1870 (Marbury)
FREEMAN, Annie E. & John P. Turner 1-30-1875
  John & Pauline Wilson 6-30-1871 (Cotton)
  Mary & Thomas Basford 12-27-1831
  Mary & Joseph Hall col^d 12-30-1881 (Rev. Mr. Aquilla)
  Mary A. & Richard T. Gardiner 2-17-1873
FRENCH, Charles & Marianne Craik Murdock 12-12-1809
  George & Margaret H. Weems 11-26-1807
  John & Mary Hawkins 6-10-1833
  Louisa Eugenia & George Taney Brent 1-16-1866 Age 19

FRENCH, Margaret & Robert Bowie 2-21-1826
Margaret A. S. & Augustus D. Brooke 5-25-1853
Mary C. & Daniel R. Dyer 5-14-1861
FRISBY, Benj. & Elizabeth Rawlings col? 4-27-1867 (Call)
Daniel & Annie Beall col? 10-26-1867 (Fr. Young)
Mary & Nicholas Brown 4-20-1872 (McDonald)
FROWMAY, Margaret & John Demcey 11-7-1784
FRY, Colemore & Mary Darcey 2-12-1821
George D. & Julia J. Magruder 8-2-1876 (Williams)
Henry & Amanda M. Allen 12-27-1865
Henry J. & Ida Marden 1-3-1881 (Rev. Solomon German)
Isaiah M. & Mary E. Thomas 4-17-1876 (Gordon)
Jeremiah & Mary Jane Thomas 10-12-1881 (Rev. Dr. Gordon)
John Henry & Susan Moor 9-13-1864
Leonard & Amey Day 12-8-1803
Noah & Lucy V. Fowler 7-23-1862
Robert & Elizabeth Alder 12-13-1792
Robert & Mary Ellen Barrs 2-18-1862
Sarah & Wm. Cook 9-4-1848
Susan & Thomas S. Ryon 2-19-1855
Thomas & Elizabeth Crandell 6-29-1795
William & Amelia Kingsbury 12-17-1846
FRYE, Elizabeth M. & William H. Thomas 6-1-1869 (Gordon)
Jennie & Thomas Duckett 3-22-1884 (Rev. Mr. Brashears)
John T. M. & Mary E. Sansbury 11-26-1873 (Johnson)
Margaret R. & John H. Peirce 8-30-1875 (West)
Mary A. & James H. Thomas 12-28-1869 (Gordon)
Noah & Alice M. Brown 4-29-1885 (Rev. C. O. Cooke)
Samuel & Hester V. Sweeny 1-26-1876 (Gordon)
FUGITT, Thomas M. & Mary H. Osbourn 1-1-1855
FULKS, Henry & Ann Dodson 10-24-1822
FULLER, Ann & John Constable 12-4-1780
Emily Augusta & John Stephen 6-20-1882 (Rev. Jno. B. Williams)
Jane Walter & James Owen Brady 12-31-1850
M. R. & William T. Davis 12-2-1869 (Kershaw)
Maggie R. & James R. Seaborn 1-4-1869
FURGESSON, Elisha B. & Victoria Richardson 6-10-1882 (Rev. Mr. Butler)
FURGUSON, Assiny Y. & Elisha Perry 9-20-1841

GADDIS, Adam Jr. & Margaret Trimble 11-24-1855
GAILOR, Milley C. & Thomas Grainger 4-7-1847
William B. & Ruth Barron 11-11-1822
GALAWAY, Jane & Thomas Watson col? 1-31-1870 (Langford)
GALER, Anne E. & Albert W. Ward 9-19-1855
GALES, Ann & William Marlin 12-27-1782
Linney & John Smith 12-30-1844
GALLAHAM, Thomas & Sarah Newton 4-5-1806
GALLOWAY, Adeline & Allen Brown 5-9-1868
Charlotte & Thomas Chase 12-27-1866 (Greenleaf)
David & Henrietta Hall col? 6-5-1868 (Greenleaf)
Jennie & Robert West 6-19-1884 (Rev. Thos H. Brooks)
John & Jane Stewart col? 8-14-1869 (Langford)
Joseph & Charlotte Edmond 3-14-1877 (Carroll)
Josephine & Charles D. Coats 10-17-1868 (Price)

GALLOWAY, Luke & Margery Craig 4-19-1873
  Matilda A. & Wm. Henry Brent col^d 12-16-1865
  Washington & Agnes Stewart 1-28-1870 (Langford)
GALLYHAM, Emily & Hendley Walker 12-22-1836
  John & Elizabeth Carrick 11-27-1841
  Nancy & William Sansbury 5-20-1839
  William M. & Elizabeth Jane Clubb 12-18-1860
GALWAY, Henry & Tracey Robinson 10-18-1873 (Dwyer)
GALWITH, Mary & Isaac Jenkins 6-5-1787
  Rachel & Joseph Simpson 1-31-1788
  Rebecca & Benjamin Morris 2-4-1783
  Susannah & James Carroll 4-6-1792
GANT, Anna & William Brown col^d 9-22-1866 (Fr. Call)
  Paul & Mary Locker 12-24-1870 (McDonald)
GANTT, A. M. L. & John Bowie 10-21-1833
  Ann & Peter Wood 4-3-1793
  Anna L. & Jonathan Prout 12-7-1832
  Eleanor & William L. Gibson 10-7-1815
  Eliza & William O.Sprigg 12-9-1802
  Elizabeth & Charles Eversfield 2-13-1786
  Elizabeth & Lloyd N. Lowe 2-15-1825
  Erasmus & Elizbeth Jane Calvert 12-26-1865 Age 21-4 mo, color dark,
    Farmhand, married Upper Marlboro by Henry J. Kershaw, Min. Prot. Ep. Ch.
  George Holdsworth & Elizabeth Davis 7-5-1806
  Henry & Wilhelmina Weems 3-3-1798
  John & Priscilla Waring 4-20-1808
  John Mackall & Mary Sprigg Hermance 12-18-1798
  Lizzie & William West 5-21-1869 (Father Maher)
  Marg^t Williammina & James B. C. Thornton 5-22-1823
  Mary & James Newborn 5-20-1791
  Mary E. & Alfred Tolson 2-14-1826
  Priscilla & Jeremiah Belt Junr 3-4-1778
  Priscilla M. & Zacharian Berry Jr. 5-13-1820
  Rachel & Charles Lee 5-16-1868 (Langford)
  Robert & Elizabeth Maynard 8-21-1790·
  Sarah & Osborn Sprigg 4-3-1779
  Sarah & John H. Beall 4-7-1808
  Thomas & Mary Hall 8-29-1816
  Thomas T. & Ann Stoddert 11-25-1811
  Wm. & Mary E. Volintine 12-12-1856
GARDINER, Abraham & Sarah Webb 4-5-1783
  Alford & Mary E. Gwynn 11-22-1847
  Benjn & Sarah Hardey 3-4-1783
  Elias & Lucinda Ford col^d 10-4-1866 (Stanley)
  Elijah & Mary Ann Langley 12-14-1822
  Elizabeth & William Poston 12-25-1797
  Elizabeth & Benjamin N. Mudd 9-6-1814
  Elizabeth & Plummer Wells 12-27-1859
  Elizabeth A. & Thomas B. Gwynn 1-24-1818
  Henrietta E. & Francis H. Clements 9-?-1843
  Henry & Mary Queen 6-30-1798
  Hezekiah & Sarah Morkabee 2-9-1857
  Ignatius A. & M. Olevia Gwynn 11-2-1871 (O'Dwyer)
  Isidore & Harriet Mudd 1-14-1822
  J. W. T. (1st U. S. Dragoons) & Annie E. West 7-3-1854

GARDINER, Joseph James & Winifred Hamilton 1-16-1795
  Joshua N. & Susan Winfield 2-5-1822
  Levin & Margaret Ann Hill 8-12-1837
  Mary & Benedict Smith 2-7-1795
  Mary Jane & Charles Curtis 6-28-1856
  Priscilla & James B. Padgett 12-20-1830
  Richard T. & Mary A. Freeman 2-17-1873
  Stephen & Mary Elizabeth Tydings 7-25-1855
  Susan & Henry Wheatly 2-20-1837
  Sylvester F. & Dolly Hardy 10-27-1812
  Tessha & John Armiger 1-27-1829
  William & Matilda Thompson 8-10-1821
GARDNER, C. Clinton & Eliza H. Middleton 10-2-1882 (Rev. Mr. Hyland)
  Eleanor & Stanislaus Boone 1-2-1796
  Peter & Rebecca Turner 5-15-1793
  Sallie & John R. Hill 6-28-1859
GARLINE, Minnie Catherine & Albert Quincy Winsor 6-30-1875
GARNER, Amelia & Trueman Rollins 2-5-1863
  Ann & William Garner 5-17-1870 (McDonald)
  Benjamin & Ann Hyde 2-8-1793
  Benjamin & Susan Cooksey 1-29-1853
  Benjamin & Sarah Rawlings 1-18-1873 (Townshend)
  Benj? & Mary L. Rawlings 2-8-1847
  Benj. R. & Mary Zora Rollings 2-8-1864
  Delilah & John Tomblesom 12-20-1830
  Edward & Sarah Jane Howard 3-16-1867 (Greenleaf)
  Elijah Thomas & Mary Susannah Devon 12-28-1859
  Eliza Ann & John Thomas Rawlings 9-15-1858
  Elizabeth & John H. Peacock 4-18-1855
  Elizabeth H. & Jas. H. Hunt 2-16-1864
  Elizth& Leond H. Boswell 1-29-1849
  Ella F. & John O. Stamp 1-9-1884 (Rev. Mr. La Roche)
  Emma & John Hyde   12-22-1868 (Smith)
  Francis & Matilda Garner 12-22-1868 (Chesley)
  Frank & Susanna R. Rawlings 2-16-1869 (Smith)
  Frederick & Martha E. Grimes 12-17-1864
  George & Mary DeVaughn 1-2-1868 (Smith)
  Henrietta & George T. Davis 4-7-1846
  Hesty & Caleb A. Rawlings 8-9-1843
  James F. & Missouri H. Rawlings 1-9-1872 (Gordon)
  James Henry & Mary Craig 1-13-1876 (Tennant)
  Jesse & Henny Hyde 2-14-1810
  John & Matilda Garner 12-16-1833
  John & Esther Downing 7-16-1839
  John & Eliza Glascow 12-18-1867 (Marbury)
  Joseph & Sarah Nowell 2-26-1794
  Joseph M. & Rosa N. Cook 6-11-1862
  Joseph P. & Hester S. Rawlings 1-3-1866 23yr-6mo, farmer. Married
    at res. of Truman Rawlings, A. J. Porter, minister
  Margaret A. & Charles L. Butler 12-3-1877
  Matilda & John Garner 12-16-1833
  Matilda & Francis Garner 12-22-1868 (Chesley)
  Michael & Sarah Boston 12-19-1798
  Michael & Elizabeth A. Rawlings 12-21-1840
  Nathan & Martha Greenfield 2-18-1878 (Homan)

GARNER, Patsy & William Wootton 6-4-1799
  Phoebe & James Hill 11-26-1819
  Rosa A. & George W. Baden 12-29-1873 (Lenaghan)
  Sam. & Mary Webster 12-27-1824
  Sarah & Henry Estep 12-4-1798
  Sarah & John T. Lynch 11-12-1849
  Sarah J. & John S. Rawlings 11-21-1871 (Watts)
  Mrs. Siss & George T. Smith 4-18-1870 (McDonald)
  Theodore & Mary Ann Mudd 4-24-1819
  Thomas & Mary Naylor 1-27-1798
  William & Ann Butler 12-30-1799
  William & Ann Garner 5-17-1870 (McDonald)
  William F. & Ann Tomlinson 12-31-1833
GARRETT, Elizabeth & William Husten 11-18-1797
GARRETTSON, Titus & Isabella Mary Mathews 6-1-1882 (Rev. Mr. Stanley)
GASSAWAY, Lethe & Hanson Greenleaf 7-19-1855
  Walter & Leathy Ann Blacklock 12-19-1846
GATES, Caroline C. & James H. Loveless 12-24-1845
  Charles & Sarah Shoemaker 5-8-1882
  Eleanor & John Ryon 3-7-1786
  Elisha & Christina A. Summers 4-12-1817
  Elizabeth & James W. Burgess 12-18-1858
  Henry & Susan Dyer 5-6-1814
  Jane & Middleton Sansbury 12-26-1803
  Jane & John Bignall 11-14-1818
  Joseph William & Maria S. Haze 12-28-1868 (Kershaw)
  Joshua & Elizabeth Fairall 2-20-1821
  Lucy & Francis Brown 7-13-1802
  Mary & Thomas Hyde 12-16-1833
  Mary Alice & Robert Burgess 11-29-1876 (Green)
  Mary C. & Stephen T. Gates 2-6-1854
  Mary S. & Henry White 4-26-1862
  Philip A. & Susanna J. Walker 1-30-1858
  Stephen T. & Mary C. Gates 2-6-1854
  Susanna & Robert Burgess 2-7-1874
  Teresa Ann & William A. Watson 3-13-1833
  Wm. F. & Margt V. Smith 8-23-1848
GATTON, Ann & Samuel Jones 10-11-1800
GAY, Susannah & Anthony Lindsey 12-13-1827
GEDDES, Charles W. & Nannie R. Hill 6-29-1869
GENERALS, Samuel & Louisa Arnell cold 9-17-1869 (Chesley)
GENERIS, John Constantine Marsollan & Jane Mary Sebastian Zephirine
  Javain de Poincy 6-2-1804
GENISENGER, Sarah E. & Benjamin Mitchell 2-2-1854
GENTLE, Linny & Perry Jones 2-6-1793
  Zachariah & Delila Cooke 12-22-1802
GEORGE, Samuel K. Jr. & Ella Carter 6-11-1863
GERMAN, Mary & James Mangun 12-22-1807
  Sarah & Andrew Tayler 5-1-1802
GHISELIN, Priscilla G. & Thomas S. Alexander 11-30-1830
  Robert & Mary E. Lansdale 12-3-1827
GHISOLIN, Rosa & Frederick Sasscer 4-17-1855
GIBBON, Elizabeth & James Wilson 3-16-1798
  Elizabeth & Richard Melcom Lamar 12-10-1808
GIBBONS, Alexander & Rebeccah Keith 10-2-1792

GIBBONS, Alexander & Mary Ann Wade 12-10-1803
 Alexander & Ann Gibbons 1-21-1820
 Ann & George Turner 9-5-1797
 Ann & Levi Mangun 12-23-1806
 Ann & Alexander Gibbons 1-21-1820
 Arabella & William Cross 8-15-1845
 Arabella Priscilla & William Marcellus Richards 12-20-1876
 Charlotte P. of P. G. Co. & Emanual Frances Acton of Charles
  County 11-24-1880 (Rev. Josiah Perrie)
 Christiana A. & Philip A. Sasscer 4-11-1855
 Daniel & Mary Ann Butler 1-16-1830
 Daniel & Mary A. Watson 4-6-1844
 Darkey & Elijah Connick 11-20-1827
 Eliza A. & Thomas E. Ball 1-7-1870 (Marbury)
 Elizabeth & Levin Clarke 12-13-1796
 Elizabeth & William Wall 8-23-1806
 Geo. & Marg.t Grear 12-31-1778
 George Wailes & Susannah Naylor 1-26-1793
 Hannah M. & Alexander McKee 4-17-1858
 Henry & Priscilla Selby 12-11-1834
 James & Elizabeth Sasscer 11-12-1833
 James H. & Jane Walls 1-25-1839
 James H. & Elizabeth A. Robinson married at residence of
  Thos. W. Robinson by Rev. Samuel R. Gordon 9-27-1865
 Jane & James Richards 1-27-1795
 Jeremiah & Mary E. Greer 5-17-1849
 John & Rebecca Wright 1-15-1799
 John A. & Margaret Ann Richardson 5-5-1856
 John Alexander & Malvina Gibbons 12-29-1823
 John R. & Susanna B. Wright 7-14-1831
 John R. & Kate Tucker 3-16-1878
 Jonathan & Rachel Mangun 1-31-1810
 Joseph H. & Mary Scott 2-3-1864
 Joseph W. & Elizabeth Ann Rawlings 1-1-1833
 Josias & Sarah Gover Baden 10-18-1819
 Julia A. & Edward T. Mark 6-21-1841
 Malvina & John Alexander Gibbons 12-29-1823
 Melvina & William Jones 7-2-1838
 Martha A. & Richard T. Robinson 11-23-1854
 Mary Anne & William C. Watson 1-9-1820
 Priscilla & Lloyd M. Scott 12-27-1841
 Rebecca & George Naylor Orme 2-17-1814
 Rebecca P. & Thomas A. Davis 11-25-1856
 Ruth & George Carter 4-19-1815
 Sarah & Alexander Baden 3-31-1804
 Sarah A. & I.N.W. Wilson Age 26 2-5-1866 (Fr. Lanahan)
 Sarah A. S. & Mr. A. McKee 4-27-1864
 Sarah Ann & James Busey 12-28-1805
 Sarah Ann & John Turton 1-28-1826
 Sarah D. & Jonathan T. Sasscer 1-16-1830
 Susannah & James Baden 12-4-1799
 Susannah & William Wilson 5-5-1800
 Susannah & John E. Richards 10-3-1868
 Tamar & Charles Howse 12-7-1779
 Thomas B. & Ella E. Rawlings 10-27-1884 (Rev. Cardon)

GIBBONS, Virlinda & John Beavin 12-6-1796
   William A. & Anna E. Grimes 4-18-1859
   William J. & Sarah A. S. Robinson 6-1-1859
   William L. & Ana Price Demar 1-17-1882 (Rev. M. La Roach)
GIBBS, Elizabeth & Alvin Osborn 5-3-1794
   George & Jane Taylor 10-22-1849
   James & Ally Jenkins 12-21-1801
   James Bennett & Bettie Boyd Wright 9-15-1857
   Jn? H. & Mary Henrietta Dyer 7-20-1778
   Sarah Ann & Jonas P, Keller 12-1-1828
GIBBSON, Elizabeth J. & James Thomas Richards 11-22-1875
GIBSON, Alexander & Mary Ann Watson 1-31-1824
   Annie E. & Thomas Crandell Ann Arundel Co. 7-5-1881
   Caleb & Susannah Merrit 11-15-1819
   Eliza & David Brown 11-30-1824
   Fannie E. of P. G. Co. Age 21 & James L. White of Washington City,
     D.C. 10-10-1866 & 10-16-1866
   Hannah M. & Walter R. Cook 12-2-1885 (Rev. Mr. Butler)
   John E. & Annie H. Jackson 1-4-1869 (Harper)
   Joshua & Martha Ann Rawlings 2-8-1840
   Margaret & Benjamin Burns 3-8-1833
   Mary Ann & James A. Vermillion 3-3-1835
   Mary Ann & Th$ D. Jackson 2-16-1864
   Minta & John W. Rawlings 2-28-1809
   Susan & Henry B. Trueman 2-8-1840
   William L. & Eleanor Gantt 10-7-1815
   William Lewis & Rebecca Hanson 3-10-1808
GIDDINGS, John Julius & Matilda Selby 2-7-1848
GIESENDAFFER, Eliz.th A. & Basil H. Harris 10-16-1843
GIL, Charity Ann & Wm. R. Barker 12-30-1828
GILES, Charles & Elizabeth Shorter 9-9-1872 (McDonald)
   Eliza & John Valentine 5-14-1853 colored
   Felix & Mary Franklin 12-26-1884 (Rev. Mr. Hendricks)
   Jacob & Linda Thomas 5-15-1869 (Gross)
   William & Teresa Holland 9-5-1872 (McDonald)
GILL, Charles H. & Alice V. Ridgeley 6-14-1870 (Maher)
   Eliz.th & John D. Bowling 4-9-1832
   German B. & Maggie Hunnicutt 4-15-1868 (Marbury)
   Joseph & Mary Fenley 12-16-1794
   Mary & Edward Marlowe 12-8-1807
   Ruth & Nathan Soper 1-18-1803
   Thomas & Sarah Jones 8-30-1777
GILLIGAN, James H. & Katie Chew 9-9-1878 (Robey)
GILLOTT, Emma J. & Wm. Walter Wilson 11-9-1883 (Rev. La Roche)
GILPIN, Margaret & Jonathan Barrett 3-20-1779
   Mary & Richard Walker 8-23-1778
GITTING, William & Lydia Higdon 9-21-1793
GITTINGS, Jeddidiah & Ann N. Clarke 11-22-1843
GIVEN, Laura J. & James F. Thompson 9-26-1885
GIVENS, Arthur & Elizabeth Givens 12-11-1800
GLAS, Elizabeth C. & Daniel C. Digges 11-27-1856
GLASCOE, Jane & Mortimer L. Green 4-4-1874 (Tennent)
GLASCOW, Ambler & Thomas Adams 9-18-1883 (Rev. N. C. Brown)
   David & Hennie Douglass 7-18-1881 (Rev. Mr. Brown)
   Eliza & John Garner 12-18-1867 (Marbury)

GLASCOW, Fanny & Walter Fowler 12-22-1876
  Lucy & George Douglass 12-26-1882 (Mr. Brown)
  Mary Eleanor & Aquila Baden 1-15-1833
  Sarah & Edward Bond 12-27-1866 (Marbury)
GLASGOW, James & Eleanor Chapman 2-19-1868
  Verlinder & Christopher Arnold 11-23-1801
GLASSCOTT, William H. & Josephine Robey 9-24-1866 born Canada, age 25;
  Gov. Employ, m. Surrattsville by Henry J. Kershaw, minister Prot. E.
GLASSGOW, Leonard & Rebecca Gray 2-18-1879 (Watkins)
  Nancy & Wesley Scott col? 4-6-1882 (Rev. Mr. Frank Wills)
  Theodore & Ann Ivington 12-1-1800
GLEN, Noble N. & Dorothy Spalding 4-7-1804
GLOVER, Mary & Thomas Mahew 4-14-1781
GLOYD, George & Rebecca Scaggs 6-11-1822
  Joanna & John Ballett 11-29-1782
GODDARD, Catherine A. & James B. Padgett 12-28-1869 (Kershaw)
  Catherine Ann & Richard Moore 11-17-1830
  Charles C. & Alice Constance 11-21-1883 (Rev. La Roche)
  Edward & Ann Humberstone 1-12-1805
  Elizabeth & Hanibal W. Richards 11-20-1876 (Gordon)
  Elizabeth A. & George Roland 1-11-1843
  Elizabeth Mahala & Daniel King 3-7-1848
  James & Priscilla Berry 12-30-1815
  John & Susannah Thorn 8-4-1787
  John & Elizabeth Knott 7-14-1795
  John W. & Elizabeth J. White 12-22-1858
  Richard L. & Ann R. Cox 1-3-1866 (Martin)
  Sarah & Hanson Thompson 3-1-1821
GODDINGS, Eliz?th T. & Josiah Trueman 5-15-1848
GODFREY, Samuel & Ann Burch 7-3-1798
GODMAN, Ann Maria & John C. Morsell 4-3-1837
  Elizabeth & Henry Duvall 1-17-1803
  Margaret A. & Mason E. McKnew 7-1-1857
  Mary Ann & Benjamin Onions 1-4-1836
  Nancy & John Tarrence 12-8-1810
  Rachael & Edmund Baldwin 12-8-1835
  Rebecca & George Beall 3-23-1805
  Samuel & Roena Baldwin 12-18-1820
  Sarah & Benedict Brashears 1-25-1810
GODY, Charlotte & John Wolfenden 12-30-1829
GOLDEN, R. A. & Belle Northern 12-4-1884 (Rev. Mr. Hamnon)
GOLDSMITH, Henrietta & George L. Segar 4-16-1884 (Rev. Mr. Chesley)
  James & Margaret A. M. Smith 6-23-1855
  John A. & Ida Baden 1-26-1880 (Rev. Perrie)
  Maggie & Joseph H. Richards 5-21-1877 (Gordon)
  Margaret & John A. Dent 12-18-1874 (Scott)
  Thomas & Susannah Crook 1-31-1828
  Uriah & Rebecca E. Clubb 11-12-1859
GOODRICH, Rev? Charles & Catharine Ogle 8-15-1838
  Miss Josephine E. C. & Joseph H. Jeferson 6-1-1864
GOODRICK, Annie Ruth & Marcus Lafayette Davis 7-16-1883 (Rev. Mr.Towle)
GORDON, Charles W. & Mary M. Forrest 10-14-1879 (Crowley)
  Dorcas & John Morsell 1-30-1817
  Elizabeth & John Wilson 2-11-1795
  Frank & Ida M. Darcy 6-17-1878 (Dorsey)

GORDON, George & Jane Kelly 6-9-1796
  John & Anna Wilson 6-5-1797
  Mary & Sabret Sollars 5-10-1781
  Mary R. & John H. Thomas 8-4-1879 (Crowley)
  Rebecca & James Marshman 10-22-1779
  Thomas & Ann Hardy 6-11-1777
  William H. & Clarissa Maddox 7-5-1848
GOSSOM, Jennie & Albert A. Sourewine Age 16 9-7-1865
GOTHERD, Stephen & Anna Osburn 4-9-1798
GOTT, Ezekial & Susannah Jackson Soper 4-23-1792
  Louis & Rachel Bowie 12-27-1883 (Rev. Mr. Barnes)
GOURLY, Elizabeth & John R. Biscoe 5-27-1858
GOVER, Elizabeth & Robert Baden 5-12-1796
  Frances & Robert Baden Jun? 11-10-1779
  Sarah Walker & Rinaldo Pindell 7-6-1811
  William A. & Verlinder P. Sasscer 1-27-1818
GRADY, Alice L. & Bennett C. Hicks 5-10-1878
  Bernard & Meta J. Wall 5-1-1877
GRAHAME, John & Susannah Hill 4-7-1808
  William & Sarah Downing 12-30-1807
GRAINGER, Thomas & Milley C. Gailor 4-7-1847
GRANT, Catherine & Hugh Mackay 2-11-1790
  John & Ephana Claud 10-21-1777
  Mary & John Riley 12-10-1788
GRAVATH, Judith M. & Richard F. Brown 4-11-1866 (Chesley)
  Age 17, 8 mos. of Washington, D. C.
GRAVES, James A. & Mrs. Georgeanna Payne 12-26-1864
GRAY, Alexius & Priscilla Vermillion 1-18-1823
  Amelia Jane & William Winfield 4-4-1853
  Ann & George Walker 12-7-1779
  Benjamin R. & Grace C. Somervill 10-27-1845
  Cassandra & John Crooke 12-23-1797
  Catherine & Benedict Padgett 4-13-1789
  Charles & Sarah Ware 12-3-1778
  Cornelia A. & James W. M. Hardisty 10-4-1861
  Darius & Mary Clubb 1-23-1819
  Dorsey & Henrietta Reeder 3-7-1884 (Rev. Frank Wills)
  Edward B. & Joanna Douglass col? 11-23-1867 (Blankford)
  Eleanor & William Kidwell 1-4-1783
  Eleanor & John Mennis 2-6-1807
  Elias & Mary Far 4-11-1785
  Elisse & James Foller 12-30-1868
  Eliza Camilla & George Allen Sims 4-4-1868
  Eliza Camilla & George Allen Spencer 5-8-1875
  Elizabeth & William Wood 12-7-1780
  Elizabeth & Cephas McDaniel 2-20-1797
  Elizabeth & James King 1-8-1819
  George & Sarah Mitchell 11-23-1816
  George & Mary Ellen King 12-28-1885 (Rev. Geo. Williams)
  George W. & Jinnie A. Brown 6-6-1883 (Rev. Mr. Walker)
  Harriet & Thomas F. Robertson 12-31-1813
  Harriet Ann & Ignatius Elias Kettle 2-16-1874
  Harriet & Henry Brooks both colored 4-27-1865
  Henrietta & Benjamin Hardey 2-12-1806
  Hezekiah & Ann Fair 1-2-1782

GRAY, Hugh & Elizabeth Stevens 8-8-1795
  James & Linny Osborn 2-7-1785
  Jane & Geo. Dodson 6-3-1876
  Jane & John F. Briscoe 10-19-1876
  John & Ann Boone 2-9-1802
  Julia Ann & Benjn Westerfield 3-27-1847
  Lavinia A. & John R. Carrick of R^d 6-1-1869 (Kershaw)
  Letty & Horatio Tenley 10-31-1804
  Louis & Annie Reeder 5-5-1884 (Rev. Francis Wills)
  Louis C. & Margaret Emma Anderson 12-2-1885
  Lyley & Joseph Mitchell 2-17-1812
  Martha A. & Thomas Hays 12-10-1862
  Mary & James Rustridge 4-7-1798
  Mary Ann & Charles Young 10-7-1871 (Evans)
  Mary Elizabeth & James Fred^k Davis 3-20-1884 (Rev. Mr. Wills)
  Mary Price & John Keadle 8-30-1805
  Mary Virginia & Thomas Evens 6-5-1876 (Price)
  Nat & Sallie Hatton 12-10-1874
  Nathaniel & Eliza Hill 10-10-1877 (Carroll)
  Rebecca & Thomas M. King 1-18-1790
  Rebecca & Leonard Glassgow 2-18-1879 (Watkins)
  Richard & Rebecca Wilson 8-30-1778
  Robert & Eliza Parker 12-26-1874
  Robert Henson & Margaret Green 4-11-1884 (Rev. Francis Wills)
  Rosetta & James Brookes 12-26-1865
  Samuel & Sally Scott 6-23-1870 (Evans)
  Samuel & Mattie A. Flanders 12-22-1884
  Sarah & Joseph Burgess 12-31-1779
  Sarah & Fielder Hays 5-4-1870 (Martin)
  Sophia M. & John W. Fowler 12-18-1878 (Perry)
  Sylvester & Vina Williams 9-6-1879 (Lewin)
  Thomas & Mary Bonifant 6-2-1781
  Thomas & Margaret Creek 4-5-1801
  Vincent & Elizabeth Jenkins 10-19-1818
  Walter & Kitty (Mary Catherine) Jenifer 12-26-1874 (Gordon)
  William & Seney McDaniel 2-14-1804
  William & Ann Huntt 12-26-1811
  William F. & Georgeanna Anderson 9-25-1876 (Kershaw)
  Zilphy & Moses Clark col^d 11-24-1866 Age 19, house servant (Fr.Young)
GREAR, Annanias & Ann Lang 2-6-1781
  Marg^t & Geo. Gibbons 12-31-1778
GREEN, Alexander & Mary Ann DeVaughn 2-22-1866 (Porter, minister)
    Age 30, farmer. Married at residence of Peyton DeVaughn
  Alice & Benjamin Wells 12-26-1877 (Homan)
  Basil & Sarah Ann Lanham 1-18-1780
  David & Priscilla Green 10-10-1879 (Butler)
  Dennis & Julia Calvert 10-22-1870 (Wheeler)
  Elisha & Mary Clarke 3-1-1783
  Henrietta & Charles H. C. Brown 10-9-1884
  James & Catharine Frank 11-9-1796
  James & Anna Hutton 5-24-1866 Age 28, colored, servant. Married
    Laurel, Jas. Alex Young, Presbyter of Ep. Ch.
  James & Sarah Ellen Franklin 12-22-1874 (Oberly)
  Jeremiah & Eliza Young 12-7-1867 (Young)
  John & Lucy Digges 10-30-1873 (Snowden)

GREEN, Joseph & Sallie Harold col^d 11-16-1872 (McDonald)
Lucian & Eliza Butler 12-26-1885 (Rev. Mr. Brooke)
Margaret & Robert Henson Gray 4-11-1884 (Rev. Francis Wills)
Martha & David Hall 8-15-1874
Mary & James Jackson 3-29-1875 (Welsh)
Mary & Frank Pinkney 7-11-1885 (Rev. Mr. Brooks)
Mary Ellen & Alexander Hanson colored 7-15-1880 (Rev. E. Lawson)
Michael & Laura Rideout 8-30-1872 (Evans)
Mortimer L. & Jane Glascoe 4-4-1874 (Tennent)
Otho & Jennie Wells 12-16-1878 (Hooman)
Philip & Sarah Talbott 5-16-1807
Pinkney & Mary Eliza Pickney 1-11-1870 (Gordon)
Pliney & Saulsbury Clagett 12-24-1872 (Ankward)
Priscilla & David Green 10-10-1879 (Butler)
Sallie & Chas. Brooks 11-29-1884 (Rev. Mr. Brooks)
Sarah & William Powell 3-17-1785
Susan & Overton Talbert 11-8-1870 (Kershaw)
W. & Martha Magruder 12-19-1867 (Langford)
William & Sophia Davis 2-26-1778
GREENE, Hiram W. & Susie P. Underwood 2-6-1866 Age 40, of Philadelphia, Pa., widower, Capt. of Coasting Vessel - James Chipchase, clergyman
Lewis & Mary Taylor 10-25-1820
GREENFIELD, Ann & John Thomas Wood 6-22-1799
John & Christianna Marshall 11-17-1877 (Hooman)
Martha & Nathan Garner 2-18-1878 (Homan)
Mary Eliz^a & John H. Tayman 2-2-1822
Sarah E. & Wm. Bean 5-8-1825
Susannah & William Baker 5-1-1789
GREENLEAF, Ann R. & Joseph Francis Ford 12-27-1882 (Rev. Mr. LaRoche)
Edmund & Emly Savoy colored 3-12-1856
Edmund & Leathe Greenleaf 10-5-1875 (Mayberry)
Emily & Henry Johnson 7-29-1869 (Lankford)
Frederick & Rachel Ann Waters 5-9-1873 (Dwyer)
Geo. & Kinah Harper 4-7-1874 (Gordon)
Hanson & Lethe Gassaway 7-19-1855
Jane & Francis Morrison 3-18-1876 (Tennant)
Jemima & James Scott 12-29-1866 (Hicks)
Leathe & Edmund Greenleaf 10-5-1875 (Mayberry)
Letitia & John H. F. Duckett col^d 9-22-1869 (Langford)
Nicholas & Catherine Duckett colored persons 11-16-1861
Peter & Eliza Calvert 10-28-1874 (O'Dwyer)
GREENWELL, Anna E. & Clarence M. Hill 10-20-1875 (Chaney)
George L. & Elizabeth Howse 5-11-1867 (Hill)
James F. & Sarah E. Armiger 12-24-1856
Jesse & Luthy Lowe 1-6-1790
Jesse & Ann Moore 1-21-1795
John D. & Sarah Ann E. Martin 3-14-1851
Joseph & Winefred Lowe 1-7-1793
Sallie J. & George W. Hardisty 10-20-1874 (Chaney)
Thomas & Rachel Armiger 2-5-1823
GREER, Alexander A. & Mary E. Hyde 2-22-1842
Edward Wilson & Letty Rawlings 2-16-1803
Elizabeth & Daniel Smith 4-8-1806
Fielder D. & Ann E. Wilson 10-15-1850
Fielder W. & Margaret V. Watson 10-1-1865 Age 45, hotel clerk. m. res. of Oze Wilson, P. G. Co. by Alex M. Marbury

GREER, Henrietta & Francis Corfries 10-14-1821
  Henry & Mary W. Downing 2-10-1816
  Jane & James Cattington 12-19-1805
  Levin & Barbara Blackburn 11-18-1815
  Margaret D. & Grafton T. Suit 12-18-1883 (Rev. Mr. Hyland)
  Martin & Mary Oliver 1-31-1807
  Mary E. & Jeremiah Gibbons 5-17-1849
  Mary M. & Josiah Davis 2-14-1817
  Sarah & George Kidwell 10-31-1818
  Susannah & Thomas Richardson 4-22-1813
  Vilette C. & John T. Tippett 8-31-1868 (Smith)
  William & Matilda Hyde 5-27-1814
  William & Jane Naylor 12-16-1838
  William Z. & Mary E. Watson 8-27-1877 (Mercer)
GREGORY, Elizabeth A. & John S. Lewis 1-17-1842
  James & Ann Jones 12-13-1792
  James A. & Mary Ann Miller 8-3-1843
  Richard & Elizabeth Tippett 12-13-1809
  Susanna C. & John L. Huntt 2-9-1841
  Susannah & Hugh Lewis 1-12-1790
GRENFEL, Eliza & Nelson Lee col^d. 8-12-1867 (Lenaghan)
GREY, Catherine & Richard Wells 8-18-1885 (Rev. Mr. Major)
GRIEB, Adalaide Virginia & Edward Jones 7-14-1859
GRIFFEN, Deborah A. V. & Joseph H. Fowler 3-12-1833
  Edward & Tomsey Harbey 12-22-1785
  Edward & Mary A. Smith 4-29-1812
  James H. & Elizth Townshend 6-17-1837
  John & Hepzebah Brown 5-30-1807
  Martha & Thomas Baden of Benjn 6-7-1811
  Mary & John G. Hoye 11-15-1817
GRIFFIN, Edward & Agnes Shekels 5-21-1781
  Edward & Frances Ryan 11-5-1819
  James H. & Mary A. Parker 11-23-1827
  Josephine E. & Richard H. C. Sunderland 10-23-1873
  Jos. R. & C. Sunderland 1-6-1881
  Pompey & Rebecca Murray 12-23-1884
  Pompey & Rebecca Thomas 6-17-1886
  Thomas & Ann Nothey 8-30-1790
  Thomas & Ann Matilda Coates 7-24-1874
  Sallie & Rousby Lyons 4-7-1871 (Marbury)
  Thomas & Elizabeth Hopkins 1-2-1804
  Walter Parker & Eleanor Ann Bryan 9-27-1853
  William & Elizabeth Adams 5-15-1869 (Langford)
  William & Rachel Ann Barney 12-26-1881 (Rev. Mr. Aquilla)
GRIFFITH, Ann & William Reynolds 12-5-1777
  Ann & Benjamin N. Walker 4-18-1794
  Emma & Wm. Armstrong 10-6-1879
  John & Mary West 12-27-1884 (Rev. Mr. Brooke) 12-27-1884
  Louis & Rosalie Proctor 10-30-1879 (De Wolfe)
  Louis A. & Bettie W. Webb 10-8-1879
  S. Allen & Mary J. Wills 12-21-1870 (Gordon)
  William H. & Laura V. Duvall 11-19-1856
GRIMES, Anna E. & William A. Gibbons 4-18-1859
  Anne E. & Jeremiah N. Ryon 3-26-1862
  Benjamin & Mary Grimes 1-17-1789

GRIMES, Charles & Ann Stone 2-17-1787
  Charles Rob? & Sarah Cox 12-24-1842
  Charlotte & Thomas Taylor 5-22-1804
  Eleanor & William Thomas Hunt 2-25-1813
  Elizabeth & James Henry Ritchie 1-8-1834
  Elizabeth E. & James M. Duckett 2-6-1877 (McNeer)
  Fannie B. & Henry A. Hyland 9-15-1885 (Rev. Mr. Hyland)
  Fielder & Martha A. Taylor 2-13-1844
  George & Elizabeth Parrett 1-11-1786
  George D. & Catherine E. Baden 2-24-1864
  George T. & Alice R. Makimsey 12-18-1877 (Kershaw)
  Hannibal & Elizabeth Price 1-27-1836
  Hannible & Mary Johnston 11-19-1863
  Harrison & Kissey Clubb 3-10-1831
  Henry Warring & Sarah Rebecca Beall 7-4-1863
  Henry Warren & Mary A. Grimes 5-21-1866 (Fr. Lenahan)
  Isaac & Elizabeth Adams 3-23-1799
  James G. & Mary F. Allen 11-10-1868 (Berry)
  James T. & Kate Grimes 1-12-1875 (Dorsey)
  Jeremiah & Susannah Talbott 1-8-1793
  Jeremiah T. & Louisa J. Lindsay 12-24-1855
  Jerry T. & B. A. King 12-1-1873
  John & Martha Clements 1-11-1785
  John & Sarah King 1-3-1789
  John & Eliza Cooke 1-26-1808
  John & Ann Ryon 1-6-1842
  John & Ann Onions 6-3-1846
  John Fielder & Maly Celestia Boswell 12-8-1873 (Lanham)
  Kate & James T. Grimes 1-12-1875 (Dorsey)
  Martha E. & William N. Beavin 9-23-1850
  Martha E. & Frederick Garner 12-17-1864
  Mary & James Short 2-9-1779
  Mary & Thomas Taylor 12-21-1785
  Mary & Benjamin Grimes 1-17-1789
  Mary & John Phelps 6-28-1822
  Mary A. & Henry Warren Grimes 5-21-1866 (Fr. Lenahan)
  Nancy Ann & Walter Phelps 9-4-1807
  P. Gibson & Kate R. Suit 6-30-1863
  Sarah E. & Richard H. Sansbury 8-12-1861
  Thomas & Elizabeth Cadle 12-16-1833
  Warren & Sarah Robey 1-20-1826
  William & Nancy Lovelace 12-17-1840
  William H. & Sarah E. Murray 4-30-1869 (Lenaghan)
GRINFIELD, Jane & Joseph Henson 10-16-1875 (Maybury)
GROCE, Edward & Matilda Ann Marshall 9-26-1868 (Lilly)
GROSS, Albert V. & Sarah Somerville 5-17-1879 (Gray)
  Ann Maria & Henry Darnall 12-29-1873 (Pinkney)
  Benjamin Thomas & Letitia Harper 12-24-1872
  Bettie & John Munroe 12-5-1878 (Watkins)
  Edward & Gracy Ann Jackson 11-13-1883 (Rev. Mr. Walker)
  Fannie Agnes & William Coates colored 12-7-1880 (Rev. Mr. Watkins)
  Fielder & Martha Duvall 12-22-1817
  George & Matilda Johnson colored 5-15-1880
  Henry & Charity Chapman 9-14-1871 (Evans)
  James & Jane Davis 9-10-1869 (Lenaghan)

GROSS, Laura & Charles Dodson 6-25-1886 (Rev. Father Cunnane)
   Lewis & Mary Simmes col? 9-8-1881 (Rev. Dr. Gordon)
   Louis & Georgeanna Jenifer 6-13-1874 (Matthews)
   Mary & John Braddy 9-2-1882
   William & Sarah Elizabeth Norfolk 3-19-1872 (Watts)
GROVE, Emma M. of Washington County & Wm. F. Blackford of
   Washington County 4-6-1878 (Williams)
GROVES, Everlina Rosetta Hammond King & Ignatius Manning 1-31-1815
GUINN, Ann & David Middleton 2-8-1821
GUMMER, Daniel & Catherine Johnson 5-5-1875 (Cotton)
   Kate & Sylvester Deal 5-31-1873
GUN, Margaret & John Reed 2-14-1801
GUNN, Rebecca & William Molleson 5-5-1781
GUNTON, Mary M. & Henry H. Carter 10-9-1873 (Stanley)
   Wm. A. & Mary R. Mullekin 6-17-1848
GUTTERICE, Louisa & John Burnill 9-8-1810
GUY, Anne & Joseph Crown 5-12-1795
   Henrietta & William Berry 10-6-1815
   Robert & Josephine Smith 12-15-1865 (Beque)
GUYN, John & Ann Eliza Dyer 2-8-1820
GUYSINGER, John & Sarah Roebe 5-18-1830
GWINN, Ann & Jon? Summers 12-23-1782
   Bennett & Susannah Hilleary 2-21-1797
   Bennett & Rebecca Edelen 8-29-1807
   Bennett F. & Ellen V. Edelen 1-31-1843
GWYNN, Celestia & Stephen Belt 11-17-1846
   Eliza Ann & John F. Summers 11-8-1852
   Ella M. & Rachel C. E. Parker 4-10-1875 (O'Dwyer)
   Emily & Walter A. Edelen 10-15-1849
   Fanny & John H. Thomas 1-15-1869 (Lenaghan)
   Harriet C. & George W. Hilleary 8-24-1855
   Louisa E. & Livingston J. Young 4-10-1875 (O'Dwyer)
   M. Olevia & Ignatius A. Gardiner 11-2-1871 (O'Dwyer)
   Maria L. & Edward W. Young 10-8-1855
   Mary E. & Alford Gardiner 11-22-1847
   Mary Pauline & Henry L. Mudd Jr. 1-20-1875 (Welsh)
   Susan Ann & Alexander St.C. Heiskell 10-11-1841
   Syenna & Henry N. Young 11-26-1849
   Thomas B. & Elizabeth A. Gardiner 1-24-1818
   William H. & Rozella Ann Boone 1-25-1825
   Wm. H.& Christiana Summers 9-22-1851

HAAS, Rachel & Osborn Vermillion 5-5-1798
HABIN, Cindrilla & William Richards 4-18-1821
HABINER, Dominick & Sarah Fergurson 11-13-1790
HAGAN, see also Hogan
   Delia & Seth Taylor 12-5-1814
   Edward & Susannah Watson 4-22-1816
   Horatio & Mary Hodges 1-1-1803
   Ignatius & Elizabeth Edelen 1-28-1792
   James & Mary Ellen Brown 5-21-1866 (Fr. Call)
   Mary Eliza & Henry Jones 4-25-1873 (O'Dwyer)
   Rachel & James Clarke 2-9-1781
   Rachel & Gusty Butler 9-27-1873 (Fowler)

HAGAN, Sarah & Samuel T. Wilson 4-10-1805
  Sarah Ann & George Shorter 12-27-1873 (Fowler)
  Virlinder & Francis E. Semmes 7-11-1814
HAGAR, Lucretia Ann & Ambrose Jackson 10-19-1867 (Call)
  Mintie & Andrew Jones 9-13-1872 (McDonald)
 HAGER, Ellen & James Washington 2-19-1870 (Dwyer)
  Louisa & Lemuel Brice 10-4-1879
  Nicholas & Ann Jackson 7-20-1872 (McDonald)
HAISLEP, Charles & Polly Scaggs 11-27-1827
HAISLIP, Andrew & Martha E. Conner 11-17-1845
HAISTIP, Humphrey & Mary Ann Wilson 5-11-1830
HAKER, Joseph & Mary Sidel 1-2-1876
HALCOCK, Jane Rebecca & John Peake 9-19-1864
HALKERSTONE, Elizabeth & Benjamin Brookes 2-18-1799
HALL, Aaron & Margaret Johnson 10-30-1873 (Snowden)
  Aaron & Sarah Jones 11-8-1873 (Jenkins)
  Amelia & John Read Magruder Junr 9-13-1794
  Ann & Thomas Clark 12-21-1781
  Ann & Lewis Hilleary 12-31-1816
  Ann & Isaac Howard 4-13-1838
  Ann E. & Charles Hill 10-3-1836
  Arabella & Samuel Henson 12-9-1873
  Benjamin & Ann Aldridge 2-19-1838
  Benjamin & Mary E. Osbourn 4-14-1857
  Benjamin & Annie Briscoe 12-25-1876
  Carrie & Joseph Wallace col^d (Rev. Mr. Langford) 8-17-1883
  Catharine & John Burgess Bowie 10-15-1803
  Catherine & Charles Evans 8-22-1882 (Rev. Mr. Butler)
  Catherine V. & Harry Sears 1-16-1886 (Rev. Father Cunane)
  Christianna & Edward W. Brice 9-6-1877 (Carroll)
  Clarence & Margaret Bowling 2-19-1884
  David & Martha Green 8-15-1874
  David & Harriet Ann Tydings 1-9-1875 (Kershaw)
  David & Mary Hall 8-26-1880 (Rev. Mr. Boteler)
  Edward & Willy Duvall 2-18-1814
  Edward & Rebecca Hall 8-16-1824
  Edward & Sarah Parker 2-23-1830
  Eleanor & David Clark 3-25-1788
  Eleanor & Francis Hall Junr 6-25-1791
  Eleanor & Notley Young 4-10-1815
  Eliza & Samuel Duvall 11-29-1826
  Elizabeth & Bennett Farr 11-28-1795
  Elizabeth & Samuel B. Anderson 12-10-1833
  Elizabeth & Charles Norfolk 12-14-1880 (Rev. Dr. Gordon)
  Elizabeth & James Dyvall 1-31-1884 (Rev. Mr. Butler)
  Elizabeth S. & Richd S. Hill 4-26-1854
  Estelle V. & Rinaldo Bryan 2-29-1884 (Father Cunane)
  Francis & Ann Elizabeth Snowden 9-15-1828
  Francis Junr & Eleanor Hall 6-25-1791
  Francis M. & Rosalie E. Carter 5-29-1851
  Francis Magruder & Mary Hill 10-20-1795
  Georgianna & Charles Adams 6-29-1885 (Fr. Cotton)
  Grafton & Rebecca Williams 11-12-1809
  Harriet P. & Wm. M. Marine 11-3-1871 (MacDonald)
  Henrietta & David Galloway col^d 6-5-1868 (Greenleaf)

HALL, Henry H. & Corenlia E. Knowles 12-30-1882 (Rev. Mr. Starr)
   Jerry & Rachel Herbert 8-7-1872 (McDonald)
   John & Eliz.ᵗʰ Boswell 9-22-1830
   John & Margaret Nicholls 3-5-1877 (Carroll)
   John Henry & Tarissa Straw 2-22-1791
   John S. & Emmeline Shaw 11-7-1849
   Joseph & Mary Freeman col? 12-30-1881 (Rev. Mr. Aquilla)
   Joseph J. & Bettie S. Young 2-26-1877 (McNeer)
   Jno. A. & Sarah Ellen Vermillon 7-29-1858
   Jno. Grafton & Ruth Adelle Beall 2-2-1878
   Laura A. & John H. Wissmann 6-5-1861
   Margaret & William T. Wootten 2-17-1819
   Margaret H. & Dennis M. Williams 2-25-1823
   Martha & Joshua Dorsey 12-17-1798
   Martha & William Hall 1-13-1779
   Mary & James Wm. Lock Weems 5-6-1786
   Mary & Thomas Gantt 8-29-1816
   Mary & James H. Boswell 8-25-1875
   Mary & Joseph T. Winsor 7-12-1877 (Kershaw)
   Mary & David Hall 8-26-1880 (Rev. Mr. Boteler)
   Mary Ann & Robert Sprigg 12-24-1872 (Evans)
   Mary D. & Thomas H. Shackels 12-9-1876 (Hodges)
   Mary S. & Dr. John C. Thomas 12-9-1877 (Perry)
   Massy & Henry Burch Thorn 2-26-1803
   Nathan Dunlop & Maria Adams 6-18-1806
   Nathaniel & Mary Hughes 12-23-1777
   Philip & Susan Mitchell 8-14-1823
   Rachel Ann & John H. Digges col? 12-31-1859
   Rebecca & Edward Hall 8-16-1824
   Rebecca & Fendall Wall 11-3-1874 (O'Dwyer)
   Rebecca F. & George W. Beall 1-24-1877 (McDonald)
   Richard & Henrietta Maria Clagett 6-20-1810
   Richard & Mary Carroll 12-29-1846
   Richard & Mary Jane Talbert 10-28-1856
   Richard D. & Elizabeth Perkins 1-8-1799
   Rich.ᵈ D. & Susann Perkins 2-1-1842
   Richard H. & Harriett Kent 3-23-1819
   Richard S. & Ann Maria Lockland 5-10-1823
   Richard T. & Ann H. P. Clagett 6-28-1827
   Sarah & William T. Calvert 7-26-1875
   Sarah Ann & George T. Clagett 9-22-1827
   Sarah R. & Wm. Alexander McDonald 6-11-1872 (Dr. Register)
   Sophia M. & Lloyd F. Harding 11-30-1830
   Susan A. & Edw.ᵈ Luther Clagett 11-2-1867 (Dr. Marbury)
   Susan Ann & Lemuel G. Beck 12-10-1822
   Susannah Virginia & Benjamin Mayhew 9-21-1864
   Thomas J. & Mary Tydings 2-22-1876 (McNeer)
   Thornton & Altzena Duvall 8-9-1842
   William & Martha Hall 1-13-1779
   William & Elizabeth Mary Waring 3-13-1826
   William & Eliz.ᵗʰ Meeks 10-12-1830
   William H. & Barbara Mangun 6-24-1851
   William H. & Harriet Curtin 12-14-1853
HALLEY, Nannie & William Bayne Jr . 6-19-1877 (J. O. Dorsey)
HALLSELL, Annastatia D. & John S. Wilson 3-12-1811

HALSAL, John & Lucy Downes 2-15-1779
HALSALL, Ruth & James Fergusson 8-23-1780
HAMILTON, And⁀ & Jane Burch 4-17-1783
  Annie & Richard Francis Butler 1-1-1876
  Arthelia & Thomas Mullan 6-22-1809
  Caroline & Samuel Peach 4-1-1822
  Cha.ˢ Edward & Catherine Beall 10-12-1867 (Young)
  Eliza & Alexius Sansbury 2-16-1789
  Eliza H. & John Oneale 1-1-1810
  Ellen L. & James Harrison 2-16-1870 (Wheeler)
  Francis & Susan Blanford 1-27-1785
  Gavin & Elizabeth Douglass 7-26-1800
  George B. & Mary E. Watson 7-24-1869 (Marbury)
  Hezekiah & Ann Higgins 11-1-1794
  Jane & Nathan Smith 10-24-1812
  John A. & Margaret Edelen 11-8-1867 (Fr. Lanahan)
  Julia & Moses Brent 12-22-1865 (Beque)
  Louisa A. & Richard John Scott 11-7-1826
  Margaret E. & James W. Fleet 12-29-1879 (Rev. Dr. Gordon)
  Maria & Henry V. Hill 4-22-1816
  Maria & Benjamin Fletcher Jr. 5-18-1871 (Stanley)
  Martha & Robert Morgan 5-30-1780
  Mary & John H. Francis 11-12-1870 (Fr. Maher)
  Matilda & Rᵈ J. Scott 4-25-1848
  Samuel H. & Elizabeth Duvall 5-7-1833
  Samuel Higgins & Mary Ann Peach 1-26-1821
  Samˡ & Anna M. Caldwell 10-25-1847
  Samˡ S. & Elizabeth M. Hill 6-8-1819
  Sarah & John Beck 11-18-1778
  Thomas & Ann Hodgkin 4-17-1781
  Wilemina & Edward Nicholls 8-15-1780
  William & Lizzie Harrison 7-10-1873 (O'Dwyer)
  Winifred & Joseph James Hardiner 1-16-1795
HAMMERSTONE, Richᵈ & Marg Wouster 12-17-1777
HAMNAN, Susan & William Caton 9-29-1832
HAMPTON, Rebecca & Daniel Howard 9-14-1878 (Carroll)
HAMSON, Bryan & Lucy Hatton 2-9-1793
HANCE, S. Elizabeth & George L. Herbert 6-5-1860
HANDLING, James & Priscilla Magruder 5-22-1787
HANES, Elizabeth & Isaac Reed 10-11-1800
HANNAH, Mary & Samuel McDowell 12-1-1805
HANSON, Alexander & Mary Ellen Green colored 7-15-1880 (Rev. E. Lawson)
  Caroline & Henry Johnson 6-16-1829
  Charles Edward & Juliet Bowie colored 6-6-1881 (Rev. Mr. Lawson)
  David & Susan Stuart 7-11-1827
  Eleanor H. & Henry A. Callis 8-28-1832
  Dr. Grafton & Arabella Beck 10-21-1818
  Josias H. & Priscilla Maddox 11-24-1832
  Margaret B. & John F. Beall 4-4-1787
  Martha & Nathaniel Wilson 6-15-1779
  Rachel & George Sebbald 1-5-1786
  Rebecca & William Lewis Gibson 3-10-1808
  Samuel & Elizabeth Fendall Marshall 7-29-1788
  Samuel & Sarah Beall 6-9-1795
  Susan & Joseph Franklin 12-20-1879 (Rev. E. Peters)

HANSON, Thomas & Mary Elizabeth Jackson col<u>d</u> 4-27-1867 (Fr. Call)
   Thomas H. & Rebecca Addison 3-21-1778
   Wesley &Kate Bowie 3-29-1869 (McDonald)
   William & Amelia Chew 2-28-1877 (Snowden)
HARBEY, Tomsey & Edward Griffen 12-22-1785
HARBIN, Charles & Sarah A. Bayne 1-12-1870
   George & Elizabeth Frazier 1-4-1821
   Rezin & Mary Macnew 11-14-1778
HARBRY, N. C. & Mary B. Beall 12-27-1884 (Rev. Mr. Butler)
HARDACRE, Susannah & William J. Rawlings 3-16-1811
HARDCASTLE, Rebecca & James Ridgeway 2-23-1797
HARDEN, Aquila & Sarah Hayes 12-23-1817
HARDESTY, Addison & Violetta Ann Connor 4-19-1847
   Eleanor Douglas & Edward W. Belt 1-16-1860
   Elisha & Sarah Wells 8-21-1780
   Eliz<u>th</u> H. & Wm. H. Clagett 12-1-1828
   Henry & Rachael Carroll 10-20-1846
   John & Henrietta Cheney 7-23-1788
   John & Susan Ennis 12-26-1828
   John H. & Ann C. Belt 6-10-1837
   John Henry & Harriet E. Clagett 11-29-1833
   John Tho<u>s</u> & Julia A. Bassford 1-6-1848
   Lethe & Benjamin Lanham 3-9-1832
   Mary & Charles Drury 1-21-1815
   Matthew & Willemina Whips 8-8-1826
   Rachael & Plummer Laddin 4-3-1826
   Richard G. & Mary Hodges 6-1-1799
   Robert & Caroline Boone 12-23-1854
   Sarah R. & James G. Sullivan 1-5-1860
HARDEY, Airry & Rezin Searce 11-3-1806
   Alice E. & Sam<u>l</u> Pinkney Sweeny 1-17-1876 (Gordon)
   Anastasa & Patrick Reynolds 12-29-1792
   Ann & John Boone 1-12-1782
   Ann & William Dorsey 1-7-1804
   Ann Virginia & John T. Lowe 2-28-1863
   Baptist & Ester Osborn 4-3-1786
   Benjamin & Henrietta Gray 2-12-1806
   Cordelia W. & Rich<u>d</u> L. Humphreys 9-6-1815
   Darkey & Isaac Dove 12-20-1802
   Eleanor & George Hughes 10-26-1797
   Elizabeth & Robert Soper 11-19-1784
   Elizabeth & Enos Schell 1-9-1808
   Elizabeth H. & William Thomas Beall 12-7-1871
   George & Priscilla Jenkins 7-13-1786
   Ignatius Lott & Lucy Darcey 7-1-1803
   James & Mary Collins 2-10-1827
   Jonathan & Mary Ann Soper 1-31-1799
   Jonathan & Lethe Davis 4-19-1837
   Juliana & Geo. T. Brown 8-11-1825
   Lucy & Amos Fox 5-12-1809
   Margaret A. & Joshua T. Clarke 1-17-1874 (Wigget)
   Mary & Basil Bowling 12-31-1799
   Mary & Benjamin Ridgway 12-14-1779
   Mary & Tho<u>s</u> Wilcoxon Jr. 4-23-1781
   Mary & Edmond Casteel 4-4-1801

HARDEY, Mary & James Summers 2-1-1817
  Mary D. & Benoni Hamilton Wade 5-31-1796
  Nathan & Terissa Coombes 5-16-1783
  Noah & Mary Stone 1-13-1794
  R. F. & Martha E. Vermillion 2-17-1880 (Stanley)
  Rachel & Francis Walker 11-4-1803
  Rebecca & Gilbert Younger 6-12-1784
  Rebecca & John Darcey 11-21-1786
  Rebecca & William Scott 2-20-1792
  Richard & Sarah Carrick 2-3-1838
  Richard & Margaret Eliza Carrick 2-6-1860
  Sarah & Benjª Gardiner 3-4-1783
  Sarah & Samuel Webb 11-15-1803
  Susannah & Richard Harvey 2-8-1798
  Terrasa Catharine & Matthais Redmond 5-21-1791
  William F. & Sarah Spalding 10-25-1806
HARDING, C. A. & Violetta E. Lee lic. 7-10-1865 44yr, 10 mo. - Physician
  residence Montgomery County. Married 7-11-1865 Oak Hill, P. G. County
  F. E Boyle, Catholic Priest
  Elizabeth & Henry Langley 2-3-1808
  Lloyd F. & Sophia M. Hall 11-30-1830
  William & Rachel Lamar 3-22-1784
HARDISTER, Ann & Benjamin Lanham 5-25-1826
HARDISTY, Albert & Catharine Ann King 1-31-1867 Age 22, wheelwright m. at
  parsonage, Upper Marlboro - Henry J. Kershaw, minister
  E. F. & Trueman C. Slingluff 8-7-1882 (Rev. Harvey Stanley)
  Edward & Martha E. Haslip 12-26-1862
  George W. & Sallie J. Greenwell 10-20-1874 (Chaney)
  James W. M. & Cornelia A. Gray 10-4-1861
  Laura Ellen & George Ignatius Seabold 5-16-1870 (Maher)
  Philip A. & Mary E. Sweeney 6-1-1886 (Father Cunnane)
  Robert & Mary Ann Cook 1-23-1821
HARDY, Ann & Thomas Gordon 6-11-1777
  Ann & Robert Ayres 9-10-1784
  Anthony & Mary Green Hatton 9-29-1796
  Arianna & Benjamin Stockett 2-8-1832
  Dolly & Sylvester F. Gardiner 10-27-1812
  Elina A. & Stephen William Suit 10-11-1880 (Herke)
  Elizª & Henry Mullican 1-13-1796
  Elizᵗʰ Jane & Samuel H. Fowler 1-12-1832
  Ella Rebecca & Richard Franklin Deal 12-27-1875 (McNeer)
  Ellen & Samuel Coe 12-20-1879
  George & Henriette Taylor 1-15-1840
  Georgianna & Robert W. Ryon 11-21-1854
  Mary Catharine & Robert Edelen 1-2-1816
  Thomas & Margᵗ Wilcoxon 2-9-1780
HARINGTON, Josephine & Andrew S. Kaldenbach 1-9-1865
HARLEY, Marcellus & Cornelia Ann Proctor 2-15-1876 (Green)
  Sarah Ann & Josias Proctor 1-15-1849
HARMAN, Abbie E. & Oswald C. Lehman 3-28-1871 (Kershaw)
  Hattie A. & George R. Dempsey 4-7-1877
  Jacob & Hannah Kerby 10-1-1872 (Kershaw)
  Olivia F. & Gustavus A. Miller 7-17-1880 (Rev. Dr. Stanley)
HARNER, Sarah J. & James L. Padgett 8-14-1882 (Rev. Edwᵈ S. Fort)
HAROLD, Sallie & Joseph Green colored 11-16-1872 (McDonald)

HARPER, Abraham & Georgeanna Hawkins 1-27-1883
  Anna & Levin Wailes 12-26-1855
  Caroline & Jacob Shorter (O'Dwyer) 1-3-1874
  Chas. Henry & Serena Forbs col.d persons 6-3-1865
  James & Ellen Whitaker 11-21-1826
  Kinah & Geo. Greenleaf 4-7-1874 (Gordon)
  Letetia & Benjamin Thomas Gross 12-24-1872
  Robert W. & Sarah Magruder Lyles 7-1-1815
  Robert W. & Laura Worthington 12-15-1856
  Sam! B. & Eliz.th Magruder 2-25-1828
HARRIS, Basil H. & Eliz.th A. Giesendaffer 10-16-1843
  Catherine & Rezin Beall 1-6-1868
  Charles & Alberta Boswell 12-22-1880 (Rev. Mr. Shoaff)
  Cora & Burdy Culley 4-6-1877
  Eleanor & Thomas Pierce 7-17-1811
  Emily & James W. Dorsey col.d Both of Ann Arundel Co. (Rev. Quiller)
  Emily & Louis Taylor 10-20-1881
  Frankie & Adolphus H. Lambert 2-17-1868
  Harriet R. & Francis Oscar Medley 12-17-1860
  James & Rosella Arnold 12-4-1838
  James & Viola Harris Age 33, clerk. M. 1-10-1867 Trinity P. E. Church
    by Henry J. Kershaw
  Jane & Randolph B. Latimer 2-13-1832
  Joseph B. & Ellen Suit 1-23-1844
  Joseph B. & Arabella Josephine Menger 10-10-1855
  O. C. & Cornelia A. E. Early 5-23-1850
  Rosa Bruce & John Waring Medley 2-17-1881 (Rev. Mr. Southgate)
  Sarah & Josias Marshall 4-18-1797
  Viola & James Harris Age 22 1-10-1867 (Kershaw)
  Walter & Laura Bolding 9-18-1878
HARRISON, Amy Ann & Washington Johnson 5-4-1867 (Call)
  Anna & John Henry Harrison col.d 4-27-1867 (Fr. Call)
  Annie E. & Alfonso R. Vermillion 8-11-1875
  Caroline & Emanuel Harrison 6-10-1870
  Cecelia & Thomas Crawford col.d 12-20-1870 (Begue)
  Cloe & Jacob Vermilion 1-29-1780
  Dennis & Kitty Sprigg 11-6-1868 (Stanley)
  Edward & Kitty Bryan 4-15-1876 (Maddox)
  Elisha & Sarah Beall 3-25-1796
  Emanuel & Caroline Harrison 6-10-1870
  Francis & Catharine Jones 8-15-1871 (McDonald)
  Hester & Wesley Brown 8-27-1875
  James & Eleanor West 7-8-1815
  James & Susanna Eliz.th Baden 10-7-1823
  James & Ellen L. Hamilton 2-16-1870 (Wheeler)
  John & Harriet Porter 11-1-1877 (Hooman)
  John & Maria Smallwood 8-4-1883
  John E. & Susan E. Trueman 2-14-1870 (Marbury)
  John Henry & Anna Harrison col.d 4-27-1867 (Fr. Call)
  Jn.o & Eliza Benson 10-23-1848
  Joseph & Rachel Perry 10-23-1778
  Josephine & Daniel Stevenson 6-14-1871 (Begue)
  Kate & Washington Williams 5-19-1877 (Bond)
  Laura & Charles Henry Lee 5-23-1874 (O'Dwyer)
  Lizzie & William Hamilton 7-10-1873 (O'Dwyer)

HARRISON, Mary & Gassaway Ford 4-15-1865 col?
  Mary & Alexander Wood 2-24-1879 (Hooman)
  Mary Henry & Plinny Davidson 8-31-1793
  Sarah Contee & Henry Waring 6-22-1802
  Susannah & James Butler col? 6-27-1868 (Fr. Lilly)
  Thomas & Jane White 12-4-1779
  Thomas & Mary Cahoe 4-15-1805
  Tho? & Mary Stamp 5-30-1783
  Trueman & Emily Holland 8-4-1877
  Walter & Rachel Young 4-26-1873 (Walsh)
  William M. & Ella Herbert 11-29-1880
  Wm. Henry & Susan Ann Watson 6-3-1872 (Marbury)
HARRON, William A. & Caroline M. Johnson 12-30-1856
  William A. & Ella Walter 6-18-1877
HARRUM, Frank & Lucy Diggs 6-16-1886 (Father Cunnane)
HARRY, Susan G. & Thomas W. Clagett 12-24-1833
HART, Margaret & Benjamin Hinton 2-17-1798
  Peter & Violetta Jones 12-19-1825
HARVEY, Alex? & Rebecca McCauley 7-19-1777
  Amanda E. & Thomas R. Taylor 11-30-1881 (Rev. Mr. Butler)
  Amelia & Cephas W. Benson 12-24-1806
  Annie L. & Thomas Bean 12-14-1875 (Rev. Mr. Hamilton)
  Barbara & William Jackson 8-20-1812
  Basil Edward & Emma Snow King 9-20-1882 (Rev. Arnsdale)
  Benjamin & Barbara Arnold 12-9-1823
  Charity Ann & Dionysius Beall 6-16-1868
  Charles W. & Emma Jane Yost 10-6-1862
  Clementine & Oliver S. Wickham 12-22-1883 (Rev. Mr. Stanley)
  Clinton & Sarah Nally 4-12-1882 (Rev. Fr. De Wolf)
  Eleanor & John Jackson 12-31-1796
  Eleanor & Colmore Jenkins 12-26-1821
  Eleanor Jane & Basil Beall 9-7-1853
  Eliza & Samuel Marlowe 2-29-1816
  Elizabeth & James Hern 4-7-1798
  Elizabeth & William Pickrell 12-1-1801
  Elizabeth Jane & James W. Pumphrey 12-28-1865 (Thomas)
  Henry & Sarah McDaniel 4-20-1791
  Howard V. & Lizzie E. Ryon 4-25-1884 (Rev. Stanley)
  James & Ann Selby 3-25-1796
  Jas. N. & Sarah Ann Ridgeway 9-3-1842
  Jennett & Benjamin Burch 7-1-1803
  Jennett C. & Benjamin B. Walls 6-12-1835
  Jennet Caroline & William Naylor 3-21-1841
  John & Willicia Earley 12-13-1814
  John & Mary Hurley 2-4-1815
  John W. & Ann E. Tayman 4-8-1837
  Laura & Israel Butler 2-28-1880 (Aquilla)
  Lenny & Thomas Burch 9-5-1794
  Lethia Ann & Judson Stewart 6-11-1831
  Louisa & Jeremiah Duckett 12-13-1842
  Lucy & John Swain 4-11-1797
  Margaret & Washington Brooke 2-15-1819
  Margaret R. & Alexander McKee 2-11-1834
  Maria & Jeremiah Mullekin Jr. 6-15-1843
  Martha & Benjamin Sweeny 1-14-1817

HARVEY, Martha & Francis Duckett 1-28-1850
  Martha Ann & Richard M. Waring 11-1-1816
  Mary & Elisha Burgess 1-29-1820
  Mary & Cephas Renaldo Beason(Benson?) 1-26-1829
  Mary Ann & John Turner 6-9-1812
  Mary Eleanor & Ellie Baldwin 1-3-1826
  Mary Elizabeth & Gonsalvo D. Mangun 7-26-1853
  Mary Jennette & John Thomas Foreacois 9-27-1881 (Rev. Mr. Thomas)
  Mary L. & Hugh Watt 1-8-1879 (Stanley)
  Moses & Clarissa Macatee 12-15-1780
  Patsey & David Owens 12-21-1807
  Rebecca & Joseph H. Selby 4-27-1832
  Rebecca & Edwin Suit 12-17-1847
  Rebecca & Richard Beall 12-18-1850
  Richard & Susannah Hardey 2-8-1798
  Rich^d & Rachel G. Beall 7-16-1845
  Rich^d & Mary Susan Yost 1-26-1852
  Sarah & Edward Willett Jr. 9-14-1815
  Susan A. & James H. King 12-13-1853
  Thomas & Eliz^a Ann Simpson 4-18-1794
  Thomas & Martha Mullican 12-21-1808
  Thomas & Martha Beall 1-20-1841
  Thomas & Anna Key 3-13-1841
  Thomas & Dorca G. Brashears 1-29-1851
  William & Jane Bean 10-15-1817
  William of Thos & Susan Mahala Lewis 12-3-1827
  William O. & Sarah V. Belt 9-27-1853
HARVIN, Rosetta & Bilsey Pickering 2-30-1824, also listed 4-29-1824
HARWOOD, Eleanor & John Smith Brookes 6-3-1786
  Elizabeth & William E. Berry 3-23-1799
  Franklin & Julia Herbert Hunter 6-25-1861
  Henry of Nich^s & Maria Harwood 10-15-1819
  Isabel & William Queen 12-26-1866
  Joseph & Matilda Sparrow 1-31-1806
  Joseph & Catherine Mullekin 1-3-1826
  Maria & Henry Harwood of Nich^s 10-15-1819
  Martha & Edward Sollers 11-30-1876 (Peters)
  Matilda & Joseph Smallwood 11-3-1875
  Mary & John Sefton 10-16-1819
  Richard & Sarah Ann Cox 10-28-1799
  Sarah & Benjamin Mulliken 10-25-1802
  Thos & Ann Whyte 10-29-1778
  William & Isabella Whittington 12-18-1876
HASLIP, Martha E. & Edward Hardisty 12-26-1862
HATHMAN, Moses & Lucy Contee cold. 7-17-1880 (Father Voltz)
HATTON, George & Eleanor Dent 6-27-1786
  Henny & Colmore Hunter 12-2-1807
  Henry D. & Emily Lyles 1-13-1812
  Jemima & Henry Davidson 10-18-1825
  John W. F. & Ann Sophia Edelen 12-13-1881 (Father Clark)
  Joseph & Martha Jones 10-4-1777
  Joseph C. & Addie L. Steed 12-2-1867 (Martin) 12-2-1867
  Joseph G. & Dorinda E. Earley 6-22-1841
  Josias & Mary Mitchell 2-22-1793
  Lucy & Bryan Hamson 2-9-1793

HATTON, Mary & Jesse Edelen of Thomas 2-7-1800
 Mary & William L. Weems 11-10-1832
 Mary C. & Gustavus R. Brown 8-21-1816
 Mary Green & Anthony Hardy 9-29-1796
 Mary R. & Zachariah B. Beall 10-26-1846
 Nathaniel & Ann N. Burch 2-15-1816
 Nathaniel & Eleanor B. Hawkins 7-31-1824
 Peter B. & Eliz^a J. Lambert 12-28-1821
 Sallie & Nat Gray 12-10-1874
 Sarah M. & Zephaniah Robey 4-22-1845
 Thomas & Sophy Carroll 12-2-1875
 William L. & Rebecca S. Lyles 5-4-1846
HAVENER, Adam & Sarah Bonafin 12-12-1792
 Anna P. & Richard B. S. Sears 2-16-1859
 Benjn & Ruth Summers 10-8-1818
 Daniel E. & Mary Ann Connick 5-19-1830
 Daniel E. & Eleanor Boswell 1-28-1826
 Dominick & Eleanor Upton 1-31-1789
 John & Linney Wheat 1-19-1788
 Mary Elizabeth & William Norfolk 1-20-1853
 Michael & Elizabeth Soper 2-5-1793
 Walter S. & Elizabeth Scasser 12-23-1841
HAVENNER, Margaret O. & Richard H. Cashell 4-7-1865
HAWKE, Charles W. & Theresa J. Collier 6-16-1873 (McKenney)
HAWKINS, Adeline Sophia of Ann Arundel County & Dennis Clark Simms col^d.
  2-3-1881 (Rev. Mr. Chaney)
 Ann & Charles Matthews col^d. 5-2-1868 (Thomas)
 Caroline H. & Edward H. Wyville 6-19-1845
 Charles & Emily Mitchell 12-27-1875 (Scott)
 Charles E. & Mary Marshall 5-28-1884
 Clarence & Harriet Brooke 4-9-1873
 Charlotte R. & John W. Jones 11-6-1876
 Edward J. & Mary J. Mitchell 5-13-1880
 Eleanor B. & Nathaniel Hatton 7-31-1824
 Eleanora & John Wesley Davis 10-22-1873 (Townshend)
 Elias & Jane Wilson 9-12-1873 (Cotten)
 Elizabeth & James Henry Bryan 10-20-1875 (Green)
 Elizabeth & Jeremiah Jenkins lic. 3-19-1884, m. 4-19-1884 (Rev. Brooks)
 Ellen & Richard Doughlas 12-23-1868 (Martin)
 Emanuel (black) & Caroline Ford (col^d.) Age 23, laborer m. 9-9-1866
  Emory Church, Wm. S. Baird, minister Also listed 9-5-1866
 Francis & Sallie Dorsey 10-9-1884
 Frank & Nancy Hicks 9-30-1871 (Marbury)
 George & Margaret Hawkins 2-19-1875 (Scott)
 George & Isabella Snowden 5-19-1877 (Barnes)
 George Leonard & Mary Eliza Thomas col^d. 1-4-1881
 Georgeanna & Abraham Harper 1-27-1883
 Georgianna & Charles Boothe 4-13-1869
 Harriet & Richard Smothers 12-20-1867 (Langford)
 Henry & Jennett Swann 12-26-1790
 Henry & Kitty Hawkins 4-1-1873 (Townshend)
 Henry J. & Sarah F. Cage 6-9-1876
 Henson & Georgianna Johnson 3-30-1885 (Rev. Jno. R. Henry)
 Isaac & Charlotte Chapman 9-14-1871 (Evans)
 James & Louisa Dent 6-22-1875 (Scott)

HAWKINS, James Alfred & Mary Priscilla Dent 12-17-1879 (Rev. Gordon)
  Jane & Michael D. Fletcher 12-27-1872 (Fr. Cotton)
  Jefferson & Nettie Carrick 12-29-1874 (Scott)
  John & Catharine Brown 2-14-1876 (Wiget)
  John R. & Mary Emma Fleet 1-29-1884 (Rev. Mr. Walker)
  John R. & Annie Brooks 12-9-1884 (Rev. John R. Henry)
  John Robert & Georgianna Sly 10-4-1876
  Kitty & Henry Carroll 6-12-1869 (Maher)
  Kitty & Henry Hawkins 4-1-1873 (Townshend)
  L. & Jane Ross 10-7-1885
  Lottie & Edward Henson 5-22-1872 (Gordon)
  Margaret & Nathaniel Washington 11-24-1790
  Margaret & George Hawkins 2-19-1875 (Scott)
  Margaret & Alfred Henson col? 2-9-1881 (Rev. Dr. Gordon)
  Maria & Allison Clagett 9-8-1876 (Gray)
  Marion & Wm. Walls 8-5-1876 (Gray)
  Mary & John French 6-10-1833
  Mary & James Burroughs 6-22-1875 (Scott)
  Minnie & Henry Pinkney col? 4-16-1881 (Rev. Sylvanus Townshend)
  Oliver & Selesta Carroll col? (Langford) 5-11-1869
  Richard & Emma Beckett 12-18-1878
  Robert & Hannah Clarke 10-9-1869 (Mahr)
  Rose Ann & George A. Boothe 1-17-1866
  Sallie & Samuel Smith 4-17-1876 (Price)
  Samuel & Mary A. Chase col? 12-1-1865
  Samuel & Nancy Johnson 1-3-1874 (Cotton)
  Sarah & Moses Snowden col? 5-11-1869 (Thompson)
  Sarah & Frederick Bond 12-6-1871
  Sarah S. & Joseph N. Baden 11-28-1826
  Sidney & Charles E. Courts 1-27-1838
  Susan Ann & James Henry Reid Age 17, black - housekeeper lic. 12-22-1865
    m 12-24-1865 (Marbury)
  Susanna A. & John F. Bowie 4-23-1784
  Susannah G. & Henderson S. Boteler 11-7-1799
  William & Eleanor Ann Belt 6-1-1870 (McDonald)
  William M. & Mary A. Miller 12-29-1885 (Rev. Jno. R. Henry)
HAWKS, Francis T. & Hannah G. Manley 1-5-1866 (Call)
  John Henry & Virginia Sewall Black, farmhand, age 25. lic. 8-3-1866
    m. 8-4-1866 at St. Thomas parsonage by Sam? R. Gordon
  also listed as Hawkins
HAY, Robert & Anna Magruder 3-9-1791
HAYDEN, Susan & Richard Alright 1-29-1822
  William J. & Elizabeth L. A. Osbourn 10-12-1854
HAYE, William & Ruth Hawkins Elder 1-6-1798
HAYES, Charles & Lucretia Coates 11-20-1845
  Ellen Frances & Richard L. Brady 4-15-1868 (Chesly)
  Mary Elizabeth & Enos F. Pumphrey 3-21-1872
  Mima & Patrick Carroll 12-31-1794
  Pamelia & George Beall 10-20-1813
  Rebecca & John S. Lynch 10-16-1818
  Sarah & Aquila Harden 12-22-1817
  Sarah & Dennis Sweeney Jr. 3-24-1845
  Thomas & Rebecca Padget 9-9-1784
  Thomas & Mary Newman 12-27-1842
  Vallinda & Nathaniel Lowe 9-9-1797

HAYES, William & Rachel Alexander 9-5-1795
HAYMAN, Henry & Rebecca Ernis of A.A. County colᵈ 12-13-1880 (Rev. Gordon)
HAYS, Amelia & Elisha B. Fergusson 10-28-1858
  Ann Elizabeth & Bushrod W. Farr 1-11-1858
  Eleanor & John Kidwell 1-5-1785
  Elizabeth & Thomas Simpson 8-14-1862
  Fielder & Sarah Gray 5-4-1870 (Martin)
  Thomas & Martha A. Gray 12-10-1862
HAYSE, Catherine & Daniel James 11-7-1777
HAYWARD, William & Sarah Thomas 5-27-1806
HAZARD, Henry & Clariet Jones 5-2-1818
  Mary & Henry Rocket 8-17-1816
HAZE, Maria S. & Joseph William Gates 12-28-1868 (Kershaw)
HAZLE, Richard T. & Alethea Ann Ridgway 12-23-1825
  Tilghman & Nancy Ridgway 4-1-1822
HAZZARD, John & Caroline Watson 12-24-1850
  Rebecca & Jnᵒ Moreland 1-12-1849
HEALLEY, Caroline & Francis Llewellyn Butler 12-13-1869 (Lenaghan)
HEATH, John & Elizabeth D. Deakins 3-20-1819
HEBBURN, Nancy & James Woodard colᵈ 5-13-1869 (Begue)
HEBORN, Alice & Samuel Snowden 1-2-1869 (Stanley)
HEDGE, Fannie & William Henry Brace colᵈ 8-8-1868
HEET, Lewis & Lizzie Ford 4-3-1869 (Gordon)
HEFFNER, William Henry & Helen May Linthecum 5-16-1885 (Rev. Strickland)
HEFLEBOWER, Caroline & Solomon G. Chaney 11-21-1860
HEIGHTMAN, Paul & Mary Brown 9-3-1875 (Green)
HEINSOOTH, Henry & Genevieve Overman 10-23-1873 (Stanley)
HEISHELL, Peter & Hester Hill 11-11-1844
HEISKELL, Alexander St.C. & Susan Ann Gwynn 10-11-1841
HEISKILL, Emma L. & Henry Lee Heiskill 12-2-1878 (Hooman)
HELLEN, Dorcus & George Beall 1?-24-1807
  Jane & James Moran 5-6-1780
  Susannah & Thomas Watt 12-5-1791
HELSELL, Catharine & Jacob Husther 3-2-1793
HEMSLEY, William W. & Margaret H. Bowie 8-23-1869 (Stanley)
HENAULT, George M. & Anne B. Brooks 8-20-1874 (Pickney)
HENDERSON, Arianna & Patrick Sim 8-28-1787
  Mary M. & John H. Dockett 12-9-1878 (Hooman)
HENDLE, Albion & Louisa J. Jenkins 8-30-1847
HENNESS, Margᵗ & William Mockbee Junʳ 12-24-1780
HENNIS, Ann & John Olbee 10-21-1786
  Rebecca & John Wight 4-15-1796
HENRY, Abraham & Cecelia Johnson 12-11-1869 (Maher)
  Benjamin & Mary Ann Lanham 12-7-1835
  Isaac & Mary Jane Fletcher 5-29-1868 (Begue)
  John & Linny Taylor 4-18-1797
  Lemuel H. & Sophy R. Davis 1-12-1861
  Lucy & William Tucker 12-18-1839
  Mary & William Lowe 4-19-1783
  Mary Ellen & Stephen Decatur Lanham 1-25-1856
  Mordicai & Ann Lanham 1-15-1805   HENRY, Richard &
  R. E. & John A. Brady 11-20-1884 (Rev. Mr. Stanley)   Louisa Johnson
  Richard N. & Martha J. Johnson 4-18-1882   12-25-1867
  Sarah & Elias Lowe 8-9-1785
  Willie Ann & Isaac W. Wood 6-24-1868 (Beque)

HENSON, Alethea & Nathaniel Simms col.^d 5-24-1878 (Gordon)
Alexander & Isabel Belt 2-28-1877 (Walker)
Alfred & Margaret Hawkins col^d 2-9-1881 (Rev. Dr. Gordon)
Alice V. & William H. Brown 2-11-1886 (Rev. Father Cunane)
Edward & Lottie Hawkins 5-22-1872 (Gordon)
Elizabeth & Pinkney Brown col^d 10-10-1881 (Rev. Mr. Wilson)
Henry & Ann Rebecca Coats 11-12-1868 (Langford)
James & Ann Rozer 5-14-1873 (Kershaw)
Jenny & Wm. H. Boothe 12-6-1875
Jeremiah & Chloe Newton 11-21-1870 (Maher)
John & Emma Barnes 10-9-1879
Joseph & Jane Grinfield 10-16-1875 (Maybury)
Joseph & Sallie Johnson 10-5-1883 (Rev. Mr. Brown)
Loveless & Elizth E. Beall 11-26-1850
Maria & George Allen 1-3-1874 (Townshend)
Mary & Henry Wiseman 3-25-1869
Mary & Robert Allen 9-6-1873 (Dwyer)
Robert & Josephine West 12-23-1874 (Mayberry)
Samuel & Arabella Hall 12-9-1873
HENWOOD, Amelia &Richard Smith 12-27-1834
HEPBURN, Henrietta Maria & Joseph Walker Jun'r 12-7-1779
James & Matilda Parker 6-7-1867 (Beque)
Maria (Butler) & Thomas M. Turner 1-6-1879
Maria & Whittington......colored, both of A. A. Co. 11-26-1880
Mary & Samuel Judson Coolidge 2-20-1798
Samuel & Jemima Brant 7-7-1871 (Stanley)
HERBERT, Andrew & Jane Barrick both col^d 4-28-1865
Ann Caroline & Henry Fairfax 10-8-1827
Dennis & Harriet Club 2-6-1823
Ella & William M. Harrison 11-29-1880
Emma & Revd William Bryant 11-10-1837
George L. & S. Elizabeth Hance 6-5-1860
Jerre & Mary Allen 5-8-1876 (Green)
John Carlyle & Mary Snowden 3-6-1805
Lizzie & Henry Sprigg col^d 12-24-1868 (Edelen)
Mary Virginia & Thomas T. Hunter lic. 4-28-1836, m. 5-2-1836
Rachel & Jerry Hall 8-7-1872 (McDonald)
HENRY, Richard & Louisa Johnson (Langford) 12-25-1867
HERBERT, Sarah & Daniel Barbour 11-6-1876 (Green)
Sarah C. & Archibald B. Fairfax 11-10-1832
Thomas & Mary Helen Sprigg 2-9-1870 (McDonald)
HERD, William & Nettie Lawson 11-30-1883 (Father Cunnanne)
HEREFORD, Dr. Jno B. & Mary L. West 9-12-1848
HERMANCE, Mary Sprigg & John Mackall Gantt 12-18-1798
HERN, James & Elizabeth Harvey 4-7-1798
HERTERLY, Savannah & James E. Dorsey 4-15-1884 (Rev. Mr. Brashaw)
HETCHERSON, Margaret & Samuel R. Stallings 6-13-1842
HEULT, Catherine & Edward Elsner 2-24-1855
HEWETT, Benjamin & Elizabeth Wilson 11-29-1810
HICKEY, Daniel G_k & Eliza Sandford 8-31-1824
Mary E. & Fred. A. Lehmann 11-12-1878
HICKMAN, John & Viana Boston 11-3-1798
Joseph & Margaret Jenkins 9-18-1780
HICKS, Bennett C. & Alice L. Grady 5-10-1878
Nancy & Frank Hawkins 9-30-1871 (Marbury)

HIDE, George & Sarah Webster 12-16-1783
HIGDON, James & Ann Rawlings 8-18-1779
  James & Anne Linton 1-28-1797
  John & Mary E. Athey 11-20-1841
  John S. & Ann E. Beall 12-12-1806
  Joshua & Mary Roberts 10-11-1783
  Lydia & William Gitting 9-21-1793
  Mary & Timothy Mayhew 3-17-1787
  Mary Ann & John Long 4-27-1798
  Nancy & John Jenkins 12-14-1804
  Phebe Eleanor & John B. Lambert 12-17-1793
  Susan & John Ward 8-24-1820
  Thomas & Ann Alby 6-10-1797
HIGGINS, Ann & Hezekiah Hamilton 11-1-1794
  Eleanor & Benjamin Duvall 7-4-1787
  John & Elizabeth Baldwin 3-31-1814
  John & Mary Compton 5-16-1853
  Louisa V. & James H. Beck 5-14-1855
  Margaret E. & Thomas S. Ferrall 6-16-1841
  Richard & Eleanor Macgill 3-21-1783
  Richard & Mary Clarke 12-17-1806
  Samuel & Tabitha Willett 12-13-1799
  Sarah & John Soper 1-5-1801
  Thomas & Smithy Murphy 5-13-1873
  William & Mary Hurley 9-15-1804
HILL, Alexander P. & Mary E Childer 4-26-1845
  Ann & Isaac Magruder 4-3-1802
  Ann & Thomas Padgett 1-5-1822
  Anna & David Dock 3-22-1877
  Charles & Margaret Smith 2-5-1816
  Charles & Susanna Clagett 6-29-1818
  Charles & Ann E. Hall 10-3-1836
  Charles C. & Emily R. Snowden 4-26-1845
  Clarence M. & Anna E. Greenwell 10-20-1875 (Chaney)
  Clement B. & Anne Maria Berry 11-22-1830
  Eliza & Nathaniel Gray 10-10-1877
  Elizabeth & Joseph Mudd 6-2-1787
  Elizabeth M. & Saml S. Hamilton 6-8-1819
  Emily R. & Gustavia M. Finnotti 6-16-1851
  Helen M. & Buchanan Beall 9-27-1875 (Kershaw)
  Henrietta J. & William L. Kennedy 4-29-1824
  Henrietta J. & Francis J. Middleton 11-23-1857
  Henry Junr. & Hetta Brooke 4-23-1781
  Henry V. & Maria Hamilton 4-22-1816
  Hester & Peter Heishell 11-11-1844
  Ida M. & Francis M. Bowie 1-14-1879 (Hooman)
  James & Phoebe Garner 11-26-1819
  John O. & Marie Hurtt 5-17-1872
  John R. & Sallie Gardner 6-28-1859
  Joseph B. & Mary Hill 11-3-1874 (O'Dwyer)
  Laura C. & Samuel Brooke 11-4-1858
  Louis Albert & Nancy Diggs 2-6-1885
  Margaret Ann & Levin Gardiner 8-12-1837
  Margaret E. & Isaac G. Magruder 10-23-1837
  Martha Eleanor & Alfred A. Eaton 12-31-1844

HILL, Mary & Francis Magruder Hall 10-20-1795
  Mary & Theodore Kidwell 1-12-1799
  Mary & Francis Darnall 4-9-1818
  Mary & Joseph B. Hill 11-3-1874 (O'Dwyer)
  Mary A. & Dionysius Sheriff 4-8-1857
  Nary A. R. & John K. Summers 10-28-1878 (Hooman)
  Mary Ann & James Brooke 10-24-1814
  Mary Ann & John B. Magruder 1-13-1834
  Mary L. & Henderson W. Magruder 1-22-1883 (Rev. Mr. Brashaw)
  Nannie R. & Charles W. Geddes 6-29-1869
  Norman F. & Carrie E. Roberts 9-28-1869 (Maguire)
  Philip W. & Sophia Magruder 4-25-1826
  Richard & Margery Wilson 6-21-1805
  Rich? S. & Elizabeth S. Hall 4-26-1854
  Sarah E. & Thomas Sprigg Blandford 10-30-1865 (Father Call)
  Sarah M. & Philip R. Edelen 5-30-1845
  Sarah M. & Wesley P. Bradley 2-25-1862
  Sophia E. & Basil T. Duckett col? 1-25-1853
  Susannah & John Grahame 4-7-1808
  Teressa Ann & Ralph Boarman 12-12-1801
  William & Martha Letchworth 12-9-1805
  William & Ann Smith 12-9-1811
  William J. & Henrietta S. Sasscer Age 30, lawyer - m. 10-11-1866
    residence of bride's mother by Sam? R. Gordon, Presbyter of P. E.Ch.
  William W. & Mary T. Magruder 11-25-1844
HILLARD, Ann & John W. Thompson 1-6-1836
HILLEARY, Ann & Samuel Wheeler 12-4-1782
  Ann & Hilleary Wilson 10-31-1814
  Ann & Samuel Magruder 3-30-1803
  Anne & John M. Hilleary 12-19-1840
  Cassandra & Richard Beall Jun. 12-16-1794
  Clement T. & Mary Mullikin 12-29-1804
  Clem? T. of Frederick County & Henrietta B. Milliken of Prince
    George's County 11-30-1818
  Eliz? & William Magruder 2-5-1796
  Elizabeth & James Waring 1-4-1787
  Elizabeth D. & Thomas T. Hurdle 4-22-1839
  Eugenia & Richard K. Osbourn 9-2-1851
  George W. & Harriet C. Gwynn 8-24-1855
  George Washington & Rebecca Magruder 1-10-1826
  H. Clotilda & Benj? H. C. Bowie 11-23-1871 (McDonald)
  Henry & Matilda Magruder 5-21-1832
  John & Verlinda Williams 2-22-1791
  John M. & Anne Hilleary 12-19-1840
  Lewis & Ann Hall 12-31-1816
  Mary & Samuel Magruder 1-11-1791
  Mary Trueman & William M. Bowie 11-29-1814
  Rebecca & Stephen Belt 1-18-1786
  Roberta R. & Doct? Richard J. Scott 11-21-1861
  Sarah & Edward Wheeler 12-21-1785
  Sarah Smith & Benjamin W. Allen 12-2-1817
  Susannah & Bennett Gwinn 2-21-1797
  Thomas & Jane Wheeler 12-6-1809
  Thomas T. & Ann Waring 1-13-1834
  Verlinda & John Wells 4-27-1831

HILLEARY, William & Mary Ann Willett 6-15-1826
HILLIARY, Eleanor & Thomas Woodward 4-18-1788
  George & Sarah Smith 11-29-1781
  Tilghman & Ann Wheeler 1-9-1782
HILLMAN, Andrew & Grace Carter   col. 1-13-1866
HILSEAGLE, Barbara & Alexander Veitch 7-11-1798
HILTON, Susannah & Henry Attchison 2-17-1800
HINES, Christian Matthew & Sarah Stuart Calvert 9-9-1871
  Elizabeth & John Peirce 2-3-1786
HINKEY, John & Nelly Mockeboy 12-20-1820
HINRICHS, Oscar & Mary Stanley 10-7-1868 (Stanley)
HINSON, Emily & John Forbes 4-11-1874
HINTON, Ann & John Miller 12-26-1800
  Benjamin & Margaret Hart 2-17-1798
  Elizabeth & John Cooke 6-25-1801
  Gideon & Priscilla Askey 12-24-1798
  John & Mary Ray 1-1-1795
  Joseph & Elizabeth Cooke 12-22-1796
  Mary & Thomas Wallis 8-22-1812
  Olevia & Chas. S. Middleton 1-6-1851
  Osborn & Margaret Irvin 1-6-1803
  Sarah & John Taylor 2-6-1784
  Sarah & Thomas Eaglen 7-25-1795
  William & Elizabeth Randall 12-22-1798
HODGE, Emily & Frank Dent 5-18-1872 (Trapnell)
  Henry & Lucey Medley 3-27-1884 (Rev. Mr. Walker)
  James & Martha Brashears 1-22-1790
  Jane & Charles Fleet 12-27-1881 (Rev. Mr. Wilson)
  Joana & Holliday Mackall 12-31-1883 (Rev. Mr. Brown)
  Joseph & Catherine Mayhew 1-13-1858
  Lucy & Dennis Osborn 12-16-1784
HODGES, Adeline & Alexander Mandell 3-20-1832
  Ann & James Prather 12-31-1790
  Ann & James Simmons 1-13-1806
  Annie R. of Prince Georges & Charles C. Bohen of Mont. Co. 12-12-1879
    (Rev. Dr. Lewin)
  Benjamin & Susanna Oden 2-6-1787
  Benjamin B. & Mary E. Hodges 6-7-1825
  Benjamin M. & Susannah Tyler 4-18-1797
  Caroline D. & Alexander Mundell 11-8-1823
  Charles Drury & Elizabeth Watkins 2-3-1798
  Cornelia & Revd William Hodges 11-14-1837
  Cornelia & Louis J. Watkins 12-11-1879 (Rev^d Dr. Hodges)
  Eliza & John Randall Jr. 12-20-1814
  Elizabeth & Walter Hodges 12-22-1794
  Elizabeth & John Clayton 4-2-1814
  Ellen & Jacob W. Bird 6-5-1886 (Rev. Wm. C. Butler)
  Ellen O. & Horatio C. Scott 10-5-1826
  Georgina & Hezekiah Dent 5-25-1869 (Father Maher)
  Jane & Joseph Young 5-16-1872
  John & Susan Ogle 6-15-1829
  John of Thomas & Rebecca Berry 1-12-1799
  John W. & Vidie E. Watson 1-1-1883
  Joseph R. & Mary Jackson 2-1-1808
  Lilly D. & James P. Bieys of A. A. Co. 4-15-1881 (Rev. Richard Brown)

HODGES, Maria R. & Tho.ˢ R. Young 4-20-1856
 Mary & Richard G. Hardesty 6-1-1799
 Mary & Horatio Hagan 1-1-1803
 Mary & George W. Craig 2-21-1860
 Mary Ann & Thomas Eversfield 2-11-1822
 Mary E. & Benjamin B. Hodges 6-7-1825
 Mary M. & Richard R. Osbourn 12-8-1846
 Nannie O. & Benjamin L. Bird, Jr. 6-8-1868 (Hodges)
 Sarah & Thomas Belt 7-25-1787
 Thomas & Elizabeth White 10-26-1797
 Thomas Ramsey & Deborah Berry 12-30-1797
 Thomas Ramsey Jr. & Sarah Magruder Clagett 3-14-1805
 Walter & Elizabeth Hodges 12-22-1794
 Rev.ᵈ William & Cornelia Hodges 11-14-1837
HODGKIN, Alexander B. & Mary E. Bourne 10-26-1861
 Amelia & John D. Ward 9-14-1816
 Ann & Thomas Hamilton 4-17-1781
 Elizabeth S. & John Bourne 6-3-1862
 Mary & Walter Skinner 1-10-1791
 Theodore & Mary J. Curcaurd 4-9-1787
 Thomas & Eliza S. Boteler 10-10-1836
HODGKINS, Barbara & John Earle 6-9-1798
HODRICK, Susanna A. & James H. Boyd 12-9-1843
HODSKINSON, Agness & Magruder Selby 2-11-1788
HOE, Abraham Barnes & Sarah Norwood Johnson 8-19-1809
HOGAN, Anne & Frederick Flemmin 12-18-1798
 Henrietta & Robert Cooke 7-27-1790
HOGUE, Sallie M. & James H. Edwards 8-15-1882 (Rev. Wm. L. Hyland)
HOKER, Jane W. & William T. Curtis 12-27-1884
HOLLAND, Abram & Martha Robinson 11-28-1874 (Billopp)
 Ann Maria & John Henry Skinner 6-5-1872
 Annie & William Briscoe 7-31-1878 (Hooman)
 Benjamin & Susan Thomas 8-11-1880 (Stanley)
 Emily & Trueman Harrison 8-4-1877
 Frank & Anna Queen 12-23-1871 (Wheeler)
 Henry & Julia Plummer 6-2-1874 (Welch)
 Henson & Mary Pinkney 5-3-1877 (Carroll)
 J. K. & Elizabeth Shanan 5-30-1868 (Langford)
 Jeremiah & Julia Ford 12-24-1875 (Tennent)
 Kitty & James Pryor 9-4-1885
 Lydia & Thomas Williams col.ᵈ 5-18-1882 (Rev. Mr. Stanley)
 Mary & Isaac Scott 9-25-1883 (Rev. Frank Wills)
 Mary E. & Daniel Barker of Wash.ⁿ City 8-28-1868
 Robert & Mary Ann Johnson col.ᵈ 12-27-1880
 Susanah & William King 10-22-1796
 Teresa & William Giles 9-5-1872 (McDonald)
HOLLEY, Thomas & Amey Downes 1-29-1800
HOLLIDAY, Mary & Marcus S. Waring 1-9-1794
 Wm. & Ann Lovelace 2-12-1822
HOLLINBERGER, Lewis & Henrietta J. Swann 1-14-1858
HOLLING, Jerry S. & Sarah Smith colored 10-22-1880
HOLLINS, Edward & Mary E. Brown 12-20-1877 (Homan)
HOLLY, Matilda & Noble Butler col.ᵈ 7-26-1852
 Penelope & William Peacock 6-28-1792
 William & Mary Ellen Boteler 1-17-1853

HOLLYDAY, Ann & Walter B. Cox 11-19-1778
  Clement & Hedwick Priggs 12-18-1784
  Clement & Martha Maria Hall Stone 12-21-1816
  Elizabeth West & Dr. Gilbert D. Wilkinson 12-18-1871 (Gordon)
  John & Rosanna Berry 5-15-1869 (Langford)
  Margarett Terrett & Thomas Truman Somerville 11-3-1807
  Urban & Amelia Skinner 6-2-1834
HOLMES, Ruffian & Margaret Dent 9-21-1866
HOLTZMAN, William F. & Mary M. Patten 3-31-1854
HOOD, Amy Ann Frances & Franklin F. Carrick 9-15-1876
  Leatha & Jacob Jeanes 4-24-1819
  Mary J. C. & Robert C. Crist 9-15-1876 (Major)
HOOE (Hove?), Peter H. & Augusta Magruder 4-3-1856
HOOE, Rice W. & Maly C. Daingerfield 8-2-1873
HOOFMAN, John & Mary Scott 4-24-1781
HOOGE, Susan & Edward Lansdale 8-26-1876 (Green)
HOOK, Mary & Benjamin Cranford 11-1-1871 (Skinner)   HOOK, Ann Eliza &
  May & Thomas Ray 1-21-1817   M. J. Kaldenback
  Richard H. & Elizabeth Ann Wells 6-2-1868 (Gordon)   8-8-1855
  Samuel P. & Ann E. Dooley 12-8-1880
  William & Caroline Swaine 9-7-1832
HOOKER, Priscilla & George Cole 5-6-1778
HOOPER, Anne & John Lang 12-17-1779
  John & Elizabeth Dove 6-6-1779
  John & Mary Ann Dove 2-20-1784
  John & Elizabeth Brown 7-7-1788
  Martha & Jonathan Bedder 5-25-1778
  Samuel & Ann Ryon 12-31-1785
  Sarah & Jesse White 12-15-1803
  Thomas & Elizabeth Bedder 8-18-1784
  William & Milley Beddow 12-19-1805
HOOPES, Alpheus C. & Julia A. Allen 2-8-1866 Age 24 of Washington, D. C.
     Artist, m. at Walter A. Allen's place 2-15-1866 Geo. M. Berry, Min.
HOOVERN, David & Catherine Miller 10-8-1819
HOPKINS, Aloysius & Sarah Eugenia Suit 1-26-1875
  Ann & Richard Tarman 5-30-1785
  Ann & James Johnson 2-2-1815
  Benjamin & Ursula M. Beckett 12-23-1826
  C. E. & W. W' Sisson 1-19-1885 (Fr. Cotton)
  Eleanor & John Crooke 1-13-1810
  Elizabeth & Thomas Dove 12-18-1797
  Elizabeth & Thomas Griffin 1-2-1804
  Elizabeth & William Hubbard 12-27-1808
  Elizabeth & John Fairall 12-13-1822
  Elizabeth & Walker Jones 2-26-1838
  Francis & Mary Sansbury 1-29-1786
  Frederick E. & Elizabeth King 3-12-1863
  Joseph D. & Fannie E. Suit 9-26-1871 (Dr. Cotton)
  Joseph T. & Joanna Betts 10-18-1875
  Mary & Rezin Beckwith 3-31-1798
  Mary & Alexander Steel 3-6-1800
  Mary Ann & Philip B. Duvall 2-26-1838
  Mary E. & Benjamin Snell black 3-12-1866 Age 20
  Mary J. & Albert H. Bevan 1-31-1873 (Cotton)
  Philip & Margaret Fowler 6-6-1794

HOPKINS, Philip & Susanna Ryon 8-22-1798
  Philip & Rebecca Weeden 11-3-1807
  Philip & Elizabeth Clark 1-9-1830
  Rachel & Levi Alley 12-30-1807
  Rich^d & Catherine R. E. Beall 12-20-1849
  Sarah Ann & Alfred Coale 2-2-1831
  Susan L. & Wm. H. Mangum 7-14-1864
  William & Eveline Cole 1-20-1836
  William A. & Elizabeth L. Robey 4-3-1855
HOPPER, Deborah & John Cooke 12-22-1802
  Lewis & Eleanor Clarke 2-7-1804
HORRELL, Thomas & Ann Somerville 9-20-1817
HORTON, Annie Josephine & James E. Cawood 11-27-1866 (Smith)
HOSKIN, Edward & Marg^t Jane Magruder 7-20-1868
HOSKINSON, Elisha & Henrietta Brashears 7-21-1777
HOUCHENS, Thomas M. & Elizth M. Miller 7-6-1869 (Lenaghan)
HOUSE, Lidia Ann & Thomas Elliott 2-4-1851
HOUSTON, Susan & James Hamilton Saville 6-6-1871
  Thomas & Mary E. Carrick 2-9-1861
HOWARD, Action & Edward Ford 6-17-1856
  Benjamin & Margaret Williams 9-3-1873 (Dwyer)
  Catherine & William Raferdy 12-1-1824
  Daniel & Rebecca Hampton 9-14-1878 (Carroll)
  Henry & Cecelia Riggs 10-2-1867
  Isaac & Ann Hall 4-13-1838
  James & Mary Fletcher (Coll.) 1-20-1866
  John & Martha Linton 9-16-1791
  John G. & Ann C. Rogers 4-16-1827
  Joseph & Elizabeth Susanna Bowie 3-31-1809
  Joseph & Sarah Ellen Clagett 10-19-1841
  Luke & Harriot Brooke 8-21-1824
  Nicholas & Emily Lewis Age 22-black, Laborer m. St. Thomas Church
    Samuel R. Gordon, Min. Presby. Ch.
  Rachel & Lewis Wood 7-17-1873 (O'Dwyer)
  Rebecca & John Walker 12-23-1831
  Rebeccah & William Adams 7-12-1796
  Sarah Jane & Edward Garner 3-16-1867 (Greenleaf)
  Thomas & Ann Mayhew 4-16-1794
  William & Priscille Coberth 6-12-1821
HOWDEN, William & Teresa Murray 6-27-1833
HOWE, Charlotte & James Johnson 5-3-1880 (Rev. Daniel Aquila)
  Ignatius & Rachel Willett 11-27-1798
  Stanislaus & Elizabeth Willett 12-6-1797
HOWEL, Henry & Ruth Magruder 6-23-1842
HOWELL, Cerina & George Johnson col^d 9-7-1867 (Stanley)
  Elizabeth & William H. Perveil 12-30-1856
  George H. & Virginia T. Magruder 3-27-1852
  James & Eliza Brown 7-30-1834
  James S. & Leticia Adams 12-12-1832
  Jane R. & Shadrach Beall 2-6-1841
  Joseph H. & Josephine V. Martin 4-7-1874
  Martha & Jesse Mangun 12-20-1841
  William F. & Elizabeth Nicholls 1-7-1839
HOWERTON, Sarah & John Owens 3-8-1780
HOWES, Elisha & Elizabeth Armiger 2-18-1834

HOWES, MacCeeny & Ann Maria Crooke 11-13-1854
  Mary & Richard Richards 5-13-1802
  Mary & Benjamin Cooley 12-17-1816
HOWSE, Charles & Tamar Gibbons 12-7-1779
  Elizabeth & George L. Greenwell 5-11-1867 (Hill)
  Henry & Sarah Tarman 12-30-1805
  Zach^a & Elizabeth Busey 11-3-1779
HOWSLEY, Henry & Martha Bayne 4-14-1783
HOXTON, Eliza & John T. Magruder 1-27-1881
  Mary & William Tolson 12-16-1823
  Mary Isabella & Charles S. Middleton 9-27-1859
  Stanislaus & Mary Semms 1-17-1799
HOY, Caroline & William Rabit 11-26-1841
HOYE, Angeline & Wilkinson Brashears 12-17-1834
  Cephas & Sarah Collings 12-27-1784
  Cephus & Elizabeth Ryon 9-9-1786
  John G. & Mary Griffen 11-15-1817
  Martha & George Booth 10-14-1805
  Mary & James H. H. Swaine 5-22-1826
  Mary & James W. Atkerson 1-12-1847
  Paul & Eleanor Rutha Mattingly 12-23-1811
  Thomas & Agnes Scott 4-22-1786
HOYLE, William S. & Susan Ann Rawlings 10-11-1848
HUBBARD, William & Elizabeth Hopkins 12-27-1808
HUGHES, Archibald & Elizabeth Reston 2-1-1811
  Elizth & Joseph Cloud 11-7-1826
  Jane & William Simms 11-24-1787
  Mary & Nathaniel Hall 12-23-1777
  Richard & Jemima Leeke 1-17-1805
  Samuel & Harriet Simpson 12-23-1885 (Rev. F. G. Hall)
  Sarah & Thomas Abbigell 2-4-1788
  William & Elizabeth Wynn 5-7-1791
  William L. & Clara B. McElfresh 3-28-1879
HUGHS, George & Eleanor Hardey 10-26-1797
HUICK, Leonard & Susan M. Scott 11-23-1857
HULL, Margaret & Joshua Farr 11-8-1800
  Samuel C. & Francis Mahew 7-5-1779
HUMBERSTONE, Ann & Edward Goddard 1-12-1805
HUMPHREYS, Alice & B. Frank Dove 12-28-1874 (Chaney)
  Ann & Allen Taylor 6-10-1799
  Joshua & Mary Smith 9-4-1838
  Mary & James Scott 2-4-1797
  Richard & Rebeccah Jones 2-1-1804
  Richard L. & Cordelia W. Hardey 9-6-1815
  Richd L. & Chloe Eleanor Tippett 1-6-1818
HUMPHRIES, Joshua & Sarah J. Dove 2-17-1873
  George & Cecelia Campbell 9-22-1868
  Thos & Marg^t Burch 11-22-1781
HUMPHRY, Pope & Eleanor Thompson 11-17-1783
  Sarah Ann & John Ranter 12-9-1778
HUNNICUTT, Maggie & German B. Gill 4-15-1868 (Marbury)
HUNT, Charles W. & Eliza E. Mills 12-8-1868 (Smith)
  James & Unie Loveless 1-12-1793
  Jas. H. & Elizabeth H. Garner 2-16-1864
  Jeremiah & Louisa Digges 6-30-1871 (McDonald)

HUNT, John & Priscilla Brown 1-10-1789
  Joseph & Mary Wilson 12-26-1812
  Martha & James Watson 3-12-1833
  Martha A. & Erasmus Bryan 6-11-1855
  William Thomas & Eleanor Grimes 2-25-1813
HUNTER, Colmore & Henny Hatton 12-2-1807
  Elizabeth & Allen Lamar 12-23-1811
  Eveline & James R. Edelen 10-4-1872 (Dwyer)
  George H. & Catharine A. Edelen 9-18-1843
  George H. & Elizabeth Edelen 7-18-1857
  Hester Bell & John L. Waring 5-21-1878 (Hooman)
  Ignatius & Sarah Smith 5-11-1822
  Janet & Francis Sheid 5-10-1831
  John & Elizabeth Alice Beasley 5-22-1867 (Martin)
  Joseph & Mary Edelen 1-13-1844
  Julia Herbert & Franklin Harwood 6-25-1861
  Margaret & John Pierce 12-10-1808
  Mary E. & John J. Lambert 9-11-1832
  Mary E. & Wm. B. Bayne 6-1-1844
  Mary R. & Jesse R. Edelen 9-9-1871 (McDonald)
  Richᵈ & Rachel Whiten 1-19-1782
  Robert W. Jr. & Grace B. Bayne 6-28-1852
  Sarah H. & Charles Demar 7-11-1828
  Thomas T. & Mary Virginia Herbert lic. 4-28-1836 m. 5-2-1836
HUNTT, Ada T. & Philip E. Sasscer 10-25-1882 (Rev. Mr. LaRoche)
  Ann & William Gray 12-26-1811
  Ann & Charles L. Steel 5-23-1814
  Basil & Lethea Ann Clagett 10-21-1871
  Ella H. & James Berry 5-5-1884 (Rev. Mr. LaRoche)
  J. Henry & Alice K. Sansbury 12-30-1884
  John L. & Susanna C. Gregory 2-9-1841
  Judson W. & Susan Purdey 4-11-1834
HURDEY, Thomas & Eliza Swaim 5-12-1843
HURDLE, Emma & Jno. W. Shaw 12-29-1863
  Lucretia & Barnaba Parsons 6-8-1799
  Mary & William Durity 1-13-1798
  Thomas T. & Elizabeth D. Hilleary 4-22-1839
HURLEY, Anna & Henry Piles 4-5-1849
  Arnold & Eleanor Neale 4-2-1803
  Barsheba & John Darnall 12-11-1782
  Basil & Mary Soper 2-3-1789
  Cornelius & Linny Wade 4-4-1795
  Daniel & Amelia Bayne 12-21-1784
  Daniel & Mary Jones 9-8-1797
  Jane & Sylvester Newman 1-20-1851
  John & Sarah Evans 12-19-1787
  Lawson & Elizᵗʰ Butler 10-30-1848
  Mary & Philip Evans 1-9-1786
  Mary & William Higgins 9-15-1804
  Mary & John Varnall Anderson 10-21-1807
  Mary & John Harvey 2-4-1815
  Rhoda & Samuel Taylor 4-10-1793
  Salem & Amma Summers 12-8-1784
  Sarah & Gerrard Darnall 1-31-1781

HURLEY, Sarah & Paul Summers 10-3-1801
  Sarah Ann & Basil Lee 3-6-1817
  William & Mary Evans 8-12-1778
  William & Rebecca Soaper 12-21-1790
  William & Sarah Soper 8-12-1795
  William & Julia Ann Boteler 12-30-1850
HURRY, Philis & Peter Sprigg 12-31-1819
HURTT, Doct. Edgar B. & Maria E. Young 10-14-1854
  Dr. Edgar D. & Harriet Ophelia Edelen 1-24-1874 (Welsh)
  Dr. Edwd & Mary M. Young 4-30-1849
  Marie & John O. Hill 5-17-1872
HUSTEN, William & Elizabeth Garrett 11-18-1797
HUSTHER, Jacob & Catharine Helsell 3-2-1793
HUTCHERSON, Alexander & Sarah Ann Caton 4-21-1840
HUTCHESON, Ann & John Littleford 5-20-1802
HUTCHINS, Frances W. & Elizabeth C. Maddox 4-29-1871
  Ignatius & Rebecca Batzel 12-20-1844
HUTCHINSON, Ann & Absalom Cater 1-7-1807
  Barbara A. & Aquila H. Wilson 11-22-1853
  Caroline & Daniel T. Redd lic. 12-26-1866, m. 12-29-1866 Age 18 (Kershaw)
  Elizabeth & Thomas Conner 2-13-1781
  Geo. & Rachel Lowe 11-13-1781
  George O. & Margaret A. M. Mullikin 9-2-1868
  John B. & Susannah Spalding 12-11-1821
  Mary & Benedict Swain 12-28-1807
  Mary & Addison Littleford 5-18-1869 (Kershaw)
  Mary Ann & George Wood 1-20-1835
  Nathan & Tracy Kidwell 6-2-1777
  Samuel & Ann Brown 6-3-1786
  Sopha R. & Jno. T. Mulliken 12-22-1863
  Theodore & Mary Kidwell 1-29-1818
  William & Christian Willett 4-18-1780
HUTCHISON, James & Sarah Ridgeway 9-5-1872 (Kershaw)
  John Thomas & Susannah Tenley 9-15-1868 (Kershaw)
HUTTON, Anna & James Green 5-24-1866 Age 18, colored, servant
HYATT, Aquila D. & Mrs. Susan Meekes 10-17-1818
  Christopher & Sarah Clarke 9-3-1793
  Christopher C. & Catherine Culver 2-25-1824
  Christopher C. & Frances R. Perkins 10-12-1846
  Eleanor & Addison Conaway 1-4-1804
  Elizabeth & William Farrall ?-26-1783
  Chris^r & Lucy Peach 9-10-1777
  Lucretia & Westley Hyatt 12-19-1828
  Mary & Marsham Duvall 8-5-1801
  Mary & Green Brashears 8-20-1806
  Mary Ellen & Reuben Middleton 7-22-1843
  Mary L. & Dr. Ch^s A. Wells 5-11-1863
  Sarah E. & Archibald P. Riddle 4-20-1863
  Westley & Lucretia Hyatt 12-19-1828
  Wm. Wesley & Sarah Elizabeth Wall 6-10-1857
HYDE, Ann & Benjamin Garner 2-8-1793
  Catharine & R^d L. Hyde 2-8-1864
  George W. & Henrietta Webster 1-27-1823
  Henny & Jesse Garner 2-14-1810
  John & Emma Garner 12-22-1868 (Smith)

HYDE, Letty & Richard Waters 3-10-1810
    Marianna & George Washington Holliday Devan 12-31-1862
    Mary Ann & William Smith 12-29-1842
    Mary E. & Alexander A. Greer 2-22-1842
    Mary Jane & M. J. Kaldenbach 4-21-1865
    Matilda & William Greer 5-27-1814
    Priscilla & Thomas Lawson 2-26-1791
    Rebecca & John Thomas Devon 3-17-1857
    Richard A. & Elizabeth A. Downing 7-2-1834
    Richard A. & Eliza M. Rawlings 10-10-1853
    R^d L. & Catharine Hyde 2-8-1864
    Sarah & Thomas Mason 7-21-1787
    Sarah A. & Jno. Davis 11-1-1841
    Thomas & Mary Gates 12-16-1833
    Thomas & Eliza King 10-7-1875 (McNeir)
    William T. & Theresa C. Kaldenback 2-27-1850
HYLAND, Henry A. & Fannie B. Grimes 9-15-1885 (Rev. Mr. Jyland)
HYSLOP, William Irving & Margaret DeHaas Pierson 12-29-1873 (Rev. Williams)

IGLEHART, John & Harriot Beall 2-11-1807
    Wm. & Susanna Soper 3-17-1781
IGLEHEART, Elizabeth & Abraham Boyd 1-23-1800
    Jemima & William Boyd 12-29-1802
    Levi & Eleanor Taylor 12-19-1808
    Susannah & Jacob Wheeler 6-2-1787
IJAMS, Isaac & Elizabeth Williams 8-4-1795
IMES, Emily & Andrew Butler 7-14-1877 (Wheeler)
IRELAND, James & Susannah Fowler 12-22-1806
    Sarah & Samuel Wood 8-18-1884
IRVIN, Margaret & Osborn Hinton 1-6-1803
IRWIN, John & Eleanor Stonestreet 6-2-1784
ISAAC, Ann & William Jenkins 12-18-1815
    Autridge & Samuel T. Belt 2-20-1832
    Caroline M. & Joseph P. Elson 1-30-1795
    Hannah & Richard Brice 11-22-1781
    Hannah & Barton Duvall 11-26-1811
    Joseph & Mary C. Williams ?-26-1821
    Katie & John L. Thompson 12-5-1877 (Still)
    Mary & John Peach 11-14-1805
    Miranda & Barton Duvall 12-23-1822
    Rachel & Samuel Farr 10-17-1795
    Rachel & John Fowler 12-16-1813
    Richard & Elizabeth Ann Riddle 1-23-1815
    Richard W. & Catherine Ann Turner 12-12-1848
    Sarah & John Ray 3-24-1787
    Sarah & John Bassford 6-2-1826
    Willy & Mordica Jacob 1-4-1821
ISAACS, John E. & Ann M. Whittington of A. A. County 1-10-1881 (Rev.Chaney)
    Martha Ann & Tilghman Crawford 4-1-1822
    Mary A. & Charles C. Brown 7-15-1867 (Stanley)
    Mary E. & Tilghman Crawford 4-14-1857
ISEMAN, George & Alia Phelps 9-29-1868 (Kershaw)
ISLE of WIGHT & Elizabeth Wilson 3-29-1783
IVES, Mary Jane & Oliver G. Besley 12-2-1864

IVES, W. W. & Elizabeth A. Cooksey 4-23-1862
IVINGTON, Ann & Theodore Glasgow 12-1-1800

JACKSON, Alexander & Margaret McLish 4-30-1784
  Alexander & Jane Sharp 12-16-1872
  Alfred & Mary Pinkney 12-24-1884 (Rev. Mr. Hendricks)
  Ambrose & Lucretia Ann Hagar 10-19-1867 (Call)
  Ann & Nicholas Hager 7-20-1872 (McDonald)
  Annie H. & John E. Gibson 1-4-1869 (Harper)
  Austin & Charlotte Matthews 12-26-1866 (Stanley)
  Belle & Gassaway Tolson 2-15-1879 (Carroll)
  Camilla & Clement Brown col^d 8-5-1869 (Maher)
  Cecelia & Andrew Boyd 7-23-1870 (Fr. McDonald)
  Charity & Daniel Jackson 5-16-1872
  Charles & Charity Brookes 11-15-1879 (Wills)
  Clarissa & Allen Spencer col^d 4-18-1881 (Rev. Frank Mills)
  Daniel & Charity Jackson 5-16-1872
  Dennis & Adaline Carrick col^d 12-21-1869 (Leneghan)
  Dorinda & Alfred West col^d 10-19-1867 (Kershaw)
  Edward & Eliza Chapman 1-13-1873 (Dwyer)
  Elizabeth D. & Th: J. Barclay 1-9-1855
  Frank & Ellen Coleman col^d 12-22-1880
  Fred. & Eliza Contee 5-3-1879 (Hooman)
  George & Nancy Butler 10-1-1884 (Rev. C. O. Cook)
  Gracy Ann & Edward Gross 11-13-1883 (Rev. Mr. Walker)
  Harriot & John Morsell 4-17-1811
  Henrietta & Clement Lewis 4-20-1878 (Kershaw)
  Henry & Rebecca Brown col^d 12-7-1878 (Wheeler)
  Hilleary & Sarah Sprigg 1-25-1868 (Fr. Call)
  Israel M. & Mary Ann Duckett 11-28-1817
  James & Frances Clarke col^d 4-19-1867 (Call)
  James & Mary Green 3-29-1875 (Welsh)
  James & Celia Simms 3-30-1877 (Carroll)
  John & Cave Williams 2-1-1788
  John & Eleanor Harvey 12-31-1796
  John & Louisa Clarke 3-13-1877 (Carroll)
  John H. & Cecelia E. Butler 12-29-1865 Age 28, black, laborer m.
    St. Peters Church by Peter Lenaghan, Cath. Priest, Charles County
    1-10-1866
  John H. & Henrietta Wood 12-27-1873 (Walsh)
  John Thomas E. & Margaret Fletcher 9-25-1868 (Begue)
  Josephine & Sandy Dent 5-25-1867 (Fr. Call)
  Juliet & James Almutt 11-12-1811
  Lucy & Lucas Tilghman col^d 7-13-1867 (Call)
  Maria & John Henry Davis col^d 1-29-1870 (Begue)
  Mary & Joseph R. Hodges 2-1-1808
  Mary & Frederick Burroughs col^d 4-18-1870 (Lenaghan)
  Mary A. & James Sedgwick 1-3-1877 (Homan)
  Mary Elizabeth & Thomas Hanson col^d 4-27-1867 (Fr. Call)
  Mary Elizabeth & Thomas Johnson col^d 1-28-1881
  Mary Jane & John Arthur Brown 12-15-1871 (Fr. McD)
  Matilda & Henry Digges 9-12-1867 (Chesley)
  Matilda & Philip Wilson 1-18-1870 (Fr. Cotton)
  Mintie & John Weldon 5-14-1875 (Cotton)

JACKSON, Robert & Nancy Batson 10-6-1871 (O'Dwyer)
  Robert & Lucretia Butler 5-29-1873 (Dent)
  Sarah & John Berry 1-1-1812
  Sarah & Charlie Chittam 5-11-1875 (Cotton)
  Thomas & Fanny Brown 8-17-1866 (Call)
  Tho's & Maria W. Mulliken 6-7-1825
  Th^S D. & Mary Ann Gibson 2-16-1864
  William & Jane Virmier 1-31-1789
  William & Barbara Harvey 8-20-1812
  William & Elizabeth Lowndes 12-17-1813
  William John & Mary Belt 4-29-1788
  William T. & Virginia Naylor 7-13-1869 (Linthicum)
JACOB, Allice & Thomas Jones Waters 7-14-1787
  Mordica & Willy Isaac 1-4-1821
  Richard & Susanna Wells 4-8-1778
JACOBS, John F. & Elizth Fairall 12-26-1825
  Mordecai & Mary Cole 6-6-1789
JAMES, Ann & Henry Sparrow 1-21-1791
  Benjamin & Harriet Blackistone 6-29-1877 (Carroll)
  Daniel & Catherine Hayse 11-7-1777
  James & Mary V. Fletcher 12-24-1872 (Evans)
  Mary E. & Alfred M. Locker 12-28-1859
JAMESON, Benedict & Margaret Boone 3-12-1796
  John M. & Margaret J. Connick 7-21-1863
JAMISON, Oswald & Terrisa Boone 1-8-1805
JANES, Ruth & George F. Finch 3-7-1879 (Gordon)
JANEY, Benjamin & Laura Scott 5-16-1866 Age 22-Black m. Bladensburg
  5-24-1866 by Saml H. Griffith, Minister M. E. Church
JARBOE, Annie V. & Francis E. Mudd 11-13-1865
  George S. & Laura A. Boone 10-29-1885
  John S. & Eliza C. McKee 10-16-1873 (Gordon)
  Sarah Josephine & Alexius Marcerone 1-27-1881 (Rev. Fr. DeWolfe)
  William A. & Elizabeth Ann Fowler 2-23-1841
JARDIN, Rose L. & C. Eugene Parker 10-23-1882 (Fr. Gallan)
JARMAIN, Ann & Geo. Lanham 2-23-1781
JARMAN, Ann & Andrew Brown 4-11-1812
  Elizabeth & Michael Robey 12-21-1790
  William & Milicent St. Clare 3-12-1781
JARVIS, Jonathan & Edelburgodis Mohorney 5-23-1787
JASPER, Henry & Miss Sprigg 12-26-1866 (Chesly)
JEAMS, Susanna & Marsh M. Duvall 6-4-1785
JEANES, Jacob & Leatha Hood 4-24-1819
JEANS, Emily & James Parker 8-1-1868 (Rev. B. Brown)
  Mary & Hugh Crawford 11-28-1780
JEFERSON, Joseph H. & Miss Josephine E. C. Goodrich 6-1-1864
JEFFERIES, Benjamin Berry & Eleanor Berry 10-18-1791
JEFFERSON, Geneva & Charles W. Johnson 6-26-1873 (Fowler)
  Jane & Michael Bowie 11-6-1851
  Thomas & Elizabeth Keader 1-29-1829
  William & Edelina D. Tippett 1-19-1821
JEFFREYS, William & Priscilla Robinson 12-14-1799
JEFFRIES, Mary & John T. Berry 2-10-1836
JENIFER, Daniel of St. Thomas Jenifer & Jane Forbes 7-5-1810
  Georgeanna & Louis Gross 6-13-1874 (Matthews)
  Kitty & Walter Gray 12-26-1874 (Mary Catherine)   (Gordon)

JENINGS, Peter & Jemima Waters 1-15-1794
JENKINS, Alice Virginia & William H. Tayman 4-23-1877
Ally & James Gibbs 12-21-1801
Amelia & John H. Beall 1-11-1836
Ann & Josey Harrison Turton 11-19-1794
Ann & Oswald Boone 4-14-1800
Ann & Benedict Thorn 10-12-1820
Ann Sarah & Martin Dooling 12-16-1822
Anna Eliza & Jno. Robert Walker 4-22-1867 (Lenahan)
Archibald & Elizabeth Webster 6-21-1821
Catherine & Philip W. Mayhew 3-18-1854
Colmore & Eleanor Harvey 12-26-1821
Colmore & Mary Pamelia Taylor 10-20-1828
Daniel A. & Caroline Turner 11-16-1859
Dorcas Maria & Thomas Jones 6-10-1822
Drusilla & Samuel Marshall 7-22-1809
Eleanor & Alexander Reed 6-20-1801
Eleanor & William P. Windsor 5-4-1875 (Billopp)
Elizabeth & Vincent Gray 10-19-1818
Francis & Martha Day 10-28-1780
Frank X. & Laura Talbott 6-24-1871
Geo. H. & Ann Maria Lisby 4-4-1850
George & Harriot Scott 1-29-1818
Isaac & Mary Galwith 6-5-1787
Jackin & Mary Edelen 2-18-1784
James L. & Mary Jane Cath. Sansbury 12-26-1867 (Martin)
Jeremiah & Elizabeth Hawkins 3-19-1884 (Rev. Mr. Brooks)also 4-19-1884
John & Nancy Higdon 12-14-1804
John D. & Mary Jane Ogle 1-3-1870
John Henry & Mary Elizabeth Jones 1-14-1876 (Gordon)
John Thomas & Mary Eliza Kidwell 11-11-1845
Joseph & Margery Wilson 6-25-1780
Jno. Z. & Mary D. Ridgeway 4-13-1843
Leonard & Martha Edelen 2-10-1798
Leonard & Sarah Clarkson 2-12-1814
Louisa J. & Albion Hendle 8-30-1847
Margaret & Joseph Hickman 9-18-1780
Martha & Nelson Ryon 2-1-1834
Mary & Zadock Summers 11-13-1794
Mary & Edward Clements 10-14-1806
Mary Elizabeth & Ignatius Windsor 2-16-1885 (Rev. Dr. Lewin)
Mary Ellen & George W. Mangun 8-12-1876 (Green)
Mary Lee & George S. Tayman 8-16-1884
Massy M. & Thomas Scott 11-23-1795
Priscilla & Wm. Beckwith 9-23-1778
Priscilla & George Hardey 7-13-1786
Priscilla Ann & William F. Masters 2-6-1823
Richard & Mary Walker 5-12-1857
Richard S. & Laura R. Edelin 1-3-1840
Robert Dalton & Mary Ann Lacey 4-12-1808
Sally & Jeremiah Edelen 2-11-1792
Theodore & Julianna M. Snowden 6-16-1835
Thomas & Mildred Atcherson 11-10-1787
Thomas & Ann Bryan 9-4-1832
Trissa & John Smith Swain 4-25-1806

JENKINS, Widman G. & Martha Ann Kidwell 6-19-1843
    William & Ann Isaac 12-18-1815
    Winifred & Nathan Masters 1-8-1794
    W^m & Dorcas Masters 12-31-1778
    Wm. & Eliz^a E. Jones 12-19-1820
    Zadock & Ann Summers 1-12-1798
JENNERS, Abrill & Deborah Young 5-17-1796
JENNIFER, Annie & Pearce Dodson 12-24-1875 (Tennant)
JERMAN, Sarah & Benjamin Robinson 5-13-1794
JESSUP, Jeremiah M. & Margaret Ann V. Sarvoy 12-20-1879 (Rev. A. B. Wilson)
JESSUPS, Mary J. & Augustus Savoy Jr. col^d 4-6-1882
JETT, Louis H. & Margaret Alice Watson 12-28-1870 (Marbury)
JEWELL, Fielder & Jane Ketlin 5-30-1817
JHONS, Fanny A. & Dr. Benjamin Berry 2-17-1857
JOHNS, Margaret & Benjn Skinner 2-4-1828
    Matilda H. & William C. Beard 8-7-1821
    Stephen S. & Elizabeth Skinner 10-9-1805
JOHNSON, Alexander & Milley Dyer 12-24-1798
    Alexander & Mary Ann Knott 1-10-1831
    Alice L. & Clifford F. Sweeney 4-16-1883 (Father Cunnane)
    Alice M. & William B. Wilson 11-29-1871 (Bush)
    Ann & Zephaniah Mitchell 1-29-1810
    Ann & Henry Sansbury 12-6-1822
    Ann M. & Leonard Malonee Age 26 m. 12-26-1866 at Elverton Hall
    Benjamin & Anne Sansbury 2-11-1792
    Benjamin & Ellen Queen 11-18-1874 (O'Dwyer)
    Capitola & William W. Phelps 6-8-1876 (McNeer)
    Caroline M. & William A. Harron 12-30-1856
    Catherine & Alexander J. J. Magruder 2-20-1836
    Catherine & Daniel Gummer 5-5-1875 (Cotton)
    Catherine & Singleton Parker 2-27-1880 (Peters)
    Catharine Ann & Francis Ayers 2-22-1881
    Cecelia & Henry Abraham 12-11-1869 (Maher)
    Charles H. & Martha Chambers 8-21-1861
    Charles W. & Geneva Jefferson 6-26-1873 (Fowler)
    Daniel C. & S. E. Atcherson 12-4-1837
    Delia A. & Horace Spencer 6-4-1883 (Rev. Mr. Wills)
    Drusella & Stephen Fairall 9-12-1806
    Eliza Ann Elizabeth & James Hanson Barton 1-7-1870 (McDonald)
    Eliz^h & Richard Tucker 1-21-1794
    Elizabeth & Valentine Lynn 9-21-1795
    Frank, see Thomas Johnson
    George of Virginia & Sarah M. Lyles 1-8-1841
    George & Cerina Howell col^d 9-7-1867 (Stanley)
    George C. & Margaret Morris 1-8-1866 Age 24, laborer m. 1-9-1866 at
        St. Peters Ch. by Peter Lenaghan, Cath. Priest
    Georgeanna & Juba. Lee 11-2-1867 (Gordon)
    Georgianna & Henson Hawkins 3-30-1885 (Rev. Jno. R. Henry)
    Hannah & Rezin Williams col^d 4-19-1867
    Hanson & Lucy Johnson 10-14-1871 (Evans)
    Harriet Ann & George Washington Abrams col^d both of A. A. Co. 12-23-1881
    Henrietta & Hendley Boswell 12-15-1792
    Henry & Caroline Hanson 6-16-1829
    Henry & Nancy Waters col^d 2-13-1858
    Henry & Emily Addison col^d 6-11-1869 (Kershaw)

JOHNSON, Henry & Emily Greenleaf 7-29-1869 (Lankford)
Hester & Josias Young 7-25-1871 col? (Marbury)
Hezakiah & Ann Maria Nowell 2-27-1826
Hezekiah & Sarah Robey 12-31-1823
James & Catherine West 12-5-1782
James & Elizabeth Carson 9-12-1800
James & Ann Hopkins 2-2-1815
James & Charlotte Howe 5-3-1880 (Rev? Daniel Aquila)
James W. & Margaret A. Briscoe 12-29-1879 (Rev? Mr. Wilson)
Jane & William Jones 12-23-1876 (Walker)
Jane & John White col? 4-5-1882 (Rev. Wm. Van Arnsdale)
John & Susanah Devaughn 2-2-1788
John & Elizabeth Tay lor 1-7-1846   JOHNSON, John Addison &
John Jr. & Mary Tyler 4-29-1823   Emma Carroll 7-24-1874 (Gordon)
John R. & Elsie Butler 8-27-1885 (Rev. Mr. Wills)
Joseph & Mary Winsett 2-2-1799
Lloyd & Matilda Boothe col? 8-9-1867 (Smith)
Lloyd & Julia Neale 12-27-1883 (Rev. Mr. Compton)
Lot & Mary West 9-27-1866 25-mulatto- carriage driver m. 10-4-1866
   Upper Marlboro, Henry J. Kershaw, Min. Prot. Ep. Ch.
Louisa & Richard Henry 12-25-1867 (Langford)
Lucy & Hanson Johnson 10-14-1871 (Evans)
Mack & Ellen Brown 12-7-1869 (Maher)
Margaret & Aaron Hall 10-30-1873 (Snowden)
Margaret & Joseph Simms 3-7-1877 (Carroll)
Maria & Thomas Johnson 5-23-1876
Martha col? & Benjamin Thomas 4-8-1871
Martha J. & Richard N. Henry 4-18-1882
Mary & James Bryan 7-21-1866 (Fr. Call)
Mary & George H. Smith 2-6-1875 (Stanley)
Mary & James G. Anderson 12-28-1877
Mary & Frederick Watson 12-26-1885 (Rev. Mr. Brookes)
Mary Ann & Jason Fearall 2-4-1800
Mary Ann & Robert Holland col? 12-27-1880
Matilda & George Gross col? 5-15-1880
Nancy & Samuel Hawkins 1-3-1874 (Cotton)
Patsey & Benedict Proctor 8-16-1833
Paul & Jennie Thomas 1-25-1876 (Gordon)
Phillis & Lawrence Wilks 6-24-1880 Black (Fr. DeWolf)
Rachel & Emory Abrams 6-16-1874 (Price)
Rebecca & James White 6-23-1871 (Budd)
Reverdy Esq. & Mary M. Bowie 11-15-1819
Richard & Drady Simpson 1-7-1822
Richard H. & Liza West 6-6-1867 (Gordon)
Rinaldo & Rebecca Truman 2-4-1779
Robert & Maria Turner 7-23-1879 (Jenkins)
Roberta & George Kidwell 1-31-1879
Sallie & Joseph Henson 10-5-1883 (Rev. Mr. Brown)
Sarah & Benjamin Brookes 11-7-1782
Sarah & Richard Barton 2-27-1875
Sarah & Benj. Fletcher 11-12-1880 (Rev. Mr. Lawson)
Sarah Ann & Weston Nalley 9-2-1871 (Trapnall)
Sarah Norwood & Abraham Barnes Hoe 8-19-1809
Susan & George Brooks 5-19-1847
Susan R. & John Riddle 8-22-1838

JOHNSON, Thomas (listed also as Frank) & Eliza Smith 12-23-1865
 Age 33, black, widower, farmhand. m. 12-25-1865 Upper Marlboro by
 Henry J. Kershaw, Prot. Epis.
 Thomas & Maria Johnson 5-23-1876
 Thomas & Mary Elizabeth Jackson color.^{d} 1-28-1881
 Washington & Amy Ann Harrison 5-4-1867 (Call)
 William & Rebecca Bruce col^d (Fr. Call) 6-10-1867
 William & Jane Robinson 7-22-1870
JOHNSTON, Mary & Hannible Grimes 11-19-1863
 Thomas & Susannah Buchanan 5-26-1807
JOINER, Joseph & Elizabeth Merrit 8-19-1800
JONES, Abraham & Margaret Williams 1-12-1802
 Abraham & Elizabeth Basford 2-12-1820
 Abraham & Elizabeth Semly 11-19-1873
 Amelia & George Brady 7-24-1845
 Amy & Josias Jones 3-23-1785
 Andrew & Mintie Hagar 9-13-1872 (McDonald)
 Ann & Thomas Reynolds 2-24-1784
 Ann & George Bayne 4-20-1779
 Ann & James Gregory 12-13-1792
 Ann & Lewin Talbott 2-13-1797
 Anna E. & Philip B. Lederer 2-1-1875
 Anne & Elisha Lovelace 1-6-1789
 Anne Richards & Richard Piles 1-27-1806
 Benjamin & Ruth Young 10-11-1786
 Benjamin & Susannah Walker 2-6-1807
 Bini & Thomas Dayley 8-23-1793
 Butler & Elizabeth Linsey 2-8-1790
 Carrie & W. R. Loveless 12-30-1885 (Rev. Father Cunane)
 Catharine & Theodore Beall 8-13-1860
 Catharine & Francis Harrison 8-15-1871 (McDonald)
 Celia & Rezin Dorsey 9-18-1876 (Gordon)
 Charles A. & Lucy Dorsey 12-20-1865 Age 21, black, farmer b. Charles
  County m. by Alex. M. Marbury, min. Prot. Ep. Ch. 12-24-1865
 Charles L. & Elizabeth S. M. Owens 2-10-1813
 Clariet & Henry Hazard 5-2-1818
 Daniel & Susanna Bradley 11-16-1779
 David & Margaret Wells 11-4-1797
 David & Mary Curtin 3-26-1806
 Deborah L. & George Beall of Ninian 9-28-1830
 Deborah S. & James H. Boswell 5-29-1858
 Edward & Susannah Jones 5-8-1799
 Edward & Sarah Darnall 1-21-1804
 Edward & Adalaide Virginia Grieb 7-14-1859
 Elijah & Elizabeth Manley 5-15-1784
 Elizabeth & John Wedderal 4-4-1786
 Elizabeth & Thomas Clark 9-20-1799
 Elizabeth of P.G. County & Aquila LanHam of Montgomery Co. 12-15-1818
 Elizabeth & George Malor col^d 5-23-1869 (McDonald)
 Eliz^a E. & Wm. Jenkins 12-19-1820
 Elizth & Benjamin Padgett 12-11-1830
 Ellen & Benedict Padgett 12-22-1835
 Florence & David Scrivener 10-23-1879 (Quiller)
 Frances & Thomas Kerr 4-10-1882 (Rev. Mr. Butler)
 Frederick & Ann Duvall 12-5-1809

124

JONES, Geo. & Beckie Murray 5-31-1873 (Peters)
  George & Elizabeth Sinclair 8-25-1787
  George & Ann Roberts 1-4-1785
  George & Elizabeth Wilson 1-29-1788
  George & Ann Tarman 6-25-1799
  George & Sally Bryan 1-18-1824
  George & Frances M. Ward 6-17-1884 (Rev. Mr. Brooks)
  Hatton Middleton & Elizabeth Lanham 11-8-1806
  Henry & Elizabeth Butler 1-3-1820
  Henry & Mary Beck 11-24-1834
  Henry & Mary Eliza Hagan 4-25-1873 (O'Dwyer)
  Horace & Airy Clarke 12-18-1869 (Mahr)
  James & Rosanah Smith 3-19-1785
  James & Mary Ann Bryan 2-15-1826
  James Jun̄ & Margaret R. Waring 11-15-1852
  James Godfrey & Rebecca Church 1-10-1823
  James H. & Georgianna Coxen 11-21-1866 Age 29, pumpmaker m. 11-22-1866
    by Rev. Henry J. Kershaw
  James S. & C. Anna Bocock 6-17-1876 (Ritter)
  Jane & Jacob Cook 11-25-1806
  John & Sarah Digges col̄ 7-31-1868 (Father Begue)
  John B. & Matilda Jones 1-13-1827
  John C. & Fannie Clark 5-31-1869 (Chesley)
  John H. & Alice Turner 12-29-1884 (Rev. Mr. Brooke)
  John Henry & Nancy Ann Bedder 8-13-1866 (Lanaham)
  John W. & Charlotte R. Hawkins 11-6-1876
  Joseph & Mary Simmons 11-25-1816
  Josias & Amy Jones 3-23-1785
  Josias & Nancy Ann Vermillion 11-3-1804
  Julius & Mary Brown col̄ 6-15-1870 (Maher)
  Letitia Jane & Elial F. Sansbury 12-15-1863
  Littey & Charles Robinson 1-21-1790
  Lizzie & Thomas Moreland 2-20-1883 (Rev. Mr. Butler)
  Louisa & Timothy N. Vaill 10-23-1818
  M. & George Washington Davis 2-22-1886 (Rev. Mr. Brooks)
  Margaret & William Wilson 11-7-1781
  Margaret & John Crosby 2-22-1881
  Margaret E. & Rousbury M. Thomas 1-26-1848
  Maria & Elema Beall 1-16-1822
  Martha & Joseph Hatton 10-4-1777
  Martha & Elkanah Cobb 9-8-1813
  Mary & William Patterson 11-23-1779
  Mary & John Tilley 3-29-1780
  Mary & Thomas Lyles 10-23-1790
  Mary & Daniel Hurley 9-8-1797
  Mary & John Rawlings 5-25-1798
  Mary & Wm. H. Ball 5-31-1862
  Mary A. & Benjamin H. Beall 2-20-1882 (Rev. Mr. Butler)
  Mary Ann & Henderson Loveless 2-7-1815
  Mary C. & John Addison col̄ 8-2-1871
  Mary E. & Francis Wood 12-5-1881 (Rev. Wm. C. Boteler)
  Mary E. & Isiah Forbes 8-10-1884 (Rev. P. H. Green)
  Mary Elizabeth & Charles Danenhower 10-30-1872
  Mary Elizabeth & John Henry Jenkins 1-14-1876 (Gordon)
  Mary M. & Stephen Clarke 3-6-1878 (Hooman)

JONES, Mary Rebecca & John D. Nally 1-12-1860
  Mary V. & Henry L. Payne 3-1-1859
  Matilda & John B. Jones 1-13-1827
  Matilda & Tobias Allen 2-1-1866 (Beque)
  Milly & George Watson 3-31-1866 (Greenleaf)
  Moses & Druscilla Ball 11-30-1790
  Nancy & Abraham Woodward 12-8-1807
  Nelson & Nancy Queen (colored folks) 3-3-1852
  Othella & Theodore Chaney 9-22-1874 (Mercer)
  Permelia & Henry Culver 1-25-1827
  Perry & Linney Gentle 2-6-1793
  Philemon & Arriana Waters 11-25-1816
  Phillis & Adam Peach 12-13-1804
  Rebecca & John Taylor 8-23-1780
  Rebecca & Richard Jones 3-29-1866 (Beque)
  Rebecca & Horace Tell 7-2-1879
  Rebeccah & Richard Humphreys 2-1-1804
  Richard & Prescilla Ladyman 1-4-1783
  Richard & Ann Wilson 12-10-1796
  Richard & Sarah Cissell 12-13-1808
  Richard & Rebecca Jones 3-29-1866 (Beque)
  Robert Anderson & Elizabeth Wheat 4-26-1803
  Samuel & Darcus Welch 11-4-1788
  Samuel & Ann Gatton 10-11-1800
  Samuel & Elizabeth Dixon 8-30-1815
  Sarah & Thomas Gill 8-30-1777
  Sarah & John Bowie Magruder 2-3-1791
  Sarah & John McKensey 2-13-1806
  Sarah & Charles Boteler 2-21-1806
  Sarah & Nathaniel Weeden 2-8-1821
  Sarah & Aaron Hall 11-8-1873 (Jenkins)
  Sarah L. & Ignatius D. Adams 4-24-1851
  Saully & Joseph Florence 6-6-1806
  Susanna & Rector Bayne 12-25-1805
  Susanna E. & Francis Morris 1-13-1862
  Susannah & Edward Jones 5-8-1799
  Susannah & Thomas Conner 3-31-1804
  Theodore & Rachel Crawford 1-25-1821
  Thomas & Dorcas Maria Jenkins 6-10-1822
  Thomas H. & Verlinda Jones 1-1-1834
  Verlinda & Thomas H. Jones 1-1-1834
  Violetta & Peter Hart 12-19-1825
  Walker & Elizabeth Hopkins 2-26-1838
  William & Darkey Mockbee 6-25-1791
  William & Sabret King 2-11-1793
  William & Eleanor Welch 1-2-1815
  William & Elizabeth Padgett 12-27-1817
  William & Eleanor Prather 6-10-1818
  William & Emily Stone 12-21-1836
  William & Melvina Gibbons 7-2-1838
  William & Jane Johnson 12-23-1876 (Walker)
  William & Matilda Selby 11-9-1877 (Valtz)
  William O. & Ann Selby 1-13-1824
  Wm. & Caroline Prather 11-22-1825
JOURNEY, Margaret & Richard Dowell 4-4-1795

126

JOY, James E. & Georgianna Demar 12-11-1883 (Rev. Mr. Sutherland)
    Joseph & Sarah Durity- 7-4-1795
    Mary F. & George W. Richardson 2-3-1881 (Rev. Mr. Brayshaw)
    Rachel Ann & Judson F. Richardson 11-9-1880 (Laney)

KAGLE, Emma Jane & Benjamin Franklin Binnex (?) 10-18-1880 (Rev. DeLaney)
    James & Henry Anna Wisman 1-16-1884 (Rev. Mr. Robey)
    Mary Ann & George Simpson 5-1-1875 (Stanley)
KALDENBACH, Andrew S. & Josephine Harington 1-9-1865
    M. J. & Ann Eliza Hook 8-8-1853
    M. J. & Mary Jane Hyde 4-21-1865
    M. J. Jr. & Annie C. Aist 3-19-1877 (Seat)
    Matthais John Kaldenback & Elizth M. Maccubbin 12-7-1846
KALDENBACK, Theresa C. & William T. Hyde 2-27-1850
KAY, Richard & Sarah Mason 2-16-1784
KAYHAWLEY, David & Elizabeth Kerrick 3-28-1780
KEADER, Elizabeth & Thomas Jefferson 1-29-1829
KEADLE, Eliz^{a} & John Moore 3-3-1783
    Humphrey & Maria Drage 12-1-1828
    John & Mary Price Gray 8-30-1805
    Mary & Casper Everheart 12-11-1792
    Thomas & Mary Perry 6-15-1784
    Wiseman & Ann Wightt 7-25-1787
KEADLES, William & Henny Taylor 4-30-1803
KEARNEY, John A. & Mary M. Forrest 12-5-1835
KEECH, Kate H. & John J. Barnard 11-7-1863
    Lily & Johnson Fitzhugh 7-13-1869
    Rose (baptised Frances) & William Scott Keech 10-31-1863
    Dr. Thomas & Miss Virginia M. Keech 4-7-1859
    Virginia M. & Dr. Thomas Keech 4-7-1859
    William & Jane Williams 9-6-1780
    William Scott & Rose (baptisted Frances) Keech 10-31-1863
KEEFFE, John & Mary Fitzgerald 7-10-1864
KEEN, Ida Luther & Robert Lee Mullikin 6-22-1886 (Rev. Mr. Shipley)
KEERL, George H. & Susanna Mundell 4-26-1820
    Joshua S. & Eleanor P. Mundell 1-24-1825
KEISER, Valentine & Dorcas Carrick 8-31-1867
KEITCH, Clarissa & Cornelius Robinson 11-29-1805
KEITH, Edward & Ann Lesby 12-9-1793
    Gerard & Eleanor Lusby 12-27-1782
    Rebeccah & Alexander Gibbons 10-2-1792
KELLER, Jonas P. & Sarah Ann Gibbs 12-1-1828
KELLEY, Addie & Scott B. Doing 4-2-1883 (Rev. E. Robet)
KELLY, Jane & George Gordon 6-9-1796
    Mary & Henry Roberts 8-10-1778
    Wm. & Mariah A. Brooke 11-30-1820
KEMP, James & Jane Spalding 10-16-1806
KENDRICK, Joseph M. & Ann R ebecca Cawood 9-6-1869 (Fowler)
    Richard H. & Martha S. Baldwin 5-14-1834
KENNEDY, James & Susanna Wailks 12-16-1799
    William L. & Henrietta J. Hill 4-29-1824 also listed 2-29-1824
KENT, Anna & Aaron Magruder 5-1-1869 (Maher)
    Daniel & Elizabeth Yates 5-15-1817

KENT, Daniel M. & Kate M. DuVal 9-21-1872 (Stanley)
Harriett & Richard H. Hall 3-23-1819
Joseph & Eleanor Lee Wallace 10-30-1804
Mary & Clement West col[d] 8-9-1867 (Call)
Sarah F. & P.A.L. Contee 3-28-1837
KERBEY, Catharine E. & Cadwalader Wickersham 10-25-1872
KERBY, Andrew Jackson & Ellen Nora Thom 9-1-1884 (Rev. J. J. Carden)
Ella S. & John R. Pumphrey 12-2-1879
Francis & Chrissy Spalding 3-17-1809
George Francis & Mary Ann Marden 8-2-1881 (Rev. Mr. Hyland)
Hannah & Jacob Harman 10-1-1872 (Kershaw)
James P. & Rebecca L. Richards 7-23-1877 (Gordon)
James P. & Susan N. Mangum 2-3-1879
John H. & Mary Jennette Mudd 10-26-1880 (Rev. Mr. Highland)
Joseph W. & Maria L. Connick 5-24-1849
Levi & Julia Ann Mattingly 5-15-1855
Levi & Ann S. Mudd 11-21-1868 (Lenaghan)
Sophia & Francis Burgen 12-18-1871
William Fred[k] & Ella Gertrude Monroe 11-3-1884 (Rev. Mr. Hyland)
KERR, James & Elizabeth Crauford 6-4-1870 (Harper)
Richard W. & Nettie E. Sweeney 1-28-1886 (Rev. Wm. C. Butler)
Thomas & Frances Jones 4-10-1882 (Rev. Mr. Butler)
KERRICK, Ann Maria & Brien O'Donnell 1-25-1856
Edward Drane & Chloe Pinkney 4-25-1873
Elizabeth & David Kayhawley 3-28-1780
KERSHAW, Henry J. & Adeline Clagett 12-16-1874 (Pinkney)
KETCHEN, Jesse A. & Annie Newman 12-18-1875
KETLAND, Annie & Edward Renna 10-9-1871 (Kershaw)
KETLIN, Jane & Fielder Jewell 5-30-1817
KETLING, Margaret & Charles Beard 7-19-1852
KETTLE, Ignatius Elias & Harriet Ann Gray 2-16-1874
KEY, Anna & Thomas Harvey 3-13-1841
Charity & James Addison 2-10-1870 (Pindell)
Edmund & Margaret J. Mackall 6-7-1814
Ignatius & Henrietta Queen 7-14-1785
Martha & Alrick McGregor 2-8-1829
Mary S. & John T. D. Compton 10-10-1850
Philip B. & Mary B. Sewall 12-1-1828
Upton S. & Mary Chew 2-13-1844
KEYS, James E. & Emma V. Connick 1-2-1884 (Rev. Mr. LaRoche)
KIDWELL, Alfred & Laura Jane Dowel 1-1-1847
Allison B. & Mary Tucker 8-17-1878 (Butler)
Ann & Nathan Perrie 12-3-1831
Ann & Joshua Watson 2-8-1834
Caroline & Leonard Taylor 1-20-1845
Catharine & Richard F. Carter 2-17-1814
Cecelia & Richard T. Lawson 1-2-1832
Deleley & John Cross 12-24-1836
Eliz[a] & Hezekiah Mobberly 12-5-1796
Elizabeth & George Joshua Naylor 3-29-1834
Elizabeth & James Curtain 4-16-1863
Elizabeth & William Curtin 4-14-1873
Elizabeth A. & Henry S. Crandell 12-11-1855
Elzear & Emily O. Lanham 9-22-1863
George & Ann Smith 12-6-1800

KIDWELL, George & Sarah Greer 10-31-1818
  George & Roberta Johnson 1-31-1879
  Harriot & Judson Sweeney 4-19-1813
  Henrietta & Joseph Lemuel Beall 3-9-1869 (Chesly)
  James & Mary Mudd 12-18-1790
  James & Matilda A. Thompson 12-24-1857
  Jane & Joseph T. Knott 1-11-1842
  John & Mary Lawson 2-22-1784
  John & Eleanor Hays 1-5-1785
  John Henry & Elizabeth V. Rawlings 2-24-1868 (Smith)
  John Henry & Mary Soper 9-4-1876 (Dorsey)
  John W. & Letty W. Moore 12-27-1828
  Joseph W. & Mary Ann Moreland 12-18-1816
  Josias & Elizabeth Ladymer 12-17-1799
  Josias & Anna Maria Bigges 10-26-1859
  Leonard & Mary Foster 8-1-1798
  Leonard & Eleanor Clarke 12-15-1826
  Margaret & John Webster 12-26-1784
  Martha & Nathaniel T. Cooksey 12-10-1821
  Martha & Geo. D. Beall 4-4-1850
  Martha Ann & Widman G. Jenkins 6-19-1843
  Mary & Theodore Hutchinson 1-29-1818
  Mary & Mordecai Taylor Boswell 5-28-1872
  Mary Ann & Benjamin F. Peacock 12-27-1883 (Rev. Mr. Dell)
  Mary Eliza & John Thomas Jenkins 11-11-1845
  Mary Ellen & Basil Ridgeway 4-14-1857
  Nath! & Presilla Moore 12-20-1781
  Pricey & Richard Smith Rawlings 6-10-1802
  Sarah & Wm. Strickland 12-20-1784
  Sarah & John F. Phillips 1-24-1853
  Theodore & Mary Hill 1-12-1799
  Thomas & Mary Ann Wentfield 3-23-1781
  Thomas & Mary E. Lanham 9-29-1859
  Tracy & Nathan Hutchinson 6-2-1777
  William & Eleanor Gray 1-4-1783
  William & Eunice Ann Thomas 10-18-1818
  Wm. Henry Phillips & Julia Ann Canter 5-17-1871 (Lenaghan)
KIERMAN, Cathrine Magdalen & Patrick H. Kiernan 11-23-1875
  Christina & George Strauss 8-5-1874
KIERNAN, Ann Isabel & George Henry Siebel 2-11-1863
  Hugh & Mazy Ann Wilson 12-27-1873
  Patrick H. & Cathrine Magdalen Kierman 11-23-1875
KILLMAN, John S. & Eva A. Birch 1-7-1878 (Cross)
KILLRIGLE, George & Ann Ferrell 11-24-1810
KILTON, George &Elizabeth Carter 9-23-1796
KINEN, Patrick & Cassandra Burch 1-1-1808
KING, Albert J. & Mary Ann Locker 2-15-1877 (Horner)
  Alfred W. & Sarah F. Stone 12-14-1878 (Cross)
  Alice J. & Robert V. Duckett 8-10-1876 (McNeer)
  Ann & Zadock Moore 3-6-1779
  Ann & Benjamin Mullekin 2-21-1838
  Ann & Richard S. Ridgeway 5-29-1841
  Anna E. & James R. Cadle 5-28-1875 (Welch)
  B. A. & Jerry T. Grimes 12-1-1873
  Benjamin & Margaret Purdy 1-28-1870 (Bird)

KING, Benjamin Edward & Jane Alice Loveless 1-31-1882
   Catherine Ann & Albert Hardisty 1-31-1867 Age 21 (Kershaw)
   Daniel & Elizabeth Mahala Goddard 3-7-1848
   Elijah & Martha Soper 2-13-1837
   Elisha & Elizabeth Spalding 2-18-1800
   Eliza & Thomas Hyde 10-7-1875 (McNeir)
   Elizabeth & Robert Simm 1-5-1786
   Elizabeth & Richard Pumphrey 2-21-1786
   Elizabeth & William Thorn 1-4-1803
   Elizabeth & Frederick E. Hopkins 3-12-1863
   Elizabeth & Arthur West col$^{\underline{d}}$ 7-27-1867
   Elizabeth & John H. Smith 2-21-1876 (Green)
   Emma Snow & Basil Edward Harvey 9-20-1882 (Rev. Arnsdale)
   Felly &Walter Thorn 9-7-1816
   Henrietta & John Brightwell 2-9-1803
   Hetty & Zadokiah Cooke 12-26-1794
   Isaac & Sarah Weaver 3-16-1799
   Jacob & Ann Soper 3-2-1802
   James & Elizabeth Gray 1-8-1819
   James H. & Susan A. Harvey 12-13-1853
   Jane & George Wise 3-7-1799
   James Swann & Sarah Lee Lanham 12-22-1800
   Jane & Theodore Mitchell 11-7-1833
   Johanna & Nathan Low 2-14-1838
   John & Susanna Leach 11-25-1777
   John & Keziah Upton 6-6-1779
   John & Ann Lewis 1-10-1791
   John of Richard & Elizabeth McDowell 7-30-1791
   John & Catharine Davis 9-23-1847
   John H. & Melvina King 1-3-1853
   John L. & Mary Payne 1-11-1831
   John R. & Gustie M. Ryon 10-15-1873 (Mercer)
   John S. & Ann C. Cissell 6-11-1859
   Joseph Alfred & Mary Ann McKenzie 2-21-1877 (Gordon)
   Julia Ann & Thomas Windsor 8-25-1873 (Welsh)
   Leonard & Susanna Watson 11-15-1780
   Lucinda & Henry Dulaney 12-24-1877 (Weems)
   Maria & John Digges 3-27-1875 (Maquire)
   Mary & Thomas Mullikin 1-5-1799
   Mary & John Parmer 10-31-1808
   Mary & Henry Tayman 2-4-1824
   Mary Ann & Zadock Riston 5-14-1818
   Mary E. & Jos. N. Arnold 4-11-1844
   Mary E. & Jonathan N. M. Laughlin 1-5-1857
   Mary Ellen & George Gray 12-28-1885 (Rev. Geo. Williams)
   Mary V. & Chas. Jacob Pfluger 9-5-1882 (Rev. Jno. Teasdale)
   Melvina & John H. King 1-3-1853
   Rebecca & George Emory Crandell 11-18-1873 (Dwyer)
   Richard & Elizabeth Brown 2-11-1795
   Richard & Anamina Weaver 2-27-1795
   Richard & Anne Clarke 11-5-1839
   Richard Oliver & Alice Elizabeth Tayler 2-19-1884 (Father Cunnane)
   Ruth & Thomas Simpson 4-7-1787
   Sabret & William Jones 2-11-1793
   Sarah & John Grimes 1-3-1789

KING, Sarah & Jesse Wilcoxen 2-9-1802
  Sarah & William H. Mitchell 11-6-1834
  Sarah & William Tayman 11-21-1855
  Sarah & Thomas Beall 12-14-1872 (Kershaw)
  Sarah E. & John Thomas Talbert 4-25-1859
  Susanna & John Biggs 12-11-1779
  Susannah & John Watson 2-28-1789
  Susannah & Caleb Thomas 4-14-1798
  Thomas & Mary Mitchell 10-16-1787
  Thomas & Elizabeth Thompson 2-26-1821
  Thomas & Cassandra Riston 3-29-1823
  Thomas A. & Alberta M. Carrick 2-15-1856
  Thomas M. & Rebecca Gray 1-18-1790
  Vinson & Sarah White 11-1-1828
  William & Susannah Holland 10-22-1796
  William A. & Margaret Compton 11-19-1883 (Rev. Laroche)
  William H. & Adelaide V. White 1-8-1876
  William Marden & Sarah Louisa Josephine Allen 4-30-1875 (West)
  Wm. Wesley & Emma Chaney 1-5-1876 (McNear)
KINGSBURY, Amelia & William Fry 12-17-1846
  Elizabeth & Luke Rawlings 1-30-1786
  Elizth & George Wells 12-30-1828
  Elizth & Erasmus Mullikin 1-16-1847
  John & Sarah Pumphrey 4-5-1827
  John & Ann Eliza Duckett 11-10-1856
  Rebecca & Benjamin L. Duckett 1-26-1857
  Sarah A. & James N. Taylor 6-2-1846
KINSOLVING, Charles James & Rachel Clagett 7-11-1870 (Kinsolving)
KIRBY, Christianna & Francis Edelen 12-9-1834
  Eleanor & Aloysius Edelen 7-14-1831
  Francis & Elizabeth Collard 1-11-1783
  George & Margaret A. Norfolk 2-25-1834
  Jane & David Middleton 2-17-1827
  John Baptist & Sarah Elson 9-23-1779
  Liliah R. & John P. Webster 9-29-1885 (Rev. Mr.Hyland)
  Richard & Susanna Talburt 9-9-1783
  Sarah & Theodore Neal 4-25-1778
  William & Henrietta A. Robinson 10-25-1836
KIRSICK, John Henry & Sarah Ann Owens 12-30-1868 (Martin)
KITLAND, John & Eliza Ann Osbourn 5-19-1845
KITLIN, William & Jane Osbourn 3-5-1832
KITTLE, John Henry & Harriet Adams col? 12-24-1881 (Rev. Dr. Gordon)
  Rachel & John Q. Adams 12-28-1878 (Gordon)
KITWELL, Amelia & Joseph Cross 6-15-1867 (Smith)
KLOCK, Ann Jennette & John Yorke AtLee 10-3-1883 (Rev. Wm. Brayshaw)
  Mary A. & George W. Salisbury 9-20-1875
  Willie Theron & Nettie J. Walker 12-21-1885 (Rev. Mr. Brayshaw)
KNIGHTEN, Samuel & Lucretia.Cattnan 1-8-1823
KNIGHTON, Elvira & Wm. H. A. Smith 4-29-1873 (Kershaw)
  Mary & James Ford 12-11-1804
  Dr. N. S. & Mattie Sasscer 11-24-1866 (Lenahan)
  Samuel & Susannah Ryon 2-11-1791
  Thompsey & John Nicholls 1-29-1791
KNOCK, Henry & Ronne Barbara Ammon 5-7-1866 69, white, widower, shop-
    keeper m. 5-28-1866 Bladensburg by John B. Ross, min. Presby Church

KNOCK, Henry C. & Maggie C. Coldenstroth 3-29-1880
KNOTT, Clement & Jane Wood 12-3-1807
   Elizabeth & John Goddard 7-14-1795
   Elizabeth & John Richard Wood 5-8-1860
   John D. & Anna Mangum 12-6-1879
   Joseph T. & Jane Kidwell 1-11-1842
   Julia Ann & Samuel Ward 4-14-1827
   Mary & William Murry 8-28-1828
   Mary Ann & Alexander Johnson 1-10-1831
   Mary Jane & Jno. H. Carrico 2-20-1865
   Richard & Christianna Webster 7-12-1840
KNOWLES, Cornelia E. & Henry H. Hall 12-30-1882 (Rev. Mr. Starr)
   David & Eleanor Barnes 1-18-1805
KNOX, Sophia & Henry W. Brown 8-11-1881
KOONES, David & Matilda Bond 5-22-1810
KREHII, Frances & Mathias Bick 2-10-1857

LACEY, Mary Ann & Robert Dalton Jenkins 4-12-1808
LACKLAND, Mary S. & Stanislaus Blandford 11-18-1832
LADDIN, Plummer & Rachael Hardesty 4-3-1826
LADYMAN, Prescilla & Richard Jones 1-4-1783
LADYMER, Elizabeth & Josias Kidwell 12-17-1799
LAIRD, John & Mary Dick 1-28-1797
LAMAR, Allen & Elizabeth Hunter 12-23-1811
   Elizabeth & Clement Craycroft 3-7-1812
   Elizabeth & William Curtain 2-6-1813
   Elizabeth Ann & Samuel Childs 5-4-1824
   Francis & Mary Watson 2-1-1808
   John W. & Nannie Demar 8-25-1883
   Mary & Benjamin Pierce 4-21-1813
   Mary & John Cross 4-26-1813
   Priscilla & James Drane 2-18-1789
   Rachel & William Harding 3-22-1784
   Richard & Ann Drane 11-9-1790
   Richard Melcom & Elizabeth Gibbon 12-10-1808
   Sarah & Levin Broten Brightwell 1-3-1820
   Susannah & Cornelius Watson 12-28-1791
   William & Sarah Pierce 3-29-1804
LAMBERT, Adolphus H. & Frankie Harris 2-17-1868 (Kershaw)
   Benjamin H. & Alice Williams 2-9-1874
   Catharine & Charles Thomas 3-13-1837
   Christopher & Rebecca Morsell 10-27-1824
   Eliz^{a} J. & Peter B. Hatton 12-28-1821
   Ellen & William Dove 3-2-1835
   John B. & Phebe Eleanor Higdon 12-17-1793
   John J. & Mary E. Hunter 9-11-1832
   Mary & John T. Boswell 12-16-1831
   Mary F. & John S. Button 3-12-1873 (Kershaw)
   Nancy & John B. Spalding 12-13-1820
   Wm. M. & E. B. McPherson 11-15-1873 (Towles)
LAMIS, John J. & Emma Jane Scotten 4-29-1867 (West)
LANCASTER, Anne & Felix Coates col^{d} 4-22-1868 (Lenaghan)
   George Washington & Sophia Quiller 12-8-1865 (Stanley)
   Sarah M. & Levin Skinner 10-27-1841

LANE, Barbara & Benjamin Berry Senr 12-19-1815
  Barbara Susannah Parker & Fielder Bowie 12-16-1811
  Charles & Eleanor Rusten 8-31-1808
  Eleanor & James Forbes 3-16-1805
  Elizabeth Bowie & Bowie Eversfield 12-13-1804
  John & Margaret Burnes 2-21-1781
  Rebecca & Jas. B. Belt 1-18-1842
LANG, Ann & Annanias Grear 2-6-1781
  Catharine & Charles Beavin 3-28-1793
  John & Anne Hooper 12-17-1779
LANGLEY, Henry & Elizabeth Harding 2-3-1808
  James & Ann Tarman 12-30-1816
  Martina & Hezekiah Curtain 12-22-1817
  Mary Ann & Elijah Gardiner 12-14-1822
  Sarah & Richard Taylor 10-21-1805
  Walter & Margaret Lanham 5-18-1804
  William & Ann Mobley 2-26-1822
LANGLY, Cornelius & SArah Clubb 12-23-1818
LANGSTER, Ignatius & Eliza Butler 2-10-1872 (O'Dwyer)
LANGSTON, John A. & Susan Bowie Duvall 8-14-1826
LANHAM, Acquilla & Ann Thompson 1-28-1788
  Ann & Henry Barnes 2-3-1790
  Ann & Mordicai Henry 1-15-1805
  Ann & Fielder Hawkins Ferral 3-5-1819
  Aquila of Montgomery County & Elizabeth Jones of P. G. C. 12-15-1818
  Benjamin & Ann Hardister 5-25-1826
  Benjamin & Lethe Hardesty 3-9-1832
  Benjn L. & Anne Maria Stewart 12-19-1855
  Catherine & Andrew Fraser 12-31-1791
  Charity & Solomon Lanham 1-14-1778
  Charity Ann & Charles Osbourn 2-14-1825
  Eleanor A. & John Sharnon 8-9-1824
  Elizabeth & Hatton Middleton Jones 11-8-1806
  Elizabeth & Edward Dixon 1-27-1818
  Ella A. & William B. Lanham 6-18-1883 (Rev. Mr. Stanley)
  Emily O. & Elzear Kidwell 9-22-1863
  Geneva A. & Humphrey Beckett 9-17-1873   (Hadaway)
  Geo. & Ann Jarmain 2-23-1781
  George & Barbara Dixon 1-27-1818
  Grafton T. & Elizabeth A. Power 6-6-1866 (Beque)
  Hilliary & Eliza Upton 4-5-1783
  John & Linna Mockbee 3-6-1800
  Josias & Chloe Mason 2-14-1790
  Layor & Charles Selby 12-18-1787
  Lucy & James Mitchell 4-3-1819
  Margaret & Walter Langley 5-18-1804
  Marianna S. & Henry F. Payne 9-22-1868 (Berry)
  Martha Ann & Wm. F. Anderson 7-2-1844
  Mary & Basil Barnes 1-22-1791
  Mary & John Mitchell 1-10-1818
  Mary & Alfred Elliott 2-7-1873 (Evans)
  Mary Ann & Benjamin Henry 12-7-1835
  Mary E. & Edward H. Bryan 11-18-1833
  Mary E. & Thomas Kidwell 9-29-1859
  Mary M. & George W. Duvall of D. 6-28-1872 (Williams)

LANHAM, Massey Ann & John Creaton 2-21-1783
  Mildred & Jesse Talbott 11-12-1794
  Robert H. & Lucy A. A. Palmer 5-20-1833
  Ruth & Charles Townley the 3rd 4-28-1817
  Sally & Benedict Barnes 3-7-1801
  Sarah & Alexander Mockbee 1-2-1808
  Sarah & William Bryan 6-24-1809
  Sarah & John Ekton 4-12-1816
  Sarah Ann & Basil Green 1-18-1780
  Sarah Lee & James Swann King 12-22-1800
  Solomon & Charity Lanham 1-14-1778
  Stephen & Eleanor Silbey 10-4-1779
  Stephen Decatur & Mary Ellen Henry 1-25-1856
  Susanna P. & William Bryan 2-28-1827
  Susannah & Hugh McShery 4-13-1790
  Trueman & Mary Beall 10-18-1825
  William & Matilda Mockbee 1-18-1813
  William & Willy Ann Clarke 4-4-1814
  William & Tabitha Beall 11-21-1820
  William B. & Ella A. Lanham 6-18-1883 (Rev. Mr. Stanley)
LANKFORD, Matilda & WilsonOwens 6-5-1875
LANSDALE, Benedict & Sophy Fletcher 12-24-1870 (Wheeler)
  Catharine & Robert W. Bowie 3-28-1818
  Cornelia & Philip Thomas 11-8-1804
  Edward & Susan Hooge 8-26-1876 (Green)
  Elizabeth & James Belt 12-2-1794
  Elizabeth M. & Dennis Boyd 11-4-1809
  Isaac & Catharine Brooke 3-27-1792
  Isaac & Elizabeth Whitaker 6-19-1794
  Isabel & William Bell 10-23-1869 (Maher)
  John W. & Miranda Stephenson 5-15-1815
  Mary E. & Robert Chiselin 12-3-1827
LANZEL, Catherine & Clement West cold 4-27-1867 (Fr. Call)
LARKINS, David & Margaret Brown cold 12-24-1881 (Rev. Mr. Butler)
  Eliza & Morris West 12-21-1875 (Denny)
  John & Charity Baddy 12-19-1878 (Watkins)
  Mary & Sullivan Douglas 5-19-1868 (Langford)
  Moses & Catherine Wallace 2-2-1885 (Mr. Green)
LARMOUR, Robert M. & Mary E. Scott 7-26-1849
LATEN, William & Eleanor Brashears 1-20-1802
LATIMER, Edwin W. & Francenia Young 10-31-1849
  James & Verlinda A. Wells 4-16-1811
  John F. & Susan R. Burch 1-4-1825
  Julia & Isaac Chaplin 8-18-1834
  M. Randolph & Anna R. Rollins 2-8-1858
  Mary & Charles Shenton 2-12-1827
  Mary Ann J. & John B. Edelen 1-1-1831
  Penelope & James H. Alder 11-23-1827
  Randolph B. & Jane Harris 2-13-1832
LATTEN, Plummer & Mary Brashears 1-25-1798
  Rebecca & Joseph Owen 6-12-1781
  Thomas Plummer & Jennett Mann 1-20-1802
LATTON, Thomas & Mary Brashears 2-12-1806
LAUGHLIN, Jonathan N. M. & Mary E. King 1-5-1857

LAWRENCE, George A. & Charlotte Lenaway 2-9-1801
  John H. & Henrietta Williams 6-3-1871
LAWRY, Elizabeth & George Sandfield 12-9-1800
LAWS, William & Martha Walker 5-26-1784
LAWSON, Benjamin & Mary Susanna Cage 12-26-1828
  Benjamin & Harriet Ann Booth 1-19-1856
  Elizabeth & John Bryan 11-19-1802
  Elizabeth & Baley Digges 3-1-1821
  James R. & Martha N. Bush 12-27-1855
  James R. & Harriet Georgianna Brown 11-26-1861
  Martha Rebecca & William Bush 9-25-1824
  Mary & John Kidwell 2-22-1784
  Nettie & William Herd 11-30-1883 (Father Cunnanne)
  Richard T. & Cecelia Kidwell 1-2-1832
  Susannah & Thomas S. Cage 1-21-1817
  Thomas & Priscilla Hyde 2-26-1791
  William & Eleanor Simpson 11-16-1778
LAYMAN, Sarah P. & Henry M. Chew 4-9-1828
LEACH, Caleb & Christianna Willett 4-1-1829
  James & Jane Watson 1-13-1790
  John & Pamelia Chaney 5-16-1807
  Mary & Isaac Ball 4-20-1799
  Susanna & John King 11-25-1777
  Verlinda & Thomas Smith 3-19-1789
  William & Elizabeth Piles 12-27-1810
LEAPLEY, George R. & Nellie Mitchellmore 2-8-1876 (McNeer)
LEATCH, Ann & John Ellis 12-22-1806
  Draden & Thomas Fowler 4-14-1804
  Tabitha & John Tippett 7-30-1796
LECOMPT, Rezin & Margaret Piper 9-6-1800
LEDERER, Annie & Thomas M. Underwood 10-23-1880
  John L. & Sarah A. M. Boswell 1-29-1858
  Philip B. & Anna E. Jones 2-1-1875
LEE, Basil & Sarah Ann Hurley 3-6-1817
  Benjamin & Mary Dolly Reynolds 7-28-1818
  Benjamin & Eleanor Lansdale Belt 12-14-1824
  Charles & Rachel Gantt 5-16-1868 (Langford)
  Charles Henry & Laura Harrison 5-23-1874 (O'Dwyer)
  Daniel & Priscilla Crawfurd 5-21-1829
  Eleanor & Nathaniel Wood 12-24-1872 (Evans)
  Elenora B. & William S. Belt 11-18-1851
  Francis Lightfoot & Elizabeth Fitzgerald 4-7-1807
  Francis Lightfoot & Jane Fitzgerald 2-2-1810
  Georgie & James West 9-4-1869 (McDonald)
  Henrietta & William Ennis 4-26-1872 (McDonald)
  Henry & Elizabeth Cave 12-15-1781
  James H. & Catharine E. Linsay 10-13-1840
  Juba. & Georgeanna Johnson 11-2-1867 (Gordon)
  Jubiter & Harriet Ann Young 6-9-1883 (Father Cunanne)
  Laura & George Anderson 10-25-1870 (Stanley)
  Mary & Thomas Lee col⁴ 5-1-1869 (Maher)
  Nelson & Eliza Grenfel col⁴ 8-12-1867 (Lenaghan)
  Richard & Mary Ambler 11-9-1779
  Sophia & Samuel Patterson 3-7-1877 (Carroll)
  Thomas & Mary Lee col⁴ 5-1-1869 (Maher)
  Violetta E. & C. A. Harding lic. 7-10-1865, m. 7-11-1865 Age 29yr-9mo.

LEE, Washington & Sallie Stewart 9-10-1870 (McDonald)
   William & Violetta Wethers 6-9-1877 (Carroll)
   William H. & Clara Smith 12-27-1875 (Scott)
LEECH, Rev. George V. (Harrisburg, Va.) & Jennie E. Beall (Beltsville)
   2-23-1861
LEEKE, Jemima & Richard Hughes 1-17-1805
   Rezin B. & Barbara Locker 4-12-1816
LEHMAN, Oswald C. & Abbie E. Harman 3-28-1871 (Kershaw)
LEHMANN, Fred'k A. & Mary E. Hickey 11-12-1878
LEITCH, Elizabeth Johnson & Benoni Trueman 4-1-1801
   Marg'r. & Wm. Sydebotham 9-23-1778
   Thomas & Ann Davis 1-8-1806
LEMON, John & Susan Smallwood black Age 33, widower, farmhand m. 7-8-1865
   Greenwood by John Chesley, Min. Prot. Ep. Ch.
LENAWAY, Charlotte & George A. Lawrence 2-9-1801
LESBY (see also Lisby and Lusby)
   Ann & Edward Keith 12-9-1793
   Mary E. & James G. Robinson 1-6-1848
LETCHWALT, Mary & Thomas Estep 3-4-1797
LETCHWORTH, John & Deborah Sothoron 12-10-1798
   Joseph & Harriot Wallace 12-1-1807
   Martha & William Hill 12-9-1805
   Susannah & Thomas Robinson 3-31-1804
LEWIS, Ann & John King 1-10-1791
   Charlotte L. & James G. Cadle 11-11-1839
   Clement & Henrietta Jackson (Kershaw) 4-20-1878
   Daniel & Mildred Martin 1-2-1792
   Elizabeth M. & John F. Thompson 4-22-1815
   Emily & Nicholas Howard 4-28-1866 Age 16, black, field hand (Gordon)
   Erosmon Fell & James Savage 12-29-1819
   Harriet A. & William J. Edelen 11-26-1843
   Hugh & Susannah Gregory 1-12-1790
   James S. & Caroline S. Richards 8-21-1837
   Jane C. & Richard R. Cadle 11-25-1833
   John S. & Elizabeth A. Gregory 1-17-1842
   John Smith & Mary Moreland 12-29-1825
   Lucinia Ann & Joseph Fowler 4-8-1820
   Mary & Clark Thompson 5-20-1783
   Mary Ann & William Swann 6-4-1833
   Mildred Mary & Benjamin Willson 5-4-1824
   Susan Mahala & William Harvey of Thos. 12-3-1827
   Thomas & Elizabeth Blandford 6-17-1815
   Wm. H. & Rachael Anne Simmons 6-19-1886 (Rev. F. G. Hall)
LIBERTY, Mitchell & Elizabeth Brown 9-11-1871 (Wheeler)
LIEBERMAN, C. L. & Jennie A. Ferrall 10-17-1867
LILLEY, Zachariah & Eugenia Nunez 6-23-1884
LINCH, Amelia & Thomas Simpson 9-17-1787
   James & Sarah Padgett 2-5-1818
   John S. & Rebecca Watson 1-5-1782
   Walter & Ann Watson 12-27-1817
LINDSAY, Eleanor & George Dyer 4-20-1815
   George & Sarah Frazier 12-6-1798
   John & Sarah Eleanor A. L. Cawood 10-11-1815
   John & Mary Barnes 7-31-1818

LINDSAY, Louisa J. & Jeremiah T. Grimes 12-24-1855
  Matilda & Charles Allen 11-25-1806
  Noble & Sarah Dove 1-18-1813
  Rachel & Samuel Moreland 1-20-1802
  Samuel & Mary Cawood 7-8-1807
  Sarah V. & Willm S. Thorne 12-12-1847
  William (no female name given) 5-30-1817
  Wm. H. & Jane E, Thompson 2-3-1845
LINDSEY, Anthony & Susannah Gay (Guy?) 12-13-1827
  Elizabeth & Henry Anderson 12-22-1815
  James T. & Mary E. Williams 2-20-1860
  Susanna & Walter Fenley 1-31-1821
  Wm. H. & Ann L. Blandford 2-15-1858
LINSAY, Catharine E. & James H. Lee 10-13-1840
LINSEY, Elizabeth & Butler Jones 2-8-1790
LINTHICUM, Helen May & William Henry Heffner 5-16-1885 (Rev. Mr. Strickland)
LINTON, Anne & James Higdon 1-28-1797
  Martha & John Howard 9-16-1791
LISBY, Ann Maria & Geo, H. Jenkins 4-4-1850
  Eleanor & John W. Lowe 10-8-1807
LITTLEFORD, Addison & Martha Ann White 12-30-1854
  Addison & Mary Hutchison 5-18-1869 (Kershaw)
  Eleanor & John T. Caroll 3-17-1846
  John & Ann Piles 1-2-1799
  John & Ann Hutcheson 5-20-1802
  John Dennis & Sarah A. Young 12-26-1839
  Martha A. E. & Julius E. Coffren 12-26-1878 (Lewin)
  Mary & Thomas Walker 12-24-1780
  Mary & Benj. Neill Walker 3-25-1788
  Mary Ann & James W. Dove 4-6-1864
  Priscilla Ann & James H. Carroll 12-21-1852
  Thomas & Eleanor Busey 2-12-1797
LIVINGSTON, John & Martha Lyle 12-19-1793
  Robert LeRoy & Ann Maria Digges 6-29-1811
LLOYD, Alexander J. & Elizabeth Stewart 7-12-1860
LOCHER, Amany & Zachariah Walker 12-24-1808
LOCKE, David & Sarah Payne 7-22-1794 see also Locker
LOCKER, Alfred M. & Mary E. James 12-28-1859
  Anne & John Walker 2-4-1808
  Barbara & Rezin B. Leeke 4-12-1816
  Caroline & Thomas Cater 1-3-1825
  Caroline Amelia & William McLean 4-12-1849
  David & Sarah Payne 7-28-1794
  Hester Ann & Francis M. Soper 5-28-1846
  Isaac & Sarah Miles 1-14-1795
  Lizzie & George Davis 4-11-1873 (Dwyer)
  Mary & Paul Gant 12-24-1870 (McDonald)
  Mary Ann & Albert J. King 2-15-1877 (Horner)
  Philip & Margaret Tongue 2-25-1785
  Rachael Ann & George A. Sansbury 12-27-1852
  Richard H. & Hessy Ridgway 12-28-1821
  Mrs. Sarah & Henry Soper 12-17-1818
  Sophia & Arsicius James Adams 9-4-1874 (Welsh)
LOCKLAND, Ann Maria & Richard S. Hall 5-10-1823
LODGE, Llewellen & Martha Ann Brown 5-21-1832

LOFLIN, Mary & Gassaway Watkins 4-17-1784
LOFTY, Frank & Rose Sellman col⁹ 5-2-1868 (Thomas)
LOGAN, Basil & Sallie Robinson 6-2-1877 (Gordon)
  James V. & Mary Elizabeth Cammel] 1-21-1866 Age 43 of Howard County,
    Md. factory employee. Minister Jas. Alex Young, Trin. Ep. Ch.
  Lloyd & Rachel Duvall 1-30-1802
LOGGANS, Sarah Ann & John Scott 5-15-1872
LOGGINS, Basil & Catharine Tolson 4-28-1865 both colored
LONG, Emily Jane & Joseph T. Owens 1-14-1873 (Kershaw)
  John & Mary Ann Higdon 4-27-1798
  Samuel & Martha Ransom 2-13-1784
  William & Rebecca Pickrell 2-11-1781
LOWDEN, Rachel & Moses Thompson 12-22-1783
LOWEREE, George E. & Margaret A. Regester 6-2-1868
LOWNDES, Eleanor & Dr. Thomas Anderson 11-29-1841
  Elizabeth & William Jackson 12-17-1813
  Eliz.ᵗʰ L. & Revᵈ William Pickney 9-27-1838
  Rebecca & Benjⁿ C. Stoddart 6-7-1781
LOWRY, John & Eleanor West Lyles 5-1-1802
  John & Mary Wilkins 4-10-1804
LOVEJOY, Alexʳ & Mary Sullivan 5-10-1779
  Alexander & Milly Boteler 9-6-1794
  Ann & Arthur Campbell 12-29-1788
  Eleanor & William Fowler 2-24-1786
  George N. & Rebecca Smallwood 6-10-1794
  Josias & Sarah Campbell 2-19-1789
  Lettice & Alexius Mitchell 10-7-1794
  Michael & Christian Poston 10-1-1788
  Michael & Elizabeth Curtain 2-10-1808
  Rebecca & William Nevitt 9-15-1803
  Samuel & Virlinda Mockbee 12-13-1793
LOVELACE, Ann & Wm. Holliday 2-12-1822
  Basil & Letty Walker 1-6-1801
  Caroline & James D. Wall 2-6-1865
  Elisha & Anne Jones 1-6-1789
  Elizabeth Sarah & John L. Frazier 5-21-1821
  George L. & Matilda A. Thomas 3-4-1872 (Gordon)
  Johannah & Josias Padgett 12-31-1796
  John & Mary Anne Taffe 1-17-1803
  Mary & John Wilson 12-24-1836
  Mary Ann & Richard Ridgeway 12-15-1803
  Nancy & William Grimes 12-17-1840
LOVELESS, Caroline & Somerville Chaney 9-2-1862
  Charles & Callie Nothey 2-11-1874 (Kershaw)
  Elisha & Sarah Ann Taylor 4-2-1839
  Elisha J. & Maggie F. Wells 1-18-1884 (Father Cunane)
  Eliza E. & Robert E. Thomas 1-6-1869 (Gordon)
  Ellen & George Stockett 5-6-1845
  Georgianna & Edmund Wells 4-2-1875
  Harriett & Richard Curtin 12-21-1839
  Henderson & Mary Ann Jones 2-7-1815
  Isaac & Sarrah Barrett 1-7-1791
  James & Sarah Ann Mangun 6-8-1831
  James H. & Caroline C. Gates 12-24-1845
  Jane & John J. Crook 12-22-1858

LOVELESS, Jane Alice & Benjamin Edward King 1-31-1882
  John & Martha Ann Lusby 12-26-1843
  John H. & Caroline Carrick 6-20-1855
  Maria A. & William A. Taylor 12-21-1830
  Martha Alice & Alfred E. Taylor 9-4-1869 (Chesley)
  Mary & John H. Smith 12-26-1853
  Mary C. & James E. Duvall 1-14-1867 (Beque)
  Millicent Ann & Alex. Francis 12-22-1783
  Rebecca & Leonard Taylor 5-10-1852
  Richard & Rosa Beall 6-2-1873 (Billup)
  Richard & Julia A. Wells 2-16-1881 (Rev. Dr. Gordon)
  Rosa M. & William Henry H. Carrick 3-1-1860
  Sarah Ann & George E. Stockett 12-5-1839
  Thomas & Elizabeth Smith 12-27-1842
  Unie & James Hunt 1-12-1793
  W. R. & Carrie Jones 12-30-1885 (Rev. Father Cunane)
  William H. & Catherine R. Thomas 2-4-1869
LOVELIS, Ignatius & Ann Calvert 12-23-1799
  Luke & Mary Ridgway 12-18-1800
LOW, James & Elizabeth Wig---- 7-26-1790
LOWE, Alice J. & Wm. A. Coale 2-4-1867 (Kershaw)
  Ann & John Urquhart 2-22-1793
  Ann & James Moore 2-3-1796
  Annie & William O'Donnell 2-12-1870
  Barbara & Elihu P. Stevens 6-19-1812
  Barsheba &Anthony Luxon 11-6-1786
  Basil & Tracey Wood 8-15-1785
  Bennett & Rebecca Deakins 12-7-1819
  Cath? & John Clarke 10-20-1843
  Charles F. & Mary B. Sutton 10-26-1795
  Daniel C. & Georganna Stone 8-13-1863
  Deborah & Walter Beckett 4-21-1813
  Elias & Sarah Henry 8-9-1785
  Emma & Wm. P. Eden 8-28-1862
  George & Mary Moore 12-12-1794
  James & Ellen Suit 3-23-1841
  James R. M. & Anna M.M.S.C. McCarty 5-14-1830
  James Rector Magruder & Christiana Arell 1-11-1803
  John & Susanna Riddle 7-10-1784
  John E. & Jane M. Perrie 12-11-1848
  John H. & Barbara Magruder 1-2-1788
  John H. & Ellen Padgett 3-12-1868 (Chesley)
  John T. & Ann Virginia Hardey 2-28-1863
  John W. & Eleanor Lisby 10-8-1807
  Keziah & Basil Talbott 6-17-1788
  Kitty & Levin Soper 2-13-1808
  Leonora & James Munroe Steed 9-20-1834
  Lloyd N. & Elizabeth Gantt 2-15-1825
  Luthy & Jesse Greenwell 1-6-1790
  Marrion E. & Jno. W. Alvey 11-19-1849
  Mary & Thomas Brown 11-9-1778
  Nathan & Johanna King 2-14-1838
  Nathaniel & Vallinda Hayes 9-9-1797
  Priscilla & Robert Wilburn 12-29-1798
  Rachel & Geo. Hutchinson 11-13-1781

LOWE, Rachel & John Willing Smith 2-27-1788
  Rachel & Joseph Wallingsford 6-22-1804
  Rebecca & Henry Pickrell 4-6-1779
  Sarah & George Allen 1-5-1782
  Warren & Ann Soper 6-1-1829
  William & Mary Henry 4-19-1783
  William & Martha Mattingly 12-30-1806
  Winefred & Joseph Greenwell 1-7-1793
LOWNDES, Eliz.th Ann & Horatio L. Edmonston 11-5-1828
LUCAS, Adam & Milley Tench 10-27-1806
  Ann & George Lutius 2-22-1816
  John & Mary Simmons 12-14-1780
  John & Rachel Duvall 9-12-1787
  John B. & Mary H. Duvall 11-22-1836
  Lucy Jane & James Pinn 5-4-1876
  Rebecca & John R. Davis 9-26-1881
LUCKER, Thomas & Rebecca Beane 2-7-1785
LUCKETT, Ann Maria L. & James T. Lusby 12-16-1858
  Mary Elizabeth & John A. Wood 10-25-1855
LUERS, Frank B. & Maggie A. Disney 2-13-1884
LUHN, Gustave & Harriet E. Medley 1-5-1863
LUSBEY, John & Martha Wilson 2-20-1778
LUSBY, Edw.d H. & Lorena Ann Taylor 4-21-1851
  Eleanor & Gerard Keith 12-27-1782
  Elizabeth E. & John L. Lusby 12-24-1850
  Ellen A. & Samuel P. Thorn 12-3-1884 (Rev. Mr. Towles)
  Emma A. & Philip P. Sweeney 2-2-1885 (Rev. Mr. Chesley)
  Essie L. & Thos. J. Watson 2-17-1879
  James R. & Walter Ann Townshend 1-25-1870 (Toles)
  James T. & Ann Maria L. Luckett 12-16-1858
  John L. & Elizabeth E. Lusby 12-24-1850
  Laura V. & Zachariah Turner 6-30-1875 (West)
  Lemuel F. & Geneva Sansbury 3-2-1868 (Martin)
  Margaret A. & Wm. L. Thompson 10-15-1872 (Fowler)
  Martha Ann & John Loveless 12-26-1843
  Mary E. & William Whitman 12-14-1857
  Mary Jane & James Simpson 12-3-1846
  Noah & Eliz.a Ana Day 12-3-1868 (Berry)
  Pliny E. & Lillie Thorn 2-15-1886 (Rev. Mr. Hyland)
  R. T. & Eliza Jane Olivia Allen 9-7-1863
  Rebecca & George W. Padgett 12-23-1882
  Richard H. & Georgie A. Sansbury 12-21-1868 (Martin)
  Rosana & Thomas A. T. Ball 9-30-1852
  Susan & James K. Simpson 2-20-1811
  Thomas H. & Caroline M. Thompson 12-21-1842
  William A. & Sarah Ann Carrick 1-30-1856
LUTIUS, George & Ann Lucas 2-22-1816
LUXON, Anthony & Barsheba Lowe 11-6-1786
LYLE, Martha & John Livingston 12-19-1793
LYLES, Eleanor West & John Lowry 5-1-1802
  Eliza & William Courts 5-17-1808
  Eliza & Thornley J. Everett 9-17-1851
  Elizabeth & Thomas Simmons 5-26-1795
  Emily & Henry D. Hatton 1-13-1812
  Frederick & Maria Chester 4-20-1866 (Fr. Call)

LYLES, Margery & Mordicai Plummer 11-14-1803
  Mary & Joseph Coombes 10-23-1797
  Priscilla & Wiseman Clagett 1-16-1779
  Rebecca S. & William L. Hatton 5-4-1846
  Richard & Harriett Magruder 1-11-1786
  Sarah M. & George Johnson of Va. 1-8-1841
  Sarah Magruder & Robert W. Harper 7-1-1815
  Sidney & John Weightman 5-25-1816
  Thomas & Eleanor Duckett 4-10-1779
  Thomas & Mary Jones 10-23-1790
  William & Caroline M. Clagett 1-4-1831
  William H. & Elizabeth Bruce 1-22-1830
  Zachariah & Henrietta Mitchell 7-27-1816
LYNCH, Charles & Mary Ann Fairall 5-28-1833
  Elizabeth B. & William J. Tippet 12-26-1838
  Henry D. & Sarah E. Pearce 12-6-1853
  James & Susannah Rawlings 10-19-1811
  James & Jane Watson 11-24-1832
  Jane & Ignatius Carroll 12-15-1800
  John S. & Rebecca Hayes 10-16-1818
  John T. & Sarah Garner 11-12-1849
  Miss Julia & Basil T. Brown 12-9-1862
  Mary Ann E. & George W. Wilson 12-26-1837
  Sarah & Lloyd Ridgely 8-6-1837
  Sarah Ann & Joshua James Edelen 2-13-1836
  V erlinda Jane & Stafford Taylor 2-24-1842
LYNN, Ann & William Buckland 11-24-1795
  Valentine & Elizabeth Johnson 9-21-1795
LYONS, John W. & Amelia Jane Dorsett 10-15-1857
  Lemuel & Bettie Brooks cold 6-25-1870 (Evans)
  Rousby & Sallie Griffin 4-7-1871 (Marbury)

MACATEE, Clarissa & Moses Harvey 12-15-1780
MACCABEE, Elizabeth & George W. Tucker 4-23-1885 (Rev. Jno. Cotton)
MACCASTLE, Mary & James Short 12-12-1791
MAC COLGIN, Catharine & Andrew Callely 3-9-1801
MACCUBBIN, Elizth M. & Matthais John Kaldenback 12-7-1846
  John M. & Ann Naylor 9-16-1826
MACDONALD, Thomas & Sarah Ann Stallings 1-12-1833
MACGILL, Ann & John McClerren 12-18-1788
  Eleanor & Richard Higgins 3-21-1783
  Elizabeth & Elijah Rawlings 8-6-1778
  Robert & Eleanor Beall 4-28-1789
MACKALL, Brooke & Bettie Brookes 2-29-1884 (Rev. C. W. Walker)
  Chloe & Augustus Franklin 7-21-1855
  Harriet & Bradley Carroll 9-12-1871
  Holliday & Joana Hodge 12-31-1883 (Rev. Mr. Brown)
  John & Jane Magruder 1-11-1788
  John G. & Susannah Somerville 4-3-1802
  Margaret & George Contee 10-17-1885 (Rev. Brooks)
  Margaret J. & Edmund Key 6-7-1814
  Mary & Alexander Magruder 2-27-1790
  Rebecca & Levin Covington 3-25-1796

MACKALL, Rebecca & The Revd Walter D. Addison 2-2-1814
  Rebecca & Fielder Bowie 3-10-1835
  Susan J. & John Thomas 2-15-1870 (Wheeler)
MACKABEE, Mary H. & Matthias Clarke 2-17-1879 (Major)
MACKAY, Hugh & Catherine Grant 2-11-1790
MACKCENEY, Zachariah & Martha Simmons 2-23-1789
MACKEBEE, Lena & Henry Orme Age 35, black, washerwoman m 11-12-1865
MACKELL, Mary J. & William Dyson 9-16-1876 (Green)
MACKENRIE, Colin & Crista S. Bowie 11-28-1853
MACKEY, Samuel D. & Annie Taylor 3-22-1880
MACKNESS, Samuel & Ann War 9-2-1779
MACNEW, Mary & Rezin Harbin 11-14-1778
MADDOCKS, Nathan & Meshal Robey 12-18-1781
MADDOX, Ann & Edward Bond 2-9-1877 (WElls)
  Catherine M. & Richard Bryan 4-1-1844
  Clarissa & William H. Gordon 7-5-1848
  Elizabeth C. & Francis W. Hutchins 4-29-1871
  Ellen & William H. Yoe 8-10-1844
  Frances & George Farr 2-12-1798
  George Franklin & Mary Suit 3-8-1882 (Rev. Dr. Lewin)
  John & Cornelia Brooks 4-11-1874 (Tennent)
  Leonard & Sarah Ann Ash 10-28-1871 (Marbury)
  Lillian M. & James W. Richardson 9-18-1883 (Rev. Mr. LaRoche)
  Margaret E. & Jarret H. Berry 1-31-1826
  Notley & Priscilla Skinner 5-5-1801
  Priscilla & Josias H. Hanson 11-24-1832
  Sarah Ann & John Ball 2-4-1802
MADISON, John & Hannah Matthews 10-11-1869 (Chesley)
MAGILL, Benjamin & Ann Yates 12-4-1826
  John & Elizabeth Belt 11-13-1786
  Julia A. & Septimas Cook 4-23-1845
  Mary Janeanna & Francis Neale Brent 11-17-1858
MAGINNES, Elizabeth & Barnabas Wilson 1-11-1786
MAGRUDER, Aaron & Anna Kent 5-1-1869 (Maher)
  Alexander & Mary Mackall 2-27-1790
  Alexander J. J. & Catherine Johnson 2-20-1836
  Ann S. & William H. Sweeny 12-24-1860
  Anna & Robert Hay 3-9-1791
  Augusta & Peter H. Hooe 4-3-1856
  Barbara & John H. Lowe 1-2-1788
  Caleb C. & Mary S. Belt 5-28-1833
  Caleb C. & Sally B. Waring 6-3-1847
  Casandra & James McKenzie 3-8-1781
  Clarissa Harlowe & James Webb 10-13-1806
  Dennis & Ann Contee 9-23-1779
  Dennis & Elizabeth G. Contee 5-29-1805
  Dennis & Frances Fitzgerald 10-4-1817
  Dennis & Mary Ann Beard 11-21-1820
  Dennis & Ellen B. Mullekin 12-16-1832
  Edward & Anne Ellen 10-23-1800
  Edward & Tracy Barnes 2-15-1813
  Edward W. & Eliza Maria Mullikin 4-23-1866 (Young)
  Edward W. & Leila Gordon Osbourn 11-18-1885 (Rev. Mr. Chesley)
  Eleanor & John M. Burgess 10-18-1779
  Eleanor B. & Robert Bowie 12-9-1850

MAGRUDER, Elizabeth & John Blackburn 2-4-1787
  Elizabeth & Osborn Williams 10-15-1787
  Elizabeth Ann & James Trueman Magruder 12-1-1803
  Elizabeth Hawkins & James Somerville 11-7-1792
  Elizth & Samuel B. Harper 2-25-1828
  Emma & Brook M. Berry 1-25-1816
  Emma C. & William W. Wilson 12-6-1875
  Enoch & Elizabeth Sprigg 2-27-1780
  Enoch & Elizabeth Sprigg 2-27-1781
  Francis & Barbara Williams 12-23-1786
  Harriette & Richard Lyles 1-11-1786
  Harriot & Alexander Covington 12-16-1797
  Haswell & Ann Allen 4-18-1802
  Henderson W. & Mary L. Hill 1-22-1883 (Rev. Mr. Brashaw)
  Henrietta & Levin Beall 1-6-1802
  Henry & Maria Tayler 11-11-1873 (Dwyer)
  Ida & Jeffrey Phillips 11-2-1864
  Isaac & Ann Hill 4-3-1802
  Isaac G. & Margaret E. Hill 10-23-1837
  J. H. & W. H. Wolfe 2-25-1884 (Rev. Wm. K. Boyle)
  James A. & Millicent Beane 6-10-1794
  James Trueman & Elizabeth Ann Magruder 12-1-1803
  Jane & John Mackall 1-11-1788
  Jane & Thomas Beall 12-28-1839
  Jane A. & J. S. Adams 1-3-1871 (Begue)
  Jane B. & John Waring 2-17-1820
  Jane Contee & William Marbury Jr. 2-3-1801
  John B. & Mary Ann Hill 1-13-1834
  John Bowie & Sarah Jones 2-3-1791
  John Read & Polly B. Magruder 11-5-1812
  John Read & Eliza Waring 4-1-1820
  John Read Junr & Amelia Hall 9-13-1794
  John T. & Eliza Hoxton 1-27-1881
  Julia J. & George D. Fry 8-2-1876 (Williams)
  Kitty & Adderton Skinner 8-29-1798
  Laura & Philip Burley 6-7-1884
  Louisa & William Wilson 9-26-1833
  Marg^t Jane & Edward Hoskin 7-20-1868
  Margaret S. & Ignatius Wheeler 3-18-1808
  Marion E. & Delano Piper 12-3-1856
  Martha & William M. Bowie 10-30-1809
  Martha & W. Green 12-19-1867 (Langford)
  Mary & Thomas Boyd Junr 10-13-1788
  Mary & Thomas Forster 6-2-1794
  Mary & William Magruder 9-3-1839
  Mary & John Duckett 1-10-1868
  Mary A. & P. Carter Dunlop 8-14-1830
  Mary A. & Washington J. Beall 7-8-1840
  Mary C. & James A. Suit 2-8-1862
  Mary T. & William W. Hill 11-25-1844
  Matilda & Henry Hilleary 5-21-1832
  Matilda Margaret Snowden & Daniel McCarty Junr 10-4-1800
  Nathan & Elizabeth Bevin 8-12-1790
  Oliver B. & Rosanna D. Crowley 11-22-1842
  Polly B. & John Read Magruder 11-5-1812

MAGRUDER, Priscilla & James Handling 5-22-1787
  R. & Mary E. Douglass 12-27-1884 (Rev. W. Williams)
  Rebecca & George Washington Hilleary 1-10-1826
  Rebecca D. & Peoly Brown 1-12-1822
  Richard & Sophronia Young 9-6-1841
  Richard A. C. & Emily C. Bowie 10-25-1824
  Ruth & Henry Howel 6-23-1842
  Samuel & Mary Hilleary 1-11-1791
  Samuel & Ann Hilleary 3-30-1803
  Sarah & Bernard Shanley 2-3-1785
  Sarah & John Osborn 1-12-1788
  Sarah Anne & Isaac Brooke 10-20-1780
  Sarah Matilda & Horace Christman 10-4-1876 (Williams)
  Sophia & Philip W. Hill 4-25-1826
  Susanna B. & Henry Phillips 5-15-1828
  Thomas & Mary Clarke 1-4-1800
  Thomas & Polly Bowie Beanes 11-21-1803
  Virginia & George H. Howell 3-27-1852
  William & Eliz^{a} Hilleary 2-5-1796
  William & Mary Magruder 9-3-1839
MAHAN, Jon^{a} & Eleanor S. Mahen 2-11-1784
  Eleanor S. & Jon^{a} Mahan 2-11-1784 MAHEN (last name), Eleanor S.
MAHEW, Alice & William Walace 4-23-1778
  Brian & Ann Conley 6-19-1779
  Francis & Samuel C. Hull 7-5-1779
  Henry & Elizabeth Bryan 7-10-1800
  Letitia & John Brightwell 1-25-1804
  Mary & William Cage 12-18-1777
  Mary Ann & Alexander Soper 12-17-1819
  Susannah & John Stone Poston 12-24-1797
  Thomas & Mary Glover 4-14-1781
  Verlinda & William Wilson Cage 12-22-1807
MAHONEY, Edward & Alis Taylor 12-18-1786
  John M. & Sarah Ann Miller 3-30-1872 (Fowler)
  Joseph & Rachel Plummer 6-5-1873 (O'Dwyer)
  Joseph S. H. & Elizabeth Matthews 12-31-1866 (Smith)
  Mary C. & James R. Pinkney 1-1-1877
  Matilda & William Digges 2-19-1876 (Green)
MAHONY, John & Elizabeth Moore 5-14-1785
MAHORNEY, Edelburgodis & Jonathan Jarvis 5-23-1787
  Geo. H. & Gwinnie Penn 2-13-1878 (Weems)
MAITLAND, James Junr. & Mary Taylor 6-17-1800
MAKIMSEY, Alice R. & George T. Grimes 12-18-1877 (Kershaw)
MALONE, Catherine & John Teasdale 5-5-1778
MALONEE, Leonard of Ann Arundel County & Ann M. Johnson m 12-26-1866 at
  Elverton Hall by John W. Chesley, Prot. Ep. minister
  Age 35, widower, farmer
MALONY, Ann & Gilbert Whitney 11-21-1794
MALOR, George & Elizabeth Jones col^{d} 5-23-1869 (McDonald)
MANDELL, Adeline & Thomas Clagett 11-13-1838
MANGER, Moses & Ann Waters 10-22-1814
MANGLER, Harriet & John Fowler 7-16-1842
MANGUM, Anna & John D. Knott 12-6-1879
  Emma A. & John H. Wilson 12-19-1882 (Rev. Mr. Wolf)
  J. Kelley & Sarah A. Coffrin 1-29-1880 (Rev. Dr. Lavin)

MANGUM, Mary & Lloyd Swaney 2-10-1790
  Mary C. & William E. Mangun 4-19-1883 (Dr. Lewin)
  Nuly & George Browning 3-16-1885
  Susan N. & James P. Kerby 2-3-1879
  Wm. H. & Susan L. Hopkins 7-14-1864
MANGUN, Barbara & William H. Hall 6-24-1851
  Dorinda V. & Otho R. Brashears 3-20-1848
  Eleanor & Norando Wilson 12-26-1785
  Eliza J. & Rich? Carr 11-8-1848
  George & Matilda Whittington 10-16-1838
  George W. & Mary Ellen Jenkins 8-12-1876 (Green)
  Gonsalvo D. & Mary Elizabeth Harvey 7-26-1853
  Henry & Eleanor Tarman 1-25-1797
  Henry & Hetta Ann Brightwell 2-7-1851
  James & Mary German 12-22-1807
  Jesse & Martha Howell 12-20-1841
  John & Elizabeth Piles 8-4-1785
  John M. & Laura Wilson 9-15-1883
  Jonas G. & Ann Selby 1-12-1803
  Levi & Ann Gibbons 12-23-1806
  Martha Ann & Gassaway W. Ridgeway 11-27-1875
  Mary & Isaac G. Brown 3-28-1818
  Mary & William Dove 2-18-1839
  Rachel & Jonathan Gibbons 1-31-1810
  Sarah & Fielder Tayman 12-18-1815
  Sarah Ann & James Loveless 6-8-1831
  William E. & Sophia Birkman 8-8-1872 (Gordon)
  William E. & Mary C. Mangun 4-19-1883 (Dr. Lewin)
  Zachariah & Elizabeth Welling 1-21-1818
  Zachariah & Mary Ann Carr 11-17-1847
MANGUNN, Ann & Jeremiah Wells 12-13-1836
MANGUS, Sarah & Theodore Mitchell 11-30-1824
MANLEY, Elizabeth & Elijah Jones 5-15-1784
  Hannah G. & Francis T. Hawks 1-5-1866 (Call)
  John & Mary Shagnasha 7-22-1786
  Thomas & Prescilla Ray 1-15-1785
  William & Sarah Brown 1-7-1789
MANN, Jennett & Thomas Plummer Latten 1-20-1802
MANNEL, Mary Virginia & Harlan P. Tabb 5-29-1885 (Rev. J. W. Wolfe)
MANNING, Ignatius & Everlina Rosetta Hammond King Groves 1-31-1815
  Jannette R. & Thomas C. Boarman 12-12-1847
  Joseph & Mary Brooke 11-5-1857
  William W. & Margaret Bryan 6-30-1800
MARBURY, Alexander & Elizth H. F. Marshall 5-31-1832
  Benjamin F. & Josephine E. Bayne 6-2-1856
  Betty D. & Calhoun Benham 4-27-1855
  Caroline & William Marshall Jr. 6-11-1810
  Cora & William A. Nimmo 1-3-1853
  Elizabeth M. & William Christian 9-23-1858
  Fendall & Sarah C. Berry 4-7-1869 (Chesley)
  Fendall Jr. & Lucy C. Berry 9-10-1883 (Rev. Dr. Lewin)
  Henrietta Beanes & Thomas Henry Clagett 11-16-1804
  Jane Contee & Hanson Penn 2-29-1824
  Jane P. & James M. Williams 1-4-1858
  John & Elizabeth Somervell 11-12-1817

MARBURY, William Jun. & Jane Contee Magruder 2-3-1801
  William A. & Annie Summerville 11-8-1882
MARCERONE, Alexius & Sarah Josephine Jarboe 1-27-1881 (Rev. Father DeWolfe)
MARDEN, Henry F, & Leonora Piles 2-25-1852
  Ida & Henry J. Fry 1-3-1881 (Rev. Solomon German)
  Mary Ann & George Francis Kerby 8-2-1881 (Rev. Mr. Hyland)
MARICA, William & Ruth Duvall 10-29-1778
MARINE, Wm. M. & Harriet P. Hall 11-3-1871 (MacDonald)
MARK, Edward T. & Julia A. Gibbons 6-21-1841
  Julia & John William Sasscer 3-26-1845
MARKLE, Harry H. & Allie F. Smith 5-7-1868
MARKWOOD, Georgeanna & Robert Downing 9-24-1850
  William & Mary Onion 12-22-1824
MARLIN, William & Ann Gales 12-27-1782
MARLOW, Abraham & Sarah Marlow 9-6-1779
  Amelia & Richard Pickrell 7-24-1779
  Amelia & Richard Pickrell 10-30-1779
  Buttler & Charlotte Foard 12-21-1782
  Clara B. & Richard Thomas Smith 12-12-1884 (Rev. Mr. Robey)
  Eliza & Thomas Prather 3-8-1817
  John & Elizabeth Baden 10-29-1791
  Martha & Benoni Earley 2-22-1816
  Mary M. & John Giles Lilburn Boswell 2-10-1826
  Sarah & Abraham Marlow 9-6-1779
  Thomas D. & Margaret Clagett 3-10-1787
  Thomas S. & Catherine E. Cawood 1-20-1844
  William & Mary Willett 12-29-1786
MARLOWE, Ann Middleton & Josias Fendall Beall 1-18-1804
  Butler D. & Elizabeth Webster 8-30-1796
  Edward & Mary Gill 12-8-1807
  John S. & Elizabeth Ann Bayne 12-1-1819
  Maria C. & George Rust 11-8-1809
  Samuel & Eliza Harvey 2-29-1816
  William & Elizabeth Smith 2-17-1803
MARR, Joshua & Joanna Speak 1-2-1779
MARRIOTT, Flavilla & John H. Blake of Calvert County 5-22-1862
  Jane W. & Nathan Waters of Henry 6-26-1838
  Jennie C. & Henry Tolson 11-19-1860
MARSHALL, Benj[a] & Sarah Upton 1-17-1778
  Caroline Sophia & Edmund Briscoe 12-2-1844
  Christianna & John Greenfield 11-17-1877 (Hooman)
  Eleanor F. & George R. Marshall 2-15-1854
  Elizabeth Fendall & Samuel Hanson 7-29-1788
  Eliz[th] H. F. & Alexander Marbury 5-31-1832
  George & Annie Dyer col[d] 12-22-1869 (Langford)
  George R. & Eleanor F. Marshall 2-15-1854
  Harriet R. & James M. Marshall 10-20-1856
  James M. & Harriet R. Marshall 10-20-1856
  James W. & Mary Smith 2-8-1878 (Homan)
  John & Elizabeth Pumphrey 1-1-1852
  Josias & Sarah Harris 4-18-1797
  Mary & Philip Steward 2-26-1787
  Mary & Joseph Pope 12-1-1817
  Mary & Charles E. Hawkins 5-28-1884
  Matilda Ann & Edward Groce 9-26-1868 (Lilly)

MARSHALL, Peter & Jane Fletcher 11-2-1870 (Maher)
  Richard H. & Ann Summers 1-7-1815
  Richard O. & Henrietta O. Summers 2-22-1851
  Robert & Ann Berry 2-25-1820
  Robert & Charlotte Brown 2-25-1839
  Samuel & Drusilla Jenkins 7-22-1809
  Sarah & Ezekial Masters 1-7-1804
  Washington & Rebecca Owens 7-18-1876
  William Jr. & Caroline Marbury 6-11-1810
MARSHMAN, James & Rebecca Gordon 10-22-1779
MARTEN, Zephaniah & Sarah Eliz^a Ford Robinson 12-30-1795
MARTIN, Alfred R. & Clara Robey 11-13-1884
  Anna Statia & Alectius Boone 11-8-1806
  Catherine A. F. & Judson S. Clements 2-17-1873 (Towles)
  Catherine R. & George R. Cooksey 11-24-1852
  Charlotte & Horace E. Nichols 4-27-1855
  Chloe & Charles Robey 2-23-1810
  Elizabeth & William Whiten 9-14-1841
  Ellen & Henry A. Williams 9-12-1865 Age 25yr-5 mo. m. 9-28-1865
    St. Barnabas Church
  George H. & Sarah Ann Adams 6-4-1867 (Kershaw)
  Jane E. & James H. Turner 1-18-1838
  Jennie C. & Lewis C. Beall 12-30-1874
  John F. A. & Sallie L. Sweeney 4-17-1883 (Father Cunnane)
  John H. & Frances E. Brashears 7-4-1870 (Kershaw)
  John M. & Catharine A. Carroll 1-24-1846
  Josephine V. & Joseph H. Howell 4-7-1874
  Julian A. & Laura C. Whitmore 5-22-1884 (Rev. Mr. Highland)
  Mildred & Daniel Lewis 1-2-1792
  Philip & Susan Ann Turner 12-16-1874 (Stanley)
  Richard & Ann Russell 1-1-1780
  Sarah Ann E. & John D. Greenwell 3-14-1851
  Smith & Catharine Burch 4-1-1822
  Thomas Jr. & Elizabeth Wall 4-29-1837
  Wallace L. & Estelle M. Beall 12-31-1875
  Wm. H. & Jane Ann Carroll 2-18-1851
MASON, Chloe & Josias Lanham 2-14-1790
  Sarah & Richard Kay 2-16-1784 MASON, Sarah & John Reives 4-19-1781
  Thomas & Sarah Hyde 7-21-1787
  Virlinda & William Wilson 1-10-1780
  Wm. & Caroline Edelen 6-30-1817
MASSEY, Mary E. & Presley N. Athey 6-6-1843
MASSON, Elizabeth & John L. Talbert 10-4-1866 Age 18 (Kershaw)
  Martha & Joseph Talbert lic. 9-5-1872 m. Oct. 29, 1872 (Kershaw)
MASTERS, Dorcas & Wm. Jenkins 12-31-1778
  Ezekiel & Cassandra Norton 4-11-1789
  Ezekial & Sarah Marshall 1-7-1804
  John & Prescella Bayne 6-3-1778
  Joshua Warren & Catherine Soper 10-28-1828
  Mary & John Waugh 11-2-1793
  Mary Ann Maria & Levin Ridgeway 10-19-1857
  Nathan & Winifred Jenkins 1-8-1794
  Nathan & Margaret Ridgeway 12-17-1857
  Nathan & Ann F. Darby 10-26-1885 (Rev. Mr. Hyland)
  William F. & Priscilla Ann Jenkins 2-6-1823

MATHANEY, Robt & Sarah P. Demar 12-9-1851
MATHES, Ann & Henson Butler 11-15-1884 (Rev. Mr. Towles)
MATHEWS, Isabella Mary & Titua Garrettson 6-1-1882 (Rev. Mr. Stanley)
MATTHASS, Thomas & Catharine Miller 1-16-1867 (Smith)
MATTHEWS, John & Sarah Alexander 12-29-1874 (Watts)
MATTHEWS, Louisa & Jacob Thomas 12-24-1883
 Charles & Ann Hawkins col^d 5-2-1868 (Thomas) MATTHEWS, Christiana &
 Charlotte & Austin Jackson 12-26-1866 (Stanley) Frank Sewall 10-16-1875
 Elizabeth & Joseph S. H. Mahoney 12-31-1866
 Fanny & Pinkney Barton 12-1-1879 (Jackson)
 Hannah & John Madison 10-11-1869 (Chesley)
 Henrietta & Thomas Williams 12-23-1871 (Wheeler)
 Hilleary & Marion Boyce 1-17-1868 (Smith)
 Russell & Mary Young col^d 12-22-1869 (Langford)
MATTINGLEY, Mary A. & Henry C. Thorn 9-16-1832
 William & Rebecca Beanes 2-7-1838
 Eleanor Rutha & Paul Hoye 12-23-1811
 Julia Ann & Levi Kerby 5-15-1855
 Martha & William Lowe 12-30-1806
 Richard Frederick & Rosa Bell Thompson 8-21-1871 (Watts)
MATTINLEY, Joseph & Margaret Scott 1-24-1785
MAULDEN, Willimina M. & Jn? Baden 1-12-1782
MAURICE, Theodore W^m & Margaret Matilda Edelen 7-16-1819
MAXLEY, Joshua & Harriot Smith 8-12-1813
MAY, Thomas & Ann Bing 4-1-1816
MAYCH, Ann & Elisha Riston 2-6-1790
MAYHEW, Ann & Thomas Howard 4-16-1794
 Basil & Henrietta Tucker 1-13-1868
 Benjamin & Susannah Virginia Hall 9-21-1864
 Catherine & Joseph Hodge 1-13-1858
 Elizabeth & John Ball 1-9-1822
 Elizabeth & William T. Elliott 3-1-1859
 James & Mary Ryon 5-14-1788
 Johne & Massy Soper 12-9-1795
 Martha Ann & Daniel Tippett 10-26-1876 (Green)
 Mary & Isaac Watson 3-21-1786
 Mary J. & E. Thomas Beall 4-15-1872 (Cotton)
 Philip W. & Catherine Jenkins 3-18-1854
 Timothy & Mary Higdon 3-17-1787
 William & Mary Cage 4-7-1794
 William & Elizabeth Talburt 12-23-1795
 Wm. Henry & Mary Julia Tucker 10-31-1865 Age 27, working hand, m. Farm
  of Richard Hill by H. J. Kershaw, min. Prot. Ep. Ch. Upper Marlboro
MAYNARD, Elizabeth & Robert Gantt 8-21-1790
MAYO, John & Ann E. Berry 10-20-1818
McATEE, Ann & Thomas Owens 4-27-1793
McATTEE, Maria & Elijah Wedge 8-24-1824
McCALLOUGH, Martha & B. N. Sweeny 3-16-1870 (Kershaw)
McCARLING, Eveline & George W. Clark 11-26-1848
McCARTEY, Sarah & Joseph Warrensford 12-20-1800
McCARTHY, Dennise & Mary Tabetha Mudd 9-16-1791
 John & Margaret P. Vermillion 6-2-1869
McCARTNEY, Fanny & William Mead 8-7-1796
McCARTY, Anna M.M.S.C. & James R.M. Lowe 5-14-1830
 Daniel Jun. & Matilda Margaret Snowden Magruder 10-4-1800
 Matilda M. S. & William G. Sanders 2-17-1815

148

McCAUGHEN, Priscilla & John Ranter 10-6-1804
McCAULEY, Rebecca & Alex.^r Harvey 7-19-1777
McCENEY, Edgar Patterson & Eliza Coombs Bowie 11-17-1873 (Billup)
McCLANE, Frederick & Jane Brown 2-5-1873
McCLERREN, John & Ann Macgill 12-18-1788
McCORMICK, Alex.^r & Elizabeth T. B. Young 10-25-1847
  Andrew T. & Sarah Ponsonby 8-27-1796
McCORMICK, Mary S. & Wm. P. Brooks 10-22-1880 (Rev. Mr. Brayshaw)
McCRAY, Farquire & Susanna Fergusson 4-21-1781
McCREADY, James & Eliz.th Mockaby 1-12-1848
McCUBBIN, Edward & Margaret Degraff 8-16-1826
McCULLOCH, Marie Louise & John Brooks Yale 5-17-1884
McCURDY, M. Tillie & DeLoss H. Smith 8-17-1870 (Rev. M. Howe)
McDANIEL, Allen & Sarah Osbourn 5-22-1823
  Archibald & Eleanor Tuel 6-25-1798
  Catharine & Richard Dement 3-1-1811
  Eleanor Jennett & Trueman Roberts 8-4-1803
  Elizabeth & David F. Beall 1-28-1800
  Elizabeth & Nicholas Farr 2-20-1816
  Janepher & Jn.? Vermilion 7-15-1780   McDANIEL, Martin N. 6-13-1808 & Ann Queen
  Mary & Ebbsworth Beane 12-12-1798
  Sarah & Henry Harvey 4-20-1791
  Sarah & Joseph Padgett 2-3-1807
  Seney & William Gray 2-14-1804
  William & Priscilla Ann Wyson 11-29-1779
McDANIELS, Cephas & Elizabeth Gray 2-20-1797
McDERMOND, Harriet & Henry Taylor 8-25-1840
McDONALD, Sarah & William Whitehead 6-11-1874
  Wm. Alexander & Sarah R. Hall 6-11-1872 (Dr. Register)
McDOUGALL, Alex.^r & Marg.^t Norwood 2-25-1783
McDOWELL, Ann & George Brown 5-27-1799
  Elizabeth & John King of Richard 7-30-1791
  Samuel & Mary Hannah 12-1-1805
  William & Mary Mitchell 10-24-1788
McELDERRY, Horatio C. & Eliza Forbes 10-29-1816
  Mary & Jacob Duckett 5-4-1799
  Patrick & Mary Clagett 6-5-1789
McELFRESH, Clara B. & William L. Hughes 3-28-1879
McEVER, Charles & Miledor Clifford 10-17-1778
McFARLEN, William & Casandra Woodward 12-13-1816
McGILL, Mary Gordon & James Belt Jun. 12-14-1813
McGREGOR, Agnes W. & Thomas T. S. Bowie 12-2-1868 (Kershaw)
McGREGOR, Alrick & Martha Key 2-8-1829
McGREGOR, Eliza & John H. Duckett col.^d 1-17-1852
  Henry & Eliza Berry 3-6-1829
  Isabella & T. Somerville Dorsett 12-2-1868 (Kershaw)
  John F. & Florence E. Wallace 6-9-1875 (Kershaw)
  Nathl M. & Susan E. Mitchell 12-22-1827
  Roderick & Ann Eaton 12-20-1831
  Roderick M. & Marg.^t Eliz.^a Bowie 10-12-1866 Age 23, farmer m. 10-16-1866
    res. of bride's mother by Henry J. Kershaw, Prot. Ep. Ch.
McILHANEY, William & Annie Sanderson 6-4-1867 (Kershaw)
McKAY, Alexander & Ann Campbell 12-16-1778
  Catharine S. & John Waters 9-29-1808
McKEE, Mr. A. & Sarah A. S. Gibbons 4-27-1864
  Alexander & Margaret R. Harvey 2-11-1834

McKEE, Alexander & Catherine M. Wall 9-3-1852
 Alexander & Hannah N. Gibbons 4-17-1858
 Ann E. & Edward Bean 4-13-1827
 Catharine M. & Edwin Stewart 11-29-1858
 Eliza C. & John S. Jarboe 10-16-1873 (Gordon)
 Irene Robertie & George F. Williams 11-20-1873 (Tennent)
 James W. & A. C. Josephine Robey 11-25-1867 (Dr. Ryan)
 Mary A. & M. R. Stamp 2-13-1855
Mc KENSEY, John & Sarah Jones 2-13-1806
McKENZIE, James & Casandra Magruder 3-8-1781
 Mary Ann & Joseph Alfred King 2-21-1877 (Gordon)
McKENZY, John & Solomy Talbott 3-19-1794
McKEVER, Bernard Lewis & Mary Elizabeth Schocberlein 1-20-1878 (Stanley)
McKNEW, Basil & Maria Frances Benson 11-21-1864
 Benjn P. & Diana Aitcheson Age 22, brick layer m. near Laurel
  11-30-1865 by J. A. Young, min. Presby. E. Ch.
 Mason E. & Margaret A. Godman 7-1-1857
McKNIGHT, John & Catharine Piercy 10-29-1799
McLEAN, William & Caroline Amelia Locker 4-12-1849
McLEOD, George & Caroline A. R. Deakins 5-7-1835
McLISH, Margaret & Alexander Jackson 4-30-1784
McNANTZ, Charles & Ann Wilson 8-19-1800
McNEMUS, John & Mary A. Dulany 11-12-1867 (Burry)
McNEW, Judson W. & Mahala Duvall 12-20-1824 .
 Thomas & Mary Summers 11-9-1802
 Thomas & Martha Maria Neall 11-23-1827
 Zadock W. & Elizabeth A. Evans 10-12-1830
McPHERSON, E. B. & Wm. M. Lambert 11-15-1873 (Towles)
 Henrietta & Peter Dejean 5-11-1816
 Mary & John Dare 11-5-1834
 Richard W. & Hellen Elizabeth Parker 1-15-1821
 Rebecca & John C. Weems 5-27-1874
 Samuel C. & Celestia Edelen 7-15-1828
 Susan E. & John A. Coe 10-20-1843
McQUILLIN, Eliza & Caleb Rawlings 7-6-1830
McSENEY, Deborah & Edward Pearce 6-3-1784
McSHERY, Hugh & Susannah Lanham 4-13-1790
McVEY, Benjamin & Mary Ray 6-15-1813
McWILLIAMS, Thomas & Emily M. Bowling 4-28-1858
MEAD, Brooke & Mary A. Talbert 12-14-1848
 George Grandon & Attaway Calvert 8-16-1873
 Theodore & Mary Ann Webster 5-29-1815
 William & Fanny McCartney 8-7-1796
MEADS, Brooke & Julia A. Orme 9-4-1873 (Townshend)
MEAGUYN, Burnett & Mary Clarke 6-11-1827
MEAKS, William & Sarah Roe 12-6-1809
MEANS, Francis & Ann Burkett 9-25-1779
MEEK, Western & Susannah Perkins 11-11-1800
MEEKE, Mary Ann & Zacharia Baldwin 4-1-1822
MEEKES, Mrs. Susan & Aquila D. Hyatt 10-17-1818
MEEKS, Elizth & William Hall 10-12-1830
MEDLEY, Elizabeth & Revd Joseph G. Bryant col^{d} 5-15-1882 (Rev. Mr. Chesley
 Francis Oscar & Harriet R. Harris 12-17-1860
 Harriet E. & Gustave Luhn 1-5-1863
 John Waring & Rosa Bruce Harris 2-17-1881 (Rev. Mr. Southgate)

150

MEDLEY, Lizzie & Thomas Ranson 6-17-1884 (Mr. Tho.ˢ H. Brooks)
  Lucey & Henry Hodge 3-27-1884 (Rev. Mr. Walker)
  Mary & William Beach 5-9-1797
MEGINNIS, J. M. & M. E. Berry 5-28-1836
MELLING, Katie J. & James S. Shedd 11-1-1876
MENGER, Arabella Josephine & Joseph B. Harris 10-10-1855
MENGERS, Eliza A. E. M. & Francis A. Ward 1-1-1831
MENNIS, John & Eleanor Gray 2-6-1807
MERCER, G. Douglass & Helen Bowling 11-10-1874
MERRICK, George C. & Alice M. Waring 1-24-1867 Age 29, lawyer - m. by
  N. D. Young, Catholic Priest
MERRILL, Milburn & Levin Olliver 2-5-1823
  Philip & Willy Oliver 10-27-1821
MERRIT, Elizabeth & Joseph Joiner 8-19-1800
  Susannah & Caleb Gibson 11-15-1819
MERROLL, Philip & Mocky Truman 2-10-1798
MERSER, Elizabeth E. & Franklin C. Padgett 9-13-1872
MESSENGER, Mary & Walter Smith Parker 3-31-1801
MIDDLETON, Ann & Anthony Soper 1-29-1844
  Catherine Hyatt & Lemuel Clark 5-17-1866 Age 20 (Dr. McCabe)
  Chas. S. & Olevia Hinton 1-6-1851
  Charles S. & Mary Isabella Hoxton 9-27-1859
  Cloe Ann & Hezekiah Miller 8-17-1818
  David & Ann Guinn 2-8-1821
  David & Jane Kirby 2-17-1827
  Eliza H. & C. Clinton Gardner 10-2-1882 (Rev. Mr. Hyland)
  Francis J. & Henrietta J. Hill 11-23-1857
  Henry O. & Ann H. Tolson 2-15-1814
  J. L. & Ada P. Parker 7-2-1867 (Lenehan)
  James W. & Virginia A. Wells 8-22-1859
  John & Eliza Soper 7-3-1828
  Laura & Andrew J. Augur 11-21-1878
  Mary & Henry Tolson 2-12-1827
  Reuben & Mary Ellen Hyatt 7-22-1843
  Sarah & Francis Tolson Jr. 9-18-1817
  Smith & Eliza Taylor 12-19-1871 (Wheeler)
  Susan & Edward Tolson 1-19-1825
  Susan Ann & Samuel T. Berry 12-29-1840
MIER, Eliz.ᵃ &Joseph Waters 8-25-1779
MILBURN, Mary A. & Wm. Henry Boswell 11-2-1864
MILES, David & Laura Dent 5-20-1873 (O'Dwyer)
  Eleanor & John Rabbitt 5-3-1778
  Frederick & Ruth Brashears 2-11-1784
  Fredᵏ & Eliz.ᵃ White 12-31-1781
  Henry & Henrietta Blanford 6-9-1783
  John & Jane Pearce 11-30-1780
  John & Rebecca Pearce 1-21-1783
  Mary & Francis Mitchell 4-26-1786
  Mary & Brock Mockbee 6-11-1788
  Mary & Joseph Delehaye 6-22-1788
  Priscilla & Wm. Miles Nevitt 1-1-1779
  Sarah & Isaac Locker 1-14-1795
MILLAR, Elizabeth & Richard H. Day 11-7-1832
  Elizabeth & Daniel Fisher 9-15-1835
  James F. & Rebecca Beall 7-28-1832

MILLAR, Leonara & Benjamin Prentis 3-14-1832
MILLARD, Eleanora & John T. Strickland 4-1-1869 (Maher)
  Elizabeth & Wm. B. Swain 10-23-1877
  George W. & Eliza Anne Scott 11-9-1867 (Fr. Call)
  Oscar A. & Mary A. Randall 2-20-1872 (Bush)
  William & Elizabeth Webb 6-22-1780
  William J. & Matilda Burgess 6-7-1862
MILLER, Ann &Robert Tilley 11-10-1801
  Catharine & Thomas Matthass 1-16-1867 (Smith)
  Catherine & David Hoovern 10-8-1819
  Cornelius J. & Eliza R. Stanton 12-12-1847
  Cornelius F. & Henrietta Ward 6-24-1855
  Elizabeth M. & John A. Wood 1-3-1840
  M. Eliz.th & Thomas M. Houchens 7-6-1869 (Lenaghan)
  Gustavus A. & Olivia F. Harman 7-17-1880 (Rev. Dr. Stanley)
  Henry S. & Fannie E. Owings 12-5-1878 (Homan)
  Hezekiah & Cloe Ann Middleton 8-17-1818
  John & Ann Hinton 12-26-1800
  Mary & Mark Duvall 1-11-1825
  Mary & Edward W. Duvall 7-11-1837
  Mary A. & Lloyd Wells 6-27-1842
  Mary A. & William M. Hawkins 12-29-1885 (Rev. Jno. R. Henry)
  Mary Ann & James A. Gregory 8-3-1843
  Philip & Elizabeth Veitch 1-24-1818
  Sarah & John W. Brown 5-11-1829
  Sarah Ann & John M. Mahoney 3-30-1872 (Fowler)
  Dr. Washington & Sophia R. Tolson 11-17-1855
MILLIKEN, see Mullican, Mullecan, Mullikin, Mulliken, Mullekin
  Henrietta B. of Prince George's County & Clem^{t} Hilleary of
    Frederick County 11-30-1818
  James & Eleanor Beanes 3-30-1781
MILLS, Eliza E. & Charles W. Hunt 12-8-1868 (Smith)
  Geo. Wm. & Julia Craig 4-23-1879 (Watkins)
  Henry & Jane R eeder col^{d} 1-13-1881 (Rev. Mr. Watkins)
  Hester & Abraham Fowler 11-28-1794
  John & Eliz^{a} Waters 1-18-1782
  John & Julia A. Batty col^{d} 11-28-1878 (Watkins)
  Mary & Benjamin Bird 2-9-1801
  Mary Jane & George F. Coffren 11-24-1869 (Linthicum)
  Philip E. & Sarah Amelia Spencer 1-15-1867 (Smith)
  Zachariah & Elizabeth Waters 12-21-1787
  Zachariah & Rachel Wells 1-7-1811
MINIS, Elizabeth & Joseph Fowler 1-15-1810
MINKER, Mary & John R. Brown 8-26-1880
MINOR, Edward & Annie C. Duckett 11-23-1885 (Rev. Mr. Smith)
MITCHELL, Alexander & Ann Simpson 9-20-1819
  Alexius & Lettice Lovejoy 10-7-1794
  Alice & Henry Brown 11-4-1871 (McDonald)
  Amelia & Benjn Ray 12-25-1782
  Ann & James Beall 5-9-1787
  Ann S. & Wm. E. Duvall 7-24-1830
  Anne J. &Charles W. Shaffer 9-17-1878
  Benjamin & Sarah E. Genisenger 2-2-1854
  Edward & Elizabeth Murphy 10-19-1812
  Edward & Elizabeth Crandall 1-19-1814

MITCHELL, Edward & Ann Richardson 1-26-1818
 Eleanor & Thomas Clark 12-9-1797
 Eleanor & Benjamin Ray 1-11-1809
 Eleanor & James Wilson 7-6-1811
 Eliza & William Courts 1-19-1822
 Elizabeth R. & John W. Taylor 2-3-1868 (Chesley)
 Eliz^h & Richd Johnson Coughland 2-28-1785
 Elizth & Notley Sweeny 11-5-1828
 Emily & Charles Hawkins 12-27-1875 (Scott)
 Emily & Henry Duvall 1-27-1885 (Fr. Cotton)
 Emily & Rinaldo Butler 12-30-1885 (Rev. Frank Wills)
 Frances & John Pool 9-4-1784
 Francis & Mary Miles 4-26-1786
 Francis & Thomas Burly 10-14-1875 (Rev. Mr. Howard)
 Francis J. & Eleanor Sewall 1-2-1809
 Geo. A. & Mary Duvall 5-2-1848
 H. G. & S. A. Owens col^d 5-11-1869 (Kershaw)
 Hannah & Zachariah Piles 8-29-1801
 Helen Woods & John Swan 4-21-1834
 Henrietta & Zachariah Lyles 7-27-1816
 Henry & Lavinia Duvall 11-22-1830
 James & Lucy LanHam 4-3-1819
 John & Drury Sweney 5-10-1788
 John & Rebeccah Clubb 1-29-1791
 John & Mary Lanham 1-10-1818
 Jno. R. & Laura Bayne 12-30-1864
 Joseph & Lyley Gray 2-17-1812
 Lucy Ann & Richard Brandtt 12-15-1792
 Margaret & Samuel Studman 5-6-1820
 Margaret Julia of New York & William Virgil Wallace of New York 9-26-1862
 Martha Ann & Robert Fletcher col^d 8-9-1867 (Beque)
 Mary & Thomas King 10-16-1787
 Mary & William McDowell 10-24-1788
 Mary & Josias Hatton 2-22-1793
 Mary A. & Joseph J. Duvall 5-12-1851
 Mary J. & Edward J. Hawkins 5-13-1880
 Massy Ann & Joseph Mullican 10-10-1797
 Medora F. & John Owens 1-12-1880 (Rev. Daniel Aquila)
 Middleton & Rebeccah Riston 4-21-1792
 Middleton F. & Sarah J. Duvall 12-9-1867 (Beque)
 Mordicai Miles & Sarah Wilson 11-26-1779
 Nancy & Elias Padgett 9-10-1828
 Polly & Leonard Davis 12-26-1812
 Priscilla & Thomas Upton 2-19-1798
 Rachel & Amos Chaney 3-12-1807
 Rector & Sarah Mockbee 12-20-1804
 Samuel & Susannah Boone 1-2-1794
 Samuel & Martha Baden 1-1-1816
 Sarah & Thomas Stallings Junr 11-25-1791
 Sarah & Robert Watson 3-25-1815
 Sarah & George Gray 11-23-1816
 Sarah & Thomas Wirt 12-21-1819
 Sarah A. & William E. Anderson 4-10-1869 (Chesley)
 Sarah Elizabeth & James Clarke 12-3-1855
 Spencer & Mary Waring 12-15-1803

MITCHELL, Spencer & Lucy Peach 11-9-1812
 Susan & Philip Hall 8-14-1823
 Susan E. & Nath⫟ M. McGregor 12-22-1827
 Theodore & Mary Wells 11-27-1777
 Theodore & Sarah Mangus 11-30-1824
 Theodore & Jane King 11-7-1833
 Thomas & Eleanor Edelen 11-9-1778
 Thomas & Eleanor Mockbee 12-22-1783
 Thomas & Elizabeth Vermillion 10-2-1802
 Thomas & Eleanor Scrivner 2-3-1823
 Thomas Lee & Elizabeth Wilson 9-29-1792
 William & Mary White 12-10-1792
 William H. & Sarah King 11-6-1834
 Wm. R. & Mary E. Brashears 1-3-1867 (Robey)
 Zephaniah & Ann Johnson 1-29-1810
 Zephaniah & Providence Shipley 5-19-1817
MITCHELLMORE, Nellie & George R. Leapley 2-8-1876 (McNeer)
MOBBERLY, Elizabeth & Luke Windsor 1-23-1797
 Hezekiah & Eli⫟.Kidwell 12-5-1796
 Mary & Ignatius Winser 12-21-1792
MOBLEY, Ann & William Langley 2-26-1822
MOBLEY, Bency & Horatio Robey 12-23-1813
 James & Ann Tayler 1-12-1811
 Jonathan & Susanna Church 2-5-1793
 Sarah Ann & Thomas Sweeney 1-3-1842
MOCKABY, Eliz^th & James McCready 1-12-1848
MOCKBEE, Alexander & Sarah Lanham 1-2-1808
 Alexander & Terrence Beall 12-24-1810
 Althea & Richard Prather 1-8-1825
 Ann & Basil Mockbee 11-5-1779
 Basil & Ann Mockbee 11-5-1779
 Brock & Mary Miles 6-11-1788
 Darkey & William Jones 6-25-1791
 Eleanor & Thomas Mitchell 12-22-1783
 Hickerson & Lethea Willson 2-13-1822
 John & Marg⫟ Robinson 8-20-1777
 John & Margaret Clarke 12-26-1833
 Linna & John Lanham 3-6-1800
 Matilda & William Lanham 1-18-1813
 Mary & Colmore Pope 5-12-1801
 Philip & Susannah Darnall 12-24-1808
 Rachel & John Ridgeway 12-2-1778
 Rebecca & Thomas Sansberry 2-25-1797
 Samuel & Mary Ann Padgett 7-11-1827
 Sarah & Anthony Beard 11-14-1801
 Sarah & Rector Mitchell 12-20-1804
 Virlinda & Samuel Lovejoy 12-13-1793
 William Junr & Marg⫟ Henness 12-24-1780
 Wm. & Ann Clarke 2-29-1780
MOCKEBOY, Nelly & John Hinkey 12-20-1820
MOLAN, James & Catherine Montgomery 10-20-1780
MOLDING, Nehemiah N. & Elizabeth A. Moore 1-3-1877 (Griffith)
MOLLESON, William & Rebecca Gunn 5-5-1781
MONGOLLIN, Wm. Fred^k & Emily Rebecca Suit 4-1-1874
MONK, Elizabeth Ann & Thomas Coffren 5-25-1854

MONKHOUSE, Howard & Elizabeth A. Tyson 6-23-1870 (Young)
MONROE, Elizabeth F. & Wm. Boswell 11-8-1851
  Ella Gertrude & William Fred⸢ᵏ Kerby 11-3-1884 (Rev. Mr. Hyland)
  Samuel R. & Kate B. Townshend 5-19-1880
  Susan & John Simmes 12-23-1885 (Rev. Mr. Brookes)
MONTGOMERY, Austin & Sarah A. E. M. Cooke 11-25-1839
  Catherine & James Molan 10-20-1780
  Margaret Ann & Richard Cook 9-18-1821
MOOR, Susan & John Henry Fry 9-13-1864
MOORE, Amelia L. & John H. Bayne 3-24-1868 (Kershaw)
  Ann & Jesse Greenwell 1-21-1795
  Barbara & Robert Dean 3-30-1861
  Charity Ann & Basil Brown 5-14-1833
  Christiana & Jesse Carter 4-2-1804
  Christopher C. & Mary Burgess 2-5-1870 (Chesley)
  David & Lizzie Digges 6-5-1870 (Mahr)
  Eliza & Overton Warner 3-24-1813
  Eliza E. & William O. Bean 4-11-1871 (Williams)
  Elizabeth & John Mahoney 5-14-1785
  Elizabeth A. & Nehemiah N. Molding 1-3-1877 (Griffith)
  Elizᵗʰ M. & William O. Tayman 11-22-1849
  Ellen Alice & James T. Young 3-30-1872 (Lanahan)
  Emma & Joshua W. Farr 6-14-1866 Age 17 (Kershaw)
  Francis E. & Louisa Ball 1-2-1866 (Porter) Age 21, farmer
    m. 1-4-1866 at Mr. Ball's by A. J. Porter, minister
  George & Eleanor Drane 11-19-1792
  George & Elizabeth Scaggs 12-30-1828
  George D. & Sarah Bayne 12-16-1795
  George M. & Mary Elizabeth Allen 5-15-1869 (Martin)
  George Washington & Martha Isabella Vermillion 4-12-1880 (Revᵈ. Mr.Butler)
  Horatio & Ann Wheat 8-10-1803
  James & Ann Lowe 2-3-1796
  James H. & Rosa Ann Booze 9-25-1884 (Rev. Mr. Williams)
  Jennie & George W. Beall 2-4-1880 (Revᵈ Mr. Butler)
  John & Elizᵈ Keadle 3-3-1783
  John C. & Lettice Eleanor Thomas 10-11-1808
  John D. & Ann Amelia Allen 11-27-1838
  Jonas & Mary Swann 3-5-1866 (Kershaw) Age 23, farmhand m. 3-6-1866
    Est. of Benj. Duvall, Henry J. Kershaw, min. P. E. Ch. Upper Marlboro
  Joseph & Elizabeth Dunn 7-11-1798
  Joseph B. & Sophia M. A. Moore 1-1-1877 (Adams)
  Josephine & Isaac Wood 5-24-1832
  Josiah & Charity Duckett 4-21-1778
  Josias & Christiana Ridgeway 12-30-1834
  Lethe Ann & Thomas H. Thompson 1-5-1870 (Gordon)
  Letty & Jonathan Ridgway 1-2-1811
  Letty W. & John W. Kidwell 12-27-1828
  Levi & Charity Scarce 12-12-1801
  Lucy & John Fowler 12-30-1802
  Marsham & Mary Allen 12-7-1842
  Marsham & Louisa Webster 12-11-1848
  Mary & George Lowe 12-12-1794
  Mary & George Cater 12-23-1815
  Mordicai & Barbara Ridgway 11-20-1805
  Mordecai J. & Elizabeth Ridgeway 1-18-1842

MOORE, Presilla & Math͟ᵂ Kidwell 12-20-1781
   Randall & Emily Boteler 12-20-1867 (Smith)
   Richard & Catherine Ann Goddard 11-17-1830
   Sarah & Jas. Fraser Thompson 6-5-1778
   Sarah & Edward C. Edelen 12-8-1801
   Sarah & William Duhays 12-24-1803
   Sophia M. A. & Joseph B. Moore 1-1-1877 (Adams)
   William & Alethia Wallingsford 6-8-1804
   Zadock & Ann King 3-6-1779
   Zadock & Mary Soper 6-6-1779
   Zadock & Rachel Elson 11-22-1782
MOORHEAD, Evis W. & Wilbur F. Smith 11-10-1875 (Nichols)
MORAN, Agnes E. & Josias R. M. Watson 12-4-1883
   Elizabeth & Samuel B. Duvall 12-15-1831
   Henrietta W. & Gabriel Duvall 11-6-1833
   James & Jane Hellen 5-6-1780
   Jesse & Elizabeth Fitzgarald 11-24-1817
   Johnson & Susan Estep 2-25-1824 also listed as 3-4-1824
   Mary & Zephaniah C. Suit 2-1-1826
   Samuel C. & Mary M. Bowie 10-8-1833
   Sarah & William Swaine 1-30-1802
   Victoria P. & William A. Roder 4-10-1880 (Rev. Mr. Butler)
MORE, William & Mary Duke 3-6-1780
MORELAND, Ann & Thomas A. Richardson 1-20-1816
   Elias & Letty Ann Tenly 2-6-1798
   Hetty & George Webster 6-29-1818
   James W. & Mary E. Webster 3-26-1862
   Jnᵒ & Rebecca Hazzard 1-12-1849
   Mary & John Smith Lewis 12-29-1825
   Mary Ann & Joseph W. Kidwell 12-18-1816
   Matilda & Edward L. Richards 1-12-1816
   Peter J. & Mary Georgiana Richardson 5-30-1861
   Rachele & Richard Piles 1-9-1816
   Samuel & Rachel Lindsay 1-20-1802
   Sarah & Benjamin Ray 9-10-1821
   Teresa & Dennis Curtin 8-25-1813
   Thomas & Lizzie Jones 2-20-1883 (Rev. Mr. Butler)
   Thomas B. & Mary Wheat 10-17-1799
MORGAN, Cornelius & M. Matilda Boswell 3-28-1864
   James E. & Norah T. Digges 6-10-1854
   John & HannahWood 4-20-1779
   Robert & Martha Hamilton 5-30-1780
MORKABEE, Sarah & Hezekiah Gardiner 2-9-1857
MORLEY, Cornlius & Elizabeth E. Boswell 3-28-1873 (Lanahan)
MORLING, Charlotte & Thomas Washington 3-26-1875 (Welsh)
MORRIS, Benjamin & Rebecca Galwith 2-4-1783
   Francis & Susanna E. Jones 1-13-1862
   James A. & Martha O'Brien 9-5-1859
   John & Lucy Payne 12-17-1799
   Margaret A. & George C. Johnson 1-8-1866 Age 26
   Mary Dent & John Simpson 4-10-1788
   Mary Norman & Henry Davis 10-23-1790
   Nathan C. & Susan Pearce 2-3-1832
   Sarah E. J. & John W. Brady 12-26-1882 (Rev. Wm. C. Butler)
   Susan & Richᵈ Spalding 2-8-1841
   Thoˢ W. & Caroline Maria Calvert 5-18-1823

MORRISON, Francis & Jane Greenleaf 3-18-1876 (Tennent)
MORRISS, Ann & Bennett Ball 1-6-1789
MORROVILL (?), Elisabeth & Richard A. Perrie 2-13-1821
MORSE, Austin & Annie Slye 1-13-1868
MORSELL, Benjamin Kidd & Mary Turner 8-21-1816
  Caroline & John Veitch 12-6-1819
  Carrie & Doct? George W. Anderson 10-1-1855
  Elizabeth Ann & John Parker 1-1-1838
  James S. Jr. & Margaret E. Baden 4-30-1839
  John & Harriot Jackson 4-17-1811
  John & Dorcas Gordon 1-30-1817
  John C. & Ann Maria Godman 4-3-1837
  Kidd & Margaret Buchan 3-29-1803
  Mary J. & Charles E. Walker 11-20-1841
  Rebecca & Christopher Lambert 10-27-1824
  Richard J. & Eleanor W. Beall 4-29-1816
  Sarah E. & John R. Taylor 11-12-1878
MORTON, Eliza E. & B. J. Thomas 11-1-1867 (Fr. Lanahan)
  Margaret & Henry Bowling 12-23-1859
  Susannah & John T. Rawlings 4-12-1816
MOSELY, Stacey & John Walker 12-16-1796
MOSS, John & Elizabeth Franklin 11-30-1866 (Young)
MOULDEN, Maria A. & James H. Dove 1-14-1853
MUDD, Alfred Benjamin & Anna Sophia Connick 2-10-1855
  Ann & Jn? F. Williams 1-9-1782
  Ann C. & Hilleary P. Mudd 9-15-1835
  Ann Louisa & Edward E. Dixon 1-4-1827
  Ann S. & Levi Kerby 11-21-1868 (Lenaghan)
  Benjamin N. & Elizabeth Gardiner 9-6-1814
  Delphina & Robert Mudd 2-4-1832
  Elizabeth & Joseph Milburn Simms 2-10-1790
  Elizabeth & William Cooke 5-28-1796
  Elizabeth & William Fletcher 1-8-1808
  Elizabeth & Sylvester Boone 11-11-1827
  Elizabeth E. & Cornelius G. Weldman 11-11-1837
  Francis E. & Mary B. Alice Mudd 7-7-1828
  Francis E. & Susanna Turton 1-23-1832
  Francis E. & Annie V. Jarboe 11-13-1865 Farmer, m. 11-14-1854
    by P. B. Lenaghan, Catholic Priest
  Georgie W. & Thomas N. Mudd 11-12-1860
  Harriet & Isidore Gardiner 1-14-1822
  Henry L. Jr. & Mary Pauline Gwynn 1-20-1875 (Welsh)
  Hester V. & Jeremiah T. Mudd 4-6-1869 (McDonald)
  Hezekiah & Elizabeth Edelon 5-12-1779
  Hilleary P. & Ann C. Mudd 9-15-1835
  Jane & George Webster 12-26-1840
  Jeremiah T. & Hester V. Mudd 4-6-1869 (McDonald)
  Joseph & Elizabeth Hill 6-2-1787
  Dr. Joseph A. & Virginia Clements 2-11-1867 (Lenahan)
  Mary & James Kidwell 12-18-1790
  Mary Ann & Theodore Garner 4-24-1819
  Mary B. Alice & Frances E. Mudd 7-7-1828
  Mary C. & Thomas H. Osbourn 6-25-1850
  Mary Jennett & John H. Kerby (Rev. Mr. Highland) 10-26-1880
  Mary Tabetha & Dennise McCarthy 9-16-1791

MUDD, Michael & Juliann Boarman 4-19-1819
   Robert & Delphina Mudd 2-4-1832
   Sarah & Alben Clarke 8-13-1812
   Thomas & Mary C. Taylor 2-25-1840
   Thomas & Elizabeth Webster 1-4-1841
   Thomas N. & Georgie W. Mudd 11-12-1860
   Thomas N. & Martha E. Wilson 11-17-1875
MULLAN, Thomas & Arthelia Hamilton 6-22-1809
MULLEKIN, Benjamin & Ann King 2-21-1838
   Catherine & Joseph Harwood 1-3-1826
   Ellen B. & Dennis Magruder 12-16-1832   MULLEKIN, Jeremiah Jr. & Maria
   Jeremiah & Louisa Ann Osbourn 7-12-1842   Harvey 6-15-1843
   Mary R. & Wm. A. Gunton 6-17-1848
MULLICAN, Henry & Eliz? Hardy 1-13-1796
   James & Mariah West Oden 1-5-1813
   Joseph & Massy Ann Mitchell 10-10-1797
   Martha & Thomas Harvey 12-21-1808
MULLIGAN, Mary & John Thomas Rogers 9-15-1876 (Major)
MULLIKEN, Ann & Zachariah Barron 12-14-1809
   Barach & Sophia Margaret Oden 2-25-1823
   Benjamin & Sarah Harwood 10-25-1802
   Eleanor & Theodore Cook 7-22-1819
   Francis & Cassy Taylor 9-5-1816
   John B. & Mary M. Weems 6-2-1812
   Jno. T. & Sopha R. Hutchinson 12-22-1863
   Lucy & Richard Thrall 12-31-1787
   Maria W. & Tho.S Jackson 6-7-1825
   Mary & Charles Clagett 11-12-1846
   Thomas J. & Fannie Tyler 12-30-1872 (Gordon)
   William & Ann Barrett 3-25-1780
   Wm. Gassaway & Juliet Ann Peacock 2-24-1846
MULLIKIN, Alice & George W. Basford 1-6-1869 (Kershaw)
   Anna & Henry Phelps 12-28-1831
   Annie & Charles Stevenson 8-19-1885 (Rev. Mr. Highland)
   Benjamin & Martha A. Beall 11-18-1872 (Gordon)
   Benjn O. & Mary E. Wootton 1-27-1846
   Catharine & Henry Bassford 2-21-1839
   Eliza Ann & Nathaniel C. Weems 12-30-1834
   Eliza Maria & Edward W. Magruder 4-23-1866 (Young)
   Elizabeth E. & Jason Baldwin 6-4-1833
   Erasmus & Elizth Kingsbury 1-16-1847
   Erasmus & Elizabeth Duckett 12-11-1854
   Francis & Adeline Duckett 8-20-1856
   George W. & Eliz.th A. Fairall 1-13-1846
   Henrietta & Robert Norton 11-16-1807
   Henrietta M. W. & James Mullikin 4-14-1841
   James & Henrietta M. W. Mullikin 4-14-1841
   James T. & Sarah Taylor 7-8-1848
   Louisa O. & John H. Mundell 1-3-1855
   Margaret A. M. & George O. Hutchinson 9-2-1868
   Margaret Alice & Francis S. Shulze 1-1-1855
   Margt & Alexander Evans 2-19-1812
   Martha Hall & Jacob Franklin Waters 2-12-1798
   Mary & James Sotherline 8-8-1799
   Mary & Clement T. Hilleary 12-29-1804

MULLIKIN, Mary & Charles Ridgely Jun. 10-18-1849
  Mary J. & Reubin W. Bunnell 4-25-1840
  Mortimer H. & Tabitha Duval 11-7-1831
  Richard B. & Ellen C. Ogle 5-19-1834
  Robert Lee & Ida Luther Keen 6-22-1886 (Rev. Mr. Shipley)
  Sarah Ann & Richard B. Taylor 2-25-1821
  Sophia Oden & Washington Custis Calvert 6-17-1851
  Thomas & Mary King 1-5-1799
  Walter & Elizabeth Russell 10-30-1799
MULLOY, Samuel G. & Almira Brown 10-26-1875
MUNDELL, Alexander & Caroline D. Hodges 11-8-1823
  Alexander & Adeline Hodges 3-20-1832
  Ann R. & Sam$\frac{1}{2}$ H. Berry 12-22-1846
  Eleanor P. & Joshua S. Keerle 1-24-1825
  John H. & Louisa O. Mulliken 1-3-1855
  Susanna & George H. Keerl 4-26-1820
  Thomas & Virlinda Eversfield 2-28-1794
MUNROE, Ally & George Dixon 8-25-1824
  Elizabeth & Thomas Taffe 1-11-1812
  Hezekiah & Rebecca Simpson 1-1-1823
  John & Bettie Gross 12-5-1878 (Watkins)
  Mary R. & John W. Webster 1-16-1856
  Townley & Mary Savage 12-27-1847
MURDOCK, Addison & Mary Anna C. Clarke 4-13-1805
  Marianne Craik & Charles French 12-12-1809
  Rebeccah & Anthony Addison 6-26-1794
MURPHY, Elizabeth & Edward Mitchell 10-19-1812
  Elizabeth & Thomas Fowler 10-21-1812
  Joseph L. & Catherine Dixon 4-11-1859
  Patrick A. & Elizabeth Dyson 1-9-1847
  Rebecca & Joseph Smith 9-4-1826
  Smithy & Thomas Higgins 5-13-1873
  Washington & Virginia Robey 9-15-1869 (Robey)
MURRAY, Beckie & Geo. Jones 5-31-1873 (Peters)
  Eliza & Bradley Bowling 10-15-1875 (Gordon)
  Henry G. & Mary Catharine Edelen 2-22-1838
  James & Delilah Cadle 1-2-1839
  James & Eliza Ann Norton 7-8-1871
  James A. & Martha A. Cage 5-21-1876 (Tennant)
  Louisa & Sylvester Bealle col$\frac{d}{d}$ 6-12-1869 (Langford)
  Marg^{t} & John Sutherland 11-30-1780
  Mary & William Franklin 4-7-1877
  Mary A. & Alpheus Downs 12-13-1882 (Rev. Mr. Towles)
  Mary Elizabeth & William Benjn Walls 9-19-1860
  Rebecca & Pompey Griffin 12-23-1884
  Sarah E. & William H. Grimes 4-30-1869 (Lenaghan)
  Teresa & William Howden 6-27-1833
  William A. & Mary E. Walls 2-18-1854
MURREY, William A. & Juliet Ann Taylor 1-11-1836
MURRY, William & Mary Knott 8-28-1828
MYERS, Elemander (Elexander?) & Mary F. Thompson 5-24-1880 (Gordon)

NALEY, Matilda Ann & Jno. Thompson 1-28-1851
NALLEY, Ann Maria & Harrison Craufurd 8-8-1867 (Father Call)
  Ignatius & Rosa Wilson 1-26-1876 (Green)
  Mary C. & William L. Stewart 6-3-1884 (Rev. Father Cotton)
  Weston & Sarah Ann Johnson 9-2-1871 (Trapnall)
NALLY, Francis L. & James W. Beall 5-27-1872 (McDonald)
  Ignatious & Elizabeth Queen 11-21-1872 (Dwyer)
  John D. & Mary Rebecca Jones 1-12-1860
  Mary Ellen & James Duckett 5-21-1863
  Philip F. & Ann Rebecca Beall 9-3-1863
  Sarah & Clinton Harvey 4-12-1882 (Rev. Fr. DeWolf)
NAYLOR, Ann & Samuel Wailes 2-8-1783
  Ann & Walter Watson 12-23-1783
  Ann & Joseph Wrightt 2-26-1788
  Ann & John M. Maccubbin 9-16-1826
  Baston & Eleanor Austin 11-6-1778
  Benjamin & Martha Beaven 12-23-1793
  Benjamin & Mary Wilson 12-14-1797
  Benjamin & Ann Perrie Wailes 2-2-1807
  Benjamin J. & Susanna Elizabeth Naylor 12-11-1857
  Christiana & Pinkney Brown 5-10-1876 (Carroll)
  Eliza & Oza Watson 11-25-1826
  Elizabeth & John Baden Jr. 3-24-1814
  Elizabeth & Francis S. Dowell 12-15-1826
  George & Eleanor Berry 6-2-1785
  George & Elizabeth Adams 1-23-1802
  George Joshua & Elizabeth Kidwell 3-29-1834
  Isaac Jones & Elizabeth Wilson 12-28-1801
  James & Priscilla Wilson 9-5-1797
  James & Mary Boteler 12-31-1800
  James & Jane Burch 7-11-1826
  James & Mary Ann Perrie 12-7-1835
  James & Margaret B. Wilson 3-29-1836
  James of Wm. & Elizabeth S. Connick 6-12-1886 (Rev. Wm. Ross)
  Jane & William Greer 12-16-1838
  Joshua & Martha Nutwell 1-17-1780
  Joshua & Martha Baden 12-2-1799
  Joshu S. & Mary L. Waters 1-19-1846
  Judson & Sarah Wilcoxen 1-16-1815
  Julia A. & William H. Townshend 4-22-1872 (Townshend)
  Lillie M. & James F. Brown 4-26-1851
  Llewellyn M. & Alice T. B. Townshend 5-14-1874 (Seat)
  Maggie J. & John S. Nichols 3-15-1860
  Margaret & Elisha Fields 2-12-1780
  Marion R. & Robert Connick 5-11-1867 (Brown)
  Martha & George Wells 2-25-1783
  Martha & Fielder Watson 6-18-1831
  Martha & George A. Baden 3-30-1832
  Martha A. E. & Lewis B. Adams 12-15-1846
  Martha L. & Benjamin J. Watson 1-22-1868 (Smith)
  Mary & Thomas Garner 1-27-1798
  Mary A. & Louis B. Adams 2-16-1866   Age 18, date of record
    22- Feb'y 1866, A. J. Porter, minister
  Mary E. & Benjamin F. Trueman 12-8-1873 (Tennent)
  Mary Jane & John L. Estep 4-26-1856

NAYLOR, Mary P. & George W. Scaggs 8-22-1856
  Nancy & James Watson 12-27-1830
  Nicholas & Mary Selby 2-15-1783
  Robert C. & Frances Selby 5-12-1883 (Mr. Wheeler)
  Susan & John T. Young 10-13-1845
  Susanna & Thomas Naylor 11-15-1824
  Susannah & George Wailes Gibbons 1-26-1793
  Susanna Elizabeth & Benjamin J. Naylor 12-11-1857
  Susie E. & J. B. Townshend 1-18-1873 (Rogers)
  Thomas & Patsey Robinson 12-14-1812
  Thomas & Susanna Naylor 11-15-1824
  Virginia & William T. Jackson 7-13-1869 (Linthicum)
  William & Jennet Caroline Harvey 3-21-1841
NEAL, Jennie & George F. Atcherson 12-21-1870 (Harper)
  John T. & Mary S. L. Robinson 6-24-1869 (Chesley)
  Susannah & Theodore O'Neal 1-12-1818
  Theadore & Sarah Kirby 4-25-1778
  Thomas & Elizabeth Whitemore 8-7-1779
NEALE, Eleanor & Arnold Hurley 4-2-1803
  Henrietta & Francis Boone 8-13-1795
  Julia & Lloyed Johnson 12-27-1883
  William & Rachel Veitch 8-1-1798
NEALL, Martha Marion & Thomas McNew 11-23-1827
NEBBIT, Alfred & Susan Diggs 7-29-1875
NEGHEN, Sarah Ann & Alverdus H. Basford 5-14-1839
NEILL, Fielder & Elizabeth Oneall 1-26-1813
NEILSON, Robert & Anne Ogle 11-19-1839
NEITZEY, Ferdinand & Dora R. Dutton 3-24-1880
NESMITH, Ebenezer & Jan Trother 5-20-1796
NEUMAN, Margaret E. & Alexander Proctor 12-12-1874 (Welsh)
NEVETT, Thomas & Henrietta Dorsey 1-3-1798
NEVILL, Ann & Thomas Bowling 8-4-1783
NEVINS, Rev? Henry V. D. & Margaret E. Ross 5-4-1843
NEVITT, Ann & Joseph Adams 11-5-1791
  Charles & Levinah Bowling 1-18-1780
  James & Ruth Conn 5-31-1777
  Lavina & Elisha Perry 9-30-1799
  Mary & Martin Yates 12-31-1798
  William & Rebecca Lovejoy 9-15-1803
  Wm. Miles & Priscilla Miles 1-1-1779
NEWBURN, James & Mary Gantt 5-20-1791
NEWCOME, William & Sarah Backett 12-19-1780
NEWHOUSE, William & Adera Conley 1-10-1786
NEWMAN, Annie & Jesse A. Ketchen 12-18-1875
  E. & Robert Dugind 10-7-1856
  Catharine & John Barrott 1-8-1799
  Francis L. & Rachael Anderson 12-20-1848
  Horatio & Eliza Alvey 1-13-1813
  James & Henrietta Booze 12-12-1818
  John & Ann Proctor 1-21-1814
  Lugene & Mary E. Proctor 10-25-1875 (Roan)
  Marcellus & Cecie Butler 10-3-1874 (Welsh)
  Mary & Leonard Soper 11-21-1801
  Mary & Thomas Hayes 12-27-1842
  Phillippena & Henry Thomas Butler 1-12-1852

NEWMAN, Sylvester & Jane Hurley 1-20-1851
NEWTON, Chloe & Jeremiah Henson 11-21-1870 (Maher)
   Eleanor & Charles Donlevy 8-12-1799
   John & Eleanor Callahan 5-27-1781
   Margaret & Jonathan H. Burch 6-11-1810
   Rachel & Ignatius Wheeler 1-28-1794
   Sarah & Thomas Gallaham 4-5-1806
NICHOLAS, Sallie & George H. Shorter 2-3-1873 (Evans)
NICHOLDSON, Frances & Henry Berckley 11-22-1788
NICHOLLS, Edward & Wilemina Hamilton 8-15-1780
   Elizabeth & William F. Howell 1-7-1839
   John & Thompsey Knighton 1-29-1791
   John & Rachel Prather 7-25-1806
   Margaret & John Hall 3-5-1877 (Carroll)
   Susanna & Samuel Tarman 1-31-1803
   William & Martha Smith 1-20-1778
NICHOLLSON, Thomas & Ann Elizabeth Pindal 5-7-1828
NICHOLS, Horace E. & Charlotte Martin 4-27-1855
   Isaac & Sarah Tolson 6-24-1871 (Wheeler)
   John S. & Maggie J. Naylor 3-15-1860
   Sophia & Matthew Deveil 7-22-1871
NICHOLSON, Isabella & William Wells 6-13-1829
   Jeremiah & Isabella Sparrow 1-30-1800
   Somervell & Cassandra Crook 1-29-1850
NIMMO, William A. & Cora Marbury 1-3-1853
NIVETT, Richard & Eleanor Ridgway 9-10-1787
NOBLE, Joseph T. & Elizabeth Turner 3-4-1802
   Richard & Rebeccah Baden 9-26-1796
NOLAND, Mary & John Wheat 12-3-1801
   Mary R. & John L. Thompson 2-3-1858
   Thomas & Mary Bayne 6-13-1796
NORFOLK, Benjamin & Mary C. Sunderland 11-15-1876 (Chaney)
   Charles & Elizabeth Hall 12-14-1880 (Rev. Dr. Gordon)
   George & Emily Smith 12-21-1875
   Georgeanna & William R. Sweeny 3-13-1878 (Miller)
   John S. & Katie Trott 11-26-1881 (Rev. Mr. Jones)
   Jno. T. & Martha Ann Swain 10-21-1874 (Gordon)
   Margaret A. & George Kirby 2-25-1834
   Mary Margaret & Edward Cornburns Burgess 7-4-1885
   Sarah Elizabeth & William Gross 3-19-1872
   Virginia & John F. Sweeny 12-20-1877 (Kershaw)
   William & Mary Elizabeth Havener 1-20-1853
NORRIS, Andrew & Sarah Fenton 10-16-1800
   Charles & Ann Simmons 2-22-1867 (Beque)
   Mary & William Shurlock 12-5-1809
NORTHERN, Belle & R. A. Golden 12-4-1884 (Rev. Mr. Hamnon)
NORTHEY, Ann & William Slye 6-19-1793
NORTHY, Mary & Clement Ryan 2-1-1779
NORTON, Ann & William T. Wilbourn 3-11-1828
   Cassandra & Ezekiel Masters 4-11-1789
   Eliza Ann & James Murray 7-8-1871
   Henrietta & James Fowler 1-1-1852
   Robert & Henrietta Mullikin 11-16-1807
   Sarah & Buttler E. Stonestreet 1-6-1778
   William & Alice Bell 2-16-1870 (Dwyer)

NORWOOD, Marg.ᵗ & Alexʳ McDougall 2-25-1783
NOTHEY, Ann & Thomas Griffin 8-30-1790
  Ann & William Clubb 1-2-1797
  Ann & John H. Burgess 2-13-1854
  Callie & Charles Loveless 2-11-1874 (Kershaw)
  Elizabeth & George Peacock 12-18-1812
  Jane & Zachariah Dunning 12-28-1816
  John & Linny Robey 12-26-1831
  John & Mary Whitmore 9-5-1855
  Jno. Henry & Sharlotte Thompson 12-29-1862
  Nathaniel & Ann Taylor 10-10-1801
  Wm. Domine & Martha A. Club 12-24-1861
NOTHIE, Mary & Horatio Club 12-11-1810
NOTHY, Mrs. Mary & F. B. Acton 1-11-1870 (Kershaw)
NOWELL, Ann Maria & Hezakiah Johnson 2-27-1826
  James & Elizabeth Ryon 2-6-1798
  Sarah & Joseph Garner 2-26-1794
NUNEZ, Eugenia & Zachariah Lilley 6-23-1884
NUTWELL, Catherine & Thomas Watson 2-11-1784
  Elias & Deborah Shekclls 5-11-1781
  Martha & Joshua Naylor 1-17-1780

O'BRIEN, Martha & James A. Morris 9-5-1859
ODEN, Benjamin & Harriet B. West 8-21-1813
  Benjamin Jun.ʳ & Henrietta P. Waring 11-12-1822
  Benj.ⁿ & Rachel Sophia West 1-25-1791
  Catharine & George Dunlop 6-27-1818
  Christianna H. & Thomas H. Clagett 11-8-1831
  Eleanor & Calvert Williams 12-20-1792
  Eliza M. & William D. Bowie 2-8-1825
  Ellen & Arthur Pen West 5-29-1821
  Hannah Sophia & George W. Biscoe 9-28-1812
  Henrietta Priscilla & Walter B. Worthington 11-6-1827
  Mariah West & James Mullican 1-5-1813
  Martha & Osburn Brashears 6-1-1785
  Mary & William D. Bowie 1-3-1854
  Michael & Sarah Estep 3-12-1796
  Sarah Biggs & Edw.ᵈ Loyd Wailes 3-22-1780
  Sophia Margaret & Barach Mulliken 2-25-1823
  Susanna & Benjamin Hodges 2-6-1787
O'DONNELL, Brien & Ann Maria Kerrick 1-25-1856
  William & Annie Lowe 2-12-1870
OGDEN, Catherine & Nathaniel Weikin 9-24-1788
  John & Salome Willett 11-2-1782
OGDON, Robert & Ann Wynn 10-17-1778
OGLE, Anne & Robert Neilson 11-19-1839
  Benjamin & Ida J. Tayman 11-29-1882 (Rev. Sam.ˡ R. Gordon)
  Catharine & Rev.ᵈ Charles Goodrich 8-15-1838
  Elizabeth & William Woodville 6-17-1822
  Elizabeth & Zadock Tayman 2-23-1858
  Ellen C. & Richard B. Mullikin 5-19-1834
  Henrietta & Wm. H. Taylor 5-3-1824
  Louisa & Upton Beall 10-9-1837
  Mary & Edward T. Taylor 12-15-1830

OGLE, Mary Jane & John D. Jenkins 1-3-1870
    Richard L. & Priscilla Bowie 12-16-1846
    Sophia & Julius Forrest 11-23-1824
    Sophia & John E. Tayman 5-4-1855
    Susan & John Hodges 6-15-1829
    William Cooke & Mary Ridout Bevins 12-15-1834
OHIO, John & Susannah Tarman 6-30-1786
OKEY, William H. & Georgianna Boone 4-17-1875 (O'Dwyer)
OLBEE, John & Ann Hennis 10-21-1786
OLIVER, Cornelius & Elizabeth Wells 1-9-1784
    Elizabeth & William Worrall 2-14-1806
    Elizabeth & Thomas Demar 12-30-1847
    Frances F. & Gamaliel Pease 8-5-1817
    Leonard C. & Ann Maria Estep 12-5-1853
    Martha & William F. R. Richardson 1-30-1836
    Mary & Martin Greer 1-31-1807
    Mary E. & Perry Craycroft 6-20-1840
    William & Lucissi Ellen Ball 6-10-1873 (Kershaw)
    Willy & Philip Merrill 10-27-1821
OLLIVER, Levin & Milburn Merrill 2-5-1823
    Martha & Samuel Wells 8-10-1778
O'MARA, Philip & Catharine Callahan 9-8-1798
O'NEAL, Theodore & Susannah Neal 1-12-1818
ONEALE, Elizabeth A. & Nathan Broomfield 1-15-1840
O'NEALE, Henry & Helen Drury 9-5-1850
ONEALE, John & Eliza H. Hamilton 1-1-1810
ONEALL, Elizabeth & Fielder Neill 1-26-1813
O'NEALL, Nathaniel & Ann Taylor 6-5-1789
    Thomas & Mary Wall 11-9-1813
ONEEL, Bernard & Eliz? Waring 1-5-1782
    William & Martha Berry 12-7-1814
ONION, Catherine & James Duckett 1-18-1844
    Mary & William Markwood 12-22-1824
    Ruth Barrow & John D. Beall 1-5-1842
    Sarah & Peter Talbert 4-3-1832
ONIONS, Ann & John Grimes 6-3-1846
    Benjamin & Mary Ann Godman 1-4-1836
    Bennetta & William Thomas Ryon 10-1-1860
    Elizabeth & Benjamin Sherbutt 12-30-1839
    Mary Ann & Thomas Beall 12-2-1845
    Rebecca & Tobias Duvall 3-5-1831
ORME, Ann & Samuel Willett 6-27-1784
    George E. & Bettie A. Briscoe 3-5-1869 (Lanahan)
    George Naylor & Rebecca Gibbons 2-17-1814
    Henry & Lena Mackebee Age 49, color yellow, farmhand m. Craufurd Estate
        11-12-1865 by John W. Chesley, minister P. E. Church
    Julia A. & Brooke Meads 9-4-1873 (Townshend)
    Lemuel L. & Ann Rebecca Wall 11-24-1855
    Moses & Elizabeth Brashears 2-27-1795
    Rebecca L. & John R. Dale 10-31-1849
    Sabinah & John Smith Selby 4-14-1780
OSBORN, Alvin & Elizabeth Gibbs 5-3-1794
OSBURN, Anna & Stephen Gotherd 4-9-1798
OSBORN, Dennis & Lucy Hodge 12-16-1784
    Dennis & Elizabeth Edelen 9-9-1801

OSBORN, Eliza. & John Osborn 1-27-1817
  Elizabeth & Zachariah Alnutt 11-26-1805
  Ester & Baptist Hardey 4-3-1786
  Francis & Charity Pope 7-19-1778
  John & Sarah Magruder 1-12-1788
  John & Eliza. Osborn 1-27-1817
  John Jun⸢ & Ariana Berry 1-2-1809
  Joseph & Rebecca Darcey 1-18-1803
  Joshua & Martha Clements 10-21-1814
  Linny & James Gray 2-7-1785
  Mary & Jacob Edelen 12-23-1806
  Sarah & James Stallions 1-1-1801
  Sarah & Wm. Davis 8-5-1816
  Usley & James Pumphry 12-23-1786
OSBOURN, Ann & Judson Scott 12-16-1823
  Charles & Charity Ann Lanham 2-14-1825
  Charles C. & Henrietta Edelen 1-29-1817
  Eliza Ann & John Kitland 5-19-1845
  Elizabeth & William Boteler 2-5-1816
  Elizabeth L. A. & William J. Hayden 10-12-1854
  Harriet M. & John Judson Sasscer 1-31-1826
  Jane & William Kitlin 3-5-1832
  John H. & Emeline Frazier 10-13-1840
  John T. & Susan Rebecca Cracklin 4-28-1856
  Leila Gordon & Edward W. Magruder 11-18-1885
  Levi & Charlotte L. Talburt 2-9-1825
  Louisa Ann & Jeremiah Mullekin 7-12-1842
  Martha Ann & E. P. Scott 2-4-1851
  Mary & William Berry 2-7-1826
  Mary E. & Benjamin Hall 4-14-1857
  Mary Ellen & Wm. Q. White 2-24-1846
  Mary H. & Thomas M. Fugitt 1-1-1855
  Mary M. & John Wallace 2-8-1882 (Rev. Dr. Gordon)
  Nicholas & Emily Scott 7-27-1831
  Richard K. & Eugenia Hilleary 9-2-1851
  Richard R. & Mary M. Hodges 12-8-1846
  Sarah & Allen McDaniel 5-22-1823
  Sophia M. & Henry White 10-4-1852
  Stephen & Dorcas Baldwin 2-3-1829
  Thomas H. & Mary C. Mudd 6-25-1850
OSBOURNE, J. B. &Mary C. Clements 2-10-1870 (Myer)
OTWAY, Eleanor & Richard Brooke 6-5-1800
OURAND, J. T. W. & Maggie Arthur 8-6-1857
OVERMAN, Genevieve & Henry Heinsooth 10-23-1873 (Stanley)
OWEN, George & Susanna Darnall 1-25-1783
  Joseph & Rebecca Latten 6-12-1781
OWENS, Alice of Ann Arundel Co. & Alfred Fisher 5-21-1877 (Wheeler)
  Annie & Charles Crown col⸢ 12-31-1880 (Rev. Mr. Butler)
  Ashby C. & Alice Crosby 1-19-1886
  David & Patsey Harvey 12-21-1807
  Elizabeth & James Atwell 9-16-1799
  Elizabeth S. M. & Charles L. Jones 2-10-1813
  Ellen & Wesley Riggs 11-26-1884 (Rev. Mr. Howard)
  Harriet & William E. Taylor 12-30-1872
  Harriet & Lloyd Brown 1-6-1877 (Walker)

OWENS, James Junior & Maria L. Bowie 8-9-1867 (Stanley)
    John & Sarah Howerton 3-8-1780
    John & Louisa Diggs 12-20-1869 (Mahr)
    John & Medora F. Mitchell 1-12-1880 (Revd Daniel Aquila)
    Joseph & Jane Waters 2-19-1787
    Joseph & Sarah Sollers colored 10-28-1880 (Rev. David Aquilla)
    Joseph T. & Emily Jane Long 1-14-1873 (Kershaw)
    Murray & Ella Robinson 12-29-1883 (Rev. Mr. Cunnane)
    Rebecca & Washington Marshall 7-18-1876
    S. A. & H. G. Mitchell col^d 5-11-1869 (Kershaw)
    Sarah Ann & John Henry Kirsick 12-30-1868 (Martin)
    Thomas & Ann McAtee 4-27-1793   OWENS, Theodore & Eliza Jane Brown col^d
    Thomas & Laura N. Rumbles 12-20-1884 (Rev. H. Green)   12-17-1880
    Wilson & Matilda Lankford 6-5-1875 (Mayberry)
OWING, Washington & Derry Prather 4-17-1804
OWINGS, Bettie col^d & Clem Dorsey 8-28-1880 (Rev. Mr. Wheeler)
    Fannie E. & Henry S. Miller 12-5-1878
    Fanny & Richard Wood 8-21-1879 (Gray)
    Simon & Mary White 4-27-1886 (Rev. Father Cotton)
OXLEY, Mary Elizabeth Estella & Philip Thomas Cheseldine 8-10-1885
    (Rev. Mr. Highland)

PACA, Elizabeth & Samuel H. Baker 6-30-1797
PADDY, John & Verlinda P. Cage 1-26-1813
    Robert & Elizabeth Cage 1-15-1817
PADGET, Rebecca & Thomas Hayes 9-9-1784
PADGETT, Ann Maria & Caleb Wedding 10-26-1868 (Smith)
    Benedict & Catherine Gray 4-13-1789
    Benedict & Ellen Jones 12-22-1835
    Benjamin & Eliz^h Jones 12-11-1830
    Charles F. & Ella C. Padgett 3-2-1885
    Elias & Nancy Mitchell 9-10-1828
    Elizabeth & William Jones 12-27-1817
    Ella C. & Charles F. Padgett 3-2-1885
    Ellen & John H. Lowe 3-12-1868 (Chesley)
    Franklin C. & Elizabeth E. Merser 9-13-1872
    George W. & Rebecca Lusby 12-23-1882
    Hester S. & George W. Carroll 1-14-1885
    James & Eleanor Ford 11-22-1817
    James B. & Priscilla Gardiner 12-20-1830
    James B. & Catherine A. Goddard 12-28-1869 (Kershaw)
    James L. & Sarah J. Garner 8-14-1882 (Rev. Edwd S. Fort)
    Jas. T. & Catherine E. Albrittain 1-3-1884 (Rev. M. M. Lewin)
    John H. & Margaret P. Rawlings 1-5-1860
    John Thos & Anne Caroline Benson 3-3-1851
    Joseph & Sarah McDaniel 2-3-1807
    Josias & Johannah Lovelace 12-31-1796
    Mary Ann & Samuel Mockbee 7-11-1827
    Mary R. & Saml. H. Thompson 2-2-1880
    Matilda & James Cooper 6-3-1820
    Robert Arthur & Fannie Elizabeth Pyles 12-11-1883 (Rev. Dell)
    Sarah & William Brian 1-13-1787
    Sarah & James Linch 2-5-1818
    Sarah T. & Jesse A. Rawlings 4-8-1882

PADGETT, Theodore & Matilda White 7-23-1807
  Thomas & Ann Hill 1-5-1822
  William & Catharine Pursley 7-30-1824
PAGE, Anthony C. & Elizabeth Cross 1-13-1838
  Daniel & Leonora Piles 11-16-1777
  George & Sophiah Beall 8-26-1813
  George W. & James Anna Sandford 5-8-1871 (Begue)
  Mary & Nathaniel Brashears 2-17-1792
  Mary & James Veatch 1-25-1798
  Verlinda & Joseph Strickland 1-19-1789
PAINE, Mary Jane & William H. Cooksey 8-19-1858
PALMER, Ann M. & William P. Pumphrey 2-12-1840
  Elizabeth & Hector Bayne 2-23-1802
  Henrietta & John W. Ward 7-25-1831
  John & Margaret Wallace 5-1-1802
  John & Elizabeth Coxe 4-30-1844
  Lucy A. A. & Robert H. Lanham 5-20-1833
  Mary E. & John R. Pumphrey 12-12-1865 (Father Call)
  William F. & Eugenia E. Bocock 2-3-1870 (Fowler)
PARISH, Robert A. & Frances Ellicott Tyson 12-19-1859
PARKER, Ada P. & J. L. Middleton 7-2-1867 (Lenehan)
  C. Eugene & Rose L. Jardin 10-23-1882 (Father Gallan)
  Charles & Elizabeth Ellen Shaw 12-14-1868 (Harper)
  Charles & Ellen Campbell 7-13-1876 (Major)
  Eliza & Robert Gray 12-26-1874
  Elizabeth & Richard Townshend 12-16-1796
  Elizabeth & James Perrie col? 4-27-1867 (Fr. Call)
  Hellen Elizabeth & Richard W. McPherson 1-15-1821
  Henry & Amelia Upton 2-7-1815
  Isabella & Thomas Brown 2-19-1870 (Maher)
  Jacob O. & Sarah Sanderson 3-9-1875
  James & Emily Jeans 8-1-1868 (Rev. B. Brown)
  James & Nancy Pindell 1-16-1873
  James Henry & Rebecca Turner 1-10-1882 (Rev. Mr. Stanley)
  John & Elizabeth Ann Morsell 1-1-1838
  Joseph & Mary Cator 11-13-1862
  Joseph M. & Olivia A. Edelen 4-15-1844
  L. E. M. & William N. Burch 12-21-1839
  Lemuel & Georgeanna Sprigg 5-6-1871 (McDonald)
  Mary & Peter B. Cage 1-20-1783
  Mary A. & James H. Griffin 11-23-1827
  Matilda & James Hepburn 6-7-1867 (Beque)
  Matilda A. & Jas. Brawner 10-30-1825
  Oden & Hannah Young col? 7-27-1867
  Rachel C. E. & Ella M. Gwynn 4-10-1875 (O'Dwyer)
  Rebecca & Edward Bartlett 12-24-1878 (Butler)
  Samuel & Sarah B. Williams 4-22-1818
  Sarah & John Turner 6-25-1810
  Sarah & Edward Hall 2-23-1830
  Singleton & Catherine Johnson 2-27-1880 (Peters)
  Thomas & Mary Shekells 3-25-1785
  Walter Smith & Mary Messenger 3-31-1801
PARKS, Elizabeth & Lemuel Douglas 1-12-1878 (Weems)
PARMER, Ebbin & Sarah Brown 4-4-1801
  John & Mary King 10-31-1808

PARRAN, Henry & Harriet Ann Barney 12-26-1881 (Rev. Mr. Aquilla)
PARRETT, Elizabeth & George Grimes 1-11-1786
PARROTT, Chris™ & Martha Clarke 1-20-1781
PARSONS, Barnaba & Lucretia Hurdle 6-8-1799
    Joseph & Ann Chatham 7-22-1798
    Susan H. & John H. Coffren 5-30-1849
PATTEN, George & Sarah Taylor col™ 6-8-1867 (Stanley)
    Mary M. & William F. Holtzman 3-31-1854
PATTERSON, Robert & Priscilla Ford 2-25-1873
    Samuel & Sophia Lee 3-7-1877 (Carroll)
    Samuel & Susan Ann Berry colored 11-11-1880 (Lawson)
    William & Mary Jones 11-23-1779
PAYNE, Mrs. Georgeanna & James A. Graves 12-26-1864
    Henry F. & Marianna S. Lanham 9-22-1868 (Berry)
    Henry L. & Mary V. Jones 3-1-1859
    Laura & Jno. R. Mitchell 12-30-1864
    Lucy & John Morris 12-17-1799
    Mary & John L. King 1-11-1831
    Milton J. & Edith N. Shaw 9-16-1885
    Sarah & David Locker 7-28-1794
    Wallace & Nellie Ritchie 4-6-1886 (Rev. Brashaw)
PEACH, Adam & Phillis Jones 12-13-1804
    John & Mary Isaac 11-14-1805
    Dr. John & Bettie Howe Wellford 1-26-1870 (Dr. Harper)
    Joseph & Mary Peach 12-24-1799
    Joseph & Lucy Wilson 2-15-1808
    Lucy & Chris™ Hyatt 9-10-1777
    Lucy & Spencer Mitchell 11-9-1812
    Mary & Joseph Peach 12-24-1799
    Mary Ann & Samuel Higgins Hamilton 1-26-1821
    Mary Ellen & Joseph Walker 10-27-1856
    Samuel & Caroline Hamilton 4-1-1822
    Sarah & Thomas Shorter 4-9-1801
PEACOCK, Benjamin F. & Susan Alice Windsor 1-20-1869 (Gordon)
    Benjamin F. & Mary Ann Kidwell 12-27-1883 (Rev. Mr. Dell)
    Christianna & Benjamin Windsor 12-23-1869 (Linthicum)
    Elizabeth & John T. Simpson 12-14-1881 (Rev. Dr. Stanley)
    George & Elizabeth Nothey 12-18-1812
    George Thomas & Mary Ellis Ridgeway 5-2-1876 (Kershaw)
    Hannah & Edward Dorsey 12-28-1799
    John & Sallie Beattey 3-3-1881 (Rev. Mr. Gordon)
    John H. & Elizabeth Garner 4-18-1855
    Juliet Ann & Wm. Gassaway Mulliken 2-24-1846
    Mary & James Richard Thomas 4-1-1839
    Mary Alice & George Wm. Winsor 6-23-1875 (Billops)
    Matilda & Daniel Thompson 9-16-1843
    Sarah & Nelson Seaburn 1-24-1846
    William & Penelope Holly 6-28-1792
PEAKE, John & Jane Rebecca Halcock 9-19-1864
    Joseph & Ann Adams 1-26-1818
PEARCE, Ann & Charles Pearce 7-31-1780
    Charles & Ann Pearce 7-31-1780
    Drusilla & Benj™ Danielson 10-26-1779
    Edward & Deborah McSeney 6-3-1784
    Elizabeth & Josephuas Amblin 10-16-1787

PEARCE, Jane & John Miles 11-30-1780
   Jane & Allen Brightwell 3-13-1802
   John & Elizabeth Taylor 4-9-1789
   Joshua & Deborah Dove 4-16-1785
   Rebecca & John Miles 1-21-1783
   Sarah E. & Henry D. Lynch 12-6-1853
   Susan & Nathan C. Morris 2-3-1832
   Thomas & Elizabeth Ambler 1-21-1783
PEARRE, Joshua & Margaret Woodward 12-6-1786
PEASE, Gamaliel & Frances F. Oliver 8-5-1817
PECK, David & Elizabeth Batson 9-17-1810
   John & Druscilla Woodward 2-17-1798
PEIRCE, Elizabeth & Thomas Cave 11-18-1786
   Elizabeth & John Venables 12-28-1808
   Jane & Leonard Ellis 11-15-1780
   John & Elizabeth Hines 2-3-1786
   John H. & Margaret R. Frye 8-30-1875 (West)
   Letetia & James P. Sheridan 6-11-1793
   Rachel & Gedion Taylor 12-29-1788
   Richard & Rhoda Beane 2-8-1819
   Richard A. & Susanna Estep 1-24-1787
PENDLETON, Charlotte T. & Mordecai Plummer 12-19-1883 (Rev. Dr. Lewin)
PENN, Edward & Elizabeth Beall 6-2-1820
   Edwd Loyd & Mary Ann Waring 1-7-1822
   Gwinnie & Geo. H. Mahorney 2-13-1878 (Weems)
   Hanson & Jane Contee Marbury 2-29-1824
   Hanson & Jane Contee 4-29-1824
PENNEFIELD, Thomas & Easther Beanes 7-20-1790
PERKINS, Elizabeth & Richard D. Hall 1-8-1799
   Frances R. & Christopher C. Hyatt 10-12-1846
   John & Fanny Ridgely 12-29-1804
   Mary & Lewis Duvall of Thomas 12-20-1802
   Rebecca & Eleazer Talburt 10-25-1805
   Samuel & Mary Warner 2-11-1797
   Sarah & Walter Smith Clarke 12-23-1808
   Sarah G. & John Ryland 8-30-1836
   Susann & Richd D. Hall 2-1-1842
   Susannah & Western Meek 11-11-1800
PERMILLION, Susanna & Ignatius Etchison 11-19-1808
PERRIE, Charles & Sophia Duvall 10-20-1830
   Charles Smith & Elizabeth Gantt Eversfield 1-18-1808
   Eliza N. & William J. F. Berry 12-22-1831
   Elizabeth A. & Joshua Watson 2-5-1818
   Elizabeth G. & John Beall 12-18-1826
   Elizth Ann & Samuel Fowler 8-4-1825
   Hugh & Ann Eastwood 1-24-1806
   Hugh & Sarah Cooksey 7-12-1817
   Hugh & Ann W. Tarman 11-20-1821
   James & Elizabeth Parker col^d 4-27-1867 (Fr. Call)
   Jane M. & John E. Lowe 12-11-1848
   John & Susannah Adams 1-1-1801
   Francis & Letty Swann 1-19-1798
   Margaret A. & Robert M. F. Tomlin 9-6-1831
   Maria & Stephen Trapnall 2-14-1873 (McDonald)
   Mary A. & Wm. F. Perrie lic. 8-25-1866 (Petherbridge) Age 24 m. 8-28-1866

PERRIE, Mary Ann & James Naylor 12-7-1835
  Nathan & Ann Kidwell 12-3-1831
  Richard A. & Elisabeth Morrovill 2-13-1821
  Richard B. & Amanda A. Waring 4-27-1863
  Richd A. & Sena W. Blackburn 7-5-1816
  Sarah & Andrew Cooksey 2-18-1800
  Susannah R. & Thomas H. Ball 8-9-1841
  Thomas & Susannah Adams 12-8-1807
  Thomas J. & Mary D. Sunderland 4-29-1858
  Wm. F. & Mary A. Perrie 8-25-1866 (Petherbridge) Age 31, res. Walker
    County, Texas, Prof. Austin College m. 8-28-1866 by Jno. F. Petherbridge
PERRY, Ann & Richd Smith Rawlings 1-17-1822
  Charles & Isabel Freeland 12-26-1874
  Easter & Benjⁿ Warman 3-20-1779
  Edward & Susana Clarke 7-12-1777
  Eleanor & Selby Scaggs 11-27-1827
  Elisha & Lavina Nevitt 9-30-1799
  Elisha & Assiny Y. Furguson 9-20-1841
  Erasmus & Ruth Ann Williams 5-7-1821
  Levi & Ann Chew 2-20-1797
  Mary & Thomas Keadle 6-15-1784
  Rachel & Joseph Harrison 10-23-1778
  Stephen & Caroline Fletcher 9-19-1879 (Crowley)
  William & Mary Soper 12-26-1796
PERVEIL, William H. & Elizabeth Howell 12-30-1856
PETER, Daniel Parke & Bettie S. Calvert 7-19-1870 (Kershaw)
PETERS, David W. & Annie S. Ritchie 9-8-1870 (Kershaw)
  John Saml & Comfort Anderson 2-27-1779
  Mary & Wm. Sharp colored 3-8-1881 (Rev. D. A. Aquilla)
PETERSON, Annie W. & Plummer L. Wells 6-25-1868 (Edwards)
PFEIL, Henry D. & Mary D. Rupley 2-12-1877 (Curtz)
PFLUGER, Chas. Jacob & Mary V. King 9-5-1882 (Rev. Jno. Teasdale)
PHELPS, Alia & George Iseman 9-29-1868 (Kershaw)
  Benjamin & Priscilla Wheat 12-10-1795
  Benj. G. W. & Mary M. Duvall 10-27-1864
  Bertha A. & Geo. J. Thompson 1-1-1851
  Caroline & John Brady 1-25-1848
  Elizabeth & Benjamin Swann 10-23-1819
  Elizabeth & Robert S. Swaine 12-22-1856
  Henry & Anna Mullikin 12-28-1831
  James & Mary Ellen Chaney 12-17-1862
  Jesse & Sarah Pumphrey 9-2-1795
  Jesse & Meeky Walker 4-15-1803
  Jesse Obleton & Caroline Elizabeth Cadle 1-22-1866 Age 23, labourer
    m. 1-26-1866 by P. B. Lenaghan, Catholic Priest
  John & Mary Grimes 6-28-1822
  John & Margaret M. Thompson 5-28-1829
  Martha Anne & John F. Danison 9-8-1857
  Sarah Ann & George D. Brady 4-22-1851
  Thomas & Ann Simpson 7-6-1829
  Walter & Nancy Ann Grimes 9-4-1807
  William & Nancy Simpson 9-11-1821
  William W. & Capitola Johnson 6-8-1876 (McNeer)
PHENIX, Thomas & Elizabeth Symmer 2-26-1791
PHILIPS, Mary & James Thompson 12-27-1790

PHILIPS, Samuel & Eleanor Butt 1-12-1790
  Samuel & Catherine Evans 6-4-1839
  Stephen & Rachel Pumphrey 11-11-1795
PHILLIPS, Anna T. & George D. Farr 10-23-1865 (Stanley)
  Henry & Susanna B. Magruder 5-15-1828
  Jeffrey & Ida Magruder 11-2-1864
  John F. & Sarah Kidwell 1-24-1853
  Matilda M. & Dionysius Sheriff 10-18-1860
  Overton C. & Cornelia Wilson 2-21-1827
  Samuel & Eveline Wilson 5-8-1827
  Susan C. & George A. Barnes 1-8-1821
  William E. & Margaret Rosine Beall 1-29-1874 (Stanley)
PHILPOT, Alexander & Sophia Smith 7-28-1803
PHIPPS, Artridge & Leonard Davy 1-30-1867
  Benjamin & Margaret Suit 12-23-1835
  Benjamin & Annie Taylor 1-31-1865
  Martha A. & Samuel B, Dove 1-5-1867 (Geo. Hildt)
PICKENS, Elizabeth & George Upton 1-6-1778
PICKEREN, William & Martha Brightwell 9-17-1806
PICKERING, Bilzey & Rosetta Harvin 2-30-1824, also listed 4-29-1824
PICKINS, William & Susanna Clarke 6-17-1777
PICKNEY, Mary Eliza & Pinkney Green 1-11-1870 (Gordon)
  Rev? William & Elizᵗʰ L. Lowndes 9-27-1838
PICKRELL, Eleaner & Henry Boswell 1-30-1811
  Henry & Rebecca Lowe 4-6-1779
  Rebecca & William Long 2-11-1781
  Richard & Amelia Marlow 7-24-1779
  Richard & Amelia Marlow 10-30-1779
  William & Elizabeth Harvey 12-1-1801
PIERCE, Ann Elizabeth & John S. Cobb 2-1-1870 (Harper)
  Benjamin & Mary Lamar 4-21-1813
  Benjamin & Mary Wood 4-16-1817
  Deborah & John Simpson 7-22-1815
  John & Rebeccah Trueman 3-29-1798
  John & Margaret Hunter 12-10-1808
  John L. & Elizabeth Ann Estep 1-15-1822
  Margaret & Bartholomew Terrasson 5-6-1781
  Sarah & William Lamar 3-29-1804
  Sophia & Josiah W. Watson 3-1-1812
  Thomas & Eleanor Harris 7-17-1811
  Thomas & Margaret Venables 12-28-1814
PIERCY, Catharine & John McKnight 10-29-1799
PIERSON, Margaret DeHass & William Irving Hyslop 12-29-1873 (Williams)
PILES, Alice & Jno. W. Cadle 1-2-1877 (McNeer)
  Ann & John Littleford 1-2-1799
  Ann Sophia & Thomas O. Chesley 12-21-1871 (Kershaw)
  Benjamin & Ann Simpson 4-17-1827
  Catharine Elizabeth & John Enoch Dunnington 1-25-1860
  Charles & Elizabeth Ratliff 2-6-1802
  Elizabeth & John Mangun 8-4-1785
  Elizabeth & William Wall 1-9-1786
  Elizabeth & William Leach 12-27-1810
  Elizabeth & Patrick A. Delmege 8-8-1868
  Emma J. & Robert T. Ball 12-10-1872
  Francis & Martha Early 4-6-1795

PILES, George F. & Mary Shaffer 11-14-1853
  Henry & Elizabeth Wallingford 8-6-1779
  Henry & Anna Hurley 4-5-1849
  Hilleary & Ariana White 1-7-1795
  Jemima & Thomas Allen 10-11-1786
  John & Mary A. Webster 1-17-1853
  John H. &Susannah E. Whitmore 1-20-1864
  John V. & Ellen Swansey 11-19-1846
  Joshua & Violetta Conner 10-24-1827
  Leonora & Daniel Page 11-16-1777
  Leonora & Henry F. Marden 2-25-1852
  Lucinda Jane & John B. Wilkinson 12-22-1840
  Martha Rebecca & James William Walker 8-21-1873
  Osceola & Mary Frances Duckett 1-3-1859
  Richard & Anne Richards Jones 1-27-1806
  Richard & Rachele Moreland 1-9-1816
  Sarah Ann & Walter Allen 2-13-1830
  Thos & Elizabeth Walker 11-19-1850
  William & Margaret Ann Ryon 4-12-1847
  Zachariah & Hannah Mitchell 8-29-1801
PINCKNEY, Delia & John Scott 7-11-1872 (Stiner)
PINDAL, Ann Elizabeth & Thomas Nicholson 5-7-1828
PINDALL, Philip & Priscilla Pratt 11-1-1796
  Thomas & Lucy B. Watkins 2-13-1817
  Nancy & James Parker 1-16-1873
PINDELL, Philip & Lucy Pratt 10-5-1787
  Rinaldo & Sarah Walker Gover 7-6-1811
' PINKNEY, Ann R. col^d & Ambrose Carroll 8-17-1883 (Rev. Mr. Mills)
  Chloe & Edward Drane Kerrick 4-25-1873
  Christianna & Wallace B. Smith 12-27-1882
  Ellen & William Briscoe col^d 12-9-1880 (Rev. Mr. Lawson)
  Elmira & Julian Carrick col^d 12-16-1868
  Frank & Mary Green 7-11-1885 (Rev. Mr. Brooks)
  Frederick & Mary Catherine Cook 8-13-1875 (Kershaw)
  Henry & Minnie Hawkins col^d 4-16-1881 (Rev. Sylvanus Townshend)
  James Arthur & Josephine Wall 12-28-1875
  James R. & Mary C. Mahony 1-1-1877 (Adams)
  John & Maria Sprigg 3-31-1877 (Carroll)
  Julia & Alexander C. Carroll 11-19-1882 (Mr. Walker)
  Kitty & John Berry 12-12-1874 (Gordon)
  Lettecia & Benjamin Boyd 2-27-1872 (Fowler)
  Mary & Enoch Burgess 2-8-1868 (Fr. Call)
  Mary & Henson Holland 5-3-1877 (Carroll)
  Mary & Alfred Jackson 12-24-1884 (Rev. Mr. Hendricks)
  Robert & Virginia Young 12-24-1872 (Evans)
  Susan & George West 1-1-1867 Age 18-mulatto, maid m. 1-22-1867
  William & Leucinda Williams 1-9-1885
PINN, James & Lucy Jane Lucas 5-4-1876
PIPER, Delano & Marion E. Magruder 12-3-1856
  Margaret & Rezin Lecompt 9-6-1800
PLATER, Caroline P. & William P. Berry 10-24-1882 (Rev. Mr. Gordon)
  Edward & Eveline Young 11-1-1836
  George & Cecelia Plowden 6-29-1875 (Welsh)
  Margaret & Thomas Talbert 6-13-1812
  Philip & Lettie Banks col^d 6-2-1869 (Fowler)

172

PLATER, Sophia R. & William Tayloe 11-20-1872 (Goodrich)
  Wilson & Sallie Bell 6-10-1867 (Smith)
PLOWDEN, Caroline & James H. Taylor 6-9-1873
  Cecelia & George Plater 6-29-1875 (Welsh)
PLUM, Lewis W. & Susannah Doxy 11-2-1799
PLUMMER, Abiezer & Susannah Wells 11-3-1795
  Ann H. & Grafton Tyler 12-14-1808
  Anthony & Emily Duckett 5-15-1872
  Christiana Jemima & John Bowling 12-15-1868 (Edelen)
  Edward S. & Rebecca A. M. Bryan 10-7-1856
  Ellen & Washington Tyler 10-1-1868
  John & Ann Digges 11-28-1780
  John & Arn Worthington 3-25-1810
  Julia & Henry Holland 6-2-1874 (Welch)
  Maggie & John Preston Brown color. 12-17-1879 (Rev. Henry Plummer)
  Mary E. & James T. Alexander 5-9-1885 (Rev. Mr. Brooks)
  Mordicai & Margery Lyles 11-14-1803
  Mordecai & Susan Waring 12-20-1842
  Mordecai & Charlotte T. Pendleton 12-19-1883 (Rev. Dr. Lewin)
  Philip & Anne Maria Waters 5-6-1823
  Rachel & Joseph Mahoney 6-5-1873 (O'Dwyer)
  Sarah & Fielder Bowie Smith 6-23-1802
  William W. & Mary L. Contee 8-31-1865 (Stanley)
PONSONBY, Sarah & Andrew T. McCormick 8-27-1796
POOL, Eugene A. & Ella C. Towles 1-6-1880 (Rev. John Fowler)
  John & Frances Mitchell 9-4-1784
  John & Lenny Beddow 1-7-1804
POOLE, Sallie & Manuel Ray 9-16-1875
POPE, Amelia & Joseph Pope Jun. 12-11-1787
  Ann & Daniel Bayne 2-4-1795
  Charity & Francis Osborn 7-19-1778
  Colmore & Mary Mockbee 5-12-1801
  Elizabeth & Phillip Evans Soper 7-30-1794
  Elizabeth & Mareen D. Soper 4-12-1814
  Joseph & Mary Marshall 12-1-1817
  Joseph Jun. & Amelia Pope 12-11-1787
  Margaret & Mareen Duvall Soper 2-13-1798
  Nathaniel & Sarah Beall 1-12-1802
  Priscilla & Joseph Soper 12-10-1822
POPHAM, Samuel & Delia Crutchly 12-25-1783
PORTER, Annie & Charles Belt col. 6-10-1873 (O'Dwyer)
  Bertie & William N. Windsor 10-21-1878 (Gordon)
  Harriet & John Harrison 11-1-1877 (Hooman)
  James & Sarah Jane Brown 12-26-1868 (Begue)
POSEY, George R.& Elizabeth Ball 7-17-1852
  Johanna & Benedict Edelen 11-21-1854
POSTON, Christian & Michael Lovejoy 10-1-1788
  Jane & Reazin Boteler 10-7-1807
  John Stone & Susannah Mahew 12-24-1797
  William & Elizabeth Gardiner 12-25-1797
POTTENGER, Robert & Mary Buchanan 2-15-1785
POWELL, Ann & Alvin Soper 1-5-1801
  Garston & Margaret Crow 10-10-1811
  George G. & Ann Turten 3-30-1813
  Georgianna & John Henry Bias 5-7-1885 (Rev. Mr. Howard)
  John & Victoria Bias 2-22-1883 (Rev. Joshua Barnes)

POWELL, Joseph & Nelly Wheeler 11-28-1804
  William & Sarah Green 3-17-1785
  William & Sally Brown 2-13-1830
POWER, Elizabeth A. & Grafton T. Lanham 6-6-1866 (Beque)
  Thomas & Elizabeth Watson 7-1-1795
POWERS, Eliz.th & Michael Deaner 8-4-1818
  Joseph & Isabella Sheckels 7-8-1871
  Mary & William Carrick 1-8-1844
  Nellie & James Fletcher 12-21-1870 (Begue)
  Thomas & Ann Smallwood 6-3-1820
POWNALL, Thomas & Sybal Selby 12-27-1787
PRATHER, Benj. & Rachel Walker 1-15-1782
  Benjamin & Easter Waring 4-3-1804
  Caroline & Wm. Jones 11-22-1825
  Columbus C. & Jane Ann Suit 4-14-1854
  Eleanor & William Jones 6-10-1818
  Derry & Washington Owing 4-17-1804
  James & Ann Hodges 12-31-1790
  John & Mary Emily Cator 6-2-1856
  Joseph & Elizabeth Welsh 6-1-1781
  Josiah & Elizabeth Drummond 10-6-1803
  Maranda & George Beane 5-13-1820
  Margaret & William Tannecliff 7-13-1810
  Rachel & John Nicholls 7-25-1806
  Rebecca & Hugh Drummond 5-16-1803
  Richard & Althea Mockbee 1-8-1825
  Richard & Susan H. Suit 2-16-1857
  Ruth & William Prather 1-31-1804
  Thomas & Eliza Marlow 3-8-1817
  William & Ruth Prather 1-31-1804
  Zach? & Rosamond Callahane 3-2-1778
PRATT. David & Teresa Burke col? 12-24-1852
  Eleanor & Cephas Shekells 9-14-1780
  John Wilks & Rachel Belt 2-12-1803
  Lucy & Philip Pindell 10-5-1787
  Priscilla & Philip Pindall 11-1-1796
  Thomas & Elizabeth Souther 12-30-1796
  Thomas & Christy Tyler 10-16-1799
PRENTIS, Benjamin & Leonora Millar 3-14-1832
PRESTON, Allen & Eliz? Easton 4-5-1779
PREUSS, Charles August.s & Louisa Anna Eleanor Savary 7-15-1805
PRICE, Elizabeth & Hannibal Grimes 1-27-1836
  Frederick & Elizabeth Fowler 10-27-1798
  James & Elizabeth Boteler 1-28-1779
  Mary & John Barrett 12-11-1781
  Mary & George Taylor 1-7-1804
  Mary & Manassah Beall 1-25-1819
  Richard & Rachel Willett 12-17-1782
  Richard & Sally R. R. Williams 4-2-1844
PRIGGS, Hedwick & Clement Hollyday 12-18-1784
PRINCE, Laura & Robert Taylor color? 10-11-1880
  William T. & Harriet E. Brown 7-12-1853
PROCTER, Elanor & ....burn Brashears 2-14-1795
  Elizabeth Ann & William Albert Butler 1-9-1875
  Mary & Richard L. Thomas 3-24-1858

PROCTER, Robert H. & Susanna Atchison 1-25-1859
PROCTOR, Alexander & Margaret E. Neuman 12-12-1874 (Welsh)
  Ally & Henry Deale 12-20-1802
  Ann & John Newman 1-21-1814
  Benedict & Patsey Johnson 8-16-1833
  Cornelia Ann & Marcellus Harley 2-15-1876 (Green)
  Eleanor & Henry Savoy 1-25-1830
  Ellen & Michael Chew 10-26-1868 (Lilly)
  Francis & Lucy Savoy 9-2-1820
  Henry & Kitty Proctor 2-6-1836
  Henry & Harriet Virginia Butler 2-9-1875 (Welch)
  John & Polly Davis 9-18-1815
  Josias & Sarah Ann Harley 1-15-1849
  Kitty & Henry Proctor 2-6-1836
  Mary E. & Lugene Newman 10-25-1875
  Rosalie & Louis Griffith 10-30-1879 (De Wolfe)
  William & Eliz^{a} Ailsea 1-11-1868
PROUT, Amelia & Rezin Williams 12-18-1832
  Elizabeth & Stephen Snowden 9-15-1869 (Thomas)
  John & Mary J. Queen col^{d} 9-4-1857
  Jonathan & Anna L. Gantt 12-7-1832
PROUTS, Sarah Ann & Moses T. Bolding 7-3-1872 (Stanley)
PRYOR, James & Kitty Holland 9-4-1885
PSHAWDER, Daniel & Fanny Franklin 1-12-1874 (Welsh)
PUMPHRAY, William & Mary Rollings 1-4-1792
PUMPHREY, Ann V. & Joseph A. Soper 12-15-1851
  Catherine E. & Christopher C. Clarke 6-15-1857
  Christie & George H. Bunnell 1-12-1870 (Kershaw)
  Daniel W. & Charlotte Cox 1-16-1878
  Eleanor & Nathaniel Soper 3-1-1840
  Elizabeth & Joseph Fowler of Wm. 1-16-1824
  Elizabeth & John Marshall 1-1-1852
  Emily C. & John H. Trabane 10-21-1856
  Enos F. & Mary Elizabeth Hayes 3-21-1872
  Georgianna & John A. Fraser 1-4-1870 (Harper)
  James & Sarah Beck 9-15-1821
  James G. & M. A. Brien 2-18-1841
  James W. & Elizabeth Jane Harvey 12-28-1865 (Thomas)
  John & Sarah Suit 1-14-1839
  John R. & Mary E. Palmer 12-12-1865 (Fr. Call)
  John R. & Ella S. Kerby 12-2-1879
  Judson C. & Priscilla Soper 5-17-1843
  Kate & Arthur B. Suit 3-13-1883
  Lloyd & Eliza Spalding 9-3-1817
  Louisa Cowle & George H. Bunnell 1-25-1877 (McNeer)
  Mary & Simon Fraser 1-10-1825
  Mary & William Suit 12-24-1843
  Mary Frances & William B. Evans 8-2-1853
  Rachel & Stephen Philips 11-11-1795
  Rachel Celestia & Joshua G. Clark 2-2-1856
  Rector & Caroline E. Soper 12-31-1839
  Richard & Elizabeth King 2-21-1786
  Sarah & Jesse Phelps 9-2-1795
  Sarah & John Kingsbury 4-5-1827
  William & Elizabeth Wilson 3-11-1815

PUMPHREY, William E. & Sarah Ryon 12-25-1809
  William E. & Sarah Ann Spalding 1-15-1819
  William P. & Ann M. Palmer 2-12-1840
  Ann & John P. Brashears 12-9-1778
  James & Usley Osborn 12-23-1786
PUMPHRY, Mary & Benj? Walker 13-31-1778
PURCE, Mary & Richard Brightwell 5-3-1785
PURCELL, William & Rebeccah Ray 1-5-1801
PURDEY, Susan & Judson W. Huntt 4-11-1834
  James F. & Elizabeth F. Chaney 12-4-1876 (Stanley)
PURDY, Margaret & Benjamin King 1-28-1870 (Bird)
PURNELL, Rachell & John Carr 2-8-1779
PURSLEY, Catharine & William Padgett 7-30-1824
PURVY, Helen & Nat. Ford 11-21-1868 (Kershaw)
PYE, Charles & Sarah Rozer 12-4-1784
PYLES, Fannie Elizabeth & Robert Arthur Padgett 12-11-1883 (Rev. Dell)
  J. Edward & Fannie Aist 2-12-1882 (Rev. Mr. Townshend)
  J. Edward & Katie Aist 9-9-1884
  Margaret Priscilla & John Oliver Stewart 12-11-1883 (Rev. Dell)
  Mattie A. & Joseph H. Selby 2-1-1881 (Rev. Mr. Cross)
  Sarah A. & Samuel G. Townshend 1-13-1875 (Ryland)

QUANDER, Charity Ann & George Beall 10-1-1873 (Dwyer)
  Mary Ellen & Fred Tolson col? 1-13-1881 (Rev. Father DeWolfe)
  Susan & Albert Bruce col? 12-8-1869 (Maher)
QUEEN, Ann & Martin N. McDaniel 6-13-1808
  Anna & Frank Holland 12-23-1871 (Wheeler)
  Elizabeth & Ignatious Nally 11-21-1872 (Dwyer)
  Ellen & Benjamin Johnson 11-18-1874 (O'Dwyer)
  Henrietta & Ignatius Key 7-14-1785
  James R. & Charlotte Young col? 7-25-1867 (Greenleaf)
  John & Elizabeth Thompson 2-7-1814
  Louisa & Charles W. H. Brown colored 11-19-1880 (DeWolfe)
  Mary & Henry Gardiner 6-30-1798
  Mary J. & John Prout col? 9-4-1857
  Nancy & Nelson Jones colored folks 3-3-1852
  Nicholas L. & Eleanor G. Boyd 1-1-1801
  Thomas & Catharine Duckett col? 12-24-1859
  William & Isabel Harwood 12-26-1866
QUILLER, Sophia & George Washington Lancaster 12-8-1865 (Stanley)
QUINN, Thomas & Elizabeth Batt 5-26-1792
QUIRK, Patrick Jr. & Johanna Delaney 1-9-1874 (Cotton)
QUYNN, William A. & Caroline A. Davis 2-18-1835

RABBITT, John & Eleanor Miles 5-3-1778
RABIT, William & Caroline Hoy 11-26-1841
RAFERDY, William & Catherine Howard 12-1-1824
RALLINGS, John Adam & Sary Cave 4-10-1787
RANDAL, Sarah & Quillar Tarman 12-25-1786
RANDALL, Abraham & Sega Tarman 12-26-1807
  Austin & Ann Tarman 12-2-1803
  Eli & Susan Burgess 12-27-1883 (Rev. Jas. Chaney)
  Elizabeth & William Hinton 12-22-1798
  John Jr. & Eliza Hodges 12-20-1814
  Martha M. & Burton Smith 3-27-1857
  Mary A. & Oscar A. Millard 2-20-1872
  Mary J. & Plummer Forrester 12-10-1884
  Rosa & Stephen Smoot col? 7-26-1881
  Virginia & Gabriel H. Fletcher 2-2-1886
RANDAM, Robert & Margery Ray 12-22-1804
RANDELL, Benjamin E. & Nancey Brooke 11-25-1867 (Fr. Young)
RANKEN, William B. & Macksey Duvall 9-15-1806
RANKINS, Walter & Milley Swaine 3-21-1805
RANSOM, George W. & Maria Ann Thomas 10-7-1879 (Watkins)
  Martha & Samuel Long 2-13-1784
  Thomas & Lizzie Medley 6-17-1884 (Mr. Thos H. Brooks)
RANTEN, John & Elizabeth Sherlock 12-3-1816
  John T. & Elizabeth E. Baldwin 12-28-1838
  John & Sarah Ann Humphrey 12-9-1778
RANTER, John & Sarah Ann Humphrey 12-9-1778
  John & Priscilla McCaughen 10-6-1804
  Sarah & Benjamin Talbott ?-6-1807
  Susannah & Paul Summers 4-11-1789
RANTIN, Elizabeth & Benjamin Simpson 12-13-1831
  Elizabeth E. & James H. Crandle 1-9-1845
  John T. & Ann H. Burnell 12-24-1836
RATCLIFF, Elizabeth & Charles Piles 2-6-1802
  Elizth N. & James P. Devaughn 9-3-1830
  Samuel & Margaret Waters 2-5-1823
  Thomas & Ann Brightwell 1-9-1805
RAWLINGS, Ann & James Higdon 8-18-1779
  Ann M. & James C. Rawlings 1-4-1853
  B. F. & Ella A. DeVaughn 4-25-1871
  Benjamin T. T. & Georgie A. Thomas 2-4-1878 (Gordon)
  Caleb & Eliza McQuillin 7-6-1830
  Caleb A. & Priscilla Scott 12-17-1838
  Caleb A. & Hesty Garner 8-9-1843
  Catherine & Allen Beddoe 6-27-1787
  Daniel & Susannah Duckett 3-27-1806
  Daniel & Monica Trueman 2-7-1812
  Elijah & Elizabeth Macgill 8-6-1778
  Eliza M. & Richard A. Hyde 10-10-1853
  Elizabeth & John Smith 8-20-1777
  Elizabeth & Benj. Frisby 4-27-1867 cold
  Elizabeth A. & Michael Garner 12-21-1840
  Elizabeth Ann & Joseph W. Gibbons 1-1-1833
  Elizabeth V. & John Henry Kidwell 2-24-1868
  Elizth & Henry Richardson 12-21-1848
  Ella E. & Thomas B. Gibbons 10-27-1884 (Rev. Gordon)
  Francis & Celia Cook 12-27-1871 (Gordon)

RAWLINGS, George W. & Sarah J. Dooley 11-17-1880 (Rev. Solomon German)
    Brandywine, Prince George's County
  Henry T. & Harriot Waters 4-8-1817
  Hester S. & Joseph T. Garner 1-3-1866 (Porter) Age 24, married
    residence Truman Rawlings
  Ignatius & Sarah Ann Duvall 1-5-1846
  James C. & Ann M. Rawlings 1-4-1853
  James H. & Martha E. Wilson 12-6-1854
  Jesse A. & Sarah T. Padgett 4-8-1882
  John & Verlinda Watson 4-12-1792
  John & Mary Jones 5-25-1798
  John L. & Elizabeth Roe 10-24-1833
  John S. & Sarah J. Garner 11-21-1871 (Watts)
  John T. & Susannah Morton 4-12-1816
  John Thomas & Eliza Ann Garner 9-15-1858
  John W. & Minta Gibson 2-28-1809
  Laura Estelle & George W. Waters 2-20-1882 (Rev. Mr. Townshend)
  Letty & Edward Wilson Greer 2-16-1803
  Luke & Elizabeth Kingsbury 1-30-1786
  Margaret P. & John H. Padgett 1-5-1860
  Maria & James Smith 11-8-1869 (Mahr)
  Martha A. & J. H. Bertram Swain 12-21-1869 (Marbury)
  Martha Ann & Joshua Gibson 2-8-1840
  Mary C. & Thomas Henry Ball 9-12-1853
  Mary C. & Sml H. Freeland 6-23-1870 (Marbury)
  Mary L. & Benjn Garner 2-8-1847
  Missouri H. & James F. Garner 1-9-1872 (Gordon)
  Paycy & Thomas Eastep 12-12-1804
  Richard Smith & Susannah Rawlings 5-17-1793
  Richard Smith & Pricey Kidwell 6-10-1802
  Richd Smith & Ann Perry 1-17-1822
  Rufus E. & Julia Birch 7-1-1884 (Mr. Chesley)
  Sarah & Benjamin Garner 1-18-1873 (Townshend)
  Susan Ann & William S. Hoyle 10-11-1848
  Susanna & Richard Waters 1-15-1824
  Susanna R. & Frank Garner 2-16-1869 (Smith)
  Susannah & Richard Smith Rawlings 5-17-1793
  Susannah & James Lynch 10-19-1811
  Virginia & Saml B. Fowler 6-5-1850
  William & Sarah Eastwood 10-9-1799
  William Cage & Ann Carrico 2-17-1807
  William Cage & Mary Davis 7-25-1809
  William J. & Susannah Hardacre 3-16-1811
RAY, Basil & Rebecca Wall 1-19-1782
  Benjamin & Eleanor Mitchell 1-11-1809
  Benjamin & Sarah Moreland 9-10-1821
  Benjn & Amelia Mitchell 12-25-1782
  Jesse & Mary Wall 1-24-1782
  John & Sarah Isaac 3-24-1787
  John & Henrietta Beall 12-8-1804
  Manuel & Sallie Poole 9-16-1875
  Margery & Robert Randam 12-22-1804
  Mary & John Hinton 1-1-1795
  Mary & Benjamin McVey 6-15-1813
  Prescilla & Thomas Manley 1-15-1785

RAY, Rebeccah & William Purcell 1-5-1801
   Thomas & May Hook 1-21-1817
   Walter & Rebeccah Br ashears 12-31-1791
RAYLAND, Virginia Cary & Donald MacNeill Fairfax 6-5-1854
REAUDON, Agnes & George Reuter 10-8-1869 (Lincham)
RED, John & Emily Jane Sweeny 12-20-1859
REDD, Daniel T. & Caroline Hutchinson 12-26-1866 Age 25, farmer
   m. 12-29-1866 by Henry J. Kershaw, Min. P. E. Ch. - Upper Marlboro
REDDEN, Mary & Joseph Duvall Jr. 8-26-1800
REDMILES, Mary & James Samuel Stewart 12-13-1865 (Stanley)
   William Jr. & Susannah Wheeler 12-10-1805
REDMOND, Matthais & Terrasa Catharine Hardey 5-21-1791
REED, Alexander & Eleanor Jenkins 6-20-1801
   Isaac & Elizabeth Hanes 10-11-1800
   John & Margaret Gun 2-14-1801
REEDER, Annie & Louis Gray 5-5-1884 (Rev. Francis Wills)
   George & Frances Brookes col? 12-21-1869 (Marbury)
   Henrietta & Dorsey Gray 3-7-1884 (Rev. Frank Wills)
   Jane & Henry Mills col? 1-13-1881 (Rev. Mr. Watkins)
   Peter & Martha Brookes 5-15-1877 (Perry)
REGESTER, Margaret A. & George E. Loweree 6-2-1868
REID, James Henry & Susan Ann Hawkins 12-22-1865 (Marbury) Age 21, black
   farmer, m. 12-24-1865 by Alex M. Marbury, Min. P. E. Ch.
REILEY, Marg? & John C. Winclar 2-22-1784
REIVES, John & Sarah Mason 4-19-1781
RENN, Sandford & Nancy Beall 4-2-1805
RENNA, Edward & Annie Ketland 10-9-1871 (Kershaw)
RESTON, Elizabeth & Archibald Hughes 2-1-1811
REUTER, George & Agnes Reaudon 10-8-1869 (Lenehan)
REYNOLDS, Annastacy & Henry Davidson 12-30-1795
   James & Mary Ann Crawford 12-9-1834
   Mary Dolly & Benjamin Lee 7-28-1818
   Patrick & Anastasa Hardey 12-29-1792
   Priscilla & Zachariah Wheat 2-4-1782
   Sarah & Joseph Boteler 12-22-1783
   Thomas & Ann Jones 2-24-1784
   William & Ann Griffith 12-5-1777
Wm. & Sarah Wells 12-19-1848
RHODES, John & Mary Bennett 1-30-1782
   Sarah Ann & John Brown 11-25-1835
RHODGERS, Eliza Ann & George Barton 7-8-1834
RICHARDS, Ann & William Willett 10-24-1814
   Barbara & Michael Devan 12-29-1812
   Caroline S. & James S. Lewis 8-21-1837
   Edward & Minerva Webster 12-28-1850
   Edward L. & Matilda Moreland 1-12-1816
   Ervin H. & Ann Worrell 11-29-1833
   Gabriel & Sarah Robey 5-12-1812
   George & Elizabeth A. Taylor 4-28-1835
   Hanibal W. & Elizabeth Goddard 11-20-1876 (Gordon)
   James & Jane Gibbons 1-27-1795
   James Thomas & Elizabeth J. Gibbson 11-22-1875 (Tennant)
   Jemima & Stephen Allingham 3-20-1781
   John E. & Susanna Gibbons 10-3-1868
   Joseph H. & Maggie Goldsmith 5-21-1877 (Gordon)

RICHARDS, Martha & Jonathan Throne Sasser 1-16-1797
　Mary E. L. & James R. Edelen 4-28-1879 (Gordon)
　Miss Richards & James Seburn 9-7-1821
　Peter Wood & Mary C. Devaughn 1-6-1879
　Rebecca L. & James P. Kerby 7-23-1877 (Gordon)
　Richard & Mary Howes 5-13-1802
　Robt & Mary Wilson 2-14-1843
　Sarah A. & J. V. Demar 1-4-1865
　Sarah Ann & James Richardson 5-22-1823
　Sarah L. & William Shaffer 2-7-1849
　William & Cindrilla Habin 4-18-1821
　William Marcellus & Arabella Priscilla Gibbons 12-20-1876
RICHARDSON, Ann & Edward Mitchell 1-26-1818
　Annie P. & William H. Soper 12-3-1883 (Rev. Mr. Hyland)
　Benj. F. & Martha E. Demar 1-8-1862
　Catharine A. & James N. Watson 12-20-1855
　Elisha & Sarah Worrald 12-3-1782
　Elizabeth & John Z. Downing 1-24-1867 (Marbury)
　Elizabeth & Elias Digges 1-27-1870 (Marr)
　George W. & Mary F. Joy 2-3-1881 (Rev. Mr. Brayshaw)
　Henry & Elizth Rawlings 12-21-1848
　James & Sarah Demar 1-22-1817
　James & Sarah Ann Richards 5-22-1823
　James & Sarah Watson 11-3-1848
　James W. & Lillian M. Maddox 9-18-1883 (Rev. Mr. LaRoche)
　Jane & James Butler 4-19-1871 (McDonald)
　John R. & Sarah B. Watson 1-2-1861
　John R. & Margaret A. Burch 5-30-1879 (Perrie)
　John W. & Martha R. Watson 12-31-1856
　John W. & Jane R. Tubman 3-2-1878 (Perry)
　John W. & Elizabeth E. Ball 10-7-1879 (Gwynn)
　Judson F. & Rachel Ann Joy 11-9-1880 (Laney)
　Mary Ann & John Canter 12-29-1840
　Margaret Ann & John A. Gibbons 5-5-1856
　Marg^t Elizabeth & John Thomas Demar 2-3-1877
　Mary Georgiana & Peter J. Moreland 5-30-1861
　Thaddeus A. & Mary A. White 2-5-1878 (Kershaw)
　Thomas & Susannah Greer 4-22-1813
　Thomas A. & Ann Moreland 1-20-1816
　Victoria & Elisha B. Furgesson 6-10-1882 (Rev. Mr. Butler)
　William F. & Mary Trueman 12-31-1834
　William F. R. & Martha Oliver 1-30-1836
　Wm. & Priscilla Estep 10-20-1821
　Wm. W. & Elizabeth S. Cahoe 1-18-1851
RICHEY, Jno. S. & Elizabeth Suit 1-31-1843
RICKETTS, Elizabeth Ann & Augustus Fillius 3-6-1857
　Jane & Zachariah Brown 4-4-1787
RIDDELL, Samuel & Susannah Baldwin 12-2-1791
RIDDLE, Archibald P. & Sarah E. Hyatt 4-20-1863
　Eliza & Jeremiah Riddle 3-1-1832
　Elizabeth Ann & Richard Isaac 1-23-1815
　Ellen & Richard Abigail 2-4-1818
　Jacob & Mary Anderson 2-1-1819
　Jacob & Sarah Anderson 2-26-1819
　Jacob & Alethea Beall 6-11-1836

RIDDLE, James & Ariana Stuart 5-8-1800
  Jeremiah & Eliza Riddle 3-1-1832
  John & Susan R, Johnson 8-22-1838
  Mary Ann & Tobias Anderson 1-5-1842
  Susanna & John Lowe 7-10-1784
  Virlinds & Samuel Tyler 1-19-1782
RIDENOUR, J. W. & Mary E. Suit 2-15-1866   Age 33, Gov. Service, m. at res.
  Kelita Suit by Henry J. Kershaw, minister P. E. Church
RIDEOUT, Laura & Michael Green 8-30-1872 (Evans)
  Sophia & Joseph Brown 4-22-1871 (Wheeler)
RIDGELEY, Alice V. & Charles H. Gill 6-14-1870 (Maher)
  Charles & Eliz⁵ʰ Sansbury 12-24-1838
  Charles Jun. & Mary Mullikin 10-18-1849
  Ella J. & George W. Ryon 2-20-1884 (Father Cunnane)
  Fanny & John Perkins 12-29-1804
  Greenberry & M. Sansberry 2-29-1840
  James & Laura Taylor 10-2-1860
  Jenevive & Hugh V. Crouse 2-27-1878 (Hooman)
  John & Ellen Talbert 6-2-1845
  Lloyd & Rachael Ann Waters 2-15-1833
  Lloyd & Sarah Lynch 8-6-1837
  Mary Ann & Andrew Beall 12-7-1832
  Mary Catherine & James A. Sweeney 12-23-1854
RIDGEWAY, Basil & Amine Castell 12-18-1798
  Basil & Mary Ellen Kidwell 4-14-1857
  Basil T. & Margaret R. Tarman 1-27-1862
  Catherine F. & Walter L. Caddington 9-20-1876 (Dorsey)
  Charles C. & Martha Cook 6-22-1852
  Christiana & Josias Moore 12-30-1834
  Eleanor & Walter Wells 1-25-1800
  Elizabeth & Mordecai J. Moore 1-18-1842
  Francis & Eleanor Ann Brooke 1-6-1868 (F. Call)
  James & Rebecca Hardcastle 2-23-1797
  John & Rachel Mockbee 12-2-1778
  Leonard S. & Mary Eliz^th Sherbert 11-7-1842
  Levi & Matty Duckett 12-22-1801
  Levin & Mary Ann Maria Masters 10-19-1857
  Margaret & Nathan Masters 12-17-1857
  Mary & William Arnold 5-29-1858
  Mary D. & Jno. Z. Jenkins 4-13-1843
  Mary Ellis & George Thomas Peacock 5-2-1876 (Kershaw)
  Mordecai & Elizabeth Clason 4-17-1832
  Overton & Sophia Watkins 8-20-1827
  Richard & Mary Ann Lovelace 12-15-1803
  Richard S. & Ann King 5-29-1841
  Ruth Ann & William Wilburn 12-15-1840
  Sarah & William Arnold 2-28-1842
  Sarah & James Hutchison 9-5-1872 (Kershaw)
  Sarah Ann & Jas. N. Harvey 9-3-1842
  Thomas & Juliet Ann Robey 6-27-1833
  W. Gassaway & Martha Ann Mangun 11-27-1875
  Warren & Sarah Swaine 11-18-1833
RIDGLEY, Caroline & John Sweeney 3-30-1850
RIDGWAY, Alethea Ann & Richard T. Hazle 12-23-1825
  Ann & Leonard Vermillion 8-12-1803

RIDGWAY, Barbara & Mordicai Moore 11-20-1805
  Basil & Eliz.^a Brashears 1-18-1779
  Benjamin & Mary Hardey 12-14-1779
  Eleanor & Richard Nivett 9-10-1787
  Eleanor & Ninian Willett 9-28-1803
  Elizabeth & Benjamin Nony Soper 7-23-1792
  Hessy & Richard H. Locker 12-28-1821
  John & Mary Bennett 11-27-1811
  Jonathan & Letty Moore 1-2-1811
  Mary & Luke Lovelis 12-18-1800
  Mordicai & Eleanor Soaper 11-24-1794
  Nancy & Tilghman Hazle 4-1-1822
  William & Elizabeth Ball 12-29-1812
RIDOUT, Louisa & Gassaway Woodward 8-1-1868 (Langford)
  Samuel & Mary Addison 12-?1-1790
RIGGINS, Mary & Richard Beddo 1-29-1816
RIGGS, Cecelia & Henry Howard 10-2-1867
  Wesley & Ellen Owens 11-26-1884 (Rev. Mr. Howard)
RIGHT, Elizabeth & William Watson 7-26-1784
  James & Elizabeth Collins 7-27-1796
RILEY, George & Alice Sansbury 12-25-1797
  John & Mary Grant 12-10-1788
  John & Willicy Clarke 8-2-1790
  Joseph & Milly Brown 7-23-1794
  Margaret & Tobias Talbert 8-9-1800
  Mary & Jesse Anderson 7-19-1800
RISSON, Elisha & Aminta Albey 1-11-1779
RISTON, Basil & Ann Bonnafill 12-4-1787
  Cassandra & Thomas King 3-29-1823
  Elisha & Ann Maych 2-6-1790
  Heziah & William Albey 1-21-1778
  Rebeccah & Middleton Mitchell 4-21-1792
  Zadock & Elizabeth Bartly 1-7-1786
  Zadock & Mary Ann King 5-14-1818
RITCHIE, Annie S. & David W. Peters 9-8-1870 (Kershaw)
  James H. & Janet Fowler 11-4-1870 (Williams)
  James Henry & Elizabeth Grimes 1-8-1834
  John & Elizabeth Cater 1-8-1816
  John S. Jr. & Georgie Sweeney 12-3-1872 (Kershaw)
  Nellie & Wallace Payne 4-6-1886 (Rev. Brashaw)
  Susie & Walter Duckett 1-23-1882
RIVES, Carrie & Samuel T. Williams 8-2-1858
ROACH, William Thomas & Elizabeth Virginia Selby 4-20-1876 (Homan)
ROBERTS, Ann & George Jones 1-4-1785
  Archibald & Ellen Rebecca Coale 5-19-1870
  Carrie E. & Norman F. Hill 9-22-1869 (Maguire)
  Edward & Ann Brent 12-29-1797
  Elizabeth & Elisha Walker 12-31-1792
  Hannah & Arch.^d Elson 11-2-1782
  Henry & Mary Kelly 8-10-1778
  James & Sarah Wells 8-27-1806
  James & Harriet Ann Clarke 2-23-1867 (Young)
  John M. & Alice Corrick 2-8-1868 (Marbury)
  Joseph K. Jr. & Edith P. Bowie 6-6-1866 Age 25, lawyer m. 6-7-1866
    at Upper Marlboro by Henry J. Kershaw, Min. P. E. Church

ROBERTS, Mary & Joshua Higdon 10-11-1783
  Rebecca & William Weaver 8-16-1877 (Butler)
  Richard & Sarah Eversfield 5-3-1847
  Sarah & Samuel Busey 7-13-1777
  T. Owen W. & Alice Bowie 11-8-1876 (Stanley)
  Trueman & Eleanor Jennett McDaniel 8-4-1803
ROBERTSON, Benjamin & Susan Craycroft 12-22-1827
  Elizabeth & Thomas Smith 11-16-1793
  Mary Ann & George Y. Bowen 2-4-1826
  Thomas F. & Harriet Gray 12-31-1813
  William B. & Rebecca M. Robinson 11-12-1855
ROBEY, A. C. Josephine & James W. McKee 11-25-1867 (Dr. Ryan)
  Adelaide & William W. Brown 4-5-1851
  Charles & Chloe Martin 2-23-1810
  Clara & Alfred R. Martin 11-13-1884
  Elizabeth L. & William A. Hopkins 4-3-1855
  George Dement & Elizabeth Athey 12-16-1791
  Horatio & Bency Mobley 12-23-1813
  John A. & Margaret R. Selby 6-5-1851
  Josephine & William H. Glasscott 9-24-1866 Age 18
  Julia A. & Pinkney A. Scaggs 1-19-1875 (Haddaway)
  Juliet Ann & Thomas Ridgeway 6-27-1833
  Linny & John Nothey 12-26-1831
  Mary & Theodore Tippett 12-24-1821
  Mary & Thomas Swann 12-23-1825
  Mary Josephine & James Richard Edelen 1-12-1882 (Rev. Mr. Hyland)
  Meshal & Nathan Maddocks 12-18-1781
  Michael & Elizabeth Jarman 12-21-1790
  Milison Louisa & Joseph Fowler 6-2-1828
  Nicholas & Elizabeth Ulle 10-15-1873
  Rebecca & John Tarvin 7-8-1808
  S. J. & James T. Devan 6-4-1884 (Rev. Mr. Chesley)
  Sarah & Gabriel Richards 5-12-1812
  Sarah & Hezekiah Johnson 12-31-1823
  Sarah & Warren Grimes 1-20-1826
  Townley B. & Mary Jane Robinson 6-17-1838
  Trueman & Eleanor Crooke 11-25-1805
  Virginia & Washington Murphy 9-15-1869 (Robey)
  Zephaniah & Sarah M. Hatton 4-22-1845
ROBINSON, Aquila T. & Sallie P. Turner 10-18-1880 (Rev. Mr. Gordon)
  Benjamin & Elizabeth Austin 2-7-1793
  Benjamin & Sarah Jerman 5-13-1794
  Benj. N. & Mary E. Craycroft 2-2-1864
  Cecelia Matilda & Nace Diggs 3-30-1874
  Charles & Littey Jones 1-21-1790
  Cornelius & Clarissa Keitch 11-29-1805
  Elijah & Ann Talburt 11-24-1788
  Elizabeth & Francis S. Edelen 3-25-1837
  Elizabeth A. & James H. Gibbons 9-19-1865 (Gordon) m. residence of
     Thomas W. Robinson 9-27-1865
  Ella & Murray Owens 12-29-1883 (Rev. Mr. Cunnane)
  Grafton & Grace Simms 10-28-1870 (Wirt)
  Harriet Ann & Anthony Brice 9-9-1876 (Green)
  Henrietta A. & William Kirby 10-25-1836
  Henry & Catharine Duckett 2-15-1868 (Kershaw)

ROBINSON, Henry & Sallie Williams 2-26-1870 (Maher)
  Isaac & Catherine Tolson 1-11-1872 (Gordon)
  James & Sarah Wynn 2-28-1801
  James F. & Mary Frazier 9-28-1825
  James G. & Mary E. Lesby 1-6-1848
  Jane & Aquilla Briscoe 4-4-1795
  Jane & William Johnson 7-22-1870
  Judith T. B. & Henry D. Edelen 1-16-1832
  Margaret & Jerry Brown 2-11-1870 (Wheeler)
  Marg† & John Mockbee 8-20-1777
  Martha & Abram Holland 11-28-1874 (Billopp)
  Mary & Martin Wells 2-26-1783
  Mary D. & John D. Thompson 1-27-1842
  Mary Jane & Townley B. Robey 6-17-1838
  Mary S. L. & John T. Neal 6-24-1869 (Chesley)
  Mary W. & Francis A. Ward 2-2-1870 (Marbury)
  Milley & Thomas Wise 12-1-1787
  Milley & John Baden 4-17-1802
  Patsey & Thomas Naylor 12-14-1812
  Priscilla & William Jeffreys 12-14-1799
  Rebecca M. & William B. Robertson 11-12-1855
  Richard T. & Martha A. Gibbons 11-23-1854
  Robert Henry & Amanda M. Baden 7-24-1872 (Marbury)
  Sallie & Basil Logan 6-2-1877 (Gordon)
  Sarah & Charles Boteler 1-22-1785
  Sarah A. S. & William J. Gibbons 6-1-1859
  Sarah Eliz⁺ Ford & Zephaniah Marten 12-30-1795
  Susannah & Jonathan Cooksey 12-27-1816
  Thomas & Susannah Letchworth 3-31-1804
  Thos⁸ W. & Martha Walls 1-12-1846
  Tracey & Henry Galway 10-18-1873 (Dwyer)
  William & Mary Ann Eleanor Turton 7-30-1828
  Zadock & Johanna Ann Townshend 12-22-1819
  Zadock & Eliza S. Baden 1-18-1840
ROCHE, Robert Frederick & Margaret Eugenia Thorn 5-28-1868
ROCKET, Henry & Mary Hazard 8-17-1816
RODER, William A. & Victoria P. Moran 4-10-1880 (Rev⁴ Mr. Butler)
ROE, Elizabeth & John L. Rawlings 10-24-1833
  Sarah & William Meaks 12-6-1809
ROEBE, Sarah & John Guysinger 5-18-1830
ROGERS, Ann C. & John G. Howard 4-16-1827
  Henry W. & Mary Dulany 6-23-1813
  John Thomas & Mary Mulligan 9-15-1876 (Major)
ROLAND, George & Elizabeth A. Goddard 1-11-1843
  William H. & Rachael E. Dixon 3-5-1845
ROLLINGS, Catherine Estep & Jn⁰ Rollings 10-22-1783
  Jn⁰ & Catherine Estep Rollings 10-22-1783
  Mary & William Pumphray 2-4-1792
  Mary Zora & Benj. R. Garner 2-8-1864
ROLLINS, Anna R. & M. Randolph Latimer 2-8-1858
  James C. & Rachel Ann Tubman 6-27-1851
  Martha Jane & Thomas G. Williams 2-10-1858
  Trueman & Amelia Garner 2-5-1863
ROSE, Thomas & Mary Smith 10-22-1777
ROSS, Ariana & John Stewart 12-13-1791

ROSS, Elizabeth & Jeremiah Smith 3-8-1797
  Elizabeth & Christopher Waters 12-23-1865
  Eliz.th Ann & Trueman Belt 4-9-1828
  Jane & L. Hawkins 10-7-1885
  John & Susan Wood 7-14-1869 (Maher)
  Margaret & Benedict Sheriff 1-28-1797
  Margaret E. & Revd Henry V. D. Nevins 5-4-1843
  Mary M. & Richard Bruce 10-9-1883 (Walker)
  Rose & Wilson Brewer 1-5-1884 (Rev. Wm. C. Butler)
  William & Harriott Tilley 3-17-1801
ROUZER, Susie & William Stineman 5-23-1868 (Markham)
ROWE, William & Ann Thompson 8-28-1802
ROWELL, Delilah A. & Benjⁿ T. P. Devaughn 2-17-1844
ROWLAND, John & Julia Ann Dyer 4-9-1819
ROZER, Ann & James Henson 5-14-1873 (Kershaw)
  Cecilia & William Hayward Foote 1-8-1801
  Eliza & Benjamin Tasker Dulaney 2-13-1796
  Francis H. & Maria Rozer 12-15-1792
  Harriot & Henry Dangerfield 5-19-1810
  Henry Jr. & Sarah Edelen 9-13-1779
  Maria & Francis H. Rozer 12-15-1792
  Maria H. H. & William Allen Daingerfield 12-12-1807
  Sarah & Charles Pye 12-4-1784
ROZIER, Francis & Ella Boston 4-20-1878 (Carroll)
RUMBLES, Laura N. & Thomas Owens 12-20-1884 (Rev. H. Green)
RUPLEY, Mary D. & Henry D. Pfeil 2-12-1877 (Curtz)
RUSSELL, Ann & Richard Martin 1-1-1780
  Ann & Sabrett Sollars 3-3-1785
  Elizabeth & Joseph Cooke Junr 12-11-1792
  Elizabeth & Walter Mullikin 10-30-1799
  Elizabeth & Thomas Cahall 5-21-1822
  Joseph & Deborah Cheney 5-16-1797
  Philip & Eliz^a Dove 2-17-1781
  William & Rachel Fitzgerald 1-6-1795
RUST, George & Maria C. Marlowe 11-8-1809
RUSTEN, Eleanor & Charles Lane 8-31-1808
  John & Eleanor Dulany 10-29-1802
RUSTRIDGE, James & Mary Gray 4-7-1798
RYAN, Clement & Mary Northy 2-1-1779
  Elizabeth & Thomas Ryon 11-8-1838
  Robert W. & Mary Swann 12-9-1852
RYLAND, John & Sarah G. Perkins 8-30-1836
  Mollie S. & Rufus Belt 11-10-1866 Age 23
RYLEY, Margaret & Luke Thompson 2-15-1793
  Thomas & Mary Webster 11-5-1811
RYON, Ann & Samuel Hooper 12-31-1785
  Ann & William Richard Sansbury 12-29-1792
  Ann & Walter Crosby 11-16-1799
  Ann & John Wilson 9-18-1802
  Ann & John Grimes 1-6-1842
  Annie V. & F. Dysen Crandell 10-8-1881
  Darby & Ann Sim 12-31-1779
  Dennis F. & Grace Burgess 3-21-1867 (Griffith)
  Eleanor & Henry Carrick 12-24-1832
  Elijah & Sarah Wilburn 1-2-1798

RYON, Elisha & Sarah Sansbury 2-16-1779
  Elizabeth & Cephus Hoye 9-9-1786
  Elizabeth & William Connock 1-31-1798
  Elizabeth & James Nowell 2-6-1798
  Elizabeth & Alexander Wilkerson 1-4-1859
  Elizabeth & Samuel B. Crauford 11-13-1861
  Fielder & Rachel Smith 6-3-1797
  Fielder Smith & Elizabeth Duckett 1-12-1818
  Frances & Edward Griffin 11-5-1819
  George W. & Ella J. Ridgeley 2-20-1884 (Father Cunnane)
  Georgianna H. & Wm. Benjamin Wilson 3-3-1863
  Gustie M. & John R. King 10-15-1873 (Mercer)
  H. M. & Agnes C. Brown 5-3-1886
  Jeremiah & Fanny Smith 12-24-1791
  Jeremiah N. & Anne E. Grimes 3-26-1862
  John & Eleanor Gates 3-7-1786
  Josephine & William T. Sherbert 12-9-1881
  Leonara & Alexander Wilkerson 1-13-1864
  Lizzie E. & Howard V. Harvey 4-25-1884 (Rev. Stanley)
  Margaret Ann & William Piles 4-12-1847
  Margery Ann & James H. Wells 9-13-1849
  Martha V. & Thomas Talbert 4-9-1844
  Mary & James Mayhew 5-14-1788
  Mary A. & John Cooksey 6-12-1871
  Mary Catharine & James Henry Coxen 3-25-1862
  Mary Ellen & Zachariah Shaw 10-14-1846
  Nelson & Martha Jenkins 2-1-1834
  Philip & Joanna Alder 3-23-1778
  Priscilla & Henry Taiman 5-2-1779
  Rachel E. & J. T. Benjamin Suit 6-23-1859
  Rachel N. & Charles T. Wood 12-12-1860
  Richard & Catherine Brown 12-19-1825
  Robert F. & Catherine A. Talbot 3-19-1866 Age 25, farmer m. 3-20-1866
    residence Thos Talbert by Henry J. Kershaw Min. P. E. Church
  Robert W. & Georgianna Hardy 11-21-1854
  Ruth E. & Wm. E. Strickland 12-28-1846
  Sarah & William E. Pumphrey 12-25-1809
  Sophia & William Strickland 5-4-1821
  Susanna & Amos Carrick 3-29-1853
  Susannah & Samuel Knighton 2-11-1791
  Susannah & Philip Hopkins 8-22-1798
  Susannah & James Duckett 12-29-1815
  Theodore & Nancy Baldwin 2-4-1823
  Thomas & Elizabeth Brown 12-7-1832
  Thomas & Elizabeth Ryon 11-8-1838
  Thomas S. & Susan Fry 2-19-1855
  Walter & Mary Ann Clarke 12-22-1830
  William S. & Christianna Wilson 12-7-1858
  William Thomas & Bennetta Onions 10-1-1860
  Wm. S. & Elizth Ann Fowler 10-16-1827

SADLER, R. H. & Emma Steiger 1-22-1870
  Rebecca & Abraham Turner 11-27-1781
ST. CLAIR, Francis O. of Washington, D. C. & Lelie C. Dent 10-24-1866
  Age 25, clerk m. 11-1-1866, James Chipchase of Calvert County, clergyman
ST. CLARE, Milicent & William Jarman 3-12-1781
SALISBURY, George W. & Mary A. Klock 9-20-1875
SANDERS, Lydia & William Fowler 11-25-1788
  Susanna & Edwin Willis 4-15-1867 (Lenahan)
  William G. & Matilda M. S. McCarty 2-17-1815
SANDERSON, Annie & William McIlhaney 6-4-1867 (Kershaw)
  Sarah & Jacob O, Parker 3-9-1875
SANDFIELD, George & Elizabeth Lowry 12-9-1800
SANDFORD, Eliza & Daniel G. Hickey 8-31-1824
  James Anna & George W. Page 5-8-1871 (Bague)
  Nancy & Alexander Leroy Sheherer 6-13-1796
  Presley & Mary Taylor 12-19-1792
  Sarah Ann & John M. Duvall 5-27-1837
  Thomas & Eleanor Clarke 12-23-1816
SANSBERRIE, Rebecca & Osborn White 12-24-1792
SANSBERRY, Joseph & Elizabeth Spalding 11-30-1798
  M. & Greenberry Ridgely 2-29-1840
  Martha & Levi Vermillion 12-28-1819
  Sarah Ann & Ignatius Adams 1-22-1816
  Thomas & Rebecca Mockbee 2-25-1797
SANSBURY, Albert Benson & Alice May Stephen 4-2-1884 (Rev. Mr. Dell)
  Alexius & Eliza Hamilton 2-16-1789
  Alice & George Riley 12-25-1797
  Alice C. & George S. Dove 2-28-1878 (Miller)
  Alice K. & J. Henry Huntt 12-30-1884
  Anne & Benjamin Johnson 2-11-1792
  Benoni & Henrietta Clubb 7-7-1873 (Coe)
  Caroline E. & Wm. B. Abigill 12-24-1878 (Mercer)
  Edward & Harriet Turner 4-10-1819
  Eleanor & Ignatius Boone 1-14-1796
  Elial F. & Letitia Jane Jones 12-15-1863
  Elizabeth J. & Aloysius B. Thorn 9-27-1867 (Martin)
  Elizth & Charles Ridgely 12-24-1838
  Emma & Joseph A. Barker 11-16-1870 (Linthicum)
  Fendall & Mary Frazier 2-10-1845
  Geneva & Lemuel F. Lusby 3-2-1868 (Martin)
  George A. & Rachael Ann Locker 12-27-1852
  Georgie A. & Richard H. Lusby 12-21-1868 (Martin)
  Henry & Ann Johnson 12-6-1822
  John B. & Sophia Simpson 12-11-1851
  John T. & Sarah E. Brown 5-16-1853
  Jno. H. & Mary E. Crawford 5-1-1850
  Margaret Ann & Enoch George Duly 4-5-1853
  Mary & Francis Hopkins 1-29-1786
  Mary & Thomas Cahaley 12-3-1807
  Mary B. & Andrew W. Brown 7-13-1876 (Kershaw)
  Mary E. & John T. M. Frye 11-26-1873 (Johnson)
  Mary Jane Cath. &James L. Jenkins 12-26-1867 (Martin)
  Middleton & Jane Gates 12-26-1803
  Minty & Edward H. Clements 1-15-1796
  Priscilla & John Winkler 3-11-1828

SANSBURY, Richard & Sarah Ann Adams 2-6-1823
  Richard H. & Sarah E. Grimes 8-12-1861
  Sarah & Elisha Ryon 2-16-1779
  Sarah & Thomas Blacklock 1-30-1783
  Sarah & William Bromley 1-29-1794
  Sarah & Charles Burgess 2-4-1807
  Sarah & William Stevens 1-29-1828
  Sarah A. & Sprigg O. Beall 1-26-1881 (Rev. Mr. Brayshaw)
  Theodore & Elizabeth Brashears 10-8-1803
  Thomas & Eliz.th V. L. Scott 12-31-1836
  William & Ann Burgess 9-8-1803
  William & Priscilla Cole 3-29-1811
  William & Nancy Gallyham 5-20-1839
  William Richard & Ann Ryon 12-29-1792
  William W. & Mary Sophronia Thorn 4-15-1867
SAPPINGTON, Jno & Jemima Fowler 1-29-1781
SARVOY, Margaret Ann V. & Jeremiah M. Jessup 12-20-1879 (Rev. A. B. Wilson)
SASSELL,....... & Anthony Thomas 1-30-1782
SASSCER, see also Scasser
  Amy & Charles Beavin 12-13-1791
  Ann & Edward Thursby 1-25-1786
  Elizabeth & James Gibbons 11-12-1833
  Frederick & Rosa Ghisolin 4-17-1855
  Frederick Jr. & Lucy Clagett 6-10-1884 (Rev. Dr. Lewin)
  Henrietta S. & William J. Hill 10-10-1866 (Fr. Call)
    Age 26, m. 10-11-1866 at residence of mother
  John Judson & Harriet M. Osbourn 1-31-1826
  John William & Julia Marker 3-26-1845
  Jonathan T. & Sarah D. Gibbons 1-16-1830
  Margaret Roberta & Dr. James L. Sutton 11-27-1856
  Martha A. & William A. Wallace 6-25-1840
  Martha J. & Jesse Selby 10-23-1832
  Mary E. & James M. Waring 12-16-1839
  Mary H. & Charles Wyckliffe 11-21-1866 (Lenahan)
  Mattie & Dr. N. S. Knighton 11-24-1866 (Lenahan)
  Philip A. & Christiana A. Gibbons 4-11-1855
  Philip E. & Ada T. Huntt 10-25-1882 (Rev. Mr. LaRoche)
  Samuel H. & Mary Eliza Smith 5-19-1841
  Sebastian & Isabella F. Berry 2-24-1873 (McDonald)
  Susan J. & Benjamin F. Duvall 11-22-1854
  Verlinder P. & William A. Gover 1-27-1818
  William & Jane Beason 5-3-1779
  William & Eliz$^{?}$ Beaven 12-5-1781
  Zadock & Henrietta S. Skinner 1-9-1827
SASSER, Elizabeth & Jon$^{?}$ T. Sasser 9-29-1783
  Elizabeth C. & Benjamin Berry of Wm. 10-23-1818
  Jon$^{?}$ T. & Elizabeth Sasser 9-29-1783
  Jonathan Throne & Martha Richards 1-16-1797
  Levin & Martha Ann Davis 7-23-1834
  Sarah & Charles Beaven 1-13-1778
  Susannah & Mackall S. Cox 12-6-1808
  Thomas & Dorinda E. Berry 12-21-1818
  Underwood & Elizth W. Wall 3-23-1818
SAUNDERS, Elizabeth & Edward Boteler 1-31-1781
SAVAGE, James & Erosmon Fell Lewis 12-29-1819

SAVAGE, Mary & Townley Munroe 12-27-1847
SAVARY, Louisa Anna Eleanor & Charles August[s] Preuss 7-15-1805
  Peter & Jane Smith 11-18-1782
SAVILLE, James Hamilton & Susan Houston 6-6-1871
SAVINGTON, Sarah & William Baldwin 11-9-1811
SAVOY, Augustus Jr. & Mary J. Jessups col[d] 4-6-1882
  Chapman & Jane A Boteler 12-30-1867 (Lanahan)
  Eliza Jane & John William Crack 3-4-1868 (Gordon)
  Emly & Edmund Greenleaf coloured 3-12-1856
  Henry & Eleanor Proctor 1-25-1830
  John & Martha Wright 5-9-1856
  Lucy & Francis Proctor 9-2-1820
  Lucy & Robert Douglass 12-23-1867 (Lankford)
  Mary & Josias Butler 10-7-1856 col[d]
  Mary & John H. Fountain 8-29-1878
  Rebecca & Nathaniel Ford 11-20-1882 (Mr. Walker)
SAWYER, Charles W. & Charlotte Webster 6-22-1816
SCAGGES, George B. & Ann Anderson 5-15-1834
SCAGGS, Alfred & Mary Duvall 3-18-1826
  Elizabeth & George Moore 12-30-1828
  George B. & Elizabeth J. Boteler 10-25-1837
  George W. & Mary P. Naylor 8-22-1856
  Pinkney A. & Julia A. Robey 1-19-1875 (Haddaway)
  Polly & Charles Haislep 11-27-1827
  Rebecca & George Gloyd 6-11-1822
  Selby & Eleanor Perry 11-27-1827
  Selby B. & Sally Ann Bounds 6-17-1850
SCARCE, Charity & Levi Moore 12-12-1801
  Milly & George Darsey 12-27-1798
  Rebeccah & John Summers 2-26-1794
  Sarah & Nathaniel Summers 1-2-1793
SCASSER, see also Sasscer, Sasser
  Elizabeth & Walter S. Havener 12-23-1841
SCEARCE, Ruthy & Jonathan Wheat 2-9-1805
SCESSALL, Eliz[a] & Bennett Woodward 12-15-1778
SCHAAFF, Annie M. & Capt. John D. R. Spencer 7-23-1864
  James L. & Flora Belle Chase 6-16-1885
  Lizzie & Dr. Williams Donally 10-26-1875 (Sweet)
SCHELL, Enos & Elizabeth Hardey 1-9-1808
SCHOCBERLEIN, Mary Elizabeth & Bernard Lewis McKever 1-20-1878
SCHOLFIELD, Ann & Wm. Ashford Scott 12-13-1796
SCHRUCNER, Hezekiah & Sarah Crain 7-21-1874 (Price)
SCISSELL, Samuel & Issabella Belt 2-21-1806
SCOTT, Adelia W. & Ninian B. Barron 4-14-1829
  Agnes & Thomas Hoye 4-22-1786
  Agnes Lucinda & Chesterfield Stewart 12-24-1872 (Evans)
  Albert H. & Elizabeth Butler 12-28-1855
  Alice & Bernard West 5-25-1872 (Evans)
  Ann & Archibald Boyd 11-9-1777
  Ann & Basil Wilson 8-9-1779
  Ariana & Ignatius Adams 1-16-1811
  Catharine & Anthony Drane 3-29-1792
  Catharine M. & Fielder Suit 9-7-1831
  E. P. & Martha Ann Osbourn 2-4-1851
  Edward & Mary Clagett 2-9-1790

SCOTT, Edward J. K. & Eliza Ann Boteler 2-25-1840
  Eleanor & Joseph Thaw 4-19-1804
  Eliza & John Wilson 12-27-1830
  Eliza Anne & George W. Millard 11-9-1867 (Fr. Call)
  Eliza^a & Thos Sherwood 2-1-1779
  Elizabeth & Edward Cross 6-19-1780
  Elizabeth & John Swain 1-30-1826
  Elizabeth & Jeremiah Fowler 7-16-1879 (Perry)
  Elizth V. L. & Thomas Sansbury 12-31-1836
  Emily & Nicholas Osbourn 7-27-1831
  Harriot & George Jenkins 1-29-1818
  Henry T. & Sarah Yost 5-18-1868
  Horatio C. & Ellen O. Hodges 10-5-1826
  Horatio C. & Henrietta M. Waring 4-21-1834
  Isaac & Mary Holland 9-25-1883 (Rev. Frank Wills)
  James & Mary Humphreys 2-4-1797
  James & Jemima Greenleaf 12-29-1866 (Hicks)
  John (Washington) & Sarah P. Selby 11-1-1866 Age 23, clerk (Marbury)
  John & Sarah Ann Loggans 5-15-1872
  John & Delia Pinckney 7-11-1872 (Stiner)
  John H. & Ann Verlinda Soper 6-15-1826
  John W. & Lucinda Benson 6-4-1836
  Judson & Ann Osbourn 12-16-1823
  Laura & Benjamin Janey 5-16-1866 Age 19, black - cook
  Lloyd M. & Priscilla Gibons 12-27-1841
  Luciffa A. & Grafton Suit 6-9-1840
  Manoah & Elizabeth Cole 2-9-1803
  Margaret & Joseph Mattinley 1-24-1785
  Maria E. & John S. Fleet 11-21-1871 (Gordon)
  Martha & Thomas Magruder Clagett 3-12-1805
  Martha Ann & Richard K. Scott 8-22-1815
  Mary & John Hoofman 4-24-1781
  Mary & Rezin Turner 12-12-1799
  Mary & Joseph H. Gibbons 2-3-1864
  Mary C. & Daniel S. Chesley 10-3-1867 (Kershaw)
  Mary E. & Robert M. Larmour 7-26-1849
  Mary Lavinia & George W. Beall 9-20-1873 (Cotton)
  Nathaniel & Rachel Ann Batson 12-27-1877 (Carroll)
  Patrick & Mary Jane Brice col^d 10-12-1868 (Langford)
  Patrick C. & Chloe A. E. Butler col^d 2-10-1881 (Rev. Mr. Lawson)
  Polydore E. & Lucy Ann Clagett 2-11-1840
  Priscilla & Caleb A. Rawlings 12-17-1838
  Rachel & Jonathan Cartwright 5-9-1843
  Rebecca M. & Columbus F. Connick 12-14-1859
  Richard & Nellie Skinner 6-3-1873 (Pinkney)
  R^d J. & Matilda Hamilton 4-25-1848
  Doct^r Richard J. & Roberta R. Hilleary 11-21-1861
  Richard John & Louisa A. Hamilton 11-7-1826
  Richard K. & Martha Ann Scott 8-22-1815
  Richard M. & Mary S. Craycroft 6-25-1863
  Robert & Ellen Thornton 3-11-1869 (Langford)
  Rose & Henson Dent 5-14-1884
  Sally & Samuel Gray 6-23-1870 (Evans)
  Samuel & Ann Dickson Wilson 11-19-1784
  Samuel & Elizabeth Free 4-19-1796

190

SCOTT, Sarah W. & William H. Compton 10-24-1855
   Susan M. & Leonard Huick 11-23-1857
   Thomas & Massy M. Jenkins 11-23-1795
   Thomas Clagett & Ann Hedwick Boone 12-8-1806
   Tilghman & Elizabeth Van Suverugh(?) Carter 2-28-1822
   Violetta & William Smitson 7-11-1876 (Stanley)
   Wesley & Nancy Glassgow col. 4-6-1882 (Rev. Mr. Frank Wills)
   William & Rebecca Hardey 2-20-1792
   William & Mary Maria Sheriff 10-27-1830
   Wm. Ashford & Ann Scholfield 12-13-1796
SCOTTEN, Emma Jane & John J. Lamis 4-29-1867 (West)
SCRIBNER, Sophia & Henry Tongue 1-4-1883 (Rev. Joshua Barnes)
SCRIVENER, David & Florence Jones 10-23-1879 (Quiller)
   Maria & Richard Stallings 7-11-1826
   William & Rebecca Watson 12-7-1802
   Eleanor & Thomas Mitchell 2-3-1823
SEABOLD, George Ignatius & Laura Ellen Hardisty 5-16-1870 (Maher)
SEABORN, Catharine H. & Henry F. Worthington 2-26-1855
   James R. & Dorinda Ann Smallwood 11-16-1846
   James R. & Maggie R. Fuller 1-4-1869
   Mary J. & Jasper P. Sweeney 9-5-1871 (Gordon)
SEABOURN, Robert B. & Mary E. Duvall 1-4-1882 (Rev. Dr. Gordon)
   William & Sophy A. Taylor 12-23-1875
SEABOURNE, James R. & Susanna Curtain 1-3-1870 (Gordon)
SEABURN, Nelson & Sarah Peacock 1-24-1846
SEAGAR, Mary Elizabeth & William Edward Seagar 12-29-1879
      William Edward & Mary Elizabeth Seagar 12-29-1879
SEARCE, Rezin & Airry Hardey 11-3-1806
SEARS, Casino & John D. Brown 8-1-1876 (Kershaw)
   Harry & Catherine V. Hall 1-16-1886 (Rev. Father Cunane)
   Richard B. S. & Anna P. Havener 2-16-1859
SEATON, Louisa D. & Henry L. Coombs 8-2-1822 m. 8-15-1822
SEBBALD, George & Rachel Hanson 1-5-1786
SEBURN, James & Miss Richards 9-7-1821
SEDGWICK, James & Mary A. Jackson 1-3-1877 (Homan)
SEDRICKS, Jane & Dorsey Dyer 12-7-1871 (Wheeler)
SEFTON, John & Mary Harwood 10-16-1819
SEGAR, George L. & Henrietta Goldsmith 4-16-1884 (Rev. Mr. Chesley)
   Thomas & Ann Maria Watson 1-24-1855
SEISSELL, Eleanor & John Smith Suit 11-28-1784
SEITZ, Alice & John Bowen 12-21-1878
   Ida B. & George M. Smith 6-13-1895
SELBY, Ann & Thomas Dorsett 12-16-1784
   Ann & James Harvey 3-25-1796
   Ann & Jonas G. Mangun 1-12-1803
   Ann & William O. Jones 1-13-1824
   Ann P. & Nathaniel M. Soper 2-6-1861
   Catherine R. & Richard H. Curtain 3-15-1866 Age 19 (Porter)
   Charles & Layor Lanham 12-18-1787
   Elizabeth A. & Joseph T. Clark 4-6-1857
   Elizabeth Virginia & William Thomas Roach 4-20-1867
   Frances & Robert C. Naylor 5-12-1883 (Mr. Wheeler)
   J. A. & Mary E. Demar 2-10-1862
   James & Rebecca Sheriff 12-12-1801
   James & Lucy Beall 2-16-1808

SELBY, James T. & Marg.^t Ellen Coffren   1-23-1872   (Gordon)
   Jesse & Ann Smith   2-13-1801
   Jesse & Martha J. Sasscer   10-23-1832
   Jesse F. & Christianna F. Swann   2-14-1859
   John H. & Elizabeth Fowler   5-23-1833
   John H. & Eleanor A. Burgess   1-12-1856
   John Smith & Sabinah Orme   4-14-1780
   Joseph H. & Rebecca Harvey   4-27-1832
   Joseph H. & Mattie A. Pyles   2-1-1881   (Rev. Mr. Cross)
   Jn? W. & Mary Jane Brady   12-20-1848
   Laura & Charles H. Adams   12-23-1876   (Gordon)
   Magruder & Agness Hodskinson   2-11-1788
   Margaret & Samuel Fowler   2-2-1798
   Margaret R. & John A. Robey   6-5-1851
   Martha & Thos. I. Selby   12-29-1828
   Mary & Nicholas Maylor   2-15-1783
   Mary Ann & John L. Estep   12-8-1821
   Matilda & John Julius Giddings   2-7-1848
   Matilda & William Jones   11-9-1877   (Valtz)
   Philip & Catherine Boteler   8-24-1778
   Priscilla & Henry Gibbons   12-11-1834
   Richard B. & Caroline E. Soper   12-23-1856
   Robert W. & Susanna Swann   2-13-1852
   Samuel & Mary Demar   1-25-1832
   Sarah P. & John Scott of Washington   11-1-1866   Age 20
      Minister, Rev. Dr. Marbury, P. E. Church
   Susannah & William Bryan   11-11-1802
   Sybal & Thomas Pownall   12-27-1787
   Thos. J. & Martha Selby   12-29-1828
SELLMAN, Rose & Frank Lofty col.^d   5-2-1868   (Thomas)
   Thomas & Mollie Coats   12-26-1878   (Wheeler)
SELTZER, John M. & Mary M. Sheriff   12-21-1885
SELVIN, Joshua & Mary Anr White   11-29-1821
SEMLY, Elizabeth & Abraham Jones   11-19-1873
SEMMES, Benedict J. & Elizabeth Emily Edelen   11-11-1823
   Francis E. & Virlinder Hagan   7-11-1814
   John & Eliz.th Wright   10-3-1848
   John B. & Edmonia Edelen   1-27-1860
   Richard A. & Permelia Webster   8-19-1822
   Thomas F. & Mary Olivia Edelen   6-1-1835
SEMMS, Mary & Stanislaus Hoxton   1-17 -1799
   Matilda & Pembroke A. Brawner   10-13-1857
SENTON, Mary & John Waine   12-24-1783
SERPALL, G. M. & Miss Georgia Clarke   9-13-1869   (Ross)
SEVOY, Henry & Angeline Batty col.^d   11-28-1878   (Watkins)
SEWALL, Charity & John Thomas Young   8-24-1876   (Carroll)
   Dolly & Louis Burls   12-13-1877   (Homan)
   Eleanor & Francis J. Mitchell   1-2-1809
   Frank & Christiana Matthews   10-16-1875
   John & Eliza Jane Dorsey   5-6-1876   (Carroll)
   Mary B. & Philip D. Key   12-1-1828
   Virginia & John Henry Hawks (also listed as Hawkins) Black,lic. 8-3-1866
      m. 8-4-1866 Age 18, yellow - farmhand
   SEWELL, Robert & Mary Brentt   2-16-1789
SEXTON, Mary A. & George W. Cousey   10-30-1869   (Mahr)

192

SHAAFF, John Thomas & Mary Sydebotham 12-18-1800
SHACKELS, Thomas H. & Mary D. Hall 12-9-1876 (Hodges)
SHAFF, Martha M. & Thomas W. Adams 12-28-1870 (Linthicum)
SHAFFER, Benjamin Franklin & Mary Estella Castle 5-30-1885
  Charles W. & Anne J. Mitchell 9-17-1878
  Mary & George F. Piles 11-14-1853
  William & Sarah L. Richards 2-7-1849
SHAGNASHA, Mary & John Manley 7-22-1786
SHAGS, Eugene H. & Susie A. Chaney 1-23-1882 (Rev. Mr. Stanley)
SHANAN, Ann & Henderson Dyson 5-30-1868 (Langford)
  Elizabeth & J. K. Holland 5-30-1868 (Langford)
SHANDLE, Anna & Clay Fergerson 4-26-1882 (Rev. M. Bryan)
SHANLEY, Bernard & Sarah Magruder 2-3-1785
SHANNON, John & Eleanor A. Lanham 8-9-1824
  Luke & Dely Wade 3-24-1794
SHARP, Charles & Margaret Sherman 12-5-1881 (Rev. Mr. Snyder)
  Jane & Alexander Jackson 12-16-1872
  Mary Elizabeth & George Washington Wedge 2-1-1872 (Evans)
  Wm. & Mary Peters 3-8-1881 (Rev. D. A. Aquilla) colored
SHARPS, Rachel Ann & John Connoway 12-27-1878
SHAW, Charles & Mary Ann Chancy 12-18-1850
  Edith N. & Milton J. Payne 9-16-1885
  Elizabeth Ellen & Charles Parker 12-14-1868 (Harper)
  Emmeline & John S. Hall 11-7-1849
  James & Elizabeth Beall 6-24-1805
  John & Harriett R. Day 6-22-1876
  Jno. W. & Emma Hurdle 12-29-1863
  Laura & Washington Thomas 7-20-1877
  Mary C. & Robert Simmons 5-11-1852
  Mary Ellen & William Beall 12-19-1846
  Nicholas & Mary A. Anderson 9-4-1856
  Rezin & Elizabeth Beall 12-21-1842
  Spencer & Clarissa Slater 3-26-1875 (Gordon)
  Thomas & Mazy Upton 4-16-1818
  William & Grace Dunkin 12-13-1797
  Zachariah & Mary Ellen Ryon 10-14-1846
SHEA, Ellen C. & John P. Turner 10-6-1885 (Fr. Caughy)
SHEAKELLS, Levi & Martha Day 2-3-1833
SHEARLOCK, Elizabeth & Thomas S. Fergusson 12-22-1856
  Thomas & Catherine Jane Earley 11-11-1823
SHECKELLS, Ann S. & Benj⁴ S. Suit 3-1-1852
  Richard & Susan Basford 1-8-1840
SHECKELS, Isabella & Joseph Powers 7-8-1871
SHECKLES, Benjamin & Mary Burch 2-6-1819
SHECKOLLS, Mary F. & William A. Cator 12-28-1858
SHEDD, James S. & Katie J. Melling 11-1-1876
SHEHERER, Alexander Leroy & Nancy Sandford 6-13-1796
SHEID, Francis & Janet Hunter 5-10-1831
  Martha & Benjamin Cawood 5-8-1798
SHEKELES, Agnes & Edward Griffin 5-21-1781
SHEKELL, Deborah & Francis Essex 8-21-1792
SHEKELLS, Cephas & Eleanor Pratt 9-14-1780
  Cephas & Eleanor Boyd 9-27-1796
  Deborah & Elias Nutwell 5-11-1781
  John & Ann Cheney 8-14-1799

SHEKELLS, Mary & Thomas Parker 3-25-1785
SHELTON, Thomas & Elizabeth Webb 8-6-1777
SHENTON, Charles & Mary Latimer 2-12-1827
SHEPPARD, Laura S. & Frank Sprigg 11-15-1876 (Homan)
  Thomas & Susan Fletcher 5-6-1876
SHEPHERD, John & Rebecca Chaney 2-27-1797
  John & Mary Lucy Smith 5-31-1880 (Rev. Thom. Gambriel)
  George W. & Mary Ann Wells 12-12-1832
  Henrietta & Charles Thomas 2-2-1831
SHERBERT, Ellen & Alfred Vermillion 9-14-1848
  Mary Elizth & Leonard S. Ridgeway 11-7-1842
  William T. & Josephine Ryon 12-9-1881
SHERBUTT, Benjamin & Elizabeth Onions 12-30-1839
SHERIDAN, James P. & Letetia Peirce 6-11-1793
SHERIFF, Alfred Thomas & Chloe Ann Cox 12-28-1840
  Benedict & Margaret Ross 1-28-1797
  Dionysius & Mary A. Hill 4-8-1857
  Dionysius & Matilda M. Phillips 10-18-1860
  Elizabeth & William Baldwin 12-7-1799
  Elizabeth & Thomas E. M. Thorn 2-23-1829
  Henry E. & Martha D. Simpson 1-24-1876 (Berry)
  John C. & Clara E. Clarke 11-25-1882 (Rev. Mr. Chew)
  Levi & Elizabeth Wilson 5-15-1810
  Margaret M. & Walter H. Wells 6-15-1868 (Stanley)
  Mary & John Brashears 1-8-1805
  Mary & Samuel Arnold 11-9-1826
  Mary M. & John M. Seltzer 12-21-1885
  Mary Maria & William Scott 10-27-1830
  Rachel & Henry Yost 3-18-1804
  Rebecca & James Selby 12-12-1801
  Ruth & Walter Brown 12-21-1799
SHERKLIFF, Dorothy & Joseph Coombes 5-4-1783
SHERLOCK, Elizabeth & John Ranten 12-3-1816
  Ralph & Ann Cooke 2-13-1805
SHERLY, Theodore & Nancy Watkins 3-28-1797
SHERMAN, Margaret & Charles Sharp 12-5-1881 (Rev. Mr. Snyder)
SHERRIFF, Mary & Samuel Arnold 11-9-1826
SHERTLIFFE, Leonard & Maria Dyer 1-30-1833
SHERWOOD, Susanna & John Callahane 2-21-1778
  Thos & Eliza Scott 2-1-1779
SHIBY, Irene M. & Robert A. Clum 2-17-1881 (Rev. Dr. Chester of Wash.D.C.)
SHIELDS, Ellen S. & Thomas Brown cold 8-7-1865 Age 20yr 8 mo, house
  servant - Adam R. Dolly, minister
SHIPLEY, Catherine Jane & Francis Brintnall 8-15-1867
  Joshua & Levinia Beall 12-4-1878
  Nicholas H. & Margaret Contee 2-19-1844
  Providence & Zephaniah Mitchell 5-19-1817
  Rachel & Samuel Welsh 2-29-1804
SHIPPS, Carrie V. & N. D. Anderson 7-13-1864
SHOEMAKEN, Ann & John Cockler 5-13-1799
SHOEMAKER, Sarah & Charles Gates 5-8-1882
SHORT, James & Mary Grimes 2-9-1779
  James & Mary Maccastle 12-12-1791
  Rhoda & Levin Club 8-25-1786
SHORTER, Albert & Alice Brown 12-24-1872 (Ankward)

SHORTER, Archibald & Anne Chew 10-26-1867 (Fa. Bayne)
  Elizabeth & Charles Giles 9-9-1872 (McDonald)
  George & Sarah Ann Hagan 12-27-1873 (Fowler)
  George H. & Sallie Nicholas 2-3-1873 (Evans)
  Jacob & Caroline Harper 1-3-1874 (O'Dwyer)
  Mary & Walter Washington col^d 5-6-1869 (Maher)
  Richard & Laura Ellen Young 12-24-1872 (Evans)
  Thomas & Sarah Peach 4-9-1801
SHREAVES, Mima & Henry Simpson 6-5-1804
SHREEVE, Domia A. S. & James A. Whitmore 6-9-1863
SHREEVES, Eliz^a & William Carrick 2-13-1795
  Mary & Humphrey Beckett 2-22-1786
SHULZE, Francis S. & Margaret Alice Mullikin 1-1-1855
SHURLOCK, William & Mary Norris 12-5-1809
SIBLEY, James Jr. & Elizabeth Cecil 4-6-1814
  Milly & Basil Benson 2-19-1850
SIDEL, Mary & Joseph Haker 1-2-1876
SIEBEL, George Henry & Ann Isabel Kiernan 2-11-1863
SILBEY, Eleanor & Stephen Lanham 10-4-1779
SILK, Samuel & Elizabeth Collings 7-26-1779
SIM, Ann & Darby Ryon 12-31-1779
  Patrick & Mary Carroll 7-11-1777
  Patrick & Arianna Henderson 8-28-1787
  Robert & Elizabeth King 1-5-1786
SIMMES, George & Mary Tolson 2-13-1813
  John & Susan Monroe 12-23-1885 (Rev. Mr. Brookes)
  Mary & Lewis Gross col^d 9-8-1881 (Rev. Dr. Gordon)
  William & Susan Bean col^d 10-21-1865 (Chesley)
SIMMINS, Charlotte & George Digges 11-18-1874 (O'Dwyer)
SIMMONS, Andrew & Charlotte Young 10-29-1870 (Maher)
  Ann & Charles Norris 2-22-1867 (Beque)
  Isaac & Susanna Simmons 11-19-1777
  Jacob & Eleanor Cross 4-19-1780
  James & Ann Hodges 1-13-1806
  Martha & Zachariah Mackceney 2-23-1789
  Mary & John Lucas 12-14-1780
  Mary & Joseph Jones 11-25-1816
  Mary & Charles Brown 8-8-1879 (Crowley)
  Rachael Anne & Wm. H. Lewis 6-19-1886 (Rev. F. G. Hall)
  Richard & Mary Willett 3-7-1779
  Robert & Eleanor Day 12-6-1805
  Robert & Mary C. Shaw 5-11-1852
  Robt & Catherine Baldwin 5-9-1781
  Susanna & Isaac Simmons 11-19-1777
  Susannah & Richard Welch 6-5-1793
  Thomas & Elizabeth Lyles 5-26-1795
SIMMS, Celia & James Jackson 3-30-1877 (Carroll)
  Charles N. & C. Ella Burroughs 6-22-1880 (Rev. Mr. Gordon)
  Dennis Clark & Adeline Sophia Hawkins of A. A. Co. col^d 2-3-1881 (Chaney)
  Elizabeth & Francis Tolson 2-27-1794
  George & Harriet Tolson 1-10-1872 (Wheeler)
  Grace & Grafton Robinson 10-28-1870 (Wirt)
  Ignatius & Sarah Ann Spalding 1-2-1810
  Joseph & Margaret Johnson 3-7-1877 (Carroll)
  Joseph Milburn & Elizabeth Mudd 2-10-1790

SIMMS, Kitty & Edward Deal 5-15-1874 (O'Dwyer)
  Margaret & John Cunningham 8-4-1792
  Nathaniel & Alethea Henson col? 5-24-1878 (Gordon)
  Samuel W. & Lizzie Benjamin 1-18-1882 (Rev. Mr. Van Arsdale)
  William & Jane Hughes 11-24-1787
SIMPSON, Ann & Henry Wornald 4-15-1780
  Ann & Clement Edelen 11-6-1780
  Ann & Fielder Turton 5-4-1799
  Ann & Alexander Mitchell 9-20-1819
  Ann & Adderton Sweeney 1-15-1821
  Ann & Benjamin Piles 4-17-1827
  Ann & Thomas Phelps 7-6-1829
  Benjamin & Elizabeth Rantin 12-13-1831
  Benjamin & Ellen Winkler 12-6-1871 (Skinner)
  Caroline & Pierce Beall 10-8-1885 (Rev. Wm. C. Butler)
  Drady & Richard Johnson 1-7-1822
  Eleanor & William Lawson 11-16-1778
  Eliz^{a} Ann & Thomas Harvey 4-18-1794
  Elizabeth & Adderton Sweeney 2-18-1830
  Elizabeth & James H. Winsor 12-27-1866 (Chesley)
  Frederick & Rebecca Sweeny 12-21-1868
  George & Mary Ann Kagle 5-1-1875 (Stanley)
  George Allen & Hettie Louisa Butler 12-26-1868 (Langford)
  Harriet & Samuel Hughes 12-23-1885 (Rev. F. G. Hall)
  Henry & Mima Shreaves 6-5-1804
  James & Lucy Wilson 12-10-1802
  James &Mary Jane Lusby 12-3-1846
  James Henry & Mary Elizabeth Winkler 4-1-1872
  James K. & Susan Lusby 2-20-1811
  John & Rebecca Whiting 9-9-1784
  John & Mary Dent Morris 4-10-1788
  John & Deborah Pierce 7-22-1815
  John T. & Elizabeth Curtain 1-9-1839
  John T. & Elizabeth Peacock 12-14-1881 (Rev. Dr. Stanley)
  Joseph & Rachel Galwith 1-31-1788
  Lloyd & Elizabeth Fowler 7-18-1819
  Martha D. & Henry E. Sheriff 1-24-1876 (Berry)
  Mary Ann & Lloyd Walker 1-19-1836
  Mary Jane & Elijah Vermillion 10-4-1860
  Nancy & William Phelps 9-11-1821
  Priscilla & William Fowler 1-29-1799
  Rebecca & John Emberson 10-25-1790
  Rebecca & Hezekiah Munroe 1-1-1823
  Richard & Draden Steel 6-6-1811
  Sarah Ann & John Cassell 12-8-1801
  Sarah Ann & Trueman Tippett 2-1-1810
  Sophia & John B. Sansbury 12-11-1851
  Susan Jane & John Clubb 9-13-1836
  Susannah & Aquila Emmerson 11-13-1792
  Thomas & Ruth King 4-7-1787
  Thomas & Amelia Linch 9-17-1787
  Thomas & Elizabeth Hays 8-14-1862
  Thomas & Beckie Chaney 12-24-1867 (Stanley)
SIMS, Christianna & William H. Creek 9-16-1878
  George Allen & Eliza Camilla Gray 4-4-1868

SIMS, John & Henrietta Forbes 5-11-1875 (O'Dwyer)
  Mary Ann & William Vermilion 4-19-1778
SINCLAIR, Elizabeth & George Jones 8-25-1787
SIPE, Joseph B. & Bettie Clarke 4-29-1882 (Rev. Dr. Stanley)
SISSON, W. W. & C. E. Hopkins 1-19-1885 (Father Cotton)
SKELLY, Levin W. & Caroline Boteler 12-20-1823
SKIDMORE, Patrick H. & Eliza Winsor 8-5-1875 (Billopp)
SKINNER, Adderton & Kitty Magruder 8-20-1798
  Amelia & Urban Hollyday 6-2-1834
  Benj? & Margaret Johns 2-4-1828
  Edward & Henny Butler 1-6-1873 (Walker)
  Elizabeth & Stephen S. Johns 10-9-1805
  Frederick & Margaret J. Wood 10-15-1880 (Rev. Mr. Gordon)
  Henrietta S. & Zadock Sasscer 1-9-1827
  John Henry & Ann Maria Holland 6-5-1872
  John S. & Martha M. H. Skinner 11-1-1837
  Levin & Sarah M. Lancaster 10-27-1841
  Margaret Johns & Peter Wood, Junior 11-23-1854
  Martha M. H. & John S. Skinner 11-1-1837
  Mary & Lamuel Dorsett 1-4-1794
  Nellie & Richard Scott 6-3-1873 (Pinkney)
  Priscilla & Notley Maddox 5-5-1801
  Richard & Eliza Young 6-25-1811
  Richard & Lizzie Spencer 12-3-1885 (Rev. Francis Wills)
  Richard Trueman & Margaret Birch 1-6-1873 (Sliner)
  Walter & Mary Hodgkin 1-10-1791
SLACK, William H. & Mrs. Carlene N. Carrick 11-25-1869 (Dr. Hancock)
SLATER, Bowling & Maria Smith col? 8-6-1881 (Rev. Mr. Lawson)
  Butler & Ellen Thomas 4-27-1871 (McDonald)
  Clarissa & Spencer Shaw 3-26-1875 (Gordon)
  David & Sarah Contee 5-29-1790
SLAYMAN, Michael J. & Sarah A. Atchison 2-6-1865
SLINGLUFF, Frank & Isabella Cross 7-13-1880 (Rev. Mr. Butler)
  Trueman C. & E. F. Hardisty 8-7-1882 (Rev. Harvey Stanley)
SLOAN, William M. & Lula E. Waldo 12-30-1885 (Rev. Mr. Chesley)
SLY, Georgianna & John Robert Hawkins 10-4-1876
SLYE, Annie & Austin Morse 1-13-1868
  Willemina & Thos. Earley 1-1-1784
  William & Ann Northey 6-19-1783
SMALL, Hetty A. & Joshua F. Beall 11-1-1881 (Rev. Mr. Hyland)
SMALLWOOD, Ann & John Wynn 12-12-1778
  Ann & Elijah Coe 10-23-1779
  Ann & Thomas Powers 6-3-1820
  Augustus & Kitty Swan 6-3-1820
  Bayne & Marsilva Coe 12-19-1780
  Christian M. & William H. Wilson 4-18-1829
  Dorinda Ann & James R. Seaborn 11-16-1846
  Elizabeth & Horatio Club 10-19-1821
  Elizabeth & John Thomas Taylor 2-23-1852
  Frank & Maria Thomas 12-19-1871 (Wheeler)
  John & Clour Wilson 12-15-1787
  John & Henrietta Contee 12-3-1869
  John R. & Letitia Fowler 12-27-1832
  Joseph & Matilda Harwood 11-3-1875
  Maria & Charles Henry Adams 3-27-1869 (Gordon)

SMALLWOOD, Maria & John Harrison 8-4-1883
Milicent & William Wynn 5-20-1778
Rebecca & George N. Lovejoy 6-10-1794
Rebecca M. & Hezekiah Wynn 1-12-1779
Samuel N. & Ruth Beall 2-28-1801
Sarah & Richard Barrott 10-14-1812
Susan & John Lemon col? 7-7-1865 (Chester) Widow, age 25, cook
Violetta S. A. & Joseph R. Douglas 12-4-1859
SMITH, Alexander & Ann Watson 1-18-1817
Alexander & Jane Bigganan 2-10-1835
Allie F. & Harry H. Markle 5-7-1868
Amze & Hannah Mary Van Patten 12-1-1869
Andrew & Emily Brown 4-29-1867
Andrew & Elizabeth Stewart 11-23-1876 (Homan)
Ann & Joseph Sparrow 12-9-1778
Ann & Anthony Drane 12-23-1778
Ann & William Willice 2-14-1780
Ann & George Kidwell 12-6-1800
Ann & Jesse Selby 2-13-1801
Ann & William Hill 12-9-1811
Ann & Lemuel Watson 10-17-1851
Ann Barbara col? & David Egling 4-20-1867 (Greenleaf)
Ann S. & John W. Canter 7-6-1878 (Perry)
Ann Sophia & John T. Berry 1-25-1827
Athena & William H. Tufts 9-21-1870 (Brown)
Barbara S. & Ignatius F. Young 1-30-1814
Benedict & Mary Gardiner 2-7-1795
Burton & Martha M. Randall 3-27-1857
C. Virginia & Alexander Turner 5-27-1880 (Aquila)
Caroline & Horace Wells 1-21-1858
Charles & Susanna Brightwell 8-4-1866 (Hoover)
Charles & Peggy Clifton col? 12-24-1868 (Stanley)
Clara & William H. Lee 12-27-1875 (Scott)
Daniel & Elizabeth Greer 4-8-1806
DeLoss H. & M. Tillie McCurdy 8-17-1870)Rev. M. Howe)
Eliza & James Club 8-16-1842
Eliza & Thomas Johnson 12-23-1865 Age 23, black, house servant
Elizabeth & Thomas Swain 2-17-1779
Elizabeth & Walter Alley 2-26-1783
Elizabeth & Edmund Warman 9-22-1788
Elizabeth & Joseph Wilson 3-17-1795
Elizabeth & William Marlowe 2-17-1803
Elizabeth & Thomas Loveless 12-27-1842
Elizabeth Ann & Hezekiah Watson 8-15-1811
Emily & George Norfolk 12-21-1875
Fannie & Francis Duckett Jr. col? 3-13-1882
Fanny & Jeremiah Ryon 12-24-1791
Fielder Bowie & Sarah Plummer 6-23-1802
Florence & J. E. Benjamin 3-2-1878 (Williams)
Francis & Kitty Baldwin 5-27-1869 (Father Maher)
George H. & Eloise Young 8-5-1841
George H. & Mary Johnson 2-6-1875 (Stanley)
George M. & Ida B. Seitz 6-13-1885
George T. & Mrs. Siss Garner 4-18-1870 (McDonald)
George W. & Mary Susannah Duvall 8-13-1859

SMITH, George W. & Josephine Boswell 1-8-1868 (Smith)
  Graceanna & Charles Beall 2-9-1880 (De Wolf)
  Harriott & Walter Smith 6-21-1802
  Harriot & Joshua Moxley 8-12-1813
  Henrietta & David Young 12-17-1784
  Henry & Matilda Beckett 12-8-1874 Hessey & Thomas Crandall 1-23-1804
  Jack & Sarah Ellis 4-17-1867
  James & Maria Rawlings 11-8-1869 (Maher)
  Jane & Peter Savary 11-18-1782
  Jane & George Summers 5-19-1787
  Jane E. T. & Wm. O. Baldwin 3-21-1848
  Jeremiah & Elizabeth Ross 3-8-1797
  Jerry & Ann Whittington 5-23-1874
  Joanna R. & George W. Curtain 8-13-1884 (Rev. Mr. Chesley)
  John & Elizabeth Rawlings 8-20-1777
  John & Anne Ellott 2-11-1796
  John & Lidia Whittington 5-25-1828
  John & Linney Gales 12-30-1844
  John H. & Mary Loveless 12-26-1853
  John H. & Margaret E. Wells 12-29-1858
  John H. & Elizabeth King 2-21-1876 (Green)
  John M. & Priscilla Watson 6-8-1819
  John Thomas & Adeline Ford 4-3-1874 (Gordon)
  John W. & Mary E. Williams 12-8-1845
  John Willing & Rachel Lowe 2-27-1788
  Johns & Mary Ann Smith 8-1-1836
  Joseph & Rebecca Murphy 9-4-1826
  Joseph S. & Ella Tayman 5-17-1880 (Father De Wolfe)
  Josephine & Walter F. Brown 8-5-1851
  Josephine & Robert Guy 12-15-1865 (Beque)
  Laura & Robt M. Tomlin 1-7-1841
  Levi & Mary Jane Beathy 2-14-1876 (Gordon)
  Linny & John Forster 2-11-1792
  Lucy & William Thos Bryan 3-23-1778
  Lucy & William N. Duvall 2-15-1814
  Lucy E. & Azel Beall 6-17-1833
  Margaret & Charles Hill 2-5-1816
  Margaret A. M. & James Goldsmith 6-23-1855
  Margaret E. & Jeremiah Sweeney 12-21-1880 (Rev. Dr. Lewin)
  Marg^t V. & Wm. F. Gates 8-23-1848
  Maria & John Fletcher 10-14-1875 (Green)
  Maria & Bowling Slater col^d 8-6-1881 (Rev. Mr. Lawson)
  Maria & James Abrams 11-28-1883
  Martha & William Nicholls 1-20-1778
  Mary & Thomas Rose 10-22-1777
  Mary & Electius Boone 1-8-1779
  Mary & Samuel Edelen 12-14-1787
  Mary & Joshua Humphreys 9-4-1838
  Mary & James W. Marshall 2-8-1878 (Homan)
  Mary A. & Edward Griffen 4-29-1812
  Mary Ann & William Barry 7-19-1778
  Mary Ann & Johns Smith 8-1-1836
  Mary Eliza & Samuel H. Sasscer 5-19-1841
  Mary Jane & Solomon M. Sweeny 5-24-1862
  Mary L. & Notley Young 4-20-1830

SMITH, Mary Lucy & John Shepherd 5-31-1880 (Gambriel)
  Mary Perry & William Watson 1-29-1806
  Mordecai F. & Jane M. Boswell 2-8-1810
  Nathan & Jane Hamilton 10-24-1812
  Nicholas & Martha Ann Dyer 10-23-1790
  Rachel & Fielder Ryon 6-3-1797
  Rebecca & Dennis Coghlan 7-18-1777
  Richard & Elizabeth Church 1-12-1785
  Richard & Amelia Henwood 12-27-1834
  Richard Thomas & Clara B. Marlow 12-12-1884 (Rev. Mr. Robey)
  Robert & Mary Jane Dockett 2-6-1872 (Evans)
  Rosanah & James Jones 3-19-1785
  Rozana & Henry W. Tomlin 12-7-1842
  Samuel & Ann Bucey 1-4-1845
  Samuel & Elizabeth Brown 11-24-1865
  Samuel & Sallie Hawkins 4-17-1876 (Price)
  Samuel Lane & Elizabeth Bowie Belt 11-26-1799
  Samuel N. & Harriet B. Webster 12-4-1843
  Samuel N. & Mrs. Mary Jane Bowie 3-29-1866 (Mark) Age 47, gardener
    res. Fort Foot, P. G. County
  Sandy & Letty Blackiston 1-8-1870 (Maher)
  Sarah & James Wear 7-19-1777
  Sarah & George Hilliary 11-29-1781
  Sarah & Ignatius Hunter 5-11-1822
  Sarah & Jerry S. Holling colored 10-22-1880
  Sophia & Alexander Philpot 7-28-1803
  Sophia & Alfred Boothe 1-13-1870 (Fowler)
  Susan Ann & James Allen 12-28-1840
  Susanna & Charles White 7-30-1777
  Susannah & Charles Crabb 2-13-1792
  Thomas & Ruth Evans 8-18-1777
  Thomas & Verlinda Leach 3-19-1789
  Thomas & Elizabeth Robertson 11-16-1793
  Thomas Barton & Leuisa Adams 1-16-1788
  Ursula & John White 8-20-1780
  Verlinda & Thomas Brunt 8-2-1796
  Wallace B. & Christianna Pinkney 12-27-1882
  Walter & Harriott Smith 6-21-1802
  Wilbur F. & Evi W. Moorhead 11-10-1875 (Nichols)
  William & Sophia Beall 2-11-1809
  William & Sarah Cooksey 9-23-1817
  William & Mary Ann Hyde 12-29-1842
  William & Margaret Ann Warfield 4-4-1844
  William & Lizzie Warren 2-6-1868 (Fr. Call)
  William & Johanna Duckett 12-17-1869 (Pindell)
  William James & Sarah Jane Burke 2-7-1854
  William N. & Elizabeth Errickson 10-14-1815
  Willy & Sarah E. Clarke 5-19-1868 (Kershaw)
  Wm. H. A. & Elvira Knighton 4-29-1873 (Kershaw)
SMITHSON, Lizzie & Frank Day 1-22-1876 (McNeer)
SMITSON, John & Martha Tucker 12-1-1885 (Rev. W. G. Davenport)
  William & Violetta Scott 7-11-1876 (Stanley)
SMOOT, Joseph & Julia A. Dement 4-5-1841
  Stephen & Rosa Randall colored 7-26-1881
SMOTHERS, Margaret & Webster Douglass 11-6-1878

SMOTHERS, Mary & Richard Ford 6-6-1882
Nancy & James Lemuel Crawford 2-26-1870 (Maher)
Richard & Harriet Hawkins 12-20-1867 (Langford)
SMYTH, Abram Hewes & Caroline Virginia Steed 11-8-1875 (Dorsey)
SNELL, Benjamin & Mary E. Hopkins black, age 35, res. Laurel m. 3-12-1866
Laurel, Presbyter E. Church
SNOW, Thomas & Henrietta Snowden col^{d}. 9-10-1868 (Stanley)
SNOWDEN, Adeline & Walter W. W. Bowie 9-1-1836
Ann Elizabeth & Francis Hall 9-15-1828
Ann Louisa & John Contee 2-16-1824
Arthur & Maria Williams 5-18-1877
Caroline Eliza & Albert Fairfax 4-7-1828
Emily R. & Charles C. Hill 4-26-1845 (Hill)
Henrietta & Thomas Snow col^{d}. 9-10-1868 (Stanley)
Isabella & George Hawkins 5-19-1877 (Barnes)
Julianna M. & Theodore Jenkins 6-16-1835
Louisa & Horace Capron 6-5-1834
Margaret & Charles H. Stanley 9-4-1884 (Rev. Dr. Stanley)
Mary & John Chew Thomas 9-16-1788
Mary & John Carlyle Herbert 3-6-1805
Moses & Sarah Hawkins col^{d}. 5-11-1869 (Thompson)
Richard & Louisa Victoria Warfield 5-16-1818
Samuel & Alice Heborn 1-2-1869 (Stanley)
Stephen & Elizabeth Prout 9-15-1869 (Thomas)
SOLLARS, Sabrett & Ann Russell 3-3-1785
Sabret & Mary Gordon 5-10-1787
SOLLERS, Edward & Martha Harwood 11-30-1876 (Peters)
Sarah & Joseph Owens colored 10-28-1880 (Rev. David Aquilla)
SOMERVELL, Amelia H. & Wm. N. Dorsett 12-18-1827
Elizabeth & John Marbury 11-12-1817
Elizabeth M. & John H. Sothoron 5-22-1834
James Jr. & Priscilla B. Beall 12-15-1846
John & Camilla Bowie 11-29-1825
SOMERVILL, Grace C. & Benjamin R. Gray 10-27-1845
Margrt & Richard W. Bowie 5-20-1836
SOMERVILLE, Ann & Thomas Horrell 9-20-1817
James & Elizabeth Hawkins Magruder 11-7-1792
Sarah & Albert V. Gross 5-17-1879 (Gray)
Susannah & John G. Mackall 4-3-1802
Thomas Truman & Margaret Terrett Hollyday 11-3-1807
SONNEMAN, Ottmar & Clara V. Walther 1-1-1883 (Rev. Geo. M. Berry)
SOPER, Alexander & Esther Belt 11-9-1796
Alexander & Mary Ann Mahew 12-17-1819
Alvin & Ann Powell 1-5-1801
Ann & Jacob King 3-2-1802
Ann & Warren Lowe 6-1-1829
Ann Verlinda & John H. Scott 6-25-1826
Anthony & Ann Middleton 1-29-1844
Artermecia & Benjamin Bean 11-16-1840
Benjamin Nony & Elizabeth Ridgway 7-23-1792
Caroline E. & Rector Pumphrey 12-31-1839
Caroline E. & Richard B. Selby 12-23-1856
Cassandra & Jesse Evans 1-13-1816
Catherine & Joshua Warren Masters 10-28-1828
Cloy Ann & William Soper 4-7-1842

SOPER, Eleanor & Joseph Childs 6-20-1793
    Eleanor & Mordicai Ridgway 11-24-1794
    Eliza & John Middleton 7-3-1828
    Elizabeth & Michael Havener 2-5-1793
    Elizabeth & William Darnall 2-20-1819
    Elizabeth & Findel Claston 3-31-1821
    Elizabeth Hill & George Washington Duvall 1-15-1820
    Esmond J. & Sarah A. Crawford 11-23-1883 (Dr. Harvey Stanley)
    Francis M. & Hester Ann Locker 5-28-1846
    Geo. P. & Margaret B. Soper 6-1-1880 (Rev. Mr. Highland)
    Henry & Mrs. Sarah Locker 12-17-1818
    Henry & Eliza Jane Anderson 3-29-1848
    Jesse & Elizabeth Beall 1-20-1813
    John & Sarah Higgins 1-5-1801
    John & Nancy Wilcoxen 2-9-1802
    Joseph & Priscilla Pope 12-10-1822
    Joseph A. & Ann V. Pumphrey 12-15-1851
    Leonard & Mary Newman 11-21-1801
    Levin & Kitty Lowe 2-13-1808
    Louisa & John L. Thompson 5-15-1882 (Rev. Mr. Fultz)
    Mareen D. & Elizabeth Pope 4-12-1814
    Mareen Duvall & Margaret Pope 2-13-1798
    Margaret & Jeremiah Brashears 4-30-1803
    Margaret B. & Geo. P. Soper 6-1-1880 (Rev. Mr. Highland)
    Martha & Azel Beall 4-13-1801
    Martha & Elijah King 2-13-1837
    Mary & Zadoch Moore 6-6-1779
    Mary & Basil Hurley 2-3-1789
    Mary & William Perry 12-26-1796
    Mary & John Henry Kidwell 9-4-1876 (Dorsey)
    Mary Ann & Jonathan Hardey 1-31-1799
    Mary Edelen & Thomas W. Soper 2-8-1836
    Massy & Johne Mayhew 12-9-1795
    Nathan & Ann Darcey 11-21-1791
    Nathan & Ruth Gill 1-18-1803
    Nathaniel & Eleanor Pumphrey 3-1-1840
    Nathaniel M. & Ann P. Selby 2-6-1861
    Philip & Ann Elizabeth Dorsey 12-27-1842
    Phillip Evans & Elizabeth Pope 7-30-1794
    Priscilla & Judson C. Pumphrey 5-17-1843
    Rachel & Edward Volumes 12-27-1796
    Rebecca & William Hurley 12-21-1790 Also spelled Soaper
    Rebecca & Benjamin Duvall Jr. 5-16-1821
    Robert & Elizabeth Hardey 11-19-1784
    Rose E. & Stephen W. Duckett 2-15-1879
    Sarah & William Hurley 8-12-1795
    Sarah & Jesse Wheat 12-2-1795
    Sarah Ann & Thomas Talbert 12-12-1843
    Susanna & Wm. Iglehart 3-17-1781
    Susannah Jackson & Ezekial Gott 4-23-1792
    Thomas & Elizabeth Duckett 1-5-1802
    Thomas W. & Mary Edelen Soper 2-8-1836
    William & Cloy Ann Soper 4-7-1842
    William W. & Annie P. Richardson 12-3-1883 (Rev. Mr. Hyland)
SOTHERLINE, James & Mary Mullikin 8-8-1799

SOTHORON, Deborah & John Letchworth 12-10-1798
  John H. & Elizabeth M. Somervell 5-22-1834
SOUREWINE, Albert A. & Jennie Gossom Age 21 - 6 mo., discharged soldier
  b. Buffalo, Erie Co. N. Y. m. 9-7-1865 at Laurel, P. G. County by
  Rev. Dr. J. A. Young, Ep. Church
SOUT (prob. Suit), Edward & Mary Wilson 7-12-1779
SOUTHER, Benj^a & Mary Ann Tyler 12-2-1778
  Elizabeth & Thomas Pratt 12-30-1796
SOUTHERLAND, John & Nelly Fraser 12-20-1777
SOUTHWELL, Lana &William Steuart 2-21-1778
SPALDING, Catharine & George Boswell 1-2-1817
  Catherine C. & Thomas S. Blandford 8-3-1857
  Chrissy & Francis Kerby 3-17-1809
  Christiana & Benjamin Burch 1-2-1809
  Dorothy & Noble N. Glen 4-7-1804
  Eliza & Lloyd Pumphrey 9-3-1817
  Elizabeth & Joseph Sansberry 11-30-1798
  Elizabeth & Elisha King 2-18-1800
  James & Eleanor Boone 12-16-1797
  Jane & James Kemp 10-16-1806
  John B. & Nancy Lambert 12-13-1820
  Matilda & Francis Coyle 5-15-1813
  Sarah & William F. Hardey 10-25-1806
  Sarah Ann & Ignatius Simms 1-2-1810
  Sarah Ann & William E. Pumphrey 1-15-1819
  Susannah & George Boswell 6-21-1811
  Susannah & John B. Hutchinson 12-11-1821
  Rich^d & Susan Morris 2-8-1841
SPARKLIN, J. Hedges & Rosa B. Cage 3-22-1880 (Cross)
SPARROW, Ann & George Bause 9-24-1796
  Henry & Ann James 1-21-1791
  Isabella & Jeremiah Nicholson 1-30-1800
  John & Bettie Ann Chew 2-10-1849
  Joseph & Ann Smith 12-9-1778
  Matilda & Joseph Harwood 1-31-1806
SPEAK, Joanna & Joshua Marr 1-2-1779
SPEAKE, Catherine & Edward Brown 3-8-1780
  Lucy & Robert Dyer 1-21-1800
SPENCER, Allen & Clarissa Jackson col^d 4-18-1881 (Rev. Frank Wills)
  Celestia M. & John A. Dixon 11-25-1872 (O'Dwyer)
  Charlotte Ann & John Berry 4-21-1883 (Mr. Walker)
  George Allen & Eliza Camilla Gray 5-8-1875
  George W. & Elizabeth M. Boocock 12-19-1842
  Horace & Delia A. Johnson 6-4-1883 (Rev. Mr. Wills)
  Capt. John D. R. & Annie M. Schaaff 7-23-1864
  Lizzie & Richard Skinner 12-3-1885 (Rev. Francis Wills)
  Sarah Amelia & Philip E. Mills 1-15-1867 (Smith)
SPICKNALL, Charles M. & Sarah Barrett 10-14-1811
SPIDEN, Robert & Ann Williams 4-3-1797
SPINK, Ignatius & Elizabeth Clarksen 12-16-1794
SPINKS, Ann & Edward Burch 10-15-1779
SPRIGG, Benjamin & Mary C.Burgess 12-26-1804
  Columbus & Harriet West 9-6-1876 (Green)
  Cornelia & Henry Clark 9-9-1874 (Wiget)
  Eliza & Cornelius Duckett col^d 11-23-1867 (Blankford)

SPRIGG, Eliza & Charles Tilghman 6-6-1879 (Crowley)
  Eliz^a & Thos Watkins Junr 1-17-1778
  Eliz^a & Wm. S. Bowie 12-18-1781
  Elizabeth & Enoch Magruder 2-27-1781
  Frank & Laura Sheppard 11-15-1876 (Homan)
  Georgeanna & Lemuel Parker 5-6-1871 (McDonald)
  Henry & Lizzie Herbert col^d 12-24-1868 (Edelen)
  Henry & Emily Addison 5-22-1875 (O'Dwyer)
  James & Caroline Contee 12-10-1884
  John Henry & Elizabeth Cook 6-10-1867 (Kershaw)
  Kitty & Dennis Harrison 11-6-1868 (Stanley)
  Maria & John Pinkney 3-31-1877 (Carroll)
  Mary C. & Frederick Addison 9-21-1878 (Carroll)
  Mary Helen & Thomas Herbert 2-9-1870 (McDonald)
  Miss & Henry Jasper 12-26-1866 (Chesly)
  Osborn & Sarah Gantt 4-3-1779
  Osborn & Caroline L. Bowie 12-22-1840
  Peter & Philis Hurry 12-31-1819
  Robert & Mary Ann Hall 12-24-1872 (Evans)
  Sally & William Thomas Carroll 10-7-1828
  Sandy & Rachel Ennis col^d 7-27-1867 (Call)
  Sarah & Hilleary Jackson 1-25-1868 (Fr. Call)
  Susan & Frederick West 5-2-1867
  Tilghman & Charlotte Ann Stewart 12-22-1873
  William O. & Eliza Gantt 12-9-1802
STALLINGS, Fanny & William Dowell 2-19-1822
  Mary & James Watson 4-12-1816
  Perry & Susannah Davis 1-29-1816
  Richard & Maria Scrivener 7-11-1826
  Samuel R. & Margaret Hetcherson 6-13-1842
  Sarah & John Strickland 2-8-1790
  Sarah Ann & Thomas Macdonald 1-12-1833
  Sophia A. & Clement R. Connie 1-12-1825
  Thomas & Rachael Ann Carr 12-23-1833
  Thomas Junr & Sarah Mitchell 11-25-1791
  William & Harriet Crosby 2-3-1838
STALLIONS, James & Sarah Osborn 1-1-1801
STALLONS, Thomas Henry & Susannah Eales 12-21-1798
STAMP, Ann & William Taylor 12-21-1808
  George B. & Mrs. Sophia E. Taylor 5-19-1862
  J. E. & Nettie Duckett 2-11-1885
  John O. & Ella F. Garner 1-9-1884 (Rev. Mr. LaRoche)
  M. R. & Mary A. McKee 2-13-1855
  Mary & Thos Harrison 5-30-1783
  Willey & Abraham Fowler 12-23-1790
  Willy & Thomas G Brightwell 1-5-1821
STANDAGE, Eleazer & Mary Wigfield 12-23-1783
  Eliz^a & Zadock Talbert 12-30-1778
  Margaret & Henry Talburt 9-26-1780
  Thomas & Lucy Arnold 9-13-1817
STANLEY, Charles H. & Margaret Snowden 9-4-1884 (Rev. Dr. Stanley)
  Mary & Oscar Hinrichs 10-7-1868 (Stanley)
STANTON, Eliza R. & Cornelius J. 12-12-1847
  John H. & Mary Isabella Taylor 10-9-1855
STARBUCK, Mary Matilda & Benj. Franklin Dement 11-19-1866 (Rev. Lanahan)

STARKS, Susan & John Bias 9-9-1874
STARLINGS, Jennie & William T. Butler 1-22-1868 (Chesley)
STARTING, Owen of A. A. Co. & Mary Caroline Butler 11-8-1880
    Rev. Father D. Woolf
STEED, Addie L. & Joseph C. Hatton 12-2-1867 (Martin)
    Caroline Virginia & Abram Hewes Smyth 11-8-1875
    James Munroe & Leonora Lowe 9-20-1834
    John J. R. & Mary P. Edelen 5-14-1861
STEEL, Alexander & Mary Hopkins 3-6-1800
    Ann & William Austin 1-23-1801
    Charles L. & Ann Huntt 5-23-1814
    Draden & Richard Simpson 6-6-1811
    Mary & Richard Bryan 9-29-1796
    Mary & Alexander Baden 6-3-1797
STEIGER, Emma & R. H. Sadler 1-22-1870
STEPHEN, Alice May & Albert Benson Sansbury 4-2-1884 (Rev. Mr. Dell)
    John & Emily Augusta Fuller 6-20-1882 (Rev. Jno. B. Williams)
    Nicholas C. & Margaret R. Day 6-10-1849
STEPHENS, James & Winefred Steward 2-3-1787
    John & Susannah Turner 2-28-1798
    Mary & Thomas Early 2-8-1810
    William & Ann Taylor 12-31-1785
STEPHENSON, Eleanor & Samuel Williams col^d 7-13-1867
    Miranda & John W. Lansdale 5-15-1815
STEPHINSON, Mary Ann & Saml Stetenius 6-18-1824
STETENIUS, Saml & Mary Ann Stephinson 6-18-1824
STEUARD, William & Jan Bryant 6-6-1783
STEUART, Ann Eustatia & Richd Watson 2-19-1781
    Charles & Elizabeth Calvert 6-14-1780
    Charles & Ann Fitzhugh Biscoe 11-1-1814
    William & Lana Southwell 2-21-1778
STEVENS, Ann & Rezin Anderson 2-19-1803
    Elihu P. & Barbara Lowe 6-19-1812
    Elizabeth & Hugh Gray 8-8-1795
    William & Rebecca Tilley 1-15-1785
    William & Sarah Sansbury 1-29-1828
STEVENSON, Charles & Annie Mullikin 8-19-1885 (Rev. Mr. Highland)
    Daniel & Josephine Harrison 6-14-1871 (Begue)
    Daniel & Sarah Colman 10-2-1875 (Green)
STEWARD, James & Massey Burgess 12-30-1790
    Philip & Mary Marshall 2-26-1787
    Winefred & James Stephens 2-3-1787
STEWART, Addison & Cerrlene Stewart 1-28-1870 (Langford)
    Agnes & Washington Galloway 1-28-1870 (Langford)
    Ann M. & Jonas Winfield 4-31-1781
    Anne Maria & Benjn L. Lanham 12-19-1855
    Ariana & Pinkney Brown 1-28-1870 (Lankford)
    Cerrlene & Addison Stewart 1-28-1870 (Langford)
    Charles & Sophia Thornton 4-2-1877 (Carroll)
    Charles & Priscilla Covington 10-10-1877
    Charlotte Ann & Tilghman Sprigg 12-22-1873
    Chesterfield & Agnes Lucinda Scott 12-24-1872 (Evans)
    David C. & Elizabeth Buchanan 8-11-1803
    Dorothy & Caroline Deville 1-28-1870 (Langford)
    Edwin & Catharine M. McKee 11-29-1858

STEWART, Edwin & Maggie R. Tayman 1-22-1867 Age 33, widower, black-
smith m. 1-23-1867 by Samuel R. Gordon, minister
 Elizabeth & Alexander J. Lloyd 7-12-1860
 Elizabeth & Andrew Smith 11-23-1876 (Homan)
 Ellen & Charles Burgess 9-8-1866 col? (Rev. Father Young)
 Henrietta & Thos. Townley 1-15-1782
 James Samuel & Mary Redmiles 12-13-1865 (Stanley)
 Jane & John Galloway col? 8-14-1869 (Langford)
 John & Mary Dove 2-3-1790
 John & Ariana Ross 12-13-1791
 John & Lydia Anderson 12-18-1822
 John Oliver & Margaret Priscilla Pyles 12-11-1883 (Rev. Dell)
 Joseph & Maria Watkins 9-1-1820
 Judson & Lethia Ann Harvey 6-11-1831
 Nancy Caroline & James W. Connick 10-23-1847
 Robert H. & Elizabeth Cross 4-5-1820
 Sallie & Washington Lee 9-10-1870 (McDonald)
 Sarah J. & Julius D. Cecil 12-30-1882 (Rev. Mr. Gordon)
 William Henry & Rebecca Brown 1-31-1880 (Rev? M. Quiller)
 William L. & Mary C. Nalley 6-3-1884 (Rev. Father Cotton)
 William M. & Laura L. Berry 8-18-1865 m. St. Matthews Church, P. G.
  Age 65 of Georgetown, D. C. - William Pinkney, minister of
  Presbyterian P. E. Church
STILSON, Frank of Washington, D. C. & Sarah E. Whiteside of
 Prince George's County 11-22-1880
STINCHECUM, Wm. H. & Mary Ann Benson 6-21-1866 Age 24 - shoemaker
 m. Presbyter E. Ch. - Laurel
STINEMAN, William & Susie Rouzer 5-23-1868 (Markham)
STOCKETT, Benjamin & Arianna Hardey 2-8-1832
 Benjamin & Emily Bean 11-20-1855
 George & Ellen Loveless 5-6-1845
 George E. & Sarah Ann Loveless 12-5-1839
STODDART, Benjn. C. & Rebecca Lowndes 6-7-1781
STODDERD, Thomas Henry & Matilda Ann Watson 2-9-1872 (Evans)
STODDERT, Arn & Thomas T. Gantt 11-25-1811
 Harriet & George Washington Campbell 7-17-1812
 Letitia Dent & Peter Dijean 1-18-1785
 Thomas James John & Cloe Hanson Dent 9-21-1790
STONE, Alice E. & James E. Farr 1-18-1876
 Amelia V. & Grafton Suit 2-27-1850
 Ann & Charles Grimes 2-17-1787
 Christopher C. & Ann M. Anderson 3-20-1850
 Emily & William Jones 12-21-1836
 Georganna & Daniel C. Lowe 8-13-1863
 John D. & Marian L. Beall 6-7-1855
 Leanoa & Nathan Talburt 4-19-1783
 Martha Marion Hall & Clement Hollyday 12-21-1816
 Mary & Edward Taylor 1-13-1784
 Mary & Noah Hardey 1-13-1794
 Mary E. & Walter Colton 1-17-1873 (Marbury)
 Mary V. & Mareen Chaney 2-2-1875 (Mercer)
 Nehemiah & Sarah Wilson 3-3-1778
 Rachel & Walter Watson 10-18-1779
 Sarah F. & Alfred W. King 12-14-1878 (Cross)
 William & Elizabeth Watkins 12-20-1794

STONESTREET, Buttler E. & Sarah Norton 1-6-1778
  Edw? & Margery Weight 5-10-1780
  Eleanor & John Irwin 6-2-1784
STORM, Leonard & Elizabeth Boose 4-20-1813
STRAINING, Lizzie & Charles H. Dean 10-18-1879
  John & Elizabeth E. Weeks 11-10-1880 (Laney)
STRANGE, Catharine C. & William Swann 11-3-1807
STRAUSS, George & Christina Kiernan 8-5-1874
STRAW, Tarissa & John Henry Hall 2-22-1791
STRICKLAND, John & Sarah Stallings 2-8-1790
  John T. & Eleanora Millard 4-1-1869 (Maher)
  Joseph & Verlinda Page 1-19-1789
  Linny & Isaac Swain 12-28-1795
  William & Elizabeth E. Beavin 6-20-1814
  William & Sophia Ryan 5-4-1821
  Wm. & Sarah Kidwell 12-20-1784
  Wm. E. & Ruth E. Ryon 12-28-1846
STUART, Ariana & James Riddle 5-8-1800
  Philip & Mary Fell Bayne 12-15-1792
  Richard H. & Julia Calvert 5-6-1833
  Susan & David Hanson 7-11-1827
STUDMAN, Samuel & Margaret Mitchell 5-6-1820
STURGEST, John & Catharine Windsor 8-9-1880 (Rev. Dr. Lavin)
SUIT, Alice Rebecca & John Edward Tolson 4-27-1874
  Ann & John H. Yost 6-21-1827
  Arthur B. & Kate Pumphrey 3-13-1883
  Benj? S. & Ann S. Sheckells 3-1-1852
  Edward & Catharine Talbert 8-1-1809
  Edwin & Rebecca Harvey 12-17-1847
  Elizabeth & James Fitzgerald 2-3-1812
  Elizabeth & Jno. S. Richey 1-31-1843
  Ellen & Horatio B. Collins 2-2-1825
  Ellen & James Lowe 3-23-1841
  Ellen & Joseph B. Harris 1-23-1844
  Emily Rebecca & Wm. Fred? Mongollin 4-1-1874
  Emma Cecelia & Charles Butler 11-14-1881 (Fr. DeWolf)
  Fannie E. & Joseph D. Hopkins 9-26-1871 (Fr. Cotton)
  Fielder & Catharine M. Scott 9-7-1831
  Grafton & Luciffa A. Scott 6-9-1840
  Grafton & Amelia V. Stone 2-27-1850
  Grafton T. & Margaret D. Greer 12-18-1883 (Rev. Mr. Hyland)
  J. T. Benjamin & Rachel E. Ryon 6-23-1859
  James A. & Mary C. Magruder 2-8-1862
  James M. & Alsa Brown 3-11-1867
  Jane Ann & O. B. Suit 7-1-1848
  Jane Ann & Columbus C. Prather 4-14-1854
  Jeffrey & Sarah Ann Brown 11-9-1831
  John A. & Jane Young 12-24-1821
  John Smith & Eleanor Seissell 11-28-1784
  Joseph Jackson & Ellen Genever Beall 1-14-1885 (Rev. Mr. Cooke)
  Josephine & George T. Cranford 10-31-1855
  Kate R. & P. Gibson Grimes 6-30-1863
  Laura A. & William Tolson 3-26-1883 (Rev. Mr. Brashaw)
  Margaret & Benjamin Phipps 12-23-1835
  Mary & Elie S. Baldwin 2-19-1834

SUIT, Mary & George Franklin Maddox 3-8-1882 (Rev. Dr. Lewin)
  Mary E. & J. W. Ridemour 2-15-1866 Age 35 m. 2-19-1866 residence
  Kelita Suit (Kershaw)
  Matilda & Peter Frances 2-22-1850
  O. B. & Jane Ann Suit 7-1-1848
  Philip & Jamima Barrott 10-14-1815
  Rebecca & John Alvy 2-11-1824
  Sarah & John Pumphrey 1-14-1839
  Sarah Catherine & Gabriel Butler 5-4-1880 (Fr. Cotten)
  Sarah Eugenia & Aloysius Hopkins 1-26-1875
  Stephen William & Elina A. Hardy 10-11-1880 (Herke)
  Susan H. & Richard Prather 2-16-1857
  Susan Jane & James A. Young 6-23-1846
  Thomas & Mary Crawfurd 11-13-1826
  William & Pumphrey, Mary 12-24-1843
  William H. & Susie R. Crandell 11-15-1877 (Miller)
  Wm. E. R. & Margueretta Eugenia Darcey 2-23-1881 (Rev. Mr. Brayshaw)
  Wm. Jesse & Sarah Ann Anderson 11-25-1844
  Zephcniah C. & Mary Moran 2-1-1826
SULLAVAN, Sarah & Thomas Bedder 1-8-1785
SULLIVAN, James G. & Sarah R. Hardesty 1-5-1860
  Mary & Alexr Lovejoy 5-10-1779
SUMMERS, Amma & Salem Hurley 12-8-1784
  Ann & Richd Fowler 1-16-1779
  Ann & Zadock Jenkins 1-12-1798
  Ann & Richard H. Marshall 1-7-1815
  Ann Maria & Aloysius Bowling 2-12-1838
  Christiana & Wm. H. Gwynn 9-22-1851
  Christina A. & Elisha Gates 4-12-1817
  Deborah & Elisha Berry 7-28-1818
  Eleven & Elizabeth Wilcoxon 12-30-1786
  Elizabeth & Thomas Brown 8-3-1854
  George & Jane Smith 5-19-1787
  Henrietta O. & Richard O. Marshall 2-22-1851
  James & Mary Hardey 2-1-1817
  John & Rebeccah Scarce 2-26-1794
  John F. & Eliza Ann Gwynn 11-8-1852
  John G. & Sarah Ann Dyer 2-8-1820
  John K. & Mary A. R. Hill 10-28-1878 (Hooman)
  Jona & Ann Gwinn 12-23-1782
  Mary & Thomas McNew 11-9-1802
  Mary & Saml Cicel 1-8-1828
  Nathaniel & Sarah Scarce 1-2-1793
  Paul & Susannah Ranter 4-11-1789
  Paul & Sarah Hurley 10-3-1801
  Ruth & Benja Havenor 10-8-1818
  Zadock & Mary Jenkins 11-13-1794
SUMMERVILLE, Annie & William A. Marbury 11-8-1882
SUNDERLAND, C. & Jos. R. Griffin 1-6-1881
  Mary C. & Benjamin Norfolk 11-15-1876 (Cheney)
  Mary D. & Thomas J. Perrie 4-29-1858 (Perry)
  Richard H. C. & Josephine E. Griffin 10-23-1873
  Wm. J. & Amy E. Dove 1-11-1856
SUTER, Annie M. & Charles E. Eversfield 8-17-1852
SUTHERLAND, Barbara & George Anderson 4-18-1788

SUTHERLAND, John & Marg⁺ Murray 11-30-1780
SUTTON, Dr. James L. & Margaret RobertaSasscer 11-27-1856
  John & Elizabeth Fenly 12-21-1797
  Mary B. & Charles F. Lowe 10-26-1795
SWAGGERT, Thomas E. & Agnes V. Westerfield 2-28-1869
SWAIM, Eliza & Thomas Hurdey 5-12-1843
SWAIN, Annie & John Weems 1-8-1883 (Rev. Mr. Gordon)
  Benedict & Mary Hutchinson 12-28-1807
  Benjamin & Hannah Ellexon 2-1-1794
  Christian & Guy Evans 9-16-1779
  Elizabeth & John Bird 9-5-1788
  Elizabeth & Henry Swain 4-4-1801
  Gabriel & Elizabeth Berry 1-3-1798
  Henry & Elizabeth Swain 4-4-1801
  Isaac & Mary Cassell 12-21-1787
  Isaac & Linny Strickland 12-28-1795
  J. H. Bertram & Martha A. Rawlings 12-21-1869 (Marbury)
  John & Lucy Harvey 4-11-1797
  John & Elizabeth Scott 1-30-1826
  John Smith & Trissa Jenkins 5-24-1806
  Laura & Pinkney Brooks 4-14-1879 (Gordon)
  Maria & Thomas Ball 1-20-1842
  Martha Ann & Jno. T. Norfolk 10-21-1874 (Gordon)
  Thomas & Elizabeth Smith 2-17-1779
  Wm. B. & Elizabeth Millard 10-23-1877
SWAINE, Caroline & William Hook 9-7-1832
  Colmore Augustus & Elizabeth Baden 12-2-1826
  James A. & Sarah Jane Swann 10-25-1839
  James H. H. & Mary Hoye 5-22-1826
  Jane & Benjamin Fowler 12-10-1839
  Maria C. & William B. Wilson 12-6-1858
  Milley & Walter Rankins 3-21-1805
  Robert S. & Elizabeth Phelps 12-22-1856
  Sarah & Andrew Austin 8-23-1832
  Sarah & Warren Ridgeway 11-18-1833
  William & Sarah Moran 1-30-1802
  William & Mary Ann Young 12-13-1832
  Zulemma & Joseph Fowler 10-25-1832
SWAN, John & Helen Woods Mitchell 4-21-1834
  Kitty & Augustus Smallwood 6-3-1820
  Thomas & Elizabeth Cater 2-11-1793
SWANEY, Lloyd & Mary Mangun 2-10-1790
SWANN, Ann & Henry T. Compton 11-17-1797
  Ann & George M. Thomas 10-2-1804
  Benjamin & Elizabeth Phelps 10-23-1819
  Benj⁹ & Margaret Fowler 5-3-1847
  Christianna F. & Jesse F. Selby 2-14-1859
  Eleanor & Henry Ball 5-21-1831
  George W. & Mary E. Fowler 8-2-1854
  Henrietta J. & Lewis Hollinberger 1-14-1858
  Henry & Minty Davis 1-8-1789
  Jennett & Henry Hawkins 12-26-1790
  Laura V. & Thomas G. Donaldson 1-19-1876 (West)
  Letty & Francis Perrie 1-19-1798
  Mary & Robert W. Ryan 12-9-1852

209

SWANN, Mary & Jonas Moore 3-5-1866 Age 21 - house servant
  m. 3-6-1866 (Kershaw)
  Mary Eliza & Geo. Henry Porter West 11-21-1870 (McCauly)
  Mary O. & Richard A. Edelen 12-17-1850
  Sarah Jane & James A. Swaine 10-25-1839
  Susanna & Robert W. Selby 2-13-1852
  Susannah & Nathaniel Taylor 2-2-1815
  Thomas & Mary Robey 12-23-1825
  William & Catharine C. Strange 11-3-1807
  William & Mary Ann Lewis 6-4-1833
SWANSEY, Ellen & John V. Piles 11-19-1846
SWEENEY, Adderton & Ann Simpson 1-15-1821
  Adderton & Elizabeth Simpson 2-18-1830
  Miss Alice & Thomas Crauford 4-27-1880 (Rev. Dr. Boteler)
  Clifford F. & Alice L. Johnson 4-16-1883 (Father Cunnane)
  Dennis Jr. & Sarah Hayes 3-24-1845
  Elizabeth & John Fowler 1-2-1844
  George A. & William T. Allen 11-21-1867 (Kershaw)
  Georgie & John S. Ritchie Jr. 12-3-1872 (Kershaw)
  James A. & Mary Catherine Ridgeley 12-23-1854
  James A. Jr. & Christiana E. Wilson 6-10-1880 (Father DeWolf)
  Jane & Joseph Tayman 2-2-1837
  Jasper P. & Mary J. Seaborn 9-5-1871 (Gordon)
  Jeremiah & Margaret E. Smith 12-21-1880 (Rev. Dr. Lewin)
  John & Marg Duvall 10-4-1819
  John & Caroline Ridgley 3-30-1850
  John F. & C. M. R. Benson 3-28-1864
  Judson & Harriot Kidwell 4-19-1813
  Loyd & Barbara Jane Crauford 2-17-1862
  Lucy & John H. Taylor 3-3-1876 (McNeer)
  Mary A. & Philip T. Sweeney 2-26-1881 (Fr. DeWolfe)
  Mary E. & Philip A. Hardisty 6-1-1886 (Father Cunnane)
  Nettie E. & Richard W. Kerr 1-28-1886 (Rev. Wm. C. Butler)
  Philip P. & Emma A. Lusby 2-2-1885 (Rev. Mr. Chesley)
  Philip T. & Mary A. Sweeney 2-26-1881 (Father De Wolfe)
  Sallie L. & Zadock Tayman 12-31-1881 (Fr. DeWolf)
  Sallie L. & John F. A. Martin 4-17-1883 (Father Cunnane)
  Thomas & Sarah Ann Mobley 1-3-1842
SWEENY Thomas & Amelia Taylor 11-14-1846
  B. N. & Martha McCallough 3-16-1870 (Kershaw)
  Benjamin & Martha Harvey 1-14-1817
  Dennis & Susannah Allen 12-12-1807
  Edward Wallace & Mary Elizabeth Coffren 2-7-1876
  Emily Jane & John Red 12-20-1859
  Hester V. & Samuel Frye 1-26-1876 (Gordon)
  John F. & Virginia Norfolk 12-20-1877 (Kershaw)
  John Lloyd & Elizabeth Ann Brashears 3-29-1848
  Judson & Felly Webster 11-15-1817
  Letty & Osborn White 1-16-1803
  Margaret & John Fowler 1-3-1840
  Notley & Eliz.th Mitchell 11-5-1828
  Rebecca & Frederick Simpson 12-21-1868
  Saml Pinkney & Alice E. Hardey 4-17-1876 (Gordon)
  Solomon M. & Mary Jane Smith 5-24-1862
  William H. & Ann S. Magruder 12-24-1860

SWEENY, William R. & Georgeanna Norfolk 3-13-1878 (Miller)
SWEETING, Emily & Alfred Butler 11-10-1879
SWENEY, Drury & John Mitchell 5-10-1788
SWOPE, J. Henry & Sallie J. Beall 1-29-1864
SYDEBOTHAM, Wm. & Marg. Leitch 9-23-1778
  Mary & John Thomas Shaaff 12-18-1800
SYMMER, Elizabeth & Thomas Phenix 2-26-1791

TABB, Harlan P. & Mary Virginia Mannel 5-29-1885 (Rev. J. W. Wolfe)
TAFFE, Eleanor & Daniel Downes 12-30-1802
  Mary Anne & John Lovelace 1-17-1803
  Thomas & Elizabeth Munroe 1-11-1812
TAIMAN, Henry & Priscilla Ryon 5-2-1779
  Richard & Mary A. Turton 2-22-1784
TAIT, Elizabeth & Joseph Boyd 1-14-1800
TALBERT, Basil C. & Sarah E. Beckett 7-11-1849
  Catharine & Edward Suit 8-1-1809
  Cath. A. & Wm. Dusief 11-2-1847
  Eliza & Henry Tenley 12-5-1820
  Elizabeth & Dennis Brown 1-10-1827
  Ellen & John Ridgely 6-2-1845
  John L. & Elizabeth Masson 10-4-1866 Age 25, farmer m. 10-4-1866
    Rectory, Upper Marlboro, Henry J. Kershaw, Min. Prot. E. Church
  John Thomas & Sarah E. King 4-25-1859
  Joseph & Martha Masson 9-5-1872 m. 10-29-1872 (Kershaw)
  Louisa & John T. Berry 1-16-1840
  Margaret A. & Samuel Fowler 11-26-1833
  Mary A. & Brooke Mead 12-14-1848
  Mary Jane & Richard Hall 10-28-1856
  Overton & Susan Green 11-8-1870 (Kershaw)
  Paul & Matilda Fowler 3-10-1823
  Peter & Sarah Onion 4-3-1832
  Susan L. & William N. Burch 6-21-1842
  Susanna P. & William Talbert 7-14-1845
  Susannah & Richard Arnold 10-16-1800
  Thomas & Margaret Plater 6-13-1812
  Thomas & Sarah Ann Soper 12-12-1843
  Thomas & Martha V. Ryon 4-9-1844
  Tobias & Margaret Riley 8-9-1800
  Virginia W. & James H. Tayman 4-20-1867 (Kershaw)
  William & Susan T. Belt 1-15-1828
  William & Susanna P. Talbert 7-14-1845
  William H. & Laura E. Wells 12-29-1884 (Rev. Father Cunane)
  Zadock & Eliz. Standage 12-30-1778
  Zadock & Sarah A. Waring 5-18-1837
TALBOT, Basil & Susannah Wilson 7-5-1800
  Catherine A. & Robert F. Ryon 3-19-1866 Age 19, m. 3-20-1866 at residence
    Tho. Talbert (Kershaw)
  Lethe & Thomas Wright 12-18-1835
TALBOTT, Basil & Keziah Lowe 6-17-1788
  Benjamin & Sarah Ranter 2-6-1807
  Eliza E. & John M. Bouse 9-2-1874 (Kershaw)
  George Washington & Nancy Brown 2-26-1814

TALBOTT, Jesse & Mildred Lanham 11-12-1794
  John & Ann Davis 10-1-1777
  Laura & Frank X. Jenkins 6-24-1871
  Lewin & Elizabeth Burch 11-17-1794
  Lewin & Ann Jones 2-13-1797
  Sarah & Thomas Tayler 11-14-1806
  Sarah & Philip Green 5-16-1807
  Solomy & John McKenzy 3-19-1794
  Susannah & Jeremiah Grimes 1-8-1793
TALBURT, Ann & Elijah Robinson 11-24-1788
  Charlotte L. & Levi Osbourn 2-9-1825
  Eleazer & Rebecca Perkins 10-25-1805
  Elizabeth & William Mayhew 12-23-1795
  Henry & Margaret Standage 9-26-1780
  Josias & Milly Bayne 6-11-1796
  Nathan & Leanoa Stone 4-19-1783
  Susanna & Thomas Burch 7-26-1780
  Susanna & Richard Kirby 9-9-1783
  Thomas & Sarah E. Turton 1-22-1833
TALBUT, Paul & Matilda Fowler 3-10-1822
TALBUTT, Paul & Sarah Ann Bryan 3-4-1791
TALL, Henry N. & Sarah Cox 1-5-1824
TANNECLIFF, William & Margaret Prather 7-13-1810
TARMAN, Ann & George Jones 6-25-1799
  Ann & Austin Randall 12-2-1803
  Ann & James Langley 12-30-1816
  Ann W. & Hugh Perrie 11-20-1821
  Benjamin & Letta Fields 3-7-1791
  Eleanor & Henry Mangrum 1-25-1797
  Henrietta & William Taylor 1-9-1794
  Margaret R. & Basil T. Ridgeway 1-27-1862
  Mary & Theodore Vanable 5-24-1799
  Mary & John Cater 1-23-1805
  Quillar & Sarah Randal 12-25-1786
  Richard & Ann Hopkins 5-30-1785
  Richard & Margaret Brant 2-12-1795
  Samuel & Susanna Nicholls 1-31-1803
  Sarah & Jonathan White 3-27-1785
  Sarah & Henry Howse 12-30-1805
  Sega & Abraham Randall 12-26-1807
  Susannah & John Ohio 6-30-1786
TARRENCE, John & Nancy Godman 12-8-1810
TARVAN, John & Mary Vertess 1-14-1805
TARVIN, John & Rebecca Robey 7-8-1808
  John & Jane Estep 1-8-1834
TATE, Margaret & Thomas Benson 2-11-1790
  Martha A. R. & Henry D. Clift 7-28-1842
TAYLER, Alice Elizabeth & Richard Oliver King 2-19-1884 (Fr. Cunnane)
  Andrew & Sarah German 5-1-1802
  Ann & James Mobley 1-12-1811
  Charles H. & Ann Maria Clubb 1-9-1837
  Charlotte & George Winder 9-29-1802
  Josias & Susetta Young 12-24-1869 (Linthicum)
  Maria & Henry Magruder 11-11-1873 (Dwyer)
  Mary Ann & Thomas Brown 6-4-1802

TAYLER, Sarah & Benjamin Estep 9-27-1793
  Thomas & Sarah Talbott 11-14-1806
TAYLOE, William & Sophia R. Plater 11-20-1872 (Goodrich)
TAYLOR, Alfred E. & Martha Alice Loveless 9-4-1869 (Chesley)
  Alice Elizabeth & Robert E. Wells 6-16-1874 (Taylor)
  Alis & Edward Mahoney 12-18-1786
  Allen & Ann Humphreys 6-10-1799
  Amelia & Thomas Sweeney 11-14-1846
  Andrew & Ann Wilson 12-24-1814
  Ann & William Stephens 12-31-1785
  Ann & Nathaniel O'Neall 6-5-1789
  Ann & William Thomas 8-12-1799
  Ann & Nathaniel Nothey 10-10-1801
  Annie & Benjamin Phipps 1-31-1865
  Annie & Samuel D. Mackey 3-22-1880
  Barbara E. & George T. Brent 2-6-1883 (Rev. Father Cunnane)
  Barbara P.& George G. Atcherson 7-14-1834
  Caleb & Milley Clarke 9-17-1803
  Cassy & Francis Mulliken 9-5-1816
  Catharine & Hezekiah Taylor 12-29-1814
  Charles & Vilinder Eastep 11-22-1819
  Charlotte & William Cox 5-25-1796
  Edward & Mary Stone 1-13-1784
  Edward & Ann H. Tyler 6-14-1825
  Edward T. & Mary Ogle 12-15-1830
  Eleanor & Levi Igleheart 12-19-1808
  Eliza & George Craycroft 7-24-1820
  Eliza & Smith Middleton 12-19-1871 (Wheeler)
  Eliza E. & Norman D. Taylor 3-28-1883 (Rev. Father Cunnane)
  Elizabeth & John Pearce 4-9-1789
  Elizabeth & Walter Wall 1-31-1801
  Elizabeth & John Johnson 1-7-1846
  Elizabeth A. & George Richards 4-28-1835
  Elizabeth R. & George W. Thorn 7-6-1850
  Eliz.th A. & John T. Boswell 11-6-1838
  Francis C. & Celestia J. Thorn 12-23-1859
  Gedion & Rachel Peirce 12-29-1788
  George & Mary Price 1-7-1804
  George W. & Emeline Yost 12-22-1852
  George W. & Mary Boswell 2-9-1881
  Harriet & Samuel Broom 1-9-1883 (Rev. Henry Walters)
  Henny & William Keadles 4-30-1803
  Henriette & George Hardy 1-15-1840
  Henry & Harriet McDermond 8-25-1840
  Hezekiah & Ann Beddo 6-15-1806
  Hezekiah & Catharine Taylor 12-29-1814
  James H. & Caroline Plowden 6-9-1873
  James N. & Sarah A. Kingsbury 6-2-1846
  Jane & George Gibbs 10-22-1849
  John & Rebecca Jones 8-23-1780
  John & Sarah Hinton 2-6-1784
  John & Mary Crook 2-16-1798
  John & Ann Boteler 1-25-1832
  John H. & Lucy Sweeney 3-3-1876 (McNeer)
  John H. & Sallie E. Wells 1-16-1883 (Rev. Father Cunnane)

TAYLOR, John R. & Sarah E. Morsell   11-12-1878
John Thomas & Elizabeth Smallwood   2-23-1852
John W. & Elizabeth R. Mitchell   2-3-1868   (Chesley)
Joseph F. & Elizabeth S. Thorn   12-23-1859
Julianna & Edward Willett Jun.   3-26-1807
Juliet Ann & William A. Murrey   1-11-1836
Laura & James Ridgely   10-2-1860
Leonard & Caroline Kidwell   1-20-1845
Leonard & Rebecca Loveless   5-10-1852
Linny & John Henry   4-18-1797
Lorena Ann & Edw. H. Lusby   4-21-1851
Lottie S. & William H. Taylor   9-24-1872
Louis & Emily Harris   10-20-1881
Martha & Samuel Anderson   2-19-1787
Martha A. & Fielder Grimes   2-13-1844
Mary & Presley Sanford   12-19-1792
Mary & James Maitland Jun.   6-17-1800
Mary & Lewis Greene   10-25-1820
Mary Ann & Norval Edwin Duley   5-24-1875   (Kershaw)
Mary C. & Thomas Mudd   2-25-1840
Mary E. & John Watson   6-29-1876
Mary Isabella & John H. Stanton   10-9-1855
Mary Pamelia & Colmore Jenkins   10-20-1828
Nathaniel &Susannah Swann   2-2-1815
Norman D. & Eliza E. Taylor   3-28-1883   (Rev. Father Cunnane)
Priscilla & James Crawford   11-9-1801
Richard & Rebecca Boyd   1-14-1801
Richard & Sarah Langley   10-21-1805
Richard B. & Sarah Ann Mullikin   2-25-1821
Robert & Mary E. Baldwin   7-23-1846
Robert & Laura Prince   colored   10-11-1880
Samuel & Rhoda Hurley   4-10-1793
Sarah & Thomas Brown   6-29-1777
Sarah & Aquila Wilson   11-21-1791
Sarah & John Club   12-23-1799
Sarah & Archibald Frazier   4-15-1800
Sarah & James T. Mullikin   7-8-1848
Sarah & George Patten   colored   6-8-1867   (Stanley)
Sarah Ann & Elisha Loveless   4-2-1839
Sarah Priscilla & James H. Brady   3-11-1868
Seth & Delia Hagan   12-5-1814
Mrs. Sophia E. & George B. Stamp   5-19-1862
Sophy A. & William Seabourne   12-23-1875
Stafford & Verlinda Jane Lynch   2-24-1842
Stephen A. & Barbara Ellen Wilburn   12-6-1860
Susannah & Albert Curtain   2-18-1878   (Kershaw)
Tabitha A. & R. W. Beall   9-2-1867   (Kershaw)
Thomas & Mary Grimes   12-21-1785
Thomas & Charlotte Grimes   5-22-1804
Thomas M. & Mary Cator   2-12-1874   (Gordon)
Thomas R. & Amanda E. Harvey   11-30-1881   (Rev. Mr. Butler)
William & Henrietta Tarman   1-9-1794
William & Elizabeth Townshend   12-30-1795
William & Ann Stamp   12-21-1808
William A. & Maria A. Loveless   12-21-1830

TAYLOR, William E. & Harriet Owens 12-30-1872
  William H. & Lottie S. Taylor 9-24-1872
  Wm. H. & Henrietta Ogle 5-3-1824
TAYMAN, Ann E. & John W. Harvey 4-8-1837
  Benjamin & Caroline Venabill 1-9-1822
  Edith of P. G. County & Richard W. Anderson of A. A. County 3-28-1881
  Ella & Joseph S. Smith 5-17-1880 (Father DeWolfe)
  Emma & John F. Wilson 1-13-1885 (Father Cunnane)
  Fielder & Sarah Mangun 12-18-1815
  George S. & Mary Lee Jenkins 8-16-1884
  Henry & Mary King 2-4-1824
  Ida J. & Benjamin Ogle 11-29-1882 (Rev. Saml R. Gordon)
  James H. & Virginia W. Talbert 4-20-1867 (Kershaw)
  John E. & Sophia Ogle 5-4-1855
  John H. & Mary Eliz^a Greenfield 2-2-1822
  Joseph & Jane Sweeney 2-2-1837
  Levi & Leona Turton 2-12-1817
  Maggie R. & Edwin Stewart 1-22-1867 Age 26 (Gorfon)
  Margaret J. & William J. Wilson 12-6-1854
  Mary & Walter Josephus DeVaughn 6-13-1877 (Gordon)
  Philip & Ann White 8-12-1857
  Richard Henry & Elennora West Devan 12-18-1883 (Rev. Mr. LaRoche)
  Robert & Rosa Cranford 12-28-1885 (Rev. Mr. Chesley)
  Samuel O. & Georgie L. Crauford 12-30-1879 (Father DeWolf)
  Sarah A. & James Wells 1-30-1845
  Sophia & Joseph C. Franklin 1-31-1883
  William & Sarah King 11-21-1855
  William H. & Alice Virginia Jenkins 4-23-1877
  William O. & Elizth M. Moore 11-22-1849
  Zadock & Elizabeth Ogle 2-23-1858
  Zadock & Sallie L. Sweeney 12-31-1881 (Father DeWolf)
TEASDALE, John & Catherine Malone 5-5-1778
TELL, Horace & Rebecca Jones 7-2-1879
TENCH, Milley & Adam Lucas 10-27-1806
TENLEY, George W. & Eliza Jane White 12-24-1884 (Rev. Mr. Brashaw)
  Henry & Eliza Talbert 12-5-1820
  Horatio & Letty Gray 10-31-1804
  Susannah & John Thomas Hutchison 9-15-1868 (Kershaw)
TENLY, Letty Ann & Elias Moreland 2-6-1798
TENNELL, James & Verlinda Townshend 10-10-1821
TERRASSON, Batholomew & Margaret Pierce 5-6-1781
TERRY, Warner & Clarissa Blackwell 2-27-1869
THAW, Joseph & Eleanor Scott 4-19-1804
THOM, Ellen Nora & Andrew Jackson Kerby 9-1-1884 (Rev. J. J. Carden)
THOMAS, Abram & Martha Ella Wallice 3-16-1886 (Rev. M. Lewin)
  Anthony & ....Sassell 1-30-1782
  B. J. & Eliza E. Morton 11-1-1867 (Fr. Lanahan)
  Benjamin & Martha Johnson col^d 4-8-1871
  Bessie & Robert E. Baden 1-18-1873 (Leneghan)
  Caleb & Mary Cave 12-29-1784
  Caleb & Susannah King 4-14-1798
  Catherine R. & William H. Loveless 2-4-1869
  Charles & Henrietta Shepherd 2-2-1831
  Charles & Catharine Lambert 3-13-1837
  Dorcas & James Robt Ennis 2-10-1876

THOMAS, Elizabeth & John Taylor Wall 5-18-1805
   Elizabeth & Nathan Walker 10-3-1810
   Ellen & Butler Slater 4-27-1871 (McDonald)
   Eunice Ann & William Kidwell 10-18-1818
   Fanoni & Richard L. Brightwell 12-26-1794
   George M. & Ann Swann 10-2-1804
   Georgie A. & Benjamin T. T. Rawlings 2-4-1878 (Gordon)
   J. L. & Caroline A. Brashears 2-6-1872 (Mr. Gordon)
   J. W. & Elizabeth Margaret Windsor 4-11-1868
   Jacob & Louisa Matthews 12-24-1883
   James H. & Mary A. Frye 12-28-1869 (Gordon)
   James Richard & Mary Peacock 4-1-1839
   Jennie & Paul Johnson 1-25-1876 (Gordon)
   John & Sarah Ann Clubb 1-12-1839
   John & Susan J. Mackall 2-15-1870 (Wheeler)
   Dr. John C. & Mary S. Hall 12-4-1877 (Perry)
   John Chew & Mary Snowden 9-16-1788
   John H. & Lizzie M. Burch 11-21-1867 (Leneghan)
   John H. & Fanny Gwynn 1-15-1869 (Lenaghan)
   John H. & Mary R. Gordon 8-4-1879 (Crowley)
   Jno. W^m & Josephine Brawner col^d 2-27-1871 (Linthicum)
   Lettice Eleanor & John C. Moore 10-11-1808
   Linda & Jacob Giles 5-15-1869 (Gross)
   Maria & William Wallace 10-3-1819
   Maria & Frank Smallwood 2-19-1871 (Wheeler)
   Maria Ann & George W. Ransom 10-7-1879 (Watkins)
   Martha A. & Joseph Boswell 12-18-1862
   Mary & Jesse T. Berry 10-27-1868
   Mary & Cornelius Evans 1-16-1869 (Langford)
   Mary E. & Isaiah M. Fry 4-17-1876 (Gordon)
   Mary Eliza & George Leonard Hawkins 1-4-1881 col^d
   Mary Elizabeth & Roger Bernard Berry 10-27-1879
   Mary Ellen & John Deveal 2-8-1883 (Rev. Mr. Walker)
   Mary Jane & Jeremiah Fry 10-12-1881 (Rev. Dr. Gordon)
   Matilda A. & George L. Lovelace 3-4-1872 (Gordon)
   Nathan & Mary Brashears 1-17-1799
   Philip & Cornelia Lansdale 11-8-1804
   Rebecca & Pompey Griffin 6-17-1886
   Richard L. & Mary Procter 3-24-1858
   Robert E. & Sarah P. Thomas 3-28-1867 (Gordon)
   Robert E. & Eliza A. Loveless 1-6-1869 (Gordon)
   Rousbury M. & Margaret E. Jones 1-26-1848
   Samuel & Mary Ellixson 4-18-1797
   Sarah & William Hayward 5-27-1806
   Sarah P. & Robert E. Thomas 3-28-1867 (Gordon)
   Susan & Benjamin Holland 8-11-1880 (Stanley)
   Susannah & Daniel Townshend 3-10-1807
   Susannah & Charles Allen 2-9-1822
   Virginia & Marrion Calis 1-9-1843
   Washington & Charlotte Morling 3-26-1875 (Welsh)
   Washington & Laura Shaw 7-20-1877
   William & Ann Taylor 8-12-1799
   William & Ann Beckett 9-27-1830
   William H. & Elizabeth M. Frye 6-1-1869 (Gordon)
   William Hanson & Mary Margaret Chesley 4-1-1881

THOMAS, William N. & Ann Elizabeth Coe 2-1-1851
  Wm. & Elizabeth U. Anderson 7-11-1842
  Zachariah & Elizabeth Sarah Wheatly 3-5-1801
THOMELSON, John & Harrison E. Boswell 7-27-1869 (Leneghan)
THOMPSON, Alizabeth & John Queen 2-7-1814
  Andrew & Elizabeth Tuel 7-20-1798
  Ann & Acquilla Lanham 1-28-1788
  Ann & William Rowe 8-28-1802
  Ann & John Adams 2-1-1803
  Caroline M. & Thomas H. Lusby 12-21-1842
  Clark & Mary Lewis 5-20-1783
  Colmore & Nancy Ann Barrott 1-11-1808
  Daniel & Matilda Peacock 9-16-1843
  Eleanor & Humphrey Pope 11-17-1783
  Electius & Eliz^a Alexander 8-14-1780
  Elizabeth & Thomas King 2-26-1821
  Elizabeth M. & Richard S. Winfield 3-10-1826
  Emily & Thomas M. Wall 1-3-1843
  George & Mary Atway Tippett 5-4-1798
  George & Annie Burgess 4-1-1872 (Skinner)
  George H. & Martha Ann Thorn 11-16-1848
  Geo. J. & Bertha A. Phelps 1-1-1851
  George Leonard & Mary Jane Duvall 1-8-1859
  George W. & Caroline R. A. Edelen 9-1-1869 (Kershaw)
  Hanson & Sarah Goddard 3-1-1821
  Henrietta & Jno H. Dixon 9-25-1848
  James & Rhodoe Athey 11-25-1788
  James & Mary Philips 12-27-1790
  James & Mary Brightwell 4-2-1803
  James E. & Annie E. Craycroft 1-25-1868 (Marbury)
  James E. & Mary L. Cheseldine 12-21-1883
  James F. & Laura J. Given 9-26-1885
  Jane & Daniel Billings 9-26-1791
  Jane E. & Wm. H. Lindsay 2-3-1845
  Jas. Fraser & Sarah Moore 6-5-1778
  John D. & Mary D. Robinson 1-27-1842
  John F. & Elizabeth M. Lewis 4-22-1815
  John L. & Mary R. Noland 2-3-1858
  John L. & Mrs. Mary Deakin 3-2-1874
  John L. & Katie Isaac 12-5-1877 (Still)
  John L. & Louisa Soper 5-15-1882 (Rev. Mr. Fultz)
  John W. & Ann Hillard 1-6-1836
  Jno. & Matilda Ann Naley 1-28-1851
  Luke & Margaret Ryley 2-15-1793
  Margaret & Edmund T. Allen 12-25-1866 Age 18 of P. G. County, date of
    record 1-11-1867 (Kershaw)
  Margaret Ann & Samuel Culver 10-30-1822
  Margaret M. & John Phelps 5-28-1829
  Martha & John Burch col^d 10-10-1868 (Fr. Lenaghan)
  Mary A. & Jas. W. Burgess 2-27-1845
  Mary Eleanor & Thomas Lewis Thompson 9-26-1809
  Mary Emily & James William Burgess 1-2-1832
  Mary F. & Alexander Myers 5-24-1880 (Gordon)
  Matilda & William Gardiner 8-10-1821
  Matilda A. & James Kidwell 12-24-1857

THOMPSON, Minta & Benjamin Yearley 2-14-1785
  Moses & Rachel Lowden 12-22-1783
  Philip & Ann Whitney 5-30-1796
  Richard & Rachel Burgess 10-20-1779
  Richard L. & Emily Berry 12-11-1826
  Rosa Bell & Richard Frederick Mattingly 8-21-1871 (Watts)
  Samuel & Ann Walker 2-10-1790
  Saml. H. & Mary R. Padgett 2-2-1880
  Sarah & Aaron Dyer Jr. 6-22-1821
  Sharlotte & Jno. Henry Nothey 12-29-1862
  Thomas & Sarah Cater 2-7-1785
  Thomas H. & Lethe Ann Moore 1-5-1870 (Gordon)
  Thomas Lewis & Mary Eleanor Thompson 9-26-1809
  Thomas O. & Matilda A. Walls 6-27-1850
  William & Martha Watson 2-10-1876 (Mayberry)
  W^m. L. & Margaret A. Lusby 10-15-1872 (Fowler)
  Zach^a & Eleanor Davis 12-9-1783
THOMSON, Strong J. & Maria Louisa Cross 12-22-1846
THORN, Aloysius B. & Elizabeth J. Sansbury 9-27-1867 (Martin)
  Benedict & Ann Jenkins 10-12-1820
  Benjamin & Letty Downes 2-19-1803
  Celestia J. & Francis C. Taylor 12-23-1859
  Elizabeth S. & Joseph F. Taylor 12-23-1859
  Filla & William Bryan of Tho§ 4-1-1839
  George W. & Elizabeth R. Taylor 7-6-1850
  Henry & Elizabeth Wilson 5-29-1779
  Henry Burch & Mary Thorn 2-25-1790
  Henry Burch & Massy Hall 2-26-1803
  Henry C. & Mary A. Mattingly 9-16-1832
  Henry F. & Mary E. Fraser 12-3-1833
  John & Emmy Downes 3-5-1803
  John A. & Ida Eugenia Whitmore 1-12-1878 (Dorsey)
  Lillie & Pliney E. Lusby 2-15-1886 (Rev. Mr. Jyland)
  Margaret Eugenia & Robert Frederick Roche 5-28-1868
  Martha Ann & George H. Thompson 11-16-1848
  Mary & Henry Burch Thorn 2-25-1790
  Mary E. & R^d D. Ball 12-19-1864
  Mary Sophronia & William W. Sansbury 4-15-1867
  Samuel P. & Ellen A. Lusby 12-3-1884 (Rev. Mr. Towles)
  Susanna & Luke Adams 6-2-1781
  Susannah & John Goddard 8-4-1787
  Thomas E. M. & Elizabeth Sheriff 2-23-1829
  Walter & Felly King 9-7-1816
  William & Elizabeth King 1-4-1803
THORNE, Willm S. & Sarah V. Lindsay 12-12-1847
THORNTON, Ellen & Robert Scott 3-11-1869 (Langford)
  James B. C. & Marg^t Williammina Gantt 5-22-1823
  Richard & Jane Young 2-17-1872 (Evans)
  Richard & Priscilla Wood 12-31-1884 (Rev. Mr. Brooke)
  Sophia & Charles Stewart 4-2-1877 (Carroll)
THRALLS, Richard & Lucy Mulliken 12-31-1787
THURSBY, Edward & Ann Sasscer 1-25-1786
TIDINGS, John H. & Ella Deale 4-19-1875 (Kershaw)
  Vinnie & Horace Wellford 1-16-1877 (McDonald)
TILGHMAN, Caroline & Thomas West 12-12-1868 (Edelin)

TILGHMAN, Charles & Eliza Sprigg 6-6-1879 (Crowley)
  Lucas & Lucy Jackson col? 7-13-1867 (Call)
  Nace & Chloe Ann Williams 10-12-1877
TILLEY, Barbara & Isaac Barrot 11-29-1809
  Eliz.th Ann & Henry Wirt Tilley 4-1-1828
  Harriott & William Ross 3-17-1801
  Henry Wirt & Eliz.th Ann Tilley 4-1-1828
  John & Barbara Wirt 1-6-1790
  John & Mary Jones 3-29-1780
  John & Martha Barron 12-9-1808
  Rebecca & William Stevens 1-15-1785
  Rebeccah & Hezekiah Athey 12-10-1799
  Robert & Ann Miller 11-10-1801
TILLMAN, Thomas & Elenor Wriston 7-1-1820
TIPPET, William J. & Elizabeth B. Lynch 12-26-1838
TIPPETT, Ann & William Wedge 8-2-1822
  Chloe Eleanor & Rich? L. Humphreys 1-6-1818
  Daniel & Martha Ann Mayhew 10-26-1876 (Green)
  Edelina D. & William Jefferson 1-19-1821
  Eleanor & John Cunningham 8-28-1811
  Eleanor & James Alder 3-24-1815
  Elizabeth & Richard Gregory 12-13-1809
  Elizabeth C. & Benjamin F. Armiger 12-10-1877 (Perry)
  John & Tabitha Leatch 7-30-1796
  John & Rozena Carter 9-1-1834
  John T. & Vilette C. Greer 8-31-1868 (Smith)
  Mary & James D. Coe 11-12-1827
  Mary Atway & George Thompson 5-4-1798
  Philip F. & Maggie V. Townshend 1-18-1868 (Smith)
  Samuel E. & Eliza R. Catterton 1-15-1873 (Townshend)
  Theodore & Mary Robey 12-24-1821
  Trueman & Sarah Ann Simpson 2-1-1810
TOGOOD, Sarah & Henry Vellum 6-29-1791
TOLLEY, Annie R. & John F. Chesley 10-29-1861
TOLSON, Alfred & Mary E. Gantt 2-14-1826
  Alfred & Martha E. Bayne 2-11-1834
  Ann H. & Henry O. Middleton 2-15-1814
  Benton & Martha M. Bowie 12-15-1860
  Bettie & James L. Addison 12-3-1860
  Catharine & Basil Loggins both colored 4-28-1865
  Catherine & Isaac Robinson 1-11-1872 (Gordon)
  Charity & Upton Bruce col? 9-28-1867 (Gordon)
  Chloe Ann & Henry Addison Callis 2-20-1810
  Chloe Ann & Daniel Ducket 2-22-1877
  Edward & Susan Middleton 1-19-1825
  Eleanor C. & Horatio Edelen 2-13-1827
  Elizabeth & Thomas Berry 12-7-1810
  Francis & Elizabeth Simms 2-27-1794
  Francis & Alice R. Bowie 11-30-1857
  Francis & Hennie Douglass 11-18-1871 (Marbury)
  Francis Jr. & Sarah Middleton 9-18-1817
  Fred & Mary Ellen Quander col? 1-13-1881 (Rev. De Wolfe)
  Gassaway & Belle Jackson 2-15-1879 (Carroll)
  Hannah Ann & George Freeland 11-30-1885 (Rev. Mr. Brooks)
  Harriet & George Simms 1-10-1872 (Wheeler)

TOLSON, Henry & Mary Middleton 2-12-1827
  Henry & Jennie C. Marriott 11-19-1860
  John & Eleanor Addison 12-18-1806
  John & Lucinda Barrette 2-12-1839
  John & Rachel Ford 8-15-1879 (Gordon)
  John Edward & Alice Rebecca Suit 4-27-1874
  Julia A. & Zeph. English 12-17-1859
  Juliet M. & Thomas E. Williams 2-1-1870 (Martin)
  Lettie & Elijah Courts 12-23-1867 (Gordon)
  Margaret & James Edelen 12-28-1829
  Mary & George Simmes 2-13-1813
  Rachel & Isaac DeVeil 10-23-1875 (Mayberry)
  Sarah & Zachariah Walker 12-8-1814
  Sarah & Isaac Nichols 6-24-1871 (Wheeler)
  Sophia R. & Dr. Washington Miller 11-17-1855
  William & Mary Hoxton 12-16-1823
  William & Jane E. Dement 9-28-1835
  William & Laura A. Suit 3-26-1883 (Rev. Mr. Brashaw)
TOMBLESOM, John & Delilah Garner 12-20-1830
TOMLIN, Henry W. & Rozana Smith 12-7-1842
  Henry W. & Jane Tomlinson 12-11-1849
  Robt M. & Laura Smith 1-7-1841
  Robert M. F. & Margaret A. Perrie 9-6-1831
TOMLINSON, Ann & William F. Garner 12-31-1833
  Jane & Henry W. Tomlin 12-11-1849
  Thomas & Ann M. Downing 7-2-1834
TONGUE..........& Rebecca Anderson 6-16-1886 (Rev. Mr. Howard)
  Margaret & Philip Locker 2-25-1785
  Mary & Milburn Coe 1-8-1783
TOUNGUE, Henry & Sophia Scribner 1-4-1883 (Rev. Joshua Barnes)
TOWLES, Ella C. & Eugene A. Pool 1-6-1880 (Rev. John Towles)
  Sophia Griffin & Charles H. Washington 12-20-1873
TOWNLEY, Charles the 3rd & Ruth Lanham 4-28-1817
  Thos & Henrietta Stewart 1-15-1782
TOWNSEND, Mary & Benjamin Burch 2-22-1784
TOWNSHEND, Alice T. B. & Llewellyn M. Naylor 5-14-1874 (Seal)
  Ann & John Watson Wright 1-8-1794
  Ann Eliza & George W. Bray 6-6-1842
  Catharine V. & Wm. L. Wall 1-19-1863
  D. W. & Martha S. Bealle 1-19-1875 (Dorcey)
  Daniel & Susannah Thomas 3-10-1807
  Eleanor A. G. & John Baden 1-21-1857
  Elizabeth & William Taylor 12-30-1795
  Elizabeth A. & John G. Townshend 2-27-1867 (Marbury)
  Elizth & James H. Griffen 6-17-1837
  George S. & Jane Wall 10-11-1838
  J. B. & Susie E. Naylor 1-18-1873 (Rogers)
  Johanna Ann & Zadock Robinson 12-22-1819
  John G. & Elizabeth A. Townshend 2-27-1867 (Marbury)
  John L. & Rebecca Baden 5-15-1838
  Kate B. & Samuel R. Monroe 5-19-1880
  Maggie V. & Philip F. Tippett 1-18-1868 (Smith)
  Margaret & Theodore Wall 12-1-1806
  Richard & Elizabeth Parker 12-16-1796
  Samuel & Elizth Brown 2-8-1831

TOWNSHEND, Samuel G. & Sarah A. Pyles 1-13-1875 (Ryland)
  Sarah R. & William N. Burch 1-14-1834
  Susanna & Joseph N. Burch Jr. 6-7-1837
  Verlinda & James Tennell 10-10-1821
  Walter Ann &James R. Lusby 1-25-1870 (Toles)
  William H. & Julia A. Naylor 4-22-1872 (Townshend)
  Wm. & Keziah Bonefant 10-12-1795
TOYE, Charles & Eliza Dorsey 9-13-1872
TRABANE, John H. & Emily C. Pumphrey 10-21-1856
TRACEY, Ann & William Webster 4-8-1831
  Ann Elizabeth & Cincinatis Fairo 11-5-1828
  Eleanor W. & John Conner 12-1-1778
TRACY, William & Mary Scissell 9-18-1777
TRAPNALL, Stephen & Maria Perrie 2-14-1873 (McDonald)
TRASS, Ann & William Collea 11-7-1786
TRAVERS, Charity & Robert Carroll 10-2-1869 (Langford)
TRIGG, David & Charity Elery 1-11-1796
TRIMBLE, Margaret & Adam Gaddis Jr. 11-24-1855
TROTHER, Jan & Ebenezer Nesmith 5-20-1796
TROTT, Katie & John S. Norfolk 11-26-1881 (Rev. Mr. Jones)
TRUE, John & Mima Waters 1-9-1797
TRUEMAN, Benjamin F. & Mary E. Naylor 12-8-1873 (Tennent)
  Benoni & Elizabeth Johnson Leitch 4-1-1801
  Henry & Ann Beavin 4-3-1790
  Henry B. & Susan Gibson 2-8-1840
  Henry T. & Ellen F. Deakins 8-19-1878 (Perry)
  John B. & Catharine B. Estep 2-8-1819
  Josiah & Eliz.th T. Goddings 5-15-1848
  Martha & George Cross 6-5-1879 (Quinn)
  Mary & William F. Richardson 12-31-1834
  Mary A. M. & John W. Young 12-19-1878 (Perry)
  Monica & Daniel Rawlings 2-7-1812
  Rebeccah & John Pierce 3-29-1798
  Susan E. & John E. Harrison 2-14-1870
TRUMAN, Jane R. & Wm. H. Tubman 1-15-1862
  Mary M. & Eli J. Watson 11-22-1873 (Townshend)
  Mocky & Philip Merroll 2-10-1798
  Rebecca & Rinaldo Johnson 2-4-1779
TRUNNELL, Rachel & Lancelot Wilson 2-14-1792
  William & Christiana Aldridge 12-19-1832
TSCHIFFELY, Frederick A. Jr. & Dollie Brown 2-15-1873 (Ernest)
TUBMAN, Henry & Eleanor Wourld 9-5-1828
  Jane R. & John W. Richardson 3-2-1878 (Perry)
  Mary Jane & Thomas E. Ball 3-9-1857
  Rachel Ann & James C. Rollins 6-27-1851
  Rachael Ann & Thos Ball of Thos 10-28-1854
  Wm. H. & Jane R.Truman 1-15-1862
TUCK, William Clem & Ruth A. Barnes 8-14-1861
  William H. & Margaret S. B. Chew 6-22-1843
TUCKER, Benjamin & Ann Wornald 2-11-1778
  Cornelia Jane & George Brown 8-13-1866 Age 22 8-13-1866 (Griffith)
  Emma S. & Columbus P. Craycroft 1-22-1876 (Tennent)
  George W. & Elizabeth Maccabee 4-23-1885 (Rev. Jno. Cotton)
  Henrietta & Basil Mayhew 1-13-1868
  James W. & Mary J. Burgess 3-10-1879 (Butler)

TUCKER, Jennie & James Evans 9-17-1878 (Butler)
 John F. & Mary E. Baker 12-20-1870 (Robey)
 Jnọ & Ellen R. Cooke 3-18-1844
 Kate & John R. Gibbons 3-16-1878
 Martha & John Smitson 12-1-1885 (Rev. W. G. Davenport)
 Mary & Allison B. Kidwell 8-17-1878 (Butler)
 Mary C. & James R. Abigail 10-16-1873 (Hatterway)
 Mary Julia & Wm. Henry Mayhew 10-31-1865 Age 21 (Kershaw)
 Rachel & Joseph Cook 11-29-1866 Age 20
 Richard & Elizạ Johnson 1-21-1794
 Sarah & Archibald Fraser 5-20-1833
 Susan & Adam C. Brown 2-17-1834
 William & Mary Baldwin 1-15-1803
 William & Ann Clubb 6-26-1824
 William & Lucy Henry 12-18-1839
TUEL, Eleanor & Archibald McDaniel 6-25-1798
 Elizabeth & Andrew Thompson 7-20-1798
TUFTS, William H. & Athena Smith 9-21-1870 (Brown)
TURNER, Abraham & Rebecca Sadler 11-27-1781
 Alexander & C. Virginia Smith 5-27-1880 (Aquila)
 Alexander W. & Martha A. Turner 8-3-1841
 Alice & John H. Jones 12-29-1884 (Rev. Mr. Brooke)
 Caroline & Daniel A. Jenkins 11-16-1859
 Catherine Ann & Richard W. Isaac 12-12-1848
 Dorens S. & Richard G. Brashears 2-21-1835
 Elizabeth & Joseph T. Noble 3-4-1802
 Elizabeth & Francis Waring 2-8-1814
 George & Ann Gibbons 9-5-1797
 Harriet & Edward Sansbury 4-10-1819
 Harriet & Robert J. Wood 12-23-1878 (Gray)
 James H. & Jane E. Martin 1-18-1838
 Jane E. & William L. Watkins 9-2-1878 (Butler)
 John & Sarah Beck 2-5-1799
 John & Sarah Parker 6-25-1810
 John & Mary Ann Harvey 6-9-1812
 John & Mary Ann Ward 5-7-1829
 John E. & Mary E. Turner 5-18-1840
 John Henry & Eliza Ann Chaney 9-7-1853
 John P. & Annie E. Freeman 1-30-1875
 John P. & Ellen C. Shea 10-6-1885 (Father Caughy)
 Lucy H. & George B. White 11-21-1868 (Boyle)
 M. J. & F. A. Wroe 12-13-1869 (Linthicum)
 Margaret D. & James W. Wood 11-26-1853
 Maria & Robert Johnson 7-23-1879 (Jenkins)
 Martha A. & Alexander W. Turner 8-3-1841
 Mary & Benjamin Kidd Morsell 8-21-1816
 Mary C. & William T. Whiting 3-23-1880 (Stanley)
 Mary E. & John E. Turner 5-18-1840
 Philip & Rachel Williams 9-14-1787
 Rebecca & Peter Gardner 5-15-1793
 Rebecca & James Henry Parker 1-10-1882 (Rev. Mr. Stanley)
 Rezin & Mary Scott 12-12-1799
 Richard & Eleanor Williams 1-10-1791
 Sallie P. & Aquila T. Robinson 10-18-1880 (Rev. Mr. Gordon)
 Samuel & Louisa Wilson 12-23-1842

TURNER, Sarah & Lancelot Anderwig 12-19-1797
  Sarah & Osborn Belt Jun. 2-10-1807
  Susan Ann & Philip Martin 12-16-1874 (Stanley)
  Susannah & John Stephens 2-28-1798
  Thomas J. & Malvina Early 12-11-1850
  Thomas M. & Maria Hepburn 1-6-1879 (Butler)
  William & Dorcas Batt 2-21-1784
  William & Catherine Brown 1-22-1873 (McDonald)
  William Albert & Sarah Elizabeth Clarke 12-24-1881 (Father Cotten)
  Zachariah & Laura V. Lusby 6-30-1875 (West)
TURTEN, Ann & George G. Powell 3-30-1813
TURTON, Fielder & Ann Simpson 5-4-1799
  John & Priscilla Fairall 12-6-1809
  John & Sarah Ann Gibbons 1-28-1826
  John A. & Almira Worthington 12-13-1839
  John E. & Elizabeth Jane Berry 3-21-1860
  John W. & Elizabeth P. Wynn 4-21-1832
  Josey Harrison & Ann Jenkins 11-19-1794
  Leona & Levi Tayman 2-12-1817
  Mary A. & Richard Taiman 2-22-1784
  Mary Ann Eleanor & William Robinson 7-30-1828
  Sarah E. & Thomas Talburt 1-22-1833
  Susanna & Francis E. Mudd 1-23-1832
  Theophilus & Ann Earley 12-24-1803
  Thomas G. & Martha J. Berry 7-20-1853
  Violetta & John L. Waring 8-31-1838
TWINE, Maria & Peter Ennis 7-26-1871 (McDonald)
TYDINGS, Harriet Ann & David Hall 1-9-1875
  Mary & Thomas J. Hall 2-22-1876 (McNeer)
  Mary Elizabeth & Stephen Gardiner 7-25-1855
  Richard T. & Alice Ann Wells 3-10-1858
  Susan & Thomas H. Deal 1-7-1852
  Susan Cordelia & Benj. J. Bassford 1-16-1877
TYLER, Ann H. & Edward Taylor 6-14-1825
  Christy & Thomas Pratt 10-16-1799
  Elizabeth & Humphrey Belt Jun. 2-4-1792
  Fannie & Thomas J. Mulliken 12-30-1872 (Gordon)
  George & Polly Bond Clagett 4-11-1803
  Grafton & Ann H. Plummer 12-14-1808
  Grafton Jr. & Mary Margaret Bowie 1-8-1836
  Henry & Lucy Crawford 2-9-1870 (Begue)
  John W. & Annic Frazier 1-9-1877 (Walker)
  Mary & John Johnson Jr. 4-29-1823
  Mary Ann & Benj. Souther 12-2-1778
  Milicent & Colmore Beanes 4-10-1778
  Priscilla & Richard Forster 4-5-1784
  Robert Bradley & Henrietta Beanes 12-1-1779
  Rob. B. & Dreyden G. Belt 3-17-1783
  Ruth & Zachariah Wood 12-2-1833
  Samuel & Virlinda Riddle 1-19-1782
  Samuel & Susanna Waters 12-25-1783
  Susannah & Benjamin M. Hodges 4-18-1797
  Tobias & Violetta Duvall 2-3-1816
  Washington & Ellen Plummer 10-1-1868

TYLER, Washington of Anne Arundel Co. & Isabella Boothes of same county colored 6-22-1881 (Rev. Daniel Aquila)
William & Mary B. Addison 7-18-1809
William & Margaret Cahall 8-2-1824
William & Annie Coats 2-28-1880 (Aquilla)
TYSON, Elizabeth A. & Howard Monkhouse 6-23-1870 (Young)
Frances Ellicott & Robert A. Parish 12-19-1859

ULLE, Edward M. & Mary E. Baker 10-1-1883 (Rev. E. Robey)
Elizabeth & Nicholas Robey 10-15-1873
UNDERWOOD, Ann & Joseph T. Boswell 1-7-1876
Elizabeth & George R. Dyar 2-8-1862
George T. & Ann Adams 1-18-1870
Henrietta & William W. Barry 2-9-1872 (Toles)
James E. & Mary J. Carroll 2-15-1873 (Leneghan)
Mary Ella & John Edward Carroll 5-8-1882 (Rev. Fr . Clarke)
Susie P. & Hiram W. Greene 2-6-1866 Age 18, married at home of mother 2-6-1866 (Chipchase)
Thomas M. & Annie Lederer 10-23-1880
UPTON, Amelia & Henry Parker 2-7-1815
Archibald & Rebeccah Ferrell 12-30-1795
Eleanor & Dominick Havener 1-31-1789
Eliz[a] & Hilliary Lanham 4-5-1783
George & Elizabeth Pickens 1-6-1778
Keziah & John King 6-6-1779
Mazy & Thomas Shaw 4-16-1818
Rebecca & Walter Deakins 2-7-1821
Sarah & Benj[a] Marshall 1-17-1778
Sarah & Francis Wheat 11-1-1780
Sarah & Joshua Bird 2-10-1806
Thomas & Priscilla Mitchell 2-19-1798
URNSHAW, John & Margery B. Brown 1-23-1843
URQUHART, John & Ann Lowe 2-22-1793

VAILL, Timothy N. & Louisa Jones 10-23-1818
VALENTINE, John & Eliza Giles colored 5-14-1853
VANETTA, Mary A. E. & Ignatius Winsor 4-11-1876 (Gordon)
VANHORN, Archibald & Alethea Elizabeth Beall 7-26-1797
Amelia Beall & Walter Trueman Greenfield Beall 6-2-1818
VAN PATTEN, Hannah Mary & Amze Smith 12-1-1869
VAUGHAN, Thomas & Ann Watson 11-6-1794
VEATCH, James & Mary Page 1-25-1798
VEITCH, Alexander & Barbara Hilseagle 7-11-1798
Elizabeth & Philip Miller 1-24-1818
John & Caroline Morsell 12-6-1819
Rachel & William Neale 8-1-1798
VELLUM, Henry & Sarah Togood 6-29-1791
VENABILL, Caroline & Benjamin Tayman 1-9-1822
VENABLE, Ann & Trueman E. Boswell 12-16-1833
Theodore & Mary Tarman 5-24-1799
VENABLES, John & Elizabeth Peirce 12-28-1808

VENABLES, Margaret & Thomas Pierce 12-28-1814
VERMILEON, Margaret E. & John H. Beall 1-5-1859
VERMILION, Eliz.ᵃ & Thomas Cross 10-14-1780
  Francis Burch & Ann Wood 8-30-1780
  Jacob & Cloe Harrison 1-29-1780
  Jn.º & Janepher McDaniel 7-15-1780
  Mary & John Baptist Farr 11-23-1780
  Penelope & Francis Burch 1-24-1783
  William & Mary Ann Sims 4-19-1778
VERMILLION, Alfonso R. & Annie E. Harrison 8-11-1875
  Alfred & Ellen Sherbert 9-14-1848
  Anna E. & Allen W. Chaney 12-9-1872 (Mercer)
  Annie & John Cox 9-23-1869 (Kershaw)
  Benjamin & Priscilla Farr 1-8-1787
  Caleb & Mary Busey 12-20-1794
  Eda & John E. Atchison 12-11-1811
  Elijah & Mary Jane Simpson 10-4-1860
  Elizabeth & Thomas Mitchell 10-2-1802
  Georgianna & George P. Barse 9-6-1877
  James A. & Mary Ann Gibson 3-3-1835
  Joseph N. & Mary Ann Earp 6-5-1873
  Julius & Emma M. Boswell 5-19-1880
  Leonard & Ann Ridgway 8-12-1803
  Levi & Martha Sansberry 12-28-1819
  Lucy & John Darcey 12-3-1825
  Margaret P. & John McCarthy 6-2-1869
  Martha E. & R. F. Hardey 2-17-1880 (Stanley)
  Martha Isabella & George Washington Moore 4-12-1880 (Rev.ᵈ Mr. Butler)
  Nancy Ann & Josias Jones 11-3-1804
  Osborn & Rachael Haas 5-5-1798
  Priscilla & Alexius Gray 1-18-1823
  Sarah Ellen & Jno. A. Hall 7-29-1858
VERNON, Bachus Lee & Mary Frances Ward 5-10-1881 (Rev. Mr. Gordon)
  Caleb & Chloe Atcreson 11-30-1790
VERTESS, Mary & John Tarvan 1-14-1805
VINCENT, Elizabeth & Humphrey Belt Sen.ᵗ 3-3-1804
VINSON, John & Julia Brown col.ᵈ 12-21-1869 (Maher)
VIRMIER, Jane & William Jackson 1-31-1789
VOLINTINE, Mary E. & Wm. Gantt 12-12-1856
VOLUMES, Edward & Rachel Soper 12-27-1796
VYRMEERS, William & Mary Edelen 6-20-1803

WADDELL, Margaret & Theophilius A. Boteler 5-8-1860
WADE, Ann Noble & John Ward Young 1-29-1806
  Benoni Hamilton & Mary D. Hardey 5-31-1796
  Dely & Luke Shannon 3-24-1794
  Elizth H. & Henry C. Boswell 11-21-1826
  Hetta & William Webster 8-13-1792
  Letty & William Fox 11-18-1794
  Linny & Cornelius Hurley 4-4-1795
  Mary Ann & Alexander Gibbons 12-10-1803
WAILES, Ann & Thomas Clark 10-29-1791
  Ann Perrie & Benjamin Naylor 2-2-1807
  Benjamin & Sophia Wilson 2-14-1816
  Edwd Loyd & Sarah Biggs Oden 3-22-1780
  Kitty B. & John Estep 5-30-1795
  Levin & Eleanor Davis 10-28-1796
  Levin & Anna Harper 12-26-1855
  Rebeccah & George Burroughs 7-6-1792
  Samuel & Ann Naylor 2-8-1783
  Samuel P. & Mary Susanna Willson 2-17-1827
  Sarah Perrie & Josiah Wilson 4-10-1807
WAILKS, Susanna & James Kennedy 12-16-1799
WAINE, John & Mary Senton 12-24-1783
WAKEFIELD, Eliza Jane & Charles H. L. West 10-24-1827
WAKEHAM, William & Mary Ann Crook 11-24-1843
WALACE, William & Alice Mahew 4-23-1778
WALDO, Lula E. & William M. Sloan 12-30-1885 (Rev. Mr. Chesley)
WALES, George & Martha Naylor 2-25-1783
  James & Virlinder Cecil 11-5-1817
WALKER, Ann & Samuel Thompson 2-10-1790
  Benjn & Mary Pumphry 12-31-1778
  Benj. Neill & Mary Littleford 3-25-1788
  Benjamin & Ann Busey 6-13-1798
  Benjamin N. & Ann Griffith 4-18-1794
  Catharine & Richard Walker 12-24-1796
  Charles E. & Mary J. Morsell 11-20-1841
  Edward S. & Sophronia Duckett 5-15-1877 (McNeer)
  Elisha & Elizabeth Roberts 12-31-1792
  Eliza & Charles W. Edwards 5-1-1878 (Cotton)
  Eliza Jane & Isaac Ball 12-5-1865
  Elizabeth & Thos Piles 11-19-1850
  Elizabeth Ann & Rezin Beck 11-11-1822
  Elizabeth B. & Jesse H. D. Wall 12-9-1816
  Esther & Walter Ball 10-9-1876 (Griffin)
  Francis & Rachel Hardey 11-4-1803
  George & Ann Gray 12-7-1779
  George & Martha Craufurd 12-16-1794
  George & Rifa Ann Conner 5-17-1807
  George P. & Elizabeth A. Allen 8-1-1833
  Hendley & Emily Gallyham 12-22-1836
  Henry & Keziah Burgess 12-8-1780
  Henry & Rachael Walker 2-3-1824
  Isaac & Eleanor Bradford 7-27-1790
  James William & Martha Rebecca Piles 8-21-1873
  Jane & Alpheus Beall 12-10-1841
  John & Stacey Mosely 12-16-1796

WALKER, John & Anne Locker 2-4-1808
  John & Mary Fowler 2-24-1830
  John & Rebecca Howard 12-23-1831
  John N. & Maria L. Duvall 10-5-1874 (Stanley)
  John R. & Mary E. Warner 1-13-1840
  Joseph & Mary Ellen Peach 10-27-1856
  Joseph Jun? & Henrietta Maria Hepburn 12-7-1779
  Jno. Robert & Anna Eliza Jenkins 4-22-1867 (Lenahan)
  Letty & Basil Lovelace 1-6-1801
  Lloyd & Mary Ann Simpson 1-19-1836
  Mareen D. & Ann Berry 1-15-1787
  Martha & William Laws 5-26-1784
  Mary & John Beckett 9-29-1778
  Mary & Humphrey Whitmore 11-30-1793
  Mary & Richard Jenkins 5-12-1857
  Mary S. & John Beall 1-19-1838
  Matilda & Hugh W. Drummond 1-1-1824
  Matilda & John Anderson 12-14-1824
  Meeky & Jesse Phelps 4-15-1803
  Nathan & Elizabeth Thomas 10-3-1810
  Nettie J. & Willie Theron Klock 12-21-1885 (Rev. Mr. Brayshaw)
  Rachel & Benj. Prather 1-15-1782
  Rachael & Henry Walker 2-3-1824
  Rebecca & Massum Duvall 1-27-1809
  Richard & Mary Gilpin 8-23-1778
  Richard & Catharine Walker 12-24-1796
  Richard B. & Mary Duvall 10-28-1823
  Richard T. & Sarah A. Wilson 9-23-1861
  Ruth Beall & Robert Clarke 8-21-1810
  Samuel & Priscilla Canter 5-5-1814
  Sarah & Richard Burgess 1-12-1802
  Susanna J. & Philip A. Gates 1-30-1858
  Susannah & Benjamin Jones 2-6-1807
- Thomas & Mary Littleford 12-24-1780
  Wm. A. & Mary E. E. Alvy 12-21-1848
  Zachariah & Amany Locher 12-24-1808
  Zachariah & Sarah Tolson 12-8-1814
  Zachariah & Eliza Berry 12-11-1817
WALL, Ann Rebecca & Lemuel L. Orme 11-24-1855
  Catherine M. & Alexander McKee 9-3-1852
  Daniel R. & Sarah J. Crauford 12-1-1855
  Elizabeth & Thomas Martin Jr. 4-29-1837
  Elizth W. & Underwood Sasscer 3-23-1818
  Fendall & Rebecca Hall 11-3-1874 (O'Dwyer)
  Harriet T. & Cephas M. Benson 10-5-1828
  Harriet T. & Fielder Cross Jr. 1-30-1856
  James D. & Caroline Lovelace 2-6-1865
  Jane D. & Thomas Clarke 12-21-1810
  Jane & George S. Townshend 10-11-1838
  Jesse H. D. & Elizabeth B. Walker 12-9-1816
  John T. & Catharine Estep 5-19-1823
  John T. & Mary Bowie 11-17-1880 (Lewin)
  John Taylor & Elizabeth Thomas 5-18-1805
  Josephine & James Arthur Pinkney 12-28-1875
  Martha Ann & William Dixon 12-24-1811

WALL, Martha Ann & Samuel T. Wall 1-20-1841
  Mary & Jesse Ray 1-24-1782
  Mary & Thomas ONeale 11-9-1813
  Meta J. & Bernard Grady 5-1-1877
  Nelson T. & Martha Ann Wells 4-19-1836
  Rebecca & Basil Ray 1-19-1782
  Robert Gordon & Mary Berry 2-7-1801
  Samuel T. & Martha Ann Wall 1-20-1841
  Sarah & Thomas Wells 5-26-1787
  Sarah Elizabeth & Wm. Wesley Hyatt 6-10-1857
  Theodore & Margaret Townshend 12-1-1806
  Thomas M. & Emily Thompson 1-3-1843
  Walter & Elizabeth Taylor 1-31-1801
  William & Elizabeth Piles 1-9-1786
  William & Elizabeth Gibbons 8-23-1806
  William L. & Anna V. Crauford 2-13-1857
  Wm. L. & Catharine V. Townshend 1-19-1863
WALLACE, Catharine & John Evans col^d 6-30-1866
  Catherine & Moses Larkins 2-2-1885 (Mr. Green)
  Eleanor Lee & Joseph Kent 10-30-1804
  Florence E. & John F. McGregor 6-9-1875 (Kershaw)
  Harriot & Joseph Letchworth 12-1-1807
  John & Mary M. Osbourn 2-8-1882 (Rev. Dr. Gordon)
  Joseph & Carrie Hall colo. 8-17-1883 (Rev. Mr. Langford)
  Margaret & John Palmer 5-1-1802
  Mary & Frank Bias 5-19-1884 (Rev. Mr. Howard)
  Michael & Eleanor Contee 8-18-1780
  Sarah & John Free 1-25-1796
  William & Maria Thomas 10-3-1819
  William & Elizabeth Beckett 3-30-1831
  William A. & Martha A. Sasscer 6-25-1840
  William Virgil of New York & Margaret Julia Mitchell of New York
    9-26-1862
WALLICE, Martha Ella & Abram Thomas 3-16-1886 (Rev. M. Lewin)
WALLINGSFORD, Alethia & William Moore 6-8-1804
  Elizabeth & Henry Piles 8-6-1779
  Emily & Peleg Brown 8-3-1836
  Joseph & Rachel Lowe 6-22-1804
WALLIS, J. William & Amy Escott 11-15-1870
  Laura Jane & Henry Wescott 10-5-1861
  Thomas & Mary Hinton 8-22-1812
WALLS, Benjamin B. & Jennett C. Harvey 6-12-1835
  Elizabeth A. & David B. Willson 12-8-1824
  George N. & Sarah Clubb 1-16-1824
  Jane & James H. Gibbons 1-25-1839
  Margaret B. & Josiah Wilson 1-18-1817
  Martha & Thos§ W. Robinson 1-12-1846
  Mary E. & William A. Murray 2-18-1854
  Matilda A. & Thomas O. Thompson 6-27-1850
  William Benjn & Mary Elizabeth Murray 9-19-1860
  W^m & Marion Hawkins 8-5-1876 (Gray)
WALTER, Ella & William A. Harron 6-18-1877
  Joseph & Lillie E. Baldwin 6-8-1886 (Rev. Wm. Brayshaw)
WALTHER, Clara V. & Ottmar Sonneman 1-1-1883 (Rev. Geo. M. Berry)
WAR, Ann & Samuel Mackness 9-2-1779

WARD, Albert W. & Anne E. Galer 9-19-1855
  Alice & Wm. Chambers 10-5-1870 (Gordon)
  Benjamin & Mary Foard 7-17-1784
  Eliza E. A. W. & James Burnell 6-14-1839
  Francis A. & Eliza A. E. M. Mangers 1-1-1831
  Francis A. & Mary W. Robinson 2-2-1870 (Marbury)
  Frances M. & George Jones 6-17-1884 (Rev. Mr. Brooks)
  Harrison Clay & Mary Edwina Wyvill 1-18-1868 (Fowler)
  Henrietta & Cornelius F. Miller 6-24-1855
  John & Susan Higdon 8-24-1820
  John D. & Amelia Hodgkin 9-14-1816
  John Mark & Sophia Ward 1-25-1825
  John W. & Henrietta Palmer 7-25-1831
  Joseph S. & Catharine E. Bunnell 2-20-1882 (Rev. Dr. Lewin)
  Mary & Scott Wood 1-31-1880 (Stanley)
  Mary Ann & John Turner 5-7-1829
  Mary Frances & Bachus Lee Vernon 5-10-1881 (Rev. Mr. Gordon)
  Samuel & Julia Ann Knott 4-14-1827
  Sophia & John Mark Ward 1-25-1825
  Stephen B. & Milly Ann Wilkinson 12-23-1813
  Stephen B. & Jane E. Berry 4-9-1834
  William & Mary White 9-3-1804
WARE, John E. & Mildred D. Adams 4-8-1868 (Smith)
  Sarah & Charles Gray 12-3-1778
WARFIELD, Eliz? & Joseph Wells 11-22-1781
  John & Ann Carrick 12-19-1784
  Louisa Victoria & Richard Snowden 5-16-1818
  Margaret Ann & William Smith 4-4-1844
WARING, Alice M. & George C. Merrick 1-24-1867 Age 26 (Young)
  Amanda A. & Richard B. Perrie 4-27-1863
  Ann & Jesse Wharton 4-6-1779
  Ann & Thomas T. Hilleary 1-13-1834
  Catharine & Edward Gantt Waring 9-8-1808
  Catherine H. & Thomas F. Bowie 11-18-1830
  Easter & Benjamin Prather 4-3-1804
  Edward Gantt & Catharine Waring 9-8-1808
  Eleanor & Henry Brooke 10-8-1798
  Eleanor & Clement Baden 8-30-1821
  Eleanor & William Cooksey 1-10-1826
  Eleanor H. & John Brookes 12-21-1841
  Eliza & John Read Magruder 4-1-1820
  Eliz? & Bernard Oneel 1-5-1782
  Elizabeth & Joshua Beall 2-3-1787
  Elizabeth L. & Richard W. W. Bowie 7-23-1852
  Elizabeth M. & Richard Duckett 6-2-1856
  Elizabeth Mary & William Hall 3-13-1826
  Francis & Elizabeth Turner 2-8-1814
  Grace H. C. & Richard H. Clagett 11-15-1837
  Henrietta M. & Horatio C. Scott 4-21-1834
  Henrietta P. & Benjamin Oden Jun? 11-12-1822
  Henry & Sarah Contee Harrison 6-22-1802
  James & Elizabeth Hilleary 1-4-1787
  James M. & Mary E. Sasscer 12-16-1839
  Jane & Walter Brooke Beall 5-1-1794
  John & Jane B. Magruder 2-17-1820

WARING, John Jun. & Elizabeth Margaret Bowie 12-30-1800
  John L. & Violetta Turton 8-31-1838
  John L. & Hester Bell Hunter 5-21-1878 (Hooman)
  Julia V. & Robert Bowie of Walter 5-17-1872
  Marcus S. & Mary Holliday 1-9-1794
  Margaret R. & James Jones Jun$\underline{r}$ 11-15-1852
  Margery & Thomas Crimpton 1-28-1779
  Marsham & Violetta Lansdale Belt 12-11-1824
  Mary & Spencer Mitchell 12-15-1803
  Mary Ann & Edw$\underline{d}$ Loyd Penn 1-7-1822
  Priscilla & John Gantt 4-20-1808
  Rebecca A. & William Edmonds 12-28-1832
  Richard M. & Martha Ann Harvey 11-1-1816
  Sally B. & Caleb C. Magruder 6-3-1847
  Sarah A. & Zadock Talbert 5-18-1837
  Susan & Mordecai Plummer 12-20-1842
  Thomas & Margaret Berry 3-21-1795
  William W. & Ida Julia Brooke 6-8-1871 (McDonald)
WARMAN, Benj$\underline{n}$ & Easter Perry 3-20-1779
  Edmund & Elizabeth Smith 9-22-1788
  Francis Hanstep & Stephen Watkins 5-18-1784
WARNER, Henry & Elizabeth Farr 12-29-1794
  Maria & John Die 11-22-1842
  Mary & Samuel Perkins 2-11-1797
  Mary E. & John R. Walker 1-13-1840
  Overton & Eliza Moore 3-24-1813
  Susan & William N. Boteler 12-16-1841
WARREN, Charles & Alice Waters 12-26-1877 (Wheeler)
  Lizzie & William Smith 2-6-1868 (Fr. Call)
  Patsy & Leonard Wheeler 12-7-1797
WARRENSFORD, Joseph & Sarah McCartey 12-20-1800
WASHINGTON, Charles H. & Sophia Griffin Towles 12-20-1873
  James & Ellen Hager 2-19-1870 (Dwyer)
  Mary & Wm. Henry Dyer 7-3-1866 (Hicks)
  Nathaniel & Margaret Hawkins 11-24-1790
  Thomas & Mary Young 9-19-1874 (Dwyer)
  Walter & Mary Shorter col$\underline{d}$ 5-6-1869 (Maher)
WATERS, Alice & Charles Warren 12-26-1877 (Wheeler)
  Ann & Moses Manger 10-22-1814
  Anne Maria & Philip Plummer 5-6-1823
  Arriana & Philemon Jones 11-25-1816
  Casandra & Thomas Bassford 4-2-1784
  Christopher & Elizabeth Ross 12-23-1865
  Eliz$\underline{a}$ & John Mills 1-18-1782
  Elizabeth & Zachariah Mills 12-21-1787
  Elkanah N. & Mary J. Brooks 11-3-1876 (Williams)
  Flavilla & Charles Duvall 12-20-1808
  Franklin & Rachael Franklin 4-30-1833
  George & Susan Brown 10-5-1872
  George H. & Julia Ann Cooksey 9-13-1831
  George W. & Laura Estelle Rawlings 2-20-1882 (Rev. Mr. Townshend)
  Harriot & Henry T. Rawlings 4-8-1817
  Henry & Mary Waters 1-30-1783
  Henry C. & Mary Watson 9-4-1816
  Jacob Franklin & Martha Hall Mullikin 2-12-1798

WATERS, Jane & Joseph Owens 2-19-1787
Jemima & Peter Jenings 1-15-1794
John & Catharine S. McKay 9-29-1808
John B. of Charles County & Martha E. Watson 11-7-1866 Age 25, widower, farmer, m. 11-8-1866 by Alex M. Marbury Presbyter P. E. Church
Joseph & Eliz^{a} Mier 8-25-1779
Joseph R. & Ellen S. Davis 2-13-1870 (Leneghan)
Lucy & Richard W. Watson 9-12-1816
Mabel & William C. Anderson 10-7-1835
Margaret & Leonard H. Early 8-7-1816
Margaret & Samuel Ratcliff 2-5-1823
Mary & Thos Whitehead 12-4-1779
Mary & Henry Waters 1-30-1783
Mary & Samuel Franklin 1-17-1807
Mary L. & Joshu S. 1-19-1846
Mima & John True 1-9-1797
Nancy & Henry Johnson col^{d} 2-13-1858
Nathan of Henry & Jane W. Marriott 6-26-1838
Rachael Ann & Lloyd Ridgeley 2-15-1833
Rachel Ann & Frederick Greenleaf 5-9-1873 (Dwyer)
Richard & Letty Hyde 3-10-1810
Richard & Susanna Rawlings 1-15-1824
Richard & Cassie Franklin 4-15-1876 (Chaney)
Robert & Caroline Butler 11-30-1868 (Lenaghan)
Stephen & Jane Duckett 3-25-1794
Susan R. & Thomas R. Brookes 12-7-1844
Susanna & Samuel Tyler 12-25-1783
Thomas Jones & Allice Jacob 7-14-1787
William & Vendalia Adams 2-6-1872 (Watson)
William & Esther Franklin, both of A. A. Co. col^{d} 1-31-1881 (Rev. Mr. Chaney)
WATHEN, Catherine & Joseph Edelen 4-4-1786
WATKINS, Charles T. & Elizabeth White 10-1-1878 (Cotton)
Elizabeth & William Stone 12-20-1794
Elizabeth & Charles Drury Hodges 2-3-1798
Gassaway & Mary Loflin 4-17-1784
Louis J. & Cornelia Hodges (white) 12-11-1879 (Rev^{d} Mr. Hodges)
Lucy B. & Thomas Pindall 2-13-1817
Maria & Joseph Stewart 9-1-1820
Nancy & Theodore Sherly 3-28-1797
Peggy & Joseph Wells 2-1-1787
Philip & Tillie Brown 11-18-1884 (Rev. Mr. Howard)
Sophia & Overton Ridgeway 8-20-1827
Stephen & Francis Hanstep Warman 5-18-1784
Thomas & Lucy Belt 12-6-1779
Thomas & Ann Wheeler 10-18-1825
Thos Junr & Eliz^{a} Sprigg 1-17-1778
William L. & Jane E. Turner 9-2-1878 (Butler)
WATSON, Alexander & Eliz^{a} Eastwood 1-9-1796
Ann & Thomas Vaughan 11-6-1794
Ann & Samuel Taylor Wilson 6-20-1795
Ann & John Cracroft 1-11-1808
Ann & Alexander Smith 1-18-1817
Ann & Walter Linch 12-27-1817
Annie F. & James T. D. Young 12-12-1870 (Linthicum)

WATSON, Ann Maria & Thomas Segar 1-24-1855
  Benjamin & Susannah Cage 2-6-1809
  Benjamin & Juliet Beaven 2-3-1819
  Benjamin J. & Martha L. Naylor 1-22-1868 (Smith)
  Benjamin T. & Maria Dorney 9-24-1832
  Caroline & John Hazzard 12-24-1850
  Charles J. & Mary A. Brown 3-15-1865
  Chloe & Charles Henry Butler 1-11-1868 (Greenleaf)
  Cornelius & Susannah Lamar 12-28-1791
  Cornelius & Elizabeth Davis 3-19-1807
  Eli J. & Mary M. Truman 11-22-1873 (Townshend)
  Eliz? & Josephus Adams 10-24-1777
  Elizabeth & Thomas Power 7-1-1795
  Elizabeth & John Wynn 9-1-1801
  Elizabeth & Hezekiah Watson 2-16-1816
  Fielder & Virlinda Brent 2-28-1817
  Fielder & Martha Naylor 6-18-1831
  Frederick & Mary Johnson 12-26-1885 (Rev. Mr. Brooke)
  George & Milly Jones 3-31-1866 (Greenleaf)
  George W. & Mary Cornelia Watson 2-4-1864
  Hezekiah & Elizabeth Ann Smith 8-15-1811
  Hezekiah & Elizabeth Watson 2-16-1816
  Isaac & Mary Mayhew 3-21-1786
  James & Sarah Watson 1-17-1780
  James & Mary Beavin 12-25-1799
  James & Elizabeth Demar 9-15-1815
  James & Mary Stallings 4-12-1816
  James & Nancy Naylor 12-27-1830
  James & Martha Hunt 3-12-1833
  James N. & Catharine A. Richardson 12-20-1855
  James N. & Sarah Ann R. Edelen 8-1-1860
  Jane & James Leach 1-13-1790
  Jane & James Lynch 11-24-1832
  John & Susannah King 2-28-1789
  John & Susannah Wilson 4-24-1819
  John & Mary E. Taylor 6-29-1876
  John F. & Mary Cross 4-8-1834
  Joshua & Elizabeth A. Perrie 2-5-1818
  Joshua & Ann Kidwell 2-8-1834
  Josiah W. & Sophia Pierce 3-1-1812
  Josias R. M. & Agnes E. Moran 12-4-1883
  Julia & Mordecai L. Boswell 12-22-1879 (white) (Rev. Cross)
  Lemuel & Ann Smith 10-17-1851
  Leonard & Sarah Cooksey 1-7-1792
  Luther E. & Mary F. Ball 8-19-1881
  Margaret Alice & Louis H. Jett 12-28-1870
  Margaret V. & Fielder W. Greer Age 20, housekeeper 10-1-1865
  Martha & William Thompson 2-10-1876 (Mayberry)
  Martha E. & John B. Waters Age 20, lic. 11-7-1866 m. 11-8-1866
  Martha R. & John W. Richardson 12-31-1856
  Mary & Francis Lamar 2-1-1808
  Mary & Henry C. Waters 9-4-1816
  Mary A. & Daniel Gibbons 4-6-1844
  Mary Ann & Alexander Gibson 1-31-1824

WATSON, Margaret Ann & John Fielder Fletcher col? 9-20-1869 (Langford)
  Mary Ann & Joseph Cross 12-23-1834
  Mary Cornelia & George W. Watson 2-4-1864
  Mary E. & George B. Hamilton 7-24-1869 (Marbury)
  Mary E. & William Z. Greer 8-27-1877 (Mercer)
  Mary Jane & Joshua J. Cooksey 4-15-1859
  Matilda Ann & Thomas Henry Stodderd 2-9-1872 (Evans)
  Nathan & Elizabeth Cross 4-6-1844
  Oza & Eliza Naylor 11-25-1826
  Philip Cooksey & Margaret Perrie Cooksey 12-12-1817
  Philip C. & Elizabeth Darnall 1-3-1820
  Priscilla & John M. Smith 6-8-1819
  Rebecca & John S. Linch 1-5-1782
  Rebecca & William Scrivener 12-7-1802
  Rich? & Ann Eustatia Steuart 2-19-1781
  Richard W. & Lucy Waters 9-12-1816
  Robert & Sarah Mitchell 3-25-1815
  Sarah & James Watson 1-17-1780
  Sarah & Jonathan Davis 12-26-1787
  Sarah & Benjamin Cooksey 2-23-1827
  Sarah & James Richardson 11-3-1848
  Sarah B. & John R. Richardson 1-2-1861
  Susan & James Beavin 12-22-1837
  Susan Ann & Wm. Henry Harrison 6-3-1872 (Marbury)
  Susanna & Elijah Ellis 12-27-1779
  Susanna & Leonard King 11-15-1780
  Susannah & Edward Hagan 4-22-1816
  Theodore W. & Elizabeth A. Cage 6-25-1879 (Perry)
  Thomas & Catherine Nutwell 2-11-1784
  Thomas & Jane Galaway col? 1-31-1870 (Langford)
  Thos. J. & Essie L. Lusby 2-17-1879
  Verlinda Watson & John Rawlings 4-12-1792
  Vidie E. & John W. Hodges 1-1-1883
  Walter & Rachel Stone 10-18-1779
  Walter & Ann Naylor 12-23-1783
  William & Elizabeth Right 7-26-1784
  William & Rebecca Cheney 12-19-1793
  William & Mary Perry Smith 1-29-1806
  William & Annie Bingham 10-9-1869 (Langford)
  William A. & Teresa Ann Gates 3-13-1833
  William C. & Mary Anne Gibbons 1-9-1820
  William F. & Sarah F. Webster 5-8-1871 (Lenaghan)
  William T. & Sarah E. Young 10-14-1844
  William Theodore & Elizabeth Ann Cross 11-10-1862
WATT, Hugh & Mary L. Harvey 1-8-1879 (Stanley)
  Thomas & Susannah Hellen 12-5-1791
WATTS James, Age 31 years, born in England & Mary Jane Anderson of
    Lauranceville, New Jersey, aged 28 years 2-16-1881 (Rev. James
    Lasey) of Bladensburgh
  Martha & William Berry 4-7-1792
WAUGH, John & Mary Masters 11-2-1793
  Warren & Susan Brown 1-7-1845
WAYSON, Virginia & John W. Armiger 10-20-1879
WEAR, James & Sarah Smith 7-19-1777

WEATHERS, Vidie & David Williams 7-31-1869 (Lankford)
WEAVER, Anamina & Richard King 2-27-1795
  Mary & Christian Wirt 9-3-1792
  Samuel T. & Emma A. Aman 7-17-1883
  Sarah & Isaac King 3-16-1799
  Thomas & Alice Ann Evans 12-24-1870 (Gordon)
  William & Rebecca Roberts 8-16-1877 (Butler)
WEBB, Ann & Levi Young 2-18-1836
  Aquilla & Anna Brown 11-27-1802
  Bettie W. & Louis A. Griffith 10-8-1879
  Elizabeth & Thomas Shelton 8-6-1777
  Elizabeth & William Millard 6-22-1780
  James & Clarissa Harlowe Magruder 10-13-1806
  Margaret & Mareen Carrick 1-17-1795
  Martha & Samuel D. Beck 8-19-1793
  Samuel & Sarah Hardey 11-15-1803
  Sarah & Abraham Gardiner 4-5-1783
  Sarah & Thomas Bryan 12-15-1807
WEBSTER, Catherine & William Downing 1-12-1847
  Charlotte & Charles W. Sawyer 6-22-1816
  Christian & Thomas Baldwin 7-23-1790
  Christianna & Richard Knott 7-12-1840
  Daniel E. & Emma A. Adams 6-3-1869 (Fowler)
  Elizabeth & Butler D. Marlowe 8-30-1796
  Elizabeth & Robert Brown 10-31-1808
  Elizabeth & Joseph Downing 12-26-1815
  Elizabeth & Archibald Jenkins 6-21-1821
  Elizabeth & Thomas Mudd 1-4-1841
  Emma Ida & Joseph Brown 8-15-1882 (Rev. Mr. W. K. Boyle)
  Felly & Judson Sweeny 11-15-1817
  George & Hetty Moreland 6-29-1818
  George & Jane Mudd 12-26-1840
  Harriet B. & Samuel N. Smith 12-4-1843
  Henrietta & George W. Hyde 1-27-1823
  James & Sarah Adams 3-3-1819
  James & Sarah Edelen 11-19-1821
  John & Margaret Kidwell 12-26-1784
  John P. & Liliah R. Kirby 9-29-1885 (Rev. Mr. Jyland)
  John W. & Mary R. Munroe 1-16-1856
  Louisa & Marsham Moore 12-11-1848
  Margaret C. & William T. Digges 6-16-1858
  Mary & Thomas Ryley 11-5-1811
  Mary & Saml Garner 12-27-1824
  Mary A. & John Piles 1-17-1853
  Mary Ann & John Wrightt 2-25-1791
  Mary Ann & Theodore Mead 5-29-1815
  Mary Ann & Benj. J. Baden 2-6-1844
  Mary E. & James W. Moreland 3-26-1862
  Milly & Isaac Beers 12-21-1818
  Minerva & Edward Richards 12-28-1850
  Permelia & Richard A. Semmes 8-19-1822
  Philip & Linny Wright 10-4-1802
  Philip Lewin & Elizabeth Beane 5-20-1793
  Sarah & George Hide 12-16-1783
  Sarah F. & William F. Watson 5-8-1871 (Lenaghan)

WEBSTER, Thomas & Sarah Barrott 2-11-1805
  William & Hetta Wade 8-13-1792
  William & Ann Wrightt 2-1-1793
  William & Ann Tracey 4-8-1831
  Zachariah & Amelia Dixon 1-5-1832
  Zephaniah & Eleanor Weedon 8-31-1801
WEDDERAL, John & Elizabeth Jones 4-4-1786
WEDDING, Caleb & Ann Maria Padgett 10-26-1868 (Smith)
  Eliza Jane & Zachariah Carrick 2-2-1859
WEDGE, Elijah & Maria McAttee 8-24-1824
  George Washington & Mary Elizabeth Sharp 2-1-1872 (Evans)
  William & Ann Tippett 8-2-1822
WEEDEN, Nathaniel & Mary Cater 12-16-1794
  Nathaniel & Sarah Jones 2-8-1821
  Rebecca & Philip Hopkins 11-3-1807
WEEDER, Catherine & John Bignell 8-21-1786
WEEDING, Mary Elizabeth & Elijah Wilson 2-1-1845
WEEDON, Eleanor & Zephaniah Webster 8-31-1801
  Henry & Sarah Young 9-23-1797
WEEKS, Elizabeth E. & John Straining 11-10-1880 (Laney)
WEEMS, Amelia Margaret & Walter Bowie 11-24-1812
  Elizabeth J. & Littleton T. Adams 9-3-1834
  James Wᵐ Lock & Mary Hall 5-6-1786
  John & Annie Swain 1-8-1883 (Rev. Mr. Gordon)
  John C. & Rebecca McPherson 5-27-1874
  Margaret H. & George French 11-26-1807
  Martha & Frederick Dockett colᵈ 5-11-1869 (Langford)
  Mary & Robert Crawford 2-22-1872 (Gordon)
  Mary M. & John B. Mulliken 6-2-1812
  Nathaniel C. & Eliza Ann Mullikin 12-30-1834
  Violetta & Joseph H. Willson 10-18-1825
  Wilhelmina & Henry Gantt 3-3-1798
  William L. & Elizabeth T. Burch 8-1-1814
  William L. & Mary Hatton 11-10-1832
WEIGHT, Margery & Edwᵈ Stonestreet 5-10-1780
WEIGHTMAN, John & Sidney Lyles 5-25-1816
  Sydney & Edward H. Edelen 7-11-1829
WEIKIN, Nathaniel & Catherine Ogden 9-24-1788
WELCH, Darcus & Samuel Jones 11-4-1788
  Eleanor & William Jones 1-2-1815
  Elizabeth & William Williams 4-4-1797
  Richard & Susannah Simmons 6-5-1793
WELDMAN, Cornelius G. & Elizabeth E. Mudd 11-11-1837
WELDON, John & Mintie Jackson 5-14-1875 (Cotton)
WELLEN, William & Mary Darcy 1-30-1793
WELLFORD, Bettie Howe & Dr. John Peach 1-26-1870 (Dr. Harper)
  F. L. & Bessie J. Clarke 1-8-1885 (Father Cotton)
  Horace & Vinnie Tidings 1-16-1877 (McDonald)
WELLING, Elizabeth & Zachariah Mangun 1-21-1818
WELLINS, Elenor & Samuel Duckett 2-18-1820
WELLS, Alice Ann & Richard T. Tydings 3-10-1858
  Benjamin & Alice Green 12-26-1877 (Homan)
  Dr. Chˢ A. & Mary L. Hyatt 5-11-1863
  Dennis & Ann Sophia Clarke 1-31-1833
  Edmund & Georgeanna Loveless 4-2-1875 (Welch)

WELLS, Eleanor & Zadock Wells 11-13-1794
   Ellen & James Clarke 4-18-1837
   Elizabeth & Cornelius Oliver 1-9-1784
   Elizabeth & Asa Anderson 1-3-1822
   Elizabeth Ann & Richard H. Hook 6-2-1868 (Gordon)
   George & Elizth Kingsbury 12-30-1828
   Horace & Caroline Smith 1-21-1858
   James & Mary Burrell 2-6-1795
   James & Sarah A. Tayman 1-30-1845
   James H. & Margery Ann Ryon 9-13-1849
   James N. & Susan E. Crandell 9-30-1867
   Jennie & Otho Green 12-16-1878 (Hooman)
   Jeremiah & Mary Becket 12-20-1819
   Jeremiah & Ann Mangunn 12-13-1836
   Joanna & William H. Clarke 2-11-1863
   John & Elizabeth Beall 1-18-1824
   John & Verlinda Hilleary 4-27-1831
   Joseph & Eliz^{a} Warfield 11-22-1781
   Joseph & Peggy Watkins 2-1-1787
   Julia A. & Richard Loveless 2-16-1881 (Rev. Dr. Gordon)
   Laura E. & William H. Talbert 12-29-1884 (Rev. Father Cunane)
   Lloyd & Mary A. Miller 6-27-1842
   Lloyd T. & Mrs. Catherine Young 1-5-1865
   Lucy & Fielder Calvert 11-16-1876 (Gordon)
   Maggie F. & Elisha J. Loveless 1-18-1884 (Father Cunane)
   Margaret & David Jones 11-4-1797
   Margaret & Edward Arnold 5-25-1854
   Margaret E. & John H. Smith 12-29-1858
   Martha & Thomas Drane 2-4-1786
   Martha Ann & Nelson T. Wall 4-19-1836
   Martin & Mary Robinson 2-26-1783
   Martin & Mary Fowler 1-5-1799
   Matilda & Henry Boswell 3-31-1834
   Mary & Theadore Mitchell 11-27-1777
   Mary Ann & George W. Shepherd 12-12-1832
   Nathan & Mary Askey 1-14-1785
   Nathan & Sophia Duley 11-12-1798
   Nathan & Sarah Clubb 11-2-1815
   Plummer & Elizabeth Gardiner 12-27-1859
   Plummer L. & Annie W. Peterson 6-25-1868 (Edwards)
   Rachel & Zachariah Mills 1-7-1811
   Rebecca & William Wells 12-22-1780
   Richard & Phoebe Deale 4-19-1830
   Richard & Catherine Grey 8-18-1885 (Rev. Mr. Major)
   Robert E. & Alice Elizabeth Taylor 6-16-1874
   Sallie E. & John H. Taylor 1-16-1883 (Rev. Father Cunnane)
   Samuel & Marth Olliver 8-10-1778
   Samuel O. & Mary E. Fowler 11-9-1878
   Sarah & Elisha Hardesty 8-21-1780
   Sarah & James Roberts 8-27-1806
   Sarah & Thomas Elliot 1-28-1812
   Sarah & Wm. Reynolds 12-19-1848
   Susanna & Richard Jacob 4-8-1778
   Susannah & Abiezer Plummer 11-3-1795
   Thomas & Sarah Wall 5-26-1787

WELLS, Tyler & Martha Wood 9-15-1884 (Rev. Mr. Butler)
  Verlinda A. & James Latimer 4-16-1811
  Virginia A. & James W. Middleton 8-22-1859
  Walter & Eleanor Ridgeway 1-25-1800
  Walter H. & Margaret M. Sheriff 6-15-1868 (Stanley)
  William & Rebecca Wells 12-22-1780
  William & Eleanor Cheney 3-30-1793
  William of George & Jemima Brashears 10-2-1816
  William & Isabella Nicholson 6-13-1829
  Zadock & Eleanor Wells 11-13-1794
WELSH, Deborah & Nathan Edmonston 12-19-1788
  Elizabeth & Joseph Prather 6-1-1781
  Samuel & Rachel Shipley 2-29-1804
WENN, Priscilla & James Butler 2-22-1867 (Hicks)
WENTFIELD, Mary Ann & Thomas Kidwell 3-23-1781
WESCOTT, Henry & Laura Jane Wallis 10-5-1861
WEST, Alfred & Dorinda Jackson col^d 10-19-1867 (Kershaw)
  Annie E. & J. W. T. Gardiner, 1st U.S. Dragoons 7-3-1854
  Arthur & Elizabeth King col^d 7-27-1867 (Greenleaf)
  Arthur Pen & Ellen Oden 5-29-1821
  Bernard & Alice Scott 5-25-1872 (Evans)
  Catherine & James Johnson 12-5-1782
  Catharine & William Chase 9-14-1868 (Fr. Lilly)
  Charles H. L. & Eliza Jane Wakefield 10-24-1827
  Clement & Catherine Lanzel col^d 4-27-1867 (Fr. Call)
  Clement & Mary Kent col^d 8-9-1867 (Call)
  Eleanor & James Harrison 7-8-1815
  Elizabeth H. & Jonathan L. Woart 7-31-1832
  Francis & Sarah Blair 5-19-1873 (Towles)
  Frederick & Susan Sprigg 5-2-1867
  George (mulatto) & Susan Pinkney 1-1-1867 married 1-22-1867 at parson-
    age St. Thomas, S. R. Gordon, min. Pr. E. Ch. Age 28, laborer
  Geo. Henry Porter & Mary Eliza Swann 11-21-1870 (McCauly)
  Harriet & Columbus Sprigg 9-6-1876 (Green)
  Harriet B. & Benjamin Oden 8-21-1813
  Henrietta & Lloyd Brown col^d 10-21-1865 (Father Call)
  James & Georgie Lee 9-4-1869 (McDonald)
  Josephine & Robert Henson 12-23-1874 (Mayberry)
  Liza & Richard H. Johnson 6-6-1867
  Mary & Lot Johnson 9-27-1866 Age 19, mulatto - servant m. 10-4-1866
  Mary & Henry Brown 2-14-1874
  Mary & John Griffith 12-27-1884 (Rev. Mr. Brooke)
  Mary & Saulsbury Brooks 4-3-1885 (Father Cotton)
  Mary L. & Dr. Jno B. Hereford 9-12-1848
  Morris & Eliza Larkins 12-21-1875 (Denny)
  Rachel Sophia & Benjn Oden 1-25-1791
  Richard & Hanna Boothe 9-4-1869 (McDonald)
  Robert & Jennie Galloway 6-19-1884 (Rev. Thos H. Brooks)
  Susan & William Clark 10-12-1867 col^d
  Thomas & Caroline Tilghman 12-12-1868 (Edelin)
  Virginia & George Driver 10-30-1872
  William & Lizzie Gantt 5-21-1869 (Father Maher)
WESTERFIELD, Agnes V. & Thomas E. Swaggert 2-28-1869
  Benj^a & Julia Ann Gray 3-27-1847
WETHERS, Violetta & William Lee 6-9-1877 (Carroll)

WHARTON, Jesse & Ann Waring 4-6-1779
WHEAT, Ann & Horatio Moore 8-10-1803
  Elizabeth & Robert Anderson Jones 4-26-1803
  Francis & Sarah Upton 11-1-1780
  Jesse & Sarah Soper 12-2-1795
  John & Mary Noland 12-3-1801
  Jonathan & Ruthy Scearce 2-9-1805
  Joseph & Rachel Brian 12-12-1791
  Linney & John Havener 1-19-1788
  Mary & Thomas B. Moreland 10-17-1799
  Noah & Eleanor Crook 9-24-1804
  Priscilla & Benjamin Phelps 12-10-1795
  Rezin & Letta Wilson 11-30-1802
  Zachariah & Priscilla Reynolds 2-4-1782
WHEATLEY, Henry A. C. & E. Anna Clements 4-1-1861
  Susan & John Crockett 6-6-1848
WHEATLY, Ann & George Wheatly 10-4-1798
  Elizabeth Sarah & Zachariah Thomas 3-5-1801
  George & Ann Wheatly 10-4-1798
  Henry & Susan Gardiner 2-20-1837
WHEELER, Acquila & Elizabeth Young 2-26-1778
  Ann & Hilliary Tilghman 1-9-1782
  Ann & Thomas Watkins 10-18-1825
  Edward & Sarah Hilleary 12-21-1785
  Eleonar & Samuel Wheeler 10-27-1780
  Eliza B. & William H. Custis 4-27-1829
  Ignatius & Rachel Newton 1-28-1794
  Ignatius & Margaret S. Magruder 3-18-1808
  Jacob & Sarah Austin 2-10-1786
  Jacob & Susannah Igleheart 6-2-1787
  Jane & Thomas Hilleary 12-6-1809
  Jemima & Thomas Bird 12-14-1780
  John & Letitia Brown 12-11-1792
  Joseph & Ann Brooke 4-23-1785
  Leonard & Patsy Warren 12-7-1797
  Nelly & Joseph Powell 11-28-1804
  Samuel & Eleonar Wheeler 10-27-1780
  Samuel & Ann Hilleary 12-4-1782
  Sarah & Nathaniel Wright 11-2-1813
  Susannah & John Farrall 1-13-1786
  Susannah & William Redmiles Jr. 10-12-1805
  Woodbury & Clara Bayne 10-26-1869 (Martin)
WHETTERS, Eva Lizzie & Edward P. Brooks 10-10-1877
WHIPS, Willemina & Matthew Hardesty 8-8-1826
WHITAKER, Ann Eleanor & Clement Brooke 4-2-1801
  Ellen & James Harper 11-21-1826
  Elizabeth & Calvert Williams 5-16-1794
  Elizabeth & Isaac Lansdale 6-19-1794
  George Washington & Nancy Brown 6-16-1801
WHITE, Adelaide V. & William H. King 1-8-1876
  Allen & Mildred Burgess 7-9-1785
  Ann & Philip Tayman 8-12-1857
  Annie & Antony Brown 5-30-1872 (McDonald)
  Annie & Jos. Davis 3-18-1875
  Ariana & Hilleary Piles 1-7-1795

WHITE, Basil & Sarah Young 6-2-1827
  Charles & Susanna Smith 7-30-1777
  Eliza Jane & George W. Tenley 12-24-1884 (Rev. Mr. Brashaw)
  Eliz^a & Fred^k Miles 12-31-1781
  Elizabeth & Thomas Hodges 10-26-1797
  Elizabeth & Charles T. Watkins 10-1-1878 (Cotton)
  Elizabeth J. & John W. Goddard 12-22-1858
  Emily & James Burgess 2-2-1853
  George B. & Lucy H. Turner 11-21-1868 (Boyer)
  Henry & Sophia M. Osbourn 10-4-1852
  Henry & Mary S. Gates 4-26-1862
  James & Mary Eleanor Burgess 12-29-1856
  James & Rebecca Johnson 6-23-1871 (Budd)
  James L. of Washington City, D. C. & Fannie E. Gibson of Prince George
    Co. 10-10-1866 Age 50-widower, m. 10-16-1866 St. Luke's, Bladensburg
    Jno. Collins McCabe, Presbyter P. E. Ch.
  James P. & Ann Craegg 1-26-1857
  Jane & Thomas Harrison 12-4-1779
  Jesse & Sarah Hooper 12-15-1803
  John & Ursula Smith 8-20-1780
  John & Mary Brown 12-20-1780
  John & Susan Beckett 12-23-1822
  John & Jane Johnson col^d 4-5-1882 (Rev. Wm. Van Arnsdale)
  John M. & Mrs. Nancy Danforth 10-30-1797
  Jonathan & Sarah Tarman 3-27-1785
  Martha Ann & Addison Littleford 12-30-1854
  Mary & William Mitchell 12-10-1792
  Mary & William Ward 9-3-1804
  Mary & Simon Owings 4-27-1886 (Rev. Father Cotton)
  Mary A. & Thaddeus A. Richardson 2-5-1878 (Kershaw)
  Mary Ann & Joshua Selvin 11-29-1821
  Matilda & Theodore Padgett 7-23-1807
  Osborn & Rebecca Sansberrie 12-24-1792
  Osborn & Letty Sweeny 1-16-1803
  Richard & Mary Branham 11-14-1798
  Samuel B. & Lethea Beall 2-21-1781
  Sarah & John Connell 12-7-1801
  Sarah & Vin son King 11-1-1828
  Sophia & Joseph F. Willett 2-6-1879 (Lewin)
  Tabitha & Nicholas Farr 2-13-1805
  Thomas & Rachel Clagett 12-26-1811
  Thomas & Emeline Fazier 3-30-1853
  Thomas O. & Elizabeth Cator 8-4-1857
  Walter & Sarah Davis 1-14-1789
  William & Rebecca Blanford 10-11-1783
  W^m. H. & Mary M. Cooksey 1-9-1867 (Smith)
  Wm. Q. & Mary Ellen Osbourn 2-24-1846
WHITEHEAD, Thos & Mary Waters 12-4-1779
  William & Sarah McDonald 6-11-1874
WHITEMORE, Elizabeth & Thomas Neal 8-7-1779
  Frances & James E. Bowie 12-21-1860
WHITEN, Rachel & Richd Hunter 1-19-1782
  William & Elizabeth Martin 9-14-1841
WHITESIDE, Sarah W. of P. G. Co. & Frank Stilson of Wash. D. C. 11-22-1880

WHITING, Rebecca & John Simpson 9-9-1784
  William T. & Mary C. Turner 3-23-1880 (Stanley)
WHITMAN, William & Mary E. Lusby 12-14-1857
WHITMORE, Humphrey & Mary Walker 11-30-1793
  Ida Eugenia & John A. Thorn 1-12-1878 (Dorsey)
  James A. & Domia A. S. Shreeve 6-9-1863
  Laura C. & Julian A. Martin 5-22-1884 (Rev. Mr. Highland)
  Mary & John Nothey 9-5-1855
  Susannah E. & John H. Piles 1-20-1864
WHITNEY, Ann & Philip Thompson 5-30-1796
  Gilbert & Ann Malony 11-21-1794
  Matilda J. & Thomas A. Austin 6-6-1811
WHITTELSEY, F. W. & Sarah E. Duvall 9-25-1862
WHITTINGTON, Ann & Jerry Smith 5-23-1874
  Ann M. & John E. Isaacs 1-10-1881 (Rev. James T. Chaney)
  Isabella & William Harwood 12-18-1876
  Lidia & John Smith 5-25-1828
  ....& Maria Hepburn colored, both of A. A. Co. 11-26-1880
  Matilda & George Mangun 10-16-1838
  Medora & Samuel Chaney 3-24-1880 (Chaney)
WHYTE, Ann & Thos Harwood 10-29-1778
WICKERSHAM, Cadwalader & Catharine E. Kerbey 10-25-1872
WICKHAM, Oliver S. & Clementine Harvey 12-22-1883 (Rev. Mr. Stanley)
  William & Mrs. Mary Duckett 6-15-1870 (Cotton)
WIG......, Elizabeth & James Low 7-26-1790
WIGFIELD, Mary & Eleazer Standage 12-23-1783
  Robert & Mary Darnall 6-29-1805
WIGHT, John & Rebecca Hennis 4-15-1786
WIGHTT, Ann & Wiseman Keadle 7-25-1787
WIGNALL, Sarah A. & Thomas H. Butler 12-24-1881 (Rev. Mr. Hyland)
WILBOURN, William T. & Ann Norton 3-11-1828
WILBURN, Barbara Ellen & Stephen A. Taylor 12-6-1860
  Robert & Priscilla Lowe 12-29-1798
  Sarah & Elijah Ryon 1-2-1798
  Theodore & Emily Deakins 11-19-1832
  William & Ruth Ann Ridgeway 12-15-1840
WILCOX, Charles G. & Anna Maria S. Forrest 10-4-1843
WILCOXEN, Nancy & John Soper 2-9-1802
WILCOXON Sarah & Judson Naylor 1-16-1815
  Elizabeth & Eleven Summers 12-30-1786
  Jesse & Sarah King 2-9-1802
  Levin & Mary Brashears 2-11-1780
  Margt & Thomas Hardy 2-9-1780
  Mary Ann & Levi Boteler 11-25-1820
  Norlinda & John Evans 12-19-1786
  Thos Jr. & Mary Hardey 4-23-1781
WILDMAN, James G. & Jennie P. Chesley 3-4-1871 (Fowler)
WILEY, Ann & Moses Dailey 10-7-1797
WILKERSON, Alexander & Elizabeth Ryon 1-4-1859
  Alexander & Leonara Ryon 1-13-1864
WILKINSON, John B. & Lucinda Jane Piles 12-22-1840
  Dr. Gilbert B. & Elizabeth West Hollyday 12-18-1871 (Gordon)
  Milly Ann & Stephen B. Ward 12-23-1813
WILKINS, Mary & John Lowry 4-10-1804
  Rebecca A. & Samuel Cooke 11-11-1839

WILKS, Lawrence & Phillis Johnson black 6-24-1880 (Father DeWolf)
WILLET, Richard Henry & Rachael Teresa Virginia Beall 10-9-1860
WILLETT, Amela & John Clerk 12-18-1788
  Christian & William Hutchinson 4-18-1780
  Christianna & Caleb Leach 4-1-1829
  Edward Jun? & Julianna Taylor 3-26-1807
  Edward Jr. & Sarah Harvey 9-14-1815
  Elizabeth & Stanislaus Howe 12-6-1797
  Joseph F. & Sophia White 2-6-1879 (Lewin)
  Margaret & George W. Dellaplane 12-28-1831
  Mary & Richard Simmons 3-7-1779
  Mary & William Childs 12-13-1781
  Mary & William Marlow 12-29-1786
  Mary Ann & William Hilleary 6-15-1826
  Ninian & Eleanor Ridgway 9-28-1803
  Ninian & Susanna Beall 11-5-1827
  Priscilla & Abraham Clarke 12-14-1786
  Rachel & Richard Price 12-17-1782
  Rachel & Ignatius Howe 11-27-1798
  Salome & John Ogden 11-2-1782
  Samuel & Ann Orme 6-27-1784
  Sarah & Tobias Duvall 2-5-1795
  Sarah & John Duckett 4-18-1816
  Susan & Howerton Cross 2-21-1931
  Susanna & Benj? Smith Bentening 5-15-1783
  Tabitha & Samuel Higgins 12-13-1799
  William & Ann Richards 10-24-1814
WILLIAMS, Abraham & Catharine Bradley 12-13-1794
  Alice & Benjamin H. Lambert 2-9-1874
  Ann & Robert Spiden 4-3-1797
  Arra Jane & Oliver Bence col? 10-16-1867 (Thompson)
  Barbara & Francis Magruder 12-23-1786
  Betsie & Thomas Williams col? 10-15-1868 (Fr. Begue)
  Calvert & Eleanor Oden 12-20-1792
  Calvert & Elizabeth Whitaker 5-16-1794
  Cave & John Jackson 2-1-1788
  Chloe Ann & Nace Tilghman 10-12-1877
  Colmore of Montgomery County & Marial H. Williams of P. G. County
    12-5-1818
  David & Vidie Weathers 7-31-1869
  Dennis M. & Margaret H. Hall 2-25-1823
  Dennis M. & Eliz.th T. Baden 7-8-1836
  Eleanor & Richard Turner 1-10-1791
  Eleanora & John L. Clarke 5-9-1832
  Eliza & Asa Anderson 2-3-1829
  Eliza T. & Washington Berry 6-17-1822
  Elizabeth & Jonathan Beale 5-6-1794
  Elizabeth & Isaac Ijams 8-4-1795
  Elizabeth & Beale Duvall 4-11-1806
  George F. & Irene Robertie McKee 11-20-1873 (Tennent)
  Henrietta & John H. Lawrence 6-3-1871
  Henry & Mary Abraham 4-7-1879
  Henry A. & Ellen Martin 9-12-1865 Age 32yr 10 mo. of Clarke Co. Va.
    farmer m. 9-28-1865 St. Barnabas Ch. by Henry B. Martin of P. E. Ch
    of Baltimore City

WILLIAMS, Hester W. & George H. Wilson 4-26-1832
  Humphrey & Sarah Beall 1-21-1794
  James & Susan Case 12-28-1840
  James M. & Jane P. Marbury 1-4-1858
  Jane & William Keech 9-6-1780
  John H. & Sarah A. Cross 1-6-1873 (Marbury)
  John W. & Eleanor Duvall of Samuel 2-15-1802
  Jnº F. & Ann Mudd 1-9-1782
  Lucy & George Clayton 12-30-1870 (Stanley)
  Margaret & Abraham Jones 1-12-1802
  Margaret & Aaron Addison 6-25-1865 colᵈ
  Margaret & Benjamin Howard 9-3-1873 (Dwyer)
  Margaret E. & John F. Davis 2-3-1882 (Rev. Mr. LaRoache)
  Maria & Arthur Snowden 5-18-1877
  Maria A. & Samuel E. Anderson 6-10-1846
  Marial H. of P.G. Co. & Colmore Williams of Mont. Co. 12-5-1818
  Mary & Thomas Berry 6-5-1815
  Mary C. & Joseph Isaac 2-26-1821
  Mary E. & John W. Smith 12-8-1845
  Mary E. & James T. Lindsey 2-20-1860
  Oden & Catherine Deal 12-13-1875
  Osborn & Elizabeth Magruder 10-15-1787
  Rachel & Philip Turner 9-14-1787
  Rebecca & Grafton Hall 11-12-1809
  Rebecca V. & Samuel Cissell 5-9-1817
  Rezin & Amelia Prout 12-18-1832
  Rezin & Hannah Johnson colᵈ 4-19-1867 (Stanley)
  Richard H. & Ann A. Biscoe 7-26-1830
  Ruth Ann & Erasmus Perry 5-7-1821
  Sallie & Henry Robinson 2-26-1870 (Maher)
  Sallie & Samuel Williams 10-19-1882
  Sally R. R. & Richard Price 4-2-1844
  Samuel & Eleanor Stephenson colᵈ 7-13-1867
  Samuel & Sallie Williams 10-19-1882
  Samuel T. & Carrie Rives 8-2-1858
  Sarah & George Douglass 8-15-1871 (McDonald)
  Sarah B. & Samuel Parker 4-22-1818
  Stephen & Harriet Digges 11-22-1867 (Fr. Call)
  Susan & Nace Boone colᵈ 7-12-1869 (Maher)
  Thomas & Bestsie Williams 10-15-1868 (Fr. Begue)
  Thomas & Henrietta Matthews 12-23-1871 (Wheeler)
  Thomas & Lydia Holland colᵈ 5-18-1882 (Rev. Mr. Stanley)
  Thomas & Jennie Freeland 12-27-1884 (Rev. Mr. Brooke)
  Thomas E. & Juliet M. Tolson 2-1-1870 (Martin)
  Thomas G. & Martha Jane Rollins 2-10-1858
  Verlinda & John Hilleary 2-22-1791
  Vina & Sylvester Gray 9-6-1879 (Lewin)
  Washington & Kate Harrison 5-19-1877 (Bond)
  William & Ruth Beck 12-11-1792
  William & Elizabeth Welch 4-4-1797
WILLIAMSON, Harriet A. E. & Wm. H. Boren 2-22-1864
  Nannie & A. M. Wilson 9-13-1875 (Ritter)
WILLICE, William & Ann Smith 2-14-1780
WILLIS, Edwin & Susanna Sanders 4-15-1867 (Lenahan)
WILLS, John & Margaret Fields 12-24-1788

WILLS, Mahala & Nathaniel Benton 6-8-1811
  Maria & Patrick Brown 1-9-1875 (Lenaghan)
  Mary J. & S. Allen Griffith 12-21-1870 (Gordon)
  Porter & Chloe Ann Ford 10-3-1885 (Rev. Mr. Wills)
WILLSON, David B. & Elizabeth A. Walls 12-8-1824
  Joseph H. & Violetta Weems 10-18-1825
  Lethea & Hickerson Mockbee 2-13-1822
  Leucinda & William Pinkney 1-9-1885
  Mary Susanna & Samuel P. Wailes 2-17-1827
WILSON, A. M. & Nannie Williamson 9-13-1875 (Ritter)
  Ann & Daniel Barnes 2-21-1783
  Ann & Richard Jones 12-10-1796
  Ann & Charles McNantz 8-19-1800
  Ann & Andrew Taylor 12-24-1814
  Ann & Benjamin Belt 1-25-1820
  Ann Dickson 11-19-1784 & Samuel Scott
  Anna & John Gordon 6-5-1797
  Ann E. & Fielder D. Greer 10-15-1850
  Aquila & Sarah Taylor 11-21-1791
  Aquila H. & Barbara A. Hutchinson 11-22-1853
  Barnabas & Elizabeth Maginnes 1-11-1786
  Basil & Ann Scott 8-9-1779
  Benjamin & Mildred Mary Lewis 5-4-1824
  Catherine & William Edelen 2-2-1843
  Christiana E. & James A. Sweeney Jr. 6-10-1880 (Fr. DeWolf)
  Christianna & William S. Ryon 12-7-1858
  Clement & Susannah Ceicel 9-5-1778
  Clour & John Smallwood 12-15-1787
  Cornelia & Overton C. Phillips 2-21-1827
  Cornelia & William Brown 1-1-1875 (Wells)
  Elijah & Mary Elizabeth Weeding 2-1-1845
  Elizabeth & Henry Thorn 5-29-1779
  Elizabeth & Isle of Wight 3-29-1783
  Elizabeth & George Jones 1-29-1788
  Elizabeth & Thomas Lee Mitchell 9-29-1792
  Elizabeth & Isaac Jones Naylor 12-28-1801
  Elizabeth & Levi Sheriff 5-15-1810
  Elizabeth & Benjamin Hewett 11-29-1810
  Elizabeth & William Pumphrey 3-11-1815
  Eveline & Samuel Phillips 5-8-1827
  George & Mary Bond Biscoe 3-3-1802
  George H. & Hester W. Williams 4-26-1832
  George W. & Mary Ann E. Lynch 12-26-1837
  Henry & Martha Fairall 12-5-1820
  Hilleary & Ann Hilleary 10-31-1814
  I. N. W. & Sarah A. Gibbons 2-5-1866 Age 30, farmer - m. 2-8-1866
    St. Peters Church P. G. Co. by Peter B. Lenaghan, Catholic Priest of
    Charles County
  James & Elizabeth Gibbons 3-16-1798
  James & Eleanor Mitchell 7-6-1811
  James B. & Suzannah Wilson 9-6-1817
  James W. L. & Emma Yost 10-25-1861
  Jane & Elias Hawkins 9-12-1873 (Cotton)
  Ja.^S C. & Mary A. Barnes 2-1-1782
  John & Elizabeth Gordon 2-11-1795

WILSON, John & Ann Ryon 9-18-1802
  John & Eliza Scott 12-27-1830
  John & Mary Lovelace 12-24-1836
  John E. & Amanda S. Duvall 10-19-1848
  John F. & Emma Tayman 1-13-1885 (Father Cunnane)
  John H. & Emma A. Mangum 12-19-1882 (Rev. Mr. Wolf)
  John S. & Annastatia D. Hallsell 3-12-1811
  Joseph & Ann S. Fergusson 8-29-1777
  Joseph & Sarah Wilson 1-8-1787
  Joseph & Ruth Ferguson 10-5-1793
  Joseph & Elizabeth Smith 3-17-1795
  Josiah & Elizabeth Burnes 4-1-1789
  Josiah & Sarah Perrie Wailes 4-10-1807
  Josiah & Margaret B. Walls 1-18-1817
  Josiah B. B. & Josephine M. Fowler 11-11-1878 (Quinn)
  Lancelot & Rachel Trunnell 2-14-1792
  Laura & John M. Mangun 9-15-1883
  Leonard D. & Eliza E. Curtin 12-24-1839
  Letta & Rezin Wheat 11-30-1802
  Lizzie & LouisCook 4-8-1871 (Gordon)
  Louisa & Samuel Turner 12-23-1842
  Lucy & James Simpson 12-10-1802
  Lucy & Joseph Peach 2-15-1808
  M. L. & Susan J. Darnall 4-26-1847
  M. Virginia & Joseph H. Coale 7-24-1877 (Kershaw)
  Margaret B. & James Naylor 3-29-1836
  Margaret J. & Thomas W. Beall 1-9-1818
  Margery & Joseph Jenkins 6-25-1780
  Margery & Richard Hill 6-21-1805
  Martha & John Lusbey 2-20-1778
  Martha E. & James H. Rawlings 12-6-1854
  Martha E. & Thomas N. Mudd 11-17-1875
  Mary & Edward Sout (prob. Suit) 7-12-1779
  Mary & Benjamin Naylor 12-14-1797
  Mary & John Duley 6-14-1800
  Mary & Joseph Hunt 12-26-1812
  Mary & Robt. Richards 2-14-1843
  Mary Ann & Humphrey Haistip 5-11-1830
  Mary C. & Charles Ash 10-25-1869 (Dr. Lowrey)
  Mazy Ann & Hugh Kiernan 12-27-1873
  Nathaniel & Martha Hanson 6-15-1779
  Norando & Eleanor Mangun 12-26-1785
  Pauline & John Freeman 6-30-1871 (Cotton)
  Philip & Matilda Jackson 1-18-1870 (Fr. Cotton)
  Priscilla & James Naylor 9-5-1797
  Priscilla E. & George Cator 12-28-1830
  Rebecca & Richard Gray 8-30-1778
  Rosa & Ignatius Nalley 1-26-1876 (Green)
  Samuel Taylor & Ann Watson 6-20-1795
  Samuel T. & Sarah Hagan 4-10-1805
  Sarah & Nehemiah Stone 3-3-1778
  Sarah & Mordicai Miles Mitchell 11-26-1779
  Sarah & Oliver Barne 2-8-1785
  Sarah & Joseph Wilson 1-8-1787
  Sarah A. & Richard T. Walker 9-23-1861

WILSON, Sophia & Benjamin Wailes 2-14-1816
  Susannah & Basil Talbott 7-5-1800
  Susannah & Samuel Burch 12-22-1809
  Susannah & John Watson 4-24-1819
  Suzannah & James B. Wilson 9-6-1817
  Thomas & Ann Beall 9-7-1783
  Thomas J. & Priscilla Brogden 3-3-1852
  Tyler & Emily Craufurd 1-28-1828
  William & Rebecca Fergusson 10-1-1777
  William & Virlinda Mason 1-10-1780
  William & Margaret Jones 11-7-1781
  William & Susannah Gibbons 5-5-1800
  William & Louisa Magruder 9-26-1833
  William B. & Maria C. Swaine 12-6-1858
  William B. & Alice M. Johnson 11-29-1871 (Bush)
  Wm. Benjamin & Georgianna H. Ryon 3-3-1863
  William H. & Christian M. Smallwood 4-18-1829
  William H. & Maggie A. Wood 1-14-1886 (Father Cunane)
  William Hall & Amelia Duvall 7-6-1802
  William J. & Margaret J. Tayman 12-6-1854
  William W. & Emma C. Magruder 12-6-1875
  Wm. Walter & Emma J. Gillott 11-9-1883 (Rev. M. Laroche)
WINCLAR, John C. & Marg^t Reiley 2-22-1784
WINDER, George & Charlotte Tayler 9-29-1802
WINDSOR, Benjamin & Christianna Peacock 12-23-1869 (Linthicum)
  Catharine & John Sturgest 8-9-1880 (Rev. Dr. Lavin)
  Elizabeth Eleanor & Rezin Harry Boteler 12-2-1844
  Elizabeth Margaret & J. W. Thomas 4-11-1868
  Ignatius & Mary Elizabeth Jenkins 2-16-1885 (Rev. Dr. Lewin)
  Ignatius & Margaret Arvin 12-23-1809
  Luke & Elizabeth Mobberly 1-23-1797
  Robert & Mary Priscilla Boswell 3-29-1880 (Rev. Josiah Perry)
  Susan Alice & Benjamin F. Peacock 1-20-1869 (Gordon)
  Thomas & Julia Ann King 8-25-1873 (Welsh)
  William N. & Bertie Porter 10-21-1878 (Gordon)
  William P. & Eleanor Jenkins 5-4-1875 (Billopp)
WINEBERGER, John & Caroline Aldridge 10-31-1836
WINFIELD, Jonas & Ann M. Stewart 4-31-1781
  Richard S. & Elizabeth M. Thompson 3-10-1826
  Susan & Joshua N. Gardiner 2-5-1822
  William & Amelia Jane Gray 4-4-1853
WINKLER, Ann & John Day 11-29-1831
  Ellen & Benjamin Simpson 12-6-1871 (Skinner)
  John & Priscilla Sansbury 3-11-1828
  Mary & Thomas Cater 1-9-1821
  Mary Elizabeth & James Henry Simpson 4-1-1872
WINSER, Ignatius & Mary Mobberly 12-21-1792
WINSETT, Mary & Joseph Johnson 2-2-1799
WINSOR, Albert Quincy & Minnie Catherine Garline 6-30-1875 (Billopp)
  Eliza & Patrick H. Skidmore 8-5-1875 (Billopp)
  Emma & Revd Benjn Franklin 4-12-1847
  George Wm. & Mary Alice Peacock 6-23-1875 (Billopp)
  Hezekiah & Mary Jane Winsor 4-22-1878 (Kershaw)
  Ignatius & Mary A. E. Vanetta 4-11-1876 (Gordon)
  James H. & Elizabeth Simpson 12-27-1866 (Chesley)

WINSOR, John J. & Celesta Ann Curten 2-21-1846
  John Thomas & Mary Eleanor Winsor 6-8-1875 (Gordon)
  John William & Emma Brightwell 10-26-1876 (Gordon)
  Joseph T. & Mary Hall 7-12-1877 (Kershaw)
  MaryEleanor & John Thomas Winsor 6-8-1875
  Mary Jane & Hezekiah Winsor 4-22-1878 (Kershaw)
  Richard & Rosanna Curtain 8-25-1863
WIRT, Barbara & John Tilley 1-6-1790
  Christian & Mary Weaver 9-3-1792
  Henry & Jennett Ferguson 1-15-1795
  Thomas & Sarah Mitchell 12-21-1819
WISE, George & Jane King 3-7-1799
  Thomas & Milley Robinson 12-1-1787
WISEMAN, Henry & Mary Henson 3-25-1869
WISMAN, Henry Anna & James Kagle 1-16-1884 (Rev. Mr. Robey)
WISSMANN, John H. & Laura A. Hall 6-5-1861
WISSMAN, Lewis O. & Louisa F. Bohleber 9-20-1866 Age 27, carpenter
  m. 9-25-1866, Vansville by J. Earnest, minister
WOART, Jonathan L. & Elizabeth H. West 7-31-1832
WOLFE, John & Elizth H. Berry 1-25-1829
  W. H. & J. H. Magruder 2-25-1884 (Rev. Wm. K. Boyle)
WOLFENDEN, John & Charlotte Gody 12-30-1829
WOOD, Alexander & Mary Harrison 2-24-1879 (Hooman)
  Alexis & Martha Clark 1-30-1817
  Ann & Francis Burch Vermilion 8-30-1780
  Barbara & John Beckett 5-1-1804
  Charles T. & Rachel N. Ryon 12-12-1860
  Dr. Edgar W. & Sarah H. Clagett 1-17-1870 (Kershaw)
  Elizabeth & Robert Alex^{r} Craine 2-4-1814
  Emanuel & Elizabeth Digges col^{d} 1-6-1881 (Rev. Mr. Lawson)
  Francis & Mary E. Jones 12-5-1881 (Rev. Wm. C. Boteler)
  George & Mary Ann Hutchinson 1-20-1835
  George T. & Jane Cage 12-26-1814
  Hannah & John Morgan 4-20-1779
  Henrietta & John H. Jackson 12-27-1873 (Walsh)
  Isaac & Josephine Moore 5-24-1832
WOODARD, Isaac & Alice Brookes 1-13-1870 (Lankford)
WOOD, Isaac N. & Willie Ann Henry 6-24-1868 (Begue)
  James G. & Sarah Allien 12-4-1798
  James G. & Martha Young 8-25-1806
  James M. & Emily R. Deakins 2-14-1855
  James W. & Margaret D. Turner 11-26-1853
  Jane & Clement Knott 12-3-1807
  Jane & Benjamin Estep 1-22-1827
  Jane & Henry Brown col^{d} 2-6-1868 (Chesley)
  John & Catherine Brightwell 4-23-1825
  John & Elizabeth Clarke 12-31-1850
  John A. & Elizabeth M. Miller 1-3-1840
  John A. & Mary Elizabeth Luckett 10-25-1855
  John G. & Sarah E. Wood 5-20-1861
  John Richard & Elizabeth Knott 5-8-1860
  John Thomas & Ann Greenfield 6-22-1799
  John W. & Alice Virginia Beall 5-19-1877 (Miller)
  Laurence & Dinah Brown 1-18-1866 Colored
  Lewis & Rachel Howard 7-17-1873 (O'Dwyer)

WOOD, Louis R. & Mary Beall 10-2-1876 (Major)
  Maggie A. & William H. Wilson 1-14-1886 (Father Cunane)
  Margaret & Richard Coe 5-8-1784
  Margaret J. & Frederick Skinner 10-15-1880 (Rev. Mr. Gordon)
  Maria & John Fletcher 1-4-1873 (Cotton)
  Martha & Tyler Wells 9-15-1884 (Rev. Mr. Butler)
  Mary & Benjamin Pierce 4-16-1817
  Mary Elizabeth & Samuel Clark 4-24-1848
  Mary S. & William H. Yoe 10-18-1880 (Rev. Mr. Gordon)
  Moses & Mary Bones 5-19-1883 (Rev. Mr. Walker)
  Nathaniel & Eleanor Lee 12-24-1872 (Evans)
  Peter & Ann Gantt 4-3-1793
  Peter Junior & Margaret Johns Skinner 11-23-1854
  Phillis & James Clarke col^d 9-1-1870 (McDonald)
  Priscilla & Richard Thornton 12-31-1884 (Rev. Mr. Brooke)
  Richard & Fanny Owings 8-21-1879 (Gray)
  Robert J. & Harriet Turner 12-23-1878 (Gray)
  Samuel & Sarah Ireland 8-18-1884
  Sarah E. & John G. Wood 5-20-1861
  Scott & Mary Ward 1-31-1880 (Stanley)
  Susan & John Ross 7-14-1869 (Maher)
  Susannah & Allen Burrell 3-18-1789
  Susannah G. & Patrick Dent 7-22-1809
  Thomas & Priscilla Clagett 3-10-1787
  Thomas & Priscilla Young 4-2-1877 (Carroll)
  Tracey & Basil Lowe 8-15-1785
  William & Elizabeth Gray 12-7-1780
  William & Margaret Felter 12-22-1818
  Zachariah & Ruth Tyler 12-2-1833
WOODALL, James R. & Priscilla E. Brown 6-28-1854
WOODARD, James & Nancy Hebburn col^d 5-13-1869 (Begue)
WOODFIELD, Dianna & Abraham Chaney 9-22-1797
WOODVILLE, William & Elizabeth Ogle 6-17-1822
WOODWARD, Abraham & Nancy Jones 12-8-1807
  Alfred & Caroline De Neil 2-8-1877 (Carroll)
  Bennett & Eliz^a Scessall 12-15-1778
  Casandra & William McFarlen 12-13-1816
  Drucilla & John Peck 2-17-1798
  Gassaway & Louisa Ridout 8-1-1868 (Langford)
  John & Eliz^a Piles Drane 11-9-1796
  Margaret & Joshua Pearre 12-6-1786
  Pamelia & William Woodward 6-14-1809
  Permella & Jacob Bassford 12-14-1814
  Thomas & Eleanor Hilliary 4-18-1788
  William & Pamelia Woodward 6-14-1809
WOOTTEN, William T. & Margaret Hall 2-17-1819
WOOTTON, Mary E. & Benjn O, Mullikin 1-27-1846
  Mary Mackall & Thomas Contee Bowie 2-7-1801
  Richard & Eloise Contee 3-23-1874 (Billup)
  Turner & Mary M. Bowie 3-27-1794
  William & Patsy Garner 6-4-1799
WORNALD, Ann & Benjamin Tucker 2-11-1778
  Henry & Ann Simpson 4-15-1780
WORRALD, Sarah & Elisha Richardson 12-3-1782
WORRALL, William & Elizabeth Oliver 2-14-1806

WORRELL, Ann & Ervin H. Richards 11-29-1833
  John & Elizabeth Adams 12-16-1833
WORTHINGTON, Almira & John A. Turton 12-13-1839
  Ann & John Plummer 3-25-1810
  Charles S. & Ellen A. Berry 9-30-1884 (Rev. Wm. Brayshaw)
  Eliza J. & Henry Brooke 5-28-1834
  Elizabeth M. & Thomas F. Bowie Jr. 12-15-1856
  Henry F. & Catharine H. Seaborn 2-26-1855
  Jane M. & Michael B. Carroll 10-9-1822
  Laura & Robert W. Harper 12-15-1856
  Walter B. & Henrietta Priscilla Oden 11-6-1827
WOURLD, Eleanor & Henry Tubman 9-5-1828
WOUSTER, Marg & Richd Hammerstone 12-17-1777
WRIGHT, Bettie Boyd & James Bennett Gibbs 9-15-1857
  Elizabeth & John Evans 8-25-1798
  Elizth & John Semmes 10-3-1848
  Ellen Clay & James Seymore Cowan 6-20-1867 (McCabe)
  Ellen G. & Robert E. Bayne 9-6-1867 (Smith)
  George & Elizabeth Beaven 1-13-1814
  James Henry & Mary Elizabeth Brown 5-23-1874 (Maybury)
  Joseph & Elizabeth Beall 5-2-1831
  Linny & Philip Webster 10-4-1802
  Martha & John Savoy 5-9-1856
  Mary & George Adams 1-21-1783
  Nathaniel & Sarah Wheeler 11-2-1813
  Rebecca & John Gibbons 1-15-1799
  Robert & Harriet E. Caldwell 10-11-1830
  Samuel & Catherine Clemmens 1-9-1786
  Susanna B. & John R. Gibbons 7-14-1831
  Thomas & Lethe Talbot 12-18-1835
  Thomas S. & Ann E. Bruce 3-26-1851
  Washington & Eleanor Caywood 8-31-1842
WRIGHTT, Ann & William Webster 2-1-1793
  John & Mary Ann Webster 2-25-1791
  John Watson & Ann Townshend 1-8-1794
  Joseph & Ann Naylor 2-26-1788
WRIGMAN, Maria & George Bailey 3-1-1843
WRISTON, Elenor & Thomas Tillman 7-1-1820
WROE, F. A. & M. J. Turner 12-13-1869 (Linthicum)
WYNN, Ann & Robert Ogdon 10-17-1778
  Ann & Thomas Blacklock 11-22-1783
  Elizabeth & William Hughes 5-7-1791
  Elizabeth P. & John W. Turton 4-21-1832
  Hezekiah & Rebecca M. Smallwood 1-12-1779
  John & Ann Smallwood 12-12-1778
  John & Elizabeth Watson 9-1-1801
  Lucy Ann & George Alder 10-31-1778
  Marlowe & Rebecca Davis 2-12-1811
  Sarah & James Robinson 2-28-1801
  William & Milicent Smallwood 5-20-1778
WYSON, Priscilla Ann & William McDaniel 11-29-1779
WYVILL, Edward & Mary T. Davis 11-26-1832
  Mary Edwina & Harrison Clay Ward 1-18-1868
WYVILLE, Edward H. & Caroline H. Hawkins 6-19-1845

248

YALE, John Brooks & Marie Louise McCulloch 5-17-1884
YATES, Ann & Benjamin Magill 12-4-1826
  Elizabeth & Daniel Kent 5-15-1817
  Jane Bruce & Luke Philip Barber 2-20-1803
  Martin & Mary Nevitt 12-31-1798
  Rebecca & Henry Young 12-17-1803
YEARLEY, Benjamin & Minta Thompson 2-14-1785
YOE, William H. & Ellen Maddox 8-10-1844
  William H. & Mary S. Wood 10-18-1880 (Rev. Mr. Gordon)
YOST, Emeline & George W. Taylor 12-22-1852
  Emma & James W. L. Wilson 10-25-1861
  Emma Jane & Charles W. Harvey 10-6-1862
  Henry & Rachel Sheriff 3-18-1804
  John H. & Ann Suit 6-21-1827
  Jno. H. & Ruth E. Burroughs 2-13-1864
  Mary Ann & Daniel Barron 12-6-1839
  Mary Susan & Richᵈ Harvey 1-26-1852
  Sarah & Henry T. Scott 5-18-1868
  William & Elizabeth Barron 9-13-1877 (Evans)
YOUNG, Bettie S. & Joseph J. Hall 2-26-1877 (McNeer)
  Mrs. Catherine & Lloyd T. Wells 1-5-1865
  Charity & Reasen Allen 12-25-1818
  Charles & Mary Ann Gray 10-7-1871 (Evans)
  Charles Jr. & Mary Dabney 8-17-1796
  Charlotte & James R. Queen colᵈ (Greenleaf)
  Charlotte & Andrew Simmons 10-29-1870 (Maher)
  David & Henrietta Smith 12-17-1784
  Deborah & Abriel Jenners 5-17-1796
  Edward T. & Katie Carlin 2-4-1884 (Rev. Mr. LaRoche)
  Edward W. & Maria L. Gwynn 10-8-1855
  Edward W. & Mary Helen Edelen 6-24-1871 (O'Dwyer)
  Eliza & Richard Skinner 6-25-1811
  Eliza & Jeremiah Green 12-7-1867 (Young)
  Elizabeth & Acquila Wheeler 2-26-1778
  Elizabeth T. B. & Alexʳ McCormick 10-25-1847
  Ellen M. & Edmund Brooke Jr. 2-1-1817
  Eloise & George H. Smith 8-5-1841
  Eveline & Edward Plater 11-1-1836
  Francenia & Edwin W. Latimer 10-31-1849
  Georgianna & A. W. Edelen 2-27-1867 (Marbury)
  Hannah & Oden Parker colᵈ 7-27-1867
  Harriet Ann & Jubiter Lee 6-9-1883 (Father Cunanne)
  Henry & Rebecca Yates 12-17-1803
  Henry N. & Syenna Gwynn 11-26-1849
  Henson & Grace Ann Dent 12-26-1867 (Greenleaf)
  Ignatius F. & Barbara S. Smith 1-30-1814
  James A. & Susan Jane Suit 6-23-1846
  James T. & EllenAlice Moore 3-30-1872 (Lanahan)
  James T. D. & Annie F. Watson 12-12-1870 (Linthicum)
  Jane & John A. Suit 12-24-1821
  Jane & Richard Thornton 2-17-1872 (Evans)
  Jane Joan G. & Fielder Dorsett 4-19-1794
  John T. & Susan Naylor 10-13-1845
  John Thomas & Charity Sewall 8-24-1876 (Carroll)
  John W. & Mary A. M. Trueman 12-19-1878 (Perry)
  John Ward & Ann Noble Wade 1-29-1806

YOUNG, Joseph & Jane Hodges 5-16-1872
  Josias & Elizabeth L. Clagett 1-22-1833 (someone later has written
    above Mary W. Clagett)
  Josias & Hester Johnson col^d 7-25-1871 (Marbury)
  Laura Ellen & Richard Shorter 12-24-1872 (Evans)
  Letty & James Findly 12-8-1801
  Levi & Ann Webb 2-18-1836
  Levi & Catherine Beans 6-20-1850
  Livingston J. & Louisa E. Gwynn 4-10-1875 (O'Dwyer)
  Margaret Ann & Joseph M. Carrick 11-10-1856
  Maria E. & Doct. Edgar B. Hurtt 10-14-1854
  Martha & James G. Wood 8-25-1806
  Mary & Nathan Darcey 9-26-1828
  Mary & Russell Matthews 12-22-1869 col^d (Langford)
  Mary & Thomas Washington 9-18-1874 (Dwyer)
  Mary Ann & William Swaine 12-13-1832
  Mary Clare & Alfred Davis 12-23-1875
  Mary E. & Charles Beall 2-5-1862
  Mary M. & Dr. Edwd Hurtt 4-30-1849
  Notley & Eleanor Hall 4-10-1815
  Notley & Mary L. Smith 4-20-1830
  Octavius & Mary Ann Cranford 2-20-1854
  Pricey A. & Jno. W. A. Davis 12-28-1885 (Rev. Geo. W. Dame)
  Priscilla & Thomas Wood 4-2-1877 (Carroll)
  Rachel & Walter Harrison 4-26-1873 (Walsh)
  Richard & Matilda Berry 10-24-1815
  Ruth & Benjamin Jones 10-11-1786
  Samuel & Ruth Ferguson 12-8-1798
  Sarah & Henry Weedon 9-23-1797
  Sarah & Basil White 6-2-1827
  Sarah A. & John Dennis Littleford 12-26-1839
  Sarah E. & William T. Watson 10-14-1844
  Sarah M. & John A. Ferrall 2-7-1872 (Marbury)
  Samuel R. & Carrie R. Brown 11-18-1862
  Sophronia & Richard Magruder 9-6-1841
  Susetta & Josias Taylor 12-24-1869 (Linthicum)
  Thomas & Lizzie Brown col^d 8-21-1869 (Maher)
  Thos R. & Maria R. Hodges 4-20-1856
  Virginia & Robert Pinkney 12-24-1872 (Evans)
  William & Elizabeth Darcey 12-20-1826
YOUNGER, Gilbert & Rebecca Hardey 6-12-1784